THE
BLACK
AND THE
RED

Translated from the French by Alan Sheridan

Harcourt Brace Jovanovich, Publishers
San Diego   New York   London

THE
BLACK
AND THE
RED

François Mitterrand
The Story of an Ambition

by

Catherine Nay

Requests for permission to make copies of any
part of the work should be mailed to:
Permissions, Harcourt Brace Jovanovich, Publishers,
Orlando, Florida 32887.

Library of Congress Cataloging-in-Publication Data
Nay, Catherine.
The black and the red.
Translation of: Le noir et le rouge.
Includes index.
1. Mitterrand, François, 1916–   .   2. France—
Politics and government—20th century.   3. France—
Presidents—Biography.   I. Title.
DC423.N3913   1987   944.083'8'0924   [B]   86-19382
ISBN 0-15-112885-5

Designed by Francesca M. Smith
Printed in the United States of America
First edition
A B C D E

For me, *Madame Bovary* is obviously the most important novel on the subject of French society. But what troubles me about the characters of the nineteenth century is their lack of magnitude. Look at the poverty of Julien Sorel's ambition.

—François Mitterrand

CONTENTS

Preface   ix

1 Happy Days at Jarnac   1

2 The Imprint   22

3 Who Am I?   36

4 To Break and to Sow   58

5 The Fourth Republic: A Career   117

6 The Fifth Republic: A Destiny   207

7 Power   338

Epilogue   359

Notes   367

Index   390

PREFACE

ON A FINE JUNE EVENING IN 1982, AMIDST GREAT POMP AND circumstance at the Château de Versailles, François Mitterrand received the heads of state and government of the major industrialized countries in a typical "show" summit put on by politicians every now and then for worldwide audiences. Not a cloud was in the sky; the ground swarmed with journalists. . . . For a brief moment, it seemed as if a state of grace had descended upon the world.

One of the most beautiful places on earth had given over its splendid setting to an unprecedented arsenal of electronic equipment. Sophisticated technological wonders had been assembled as if to convince the world's leaders that the French president's vision bespoke modernity. But the distinguished guests of Socialist France were far more dazzled by the unparalleled setting of the Hall of Mirrors than the marvels of technology or the choreographic feats of helicopters. Amid the Sun King's golden splendor, the president of the Republic seemed to take intense pleasure in the moment. With head proudly erect, a look of confident authority in his eyes, and a constrained smile, Mitterrand himself seemed to possess a royal bearing there, in that very symbol of privilege. "I wasn't

aware that Louis XIV had succeeded Louis XV," remarked the
most impertinent of the Socialist ministers, alluding to the discreetly
claimed ancestry of the former president, Valéry Giscard d'Estaing.
With his Bourbon-like thickness and dignified airs, François Mitterrand certainly did seem more at home than his aristocratic predecessor.

That evening, the natural yet paradoxical manner of the new
president (a Communist minister was in attendance at the court)
made me want to learn more about this man who was to be responsible for France's destiny in the next seven years. I did not
know much about him then, and what I felt was neither attraction
nor repulsion, but I resolved to find out where he had come from,
what had influenced him, what his life had been like before he
came to power—in short, what events had shaped François Mitterrand before he, in turn, shaped events.

—C.N.

THE
BLACK
AND THE
RED

1

HAPPY DAYS AT JARNAC

NO SOONER HAD HE BEEN HOISTED TO THE PINNACLE OF power than François Mitterrand chose, on May 21, 1981, to descend alone into the tomb. As he wandered through the icy depths of the Panthéon, half of France—his half—went wild with joy, abandoning itself to profane celebration. His supporters would no doubt have understood him better had they known he was actually trying to outdo an earlier scene: seven years before Valéry Giscard d'Estaing had sealed his fresh victory by walking the entire length of the Champs-Elysées to the Etoile, to the acclamation of his supporters.

Mitterrand's closest colleagues were not surprised, knowing of the new president's taste for burial places. Some scholarly politicians can reel off a few verses of Racine or wax eloquent about the depth of blue or density of vermilion in a given painting. When François Mitterrand refers to a great poet or painter, he adds, almost automatically, the location of his last resting place. "Bernanos? Buried at Pellevoisin, in the Indre, next to his mother. Mallarmé? At Samoreau, near Fontainebleau. Van Gogh? At Auvers-sur-Oise. Romain Rolland? At Brèves. And Braque? At Varangeville, near Dieppe, under a stone decorated with a bird, wings spread for eternity." He once explained: "Where are the bodies of those who invented the world as we know it? Where are they now? The question interests me. He who loves death loves life."[1]

But, on that May day, more than one Frenchman, more than one left-wing voter, unaware of this strange predilection, wondered what this visit symbolized. Was it the humility of the mystic already aware of the vanities of power? Or the haste of a superstitious man anxious to exorcize evil spirits? Or the desire of a man on the brink of a mysterious future to open up an appeasing dialogue with great ancestors who would never be rivals or traitors?

The new president's inspiration may have been quite simply political. For a century, the Left had been excluded from power, sharing it only on a few brief occasions. In going to the Panthéon and bowing his head before the tombs of Jean Jaurès, Jean Moulin, and Victor Schoelcher, the Socialist victor was reforging a link that for many years had been broken. He was planting the roots of the Left in the compost of history once more. Half a century before, in an identical ritual, the three Normaliens,[2] Paul Painlevé, Edouard Herriot, and Léon Blum, who had just brought the Cartel of the Left[3] to power, had similarly followed, in great pomp, the transfer of the remains of Jean Jaurès from the Palais-Bourbon[4] to the secular temple.[5]

Mitterrand's choice of these three tombs was a marvelous illustration of the hopes his success had raised and the equivocations that had made that success possible. Jean Jaurès represented the union of the working-class movement. Assassinated a few days before the outbreak of World War I, the inspired prophet of French socialism—a man of generous instincts and modest background (like the newly elected president), patriotic but pacifist, left-wing but tolerant—faced none of the great questions that were later to divide the Left. He did not have to opt at the crucial moment for or against national defense, for or against bolshevism, for or against a break with those who were to form the Communist party and who today noisily claim to be his heirs. In 1981, Jean Jaurès was still the ideal hero.

The second tomb was that of Jean Moulin, who represented the French Resistance in World War II. A former prefect[6] under the Third Republic who had become General Charles de Gaulle's secret delegate in occupied France, Moulin had also succeeded in coming to an agreement with the Communists. But although he appreciated their contribution to the Resistance, he knew they could not always be counted on. The Communists chose the time either to work with others or stand apart according to criteria they alone knew. General de Gaulle's heirs could not fail to recognize themselves in Jean Moulin.

Finally, there was the tomb of Victor Schoelcher, minister of the navy under the Revolution of 1848 and liberator of slaves.[7] The edifying example of "the good white," liberator of the oppressed of all races and conditions, must have gone straight to the hearts of many fervent advocates of the Third World in and around the Socialist party.

As for members of the Right, who had embarked on a new era, as people of the minority, that official route up the rue Soufflot through the historical and intellectual heart of Paris, that celebration in the crypt of left-wing republicanism, caused mixed feelings. The Right felt the bitterness of the defeated, excluded as they were from a power they had believed would be theirs forever. They felt, too, perhaps, the instinctive deference of legitimists toward a democratically elected adversary. But surely they also felt a strong desire to mock what seemed a piece of irresistibly corny theater.

Indeed, through the magic of television, the whole of France looked on, staring first into the tomb, then at the pilgrim. It was an astonishing sight: the most secretive of politicians, a jealous guard of his privacy, was soliciting the intrusion of millions in a face-to-face encounter with destiny. He had made them voyeurs into the emotion, pride, revenge, certitudes, and doubts that assailed him at that singular moment.

The choreography was almost surrealistic. What exactly did people see? An astonishing illusion: a never-ending stream of roses. Like a fashionable priest going to lunch at the château, the president entered the Panthéon holding a single flower (a bunch would have made him look too much like a young bride). No sooner had he laid it on the tomb of one of his heroes than another thornless rose seemed to spring from his sleeve. The explanation came later: an anonymous crew, hidden behind the pillars, had been entrusted with the task of guiding the new president through the labyrinth and keeping him supplied with flowers.

Quite shamelessly, the cameras zoomed in on Mitterrand's frozen features, lit as if from within by that rare happiness called ecstasy. But his marble bust was carried on legs—the only sign of life in that petrified edifice—that moved forward in short, cautious steps, as if afraid of dropping their prodigious load. Mitterrand's short figure threw extended shadows on the infinite colonnades as his steps echoed through the vaults and Beethoven's "Ode to Joy" grew louder.

Touches of Fritz Lang or Cecil B. de Mille? On that day the production was in the hands of another Lang, the future minister of culture then unknown to the masses, who was about to assume the nickname Jack.

Once the new president had finished that journey through the night and returned to the land of the clamoring living, how did he see himself? As a participant, or as an observer? Intoxicated with his triumph, did he feel the first few drops of rain that at precisely that moment happened to fall? Did he even hear the "Marseillaise," sung by the tenor Placido Domingo under the baton of the conductor Daniel Barenboim?

"He might have chosen *French* artists," came the predictable complaint from the new opposition. They duly noted that the head of state's personal guests had been chosen from among the international, leftist firmament of arts and letters: Americans William Styron, Arthur Miller, and Elie Wiesel; Colombian Gabriel García Márquez; Mexican Carlos Fuentes; Argentine Julio Cortázar; and Turk Yachar Kemal. Régis Debray, Paul Guimard, and Jean-Edern Hallier, all representing French literature, were the only three symbols of the intellectual reconquest of the home market that day.

It was eight o'clock in the evening, the pilgrimage was over, the new reign was beginning. What would it be like? What could France expect? On the Left, people stifled their doubts. For as long as anyone could remember, the formula had been that socialism and happiness went together. "We must dream life," the election posters had blithely urged. The advent of François Mitterrand was to put an end to economic crisis, inequality, and unemployment, giving everybody a hoped-for second chance and ensuring even the poorest security and dignity. The bosses were to be thrown out: people would work less and earn more. Daring at last to give a salutary and liberating kick in the teeth to the cruel world of profit, France would regain strength and prosperity. Everything would be changed: history required it. Let all the idealists in the world join hands!

The opposite camp continued to ask questions. If this victorious Mitterrand had succeeded in convincing everybody, it was because he had played on the most ambiguous of registers. With him, one had to learn to distinguish the tune from the refrain of words, words, words. Mitterrand had announced a break with capitalism, which would bring an end to the rich and result in the birth of a new world, one in which the first would be last and the last would be first. It was enough to scare more than a few, though the words had been sung to the most melodious, most seraphic of tunes. But the man who had made people fear for the future of private education was now appearing in front of a Romanesque church.[8] The man who for years had scrapped with others fiercely now seemed appeased, even gentle. The man who had always cast a skeptical eye had now won people over to his quasi-religious ardor for socialism. He was acting as if all ought to accept him, as if morality had triumphed at last. With François Mitterrand in power, went the message, all would be protected from grand inquisitions that disfigure times of fervor, zeal, and passion. The new president gave an almost elegiac style to an almost sectarian content.

The defeated certainly expected change, but had no idea how far it would go. Would there be a major upheaval? Socialism with a force of ten on the Richter scale? Or would there be a slow, gradual evolution? Nobody knew. Would Mitterrand turn out to be a Robespierre, Blanqui, Guesde, Danton, Gambetta, Proudhon, or even Victor Considérant? The betting was wide open.

"Didn't he once belong to the Right?" a few worried souls hazarded, largely to reassure themselves. "Then he'll have all the fire of a recent convert," others replied, largely to frighten themselves. And they proceeded to forget all that the victor had written, all that he was, and all he had done.

If it is true that childhood contains the seed of the adult personality, could it be that François Mitterrand's childhood offered the key to his character? A clue to what was in store for France? Mitterrand's early years opened up a range of possible futures for him, many mutually exclusive. His family background and upbringing suggest a kind of conformism that leads naturally to political conservatism (a happy childhood does not necessarily bring a teenager into opposition with social order). But his character, evincing a tendency to contention and a restless desire to be noticeably unique, drove him instinctively toward rebellion. On the other hand, his temperament—his natural sense of leadership, his liking for authority, his wish to be first—was a sure indication that François Mitterrand was a natural monarch.

Born at Jarnac on Thursday, October 26, 1916, François was the second son and fifth child of Joseph Mitterrand, stationmaster at Angoulême, and Yvonne (née Lorrain) Mitterrand, a very devout mother whom François was to revere. His was to be a privileged childhood. The Mitterrand family was sufficiently well-off for money never to be mentioned. It was large enough—eight brothers and sisters and two cousins of the same age—for there to be a permanent atmosphere of gaiety. It was religious enough to inculcate into the children the morality and principles necessary to get through life. It was warm and caring enough to prevent any desire to break with it. It was strict enough to lay down how things were to be done, yet flexible enough not to infringe on liberty. And it was bookish and open-minded enough for the children to grow up fully conversant with concerns of the mind.

To live in Jarnac in the years following the Great War was not to have been locked away in some provincial backwater where the unexpected might provide a novelist with exotic raw material. The little township of four thousand inhabitants, well anchored to its barrels of cognac, was traditionally open to the outside world with which it traded. English, Swedish, and German merchants came to buy Jarnac's precious commodity, and were received by those enigmatic households in their solid white stone houses. The merchants came as customers, but left as friends. The summers were warm and the winters mild. Even at Jarnac, one could sometimes smell the sea.

The people of the Charente, in which Jarnac is located, lived in harmony in those times. The sound and fury of the class struggle had not yet taken hold of people's minds. The region was without heavy industry and had no proletariat. The rich were very rich—"they believed they deserved their advantages and the others agreed with them."[9] The poor were not wretched. Nothing seemed to of-

fend natural justice. Here the largest fortunes were Protestant, and
therefore Republican. The Huguenot patricians and Catholic bourgeois, very often Royalist by tradition, greeted one another, sometimes expressed esteem for one another, but seldom met socially:
"The Protestants tended to marry into the porcelain-manufacturing
families of Limoges or the Bordeaux châteaux."[10] Until the Liberation, mixed marriages between religions were almost inconceivable.

The devoutly Catholic Mitterrand-Lorrain family held an honorable place in this small world. They were notables, but not among
the first rank. Regarded as *petits bourgeois* by the rich and as
grands bourgeois by the humble, they could be doubly proud: their
closeness to the ordinary people was based on charity; their relations with those who mattered, on reserve. Their lack of arrogance
toward the humble allowed them to maintain a certain distance,
tinged with disapproval, toward the better-off, who in turn were
not very inclined to narrow the gap.

The Mitterrands and Lorrains were respected, praised for their
generosity and for the unostentatious way they would take in some
needy old cousin or nun in poor health. They had property, but
did not flaunt it. Without feeling the pinch, they could afford to
send one of their daughters, a war widow, and her nurse to rest
for a year and a half in a Swiss hotel.

Jules Lorrain, the maternal grandfather, owned several fine
apartment blocks at Jarnac—"a whole district of the town," some
townspeople claim to remember. The family divided its time between two solidly built, rather than elegant, houses. Each had two
stories, with small, narrow doorways and windows, as is common
in the Charente. The houses were separated by a huge garden of
geraniums, stocks ("which provide better arguments for the existence of God than are ever given at Notre-Dame"[11]), a palm tree,
and even a *Pinus pinaster soland*, the sea pine symbolizing eternal
life for the Reformed church. That tree was an irrefutable sign of
origin: the grandfather had bought one of the houses adjoining the
Protestant church from the pastor's heirs. There lived M. and Mme
Lorrain; their daughter Antoinette Sarrazin, a war widow; her two
children, Pierre and Yvonne (nicknamed Lolotte). A permanent
smell of polish clung to the long, shadowy, chapel-like corridors,

which the children said were haunted. The huge rooms were filled with furniture in the rustic or Louis-Philippe styles, and scattered with porcelain imported by the Compagnie des Indes or English knickknacks brought back from foreign travel.

In the other house lived the ten Mitterrands. When the president's brothers and sisters remember their childhoods, they mention how fond their father was of converting furniture to unexpected uses. Joseph Mitterrand once brought an old carved Breton bed back from Quimper and turned it into a bookcase, and the drawing-room chimney was decorated with cupboards, also of Breton origin. "He had a taste for beautiful things," they say.

With girls on one side and boys on the other, the children slept together in large, airy bedrooms. While still very young, François plotted to get his own space in the *chambre aux oiseaux* (the bird room), so called because the red and green chintz wallpaper depicted sparrows.

The grandfather, Jules Lorrain, also owned a small property of about 60 acres at La Treille, on the edge of the township. There, grapes were grown and the produce sold to cognac makers. But it was at Touvent, near Aubeterre on the edge of the Dordogne, that his true estate was to be found—about 250 acres surrounding a comfortable country house, with an ornamental garden in front and ancient elms towering above. There Jules Lorrain spent eight months out of the year, from primroses in early spring to *foie gras* in late fall. They did not live in luxury: there was no hot water, the lighting was by gas, and a rustic lavatory was enthroned in the garden. All this was quite usual at the time in that milieu. But the Lorrains wanted for nothing. They had servants—a cook, linen maid, and coachman—and the wives of the three sharecroppers added their labor when necessary.

For Jarnac, Mme Lorrain got her maids from Brittany. She would choose them from photographs. The whole family still laughs about a certain Marie who had sent a full-length portrait of herself in her sister's wedding dress. An attractive proposition judging from the photograph, she was duly chosen; upon arrival, however, Marie turned out to be tiny and deformed. Then there was the irritating Simone, who sang "La Fille du bédouin" from morning till night, and the beautiful Henriette, who had an interesting effect on the boys.

On Sundays, the whole family would go off in an upholstered carriage to mass at Nabinaud.[12] They might then be invited to lunch with the parish priest, the Abbé Marcellin, who tended to be a Bonapartist politically, and M. Delugin, the town's liberal, anticlerical mayor.

The food was pleasant and varied, with a plentiful supply of calves, cows, pigs, hens, and seasonable fruit and vegetables. *Canard à l'orange* was a dish for high days and holidays.[13] The Dronne, a small, slow-moving river on which the children sailed in flat-bottomed boats, crossed the estate, providing the family with rainbow perch and eel. The nets sometimes collected up to 450 pounds of fish in a single night, which were then taken off to be sold at Angoulême. A press provided walnut oil. The neighbors talked with great interest about the model piggery built by Jules Lorrain and, not without a touch of surprise for such paternalism was not common in the region, about the houses he had built for his sharecroppers.

For two terms (seven years in a row), until entering the Catholic secondary school at Angoulême, young François, his younger brother Jacques, his younger sister Geneviève, and their cousins Pierre and Lolotte lived with their grandparents in this setting "where time and things spoke of God as self-evident."[14] They hardly attended the local primary school, since they spent only a term a year at Jarnac. The parish priests of La Prade and Pillac came and gave them private lessons, as they might to children at the château. The timetable was strict—9:00 A.M. to midday, then 2:00 till 4:00 P.M.—with no messing about. A big chiming clock, stuck on the roof, regulated the children's days. It was set in motion from the hall at the foot of the stairs. "There go the young gentlemen to their lunch" or "there go the young gentlemen back to class" the farm laborers' children would say to one another upon hearing the bell.

"At Touvent one followed the rhythm of the seasons and the curve of the days without thinking. In the evening, the lamp was lowered to light the gas jet. The wood stove roared from October onward. Everyday life followed its course, with wet paths in November, the ground hard in February, and one's unexercised, soft legs in spring. At that time, one died at home, if not in war. The physician came on horseback. The parish priest, a younger man, rode a bicycle—a woman's bicycle, of course, on account of his cassock. To give death its metaphysical dimension, one had to force oneself a little," wrote François Mitterrand in *Ici et maintenant*. "I lived my childhood in another century; I had to make an effort to jump into ours," the Socialist leader admitted fifty years later.[15]

Two men marked the childhood of the future president: the grandfather, known as Papa Jules, and the father, Papa Joseph. Whenever someone asked the young François, "How's your papa?" he would reply innocently, "Which one?"

Papa Jules, born in 1854, was the cornerstone of the family and lived a happy life. "He had everything," one of his granddaughters, still dazzled by his memory, says of him. He was generous, popular, jolly, and a good husband and father; he also appreciated pretty girls and new ideas. He was of average height, but always stood erect so as not to lose an inch; his hair was thick and white, and he sported a full, smooth mustache. This accomplished sportsman, a good swimmer[16] and excellent fencer, was extremely careful of his person. He rubbed himself every day with a friction glove and exuded a fragrance of lavender. "He could charm an audience by recounting in perfect patois delicious Charente stories that were the delight of the family on winter evenings. The minor reputation this earned him meant more to him than any decoration."[17]

Papa Jules loved human contact, was fond of traveling, and had great commercial sense. Fortune smiled on him. When his father's wood business was floundering (François Mitterrand was then only a teenager), Jules Lorrain was made the representative in England of Pellisson, a large cognac firm, for "although he did not drink it [cognac], he had a reputation for an infallible nose and could accurately guess the vineyard and the year."[18] He spoke English with ease and was fond of entertaining. Each Christmas, black puddings and golden shortbreads were eaten—toys were not given out until New Year's Day.

An independent man with superabundant energy, he opened a vinegar factory at Jarnac, and with the help of Mme Lorrain, the business did extremely well. Together with the great condiment king Dessaux of Orléans, Jules Lorrain started the National Federation of Vinegar Manufacturers, of which he remained honorary president until his death. He was also a member of Jarnac's city council alongside those of the Bisquit cognac dynasty. With the Bisquits, he started the first free school for girls.

Politically, the family regarded Papa Jules as a republican. His great heroes, it is said, were Clemenceau and Poincaré. But at the age of twenty, as the story goes, he was given a front-row seat at the funeral of Napoleon III in the little church of Sainte-Marie in Chislehurst, near London. His descendants insist he must have been pushed forward by the crowd. In any case, his political outlook accommodated the cut and thrust of commerce, provided it was accompanied by a social conscience. This nationalist, who never hesitated to voice dreams of revenge against Germany, was also liberal-minded and quite willing to admit that not everybody had to agree with him. When the Dreyfus affair split France in two, Jules Lorrain, though not in Dreyfus's camp, did not refuse to listen to the arguments of his defenders. Above all, he practiced tolerance—the euphemism for skepticism. At Touvent he might have a political argument with one of the sharecroppers (a "wicked Red"), but in Jarnac he would look up the local eccentric—the only reader of *L'Humanité*[19] in the area—to discuss politics.

Above all, Jules Lorrain liked important people. He was particularly fond of the company of soldiers (officers, of course), and in the country he called himself Commandant (Major) Lorrain. The great of the world fascinated him. He was immensely proud of a very distant, but indisputable, kinship with the English royal family through a certain Léonore, born in the 1650s, who became, by marriage, Duchess of Brunswick-Lüneburg-Celle. Later, as a Socialist president, François Mitterrand would be prudent enough not to indulge in any hasty vainglory, even attending the wedding of the Prince of Wales and Lady Diana without revealing himself as a relation of the future king. None of his predecessors would have been so modest.

Grandfather Lorrain, to whom life seemed to have been kind, nevertheless had his share of tragedy. He lost two sons: one died at the age of four; another, Robert, died of tuberculosis at twenty. Robert, whose memory was to haunt the family for years, had been deeply religious. While still very young, he had been introduced into Paris's literary world—he was a close friend of François Mauriac—and had taken a great interest in the social Catholic movement. Jules Lorrain, who wrote to him in Paris every day, would have loved for him to have taken up a political career and, perhaps, to have been honored by the Republic. After Robert's death, this skeptic began to attend church. Following his example, the whole family became imbued with the ideas of social Catholicism—with the dream of a society that combined social cohesion with respect for the individual. Each in his own way, Jules Lorrain's grandsons were to keep those beliefs alive.

Joseph Mitterrand, or Papa Joseph, was not at all like Papa Jules. Where the grandfather was exuberant and voluble, the father was secretive, reserved, and misanthropic. Joseph Mitterrand's distinguished appearance commanded respect. He was feared. He was "cold, even icy," a man who "never spoke about himself."[20] One of his daughters admitted that she feared the time when, after her mother's death, she would have to live with him under the same roof. He would go out for long, solitary walks. He confided in no one and began to speak with his sons only after his wife's death, when he came to visit them in Paris while they were students. "Beauty doesn't matter in a woman," he would advise. "Only moral worth." In his own way, though, Joseph Mitterrand was a proud and loving father. As a reward for a good school report, he would invite his children to lunch at Dubern's in Bordeaux, the three-star restaurant of the time, whose old woodwork was particularly admired. Fifteen years later, the current president still makes pilgrimages there.

Joseph Mitterrand was a native of the Berry. An ancestor on his father's side called de Laroche had dropped the aristocratic *de* before the revolution out of "a sort of ostentatious modesty"[21]— or prudent foresight. Thereafter, there was a sprinkling of lawyers and minor businessmen in the family, but by the time Joseph came into the world, the family was in straitened circumstances. As a result, he was not to go on to higher education.

When he finished his studies at Notre-Dame-des-Aides at Blois, this first-class pupil, who particularly excelled in Latin and Greek and dreamed of entering journalism, joined the Paris-Orléans Railway Company. It was the beginning of a management career that was to take him from town to town: Nantes-Chantenay, Montluçon, Quimper, and, finally, Angoulême, where he became stationmaster.

According to his children, Joseph was about to be promoted to the supreme post at the Gare d'Austerlitz[22] in Paris when, in 1919, he was forced to resign to take over for his father-in-law at the vinegar factory. Joseph was forty-six at the time; young François was just three.[23]

According to others in the family, Joseph's wife had persuaded him to give up a profession in which he was not fulfilling himself. Or perhaps together they had decided that he should be closer to his children and put an end to his nomadic existence. Her father, she swore to him, would surely make room in the family business. In fact, M. Lorrain was far less well disposed to the idea than his daughter imagined.

Relations between the introverted son-in-law and exuberant father-in-law could not have been easy. Just as Joseph Mitterrand gave in to his wife and abandoned the railways, Papa Jules signed on again at the vinegar factory for another ten years. In business as in politics, it seems, the successor is always more or less an impostor, even in the best of families.

In order to bolster the family's finances, Papa Joseph then launched into insurance. He became the regional representative of the union group. He also opened a small broom factory. But although others might start with a modest workshop and carve out an empire, Joseph Mitterrand never got beyond the initial stage. For him, profit was a vulgar concern and selling an unsuitable occupation. When, after 1929, Grandfather Jules divided up his property[24] and Joseph took over running the vinegar factory, Joseph actually managed never to visit a single client. His children would not inherit a spirit of enterprise, nor a fondness for commerce and finance. Running the National Federation of Vinegar Manufacturers was for him a much more constructive occupation. "I believe he found satisfaction in representing his profession in the business world of the Charente. . . ." François later wrote. "My father was a very intelligent man. He always regarded himself as an exile in the Charente. He knew he was living at the end of a period and endured in silence the outmoded rituals and empty formalities that accompanied that period in its death throes."[25]

The taciturn, complex Joseph Mitterrand must sometimes have felt submerged under the flood of his wife's family. Indeed, in the

eternal quarrel between ancients and moderns, Grandfather Lorrain represented audacity and innovation far more than his son-
in-law. "Instead of building model piggeries, your grandfather would
do better to bring a little comfort to his own home," Joseph Mitterrand remarked gently, but caustically, to his children. "Rather
than flatter himself that he never sees them, my son-in-law would
do better to cultivate his clients," Papa Jules must have thought
to himself, though refraining from telling his taciturn son-in-law
what he thought to his face.

In fact, each was typical of his period and generation. Joseph
Mitterrand was one of the first men in Jarnac to drive a car—a
gleaming Chenard-Walker, whose spark plugs, the whole family
still remembers, constantly needed cleaning. When he took his
father-in-law to make a few purchases at Aubeterre, the old man,
who knew little about mechanics, remarked: "You won't need to
turn off the engine—I won't be more than half an hour." The
grandfather had belonged to that part of the Charente bourgeoisie
that had come under the sway of Bonapartism and been won over
to the ideas of expansion and free trade, social improvement, and
commercial conquest. The father represented the bourgeoisie of a
France that had emerged bloodless from victory only to enter the
great economic and financial depression of the 1930s. It was an
impoverished, frightened class more intent on cutting its losses and
awaiting better days than on reacting with new initiatives. The new
circumstances comforted Joseph Mitterrand in his melancholy and
regret that he had been unable to follow a more intellectual career.

Although both were men of order, Joseph Mitterrand was politically more conservative, more traditionalist than his father-in-law.
His children now describe him as a Christian democrat. "He would
have been quite happy to accept the monarchy," his son Robert
notes.[26] He was regional head of the Saint-Vincent-de-Paul group
and very active regional president of the National Catholic Federation, a group set up in 1924 in opposition to the Cartel of the
Left, which threatened to restore the anticlerical laws. Under the
patronage of General de Castelnau—a much respected soldier of
Royalist convictions, a vigilant patriot, and a man of the Right if
ever there was one—this group set out to mobilize the faithful to
preserve Catholic interests. The plans for outlawing private (largely

Catholic) education never had more determined opponents than the members of the National Catholic Federation.

Although he had never belonged to any party,[27] Joseph Mitterrand liked to attend political meetings and was not averse to doing a bit of heckling himself. At Jarnac, he supported the honorable councillor Rambaud de La Roque, the grandfather of Pierre Marcilhacy, the famous lawyer who was a candidate in the presidential elections of 1965 against de Gaulle—and François Mitterrand. In the mid-1930s, Joseph was interested in the views of Colonel de La Roque, leader of the Croix-de-Feu league,[28] and attended many of the colonel's meetings, his daughters remember. Was he tempted by Action française,[29] as local rumor sometimes has it? Those close to him vehemently deny this could ever have been so, especially after 1926, when the movement was condemned in an encyclical from Pope Pius XI.

Though they might have differed on details, Papa Jules and Papa Joseph were both Catholic and conservative (with a small *c*), and all the Lorrains and Mitterrands were with them. In the family, they loved God and France *terre et chair* (soil and flesh). They did not care for Freemasons, Germans, Bolsheviks—nor for socialists. "Before I was about fifteen, the names of socialist and liberal leaders were always objects of criticism in our house,"[30] Robert, the president's oldest brother, remembers. "I never heard anything harsh said about the socialists or communists at home,"[31] François Mitterrand claims, however. Of course, one can be brothers and not hear the same things between the pear and the cheese.

But it was a well-known fact at Jarnac that Joseph Mitterrand had no love for the Left. During the demonstration of July 13, 1936, that brought supporters and opponents of the Popular Front into conflict in the small town, he was among the opponents. Fred Bourgignon, then a young, left-wing dyeworker and now an artist living in the Dordogne, remembers very clearly how the day after the clashes Joseph Mitterrand went to see his boss to warn him that he was employing a dangerous revolutionary. "Nowadays I can't help but laugh," says Bourgignon wryly, "when I hear Mitterrand referring to Blum as his great ancestor!"

And yet that Catholic family cared even less for the "rich" and the nouveaux riches than they did for the Left. Though they were

not without money themselves, "they considered hierarchies based
on the privileges of money to be the worst kind of disorder. Money
was the enemy, the corrupter . . . their Christian faith reinforced
that view," François Mitterrand notes. He adds: "My father took
a harsh view of bosses, capital, money. I was deeply affected by
his opinions. As a result, I have never felt I belonged to that milieu.
I have always had a sort of mistrust of it, though no doubt certain
elements in my own character had something to do with that. . . .
Despite my bourgeois existence, I have never had any link of any
kind with the world of business."[32]

In the family folklore, the best stories are at the expense of the
local people. The Mitterrands often made fun of those who seemed
to them to be overkeen to make money: how could they be so
obvious and shallow? They respected the old dynasties, but made
sarcastic remarks about the children of the Protestant cognac families with their ostentatious ways and intellectual superficiality.

And for their part, the smart, well-dressed Protestant youth looked
down on the Mitterrand children. At Jarnac, where he never knew
poverty, insecurity, or indignity, the future leader of the Left may
have been affected, at least to some degree, by social envy—the
kind that breeds inferiority complexes and socialist ideas.

It was in this sometimes quite venomous struggle between castes
that Mitterrand learned how rigid the frontier was between the
clans. One is reminded of Maurice Barrès's words: "Young, infinitely sensitive, and perhaps humiliated, you are ready for ambition."

Although they barricaded themselves against what they considered superficiality, the Mitterrands and Lorrains were not at all
strangers to humor and gaiety. On the contrary, there was fun to
be had in the Mitterrand household. There were never fewer than
twelve around the table. Robert, the oldest of the boys and also
the most outgoing, was an excellent mimic. He would launch into
eloquent pastiches of Verlaine or Rimbaud; his range of talents
even included tap dancing. The Mitterrands were fond of puns and
witticisms, but jokes in poor taste were abhorred. "When François's
father was around, you were always afraid to say something stupid
or let some silly remark pop out," François Dalle, who often spent
the holidays in Jarnac, recalls.[33]

Conversation, which was always lively, often concerned cultural matters. There were interminable arguments between François and Robert, one of their sisters remembers, on such highly speculative subjects as: What is more important for mankind, a scientific discovery or accuracy in a Latin translation? Robert argued for science; François, for syntax. Such arguments could go on for hours, it seems, as if they were questions of life and death.

Papa Jules and Papa Joseph had the same ambitions for their descendants, though both were too respectful of self-determination to lay down precise careers for them. Of course, the children were expected to work hard and strive to get top marks. The family was too large for any of them to expect a large inheritance, so they had to prepare themselves for the struggle of life.

Jules Lorrain often browsed in a big book, the *Carus*, a sort of guide to occupations of the future. He noted with pleasure that commerce offered the most attractive possibilities. But he read that in a period of economic disorder it was better not to risk one's future in industry, being safer to work for the state, in the civil service, or in the army. Two of his grandsons who also had a gift for commerce, Pierre Sarrazin and Philippe Mitterrand (the youngest member of the family),[34] were interested in the cognac business. But it was no accident that, of the Mitterrand brothers, Robert entered the Ecole Polytechnique, France's major engineering school, and Jacques went to Saint-Cyr, the military academy. Both choices delighted the grandfather, of course, who set great store by uniforms and the giant corporations of the state. His ideal would have been to have another grandson rise to the Cour des Comptes (Audit Office)—*conseiller-maître* was such a fine title!

Joseph Mitterrand more or less shared his father's preferences. He still looked back fondly on his years of public service, according to his children. He was attracted to the bar. A career in politics, perhaps? Nobody would have dared look in that direction (except Papa Jules, possibly). There was a great wave of antiparliamentarianism at the time, as France lurched from one scandal to another. Everybody agreed the perilous road was more suited to mountebanks than to prudent sons of good families. Anyway, as Maman Ninie had always said: "Politics? It goes to men's heads and divides families."

The three women of the household were no less important than the men. Ninie, the wife of Jules Lorrain, came from a well-off family and had nearly married Ernest Monis, a Charentais who was to become minister of justice, and then, in 1911, prime minister. In the family albums, Ninie looks small and nearsighted behind her pince-nez; she always dressed in black. She did not stint her time where her grandchildren's religious education was concerned and prepared them assiduously for their first communion. Armed with firmly held principles, she ruled her tiny world of domestics and children. She was not to be interrupted. One had to say thank you, sit up at table, and keep one's hands clean. More austere and less outgoing than her husband, Maman Ninie did not share his taste for social intercourse. Nevertheless, she played an important part in family affairs. She said little, in this showing some affinity with her son-in-law. This thrifty and prudent woman admitted to only one extravagance: fine silver.

The mother, Maman Yvonne, reigned over the home. When she is remembered at Jarnac or Angoulême, the image always conjured is that of the "admirable mother." Unlike her husband, Joseph, she appears rarely in François Mitterrand's writings, yet still meant a great deal to him. "In fact, I did not know her very well," the president now admits. The reader of Mitterrand's writings meets her almost by chance, in the middle of a sentence, when her son remembers her saying: "All wars are wars of religion." It was a quotation borrowed from Montalembert, the nineteenth-century leader of the Orléanist liberal Catholics (they would now be regarded as centrists). In 1974, Mme Mitterrand might well have been pro-Giscard d'Estaing. She shared her husband's political ideas. In her youth, like so many young ladies of her time, "she was very enthusiastic about General Boulanger,"[35] her oldest son Robert reports. "She was a great communicator," one of her daughters insists.

Mme Mitterrand, a dark-haired woman with somewhat heavy features, was cultured and musical, outgoing and domineering, and showed a certain tendency to excess. Bringing eight children into the world (four boys and four girls) in ten years of marriage was rather reckless for a woman with a weak heart. All her life she imposed a severe discipline upon herself, rising at five o'clock in the summer, six in the winter, attending mass daily, and praying for long periods each day. "Is it not rather Spartan to raise one's heart to God four times in each hour?" she confided in her diary.

Yvonne took great care to teach her principles to her children—"but, for her, a child was never in the wrong," one of her cousins observed. When the children were away, they received a letter from her every day. Always conscious of their education, she was an early subscriber to the *Nouvelle revue française*, already a great literary review, and she guided them in their reading: Claudel, Bernanos, Jules Romain, Maurice Barrès, Marie Noël, without forgetting, of course, such regional writers as Jacques Chardonne, François Mauriac, the brothers Tharaud, and Alfred de Vigny. Yvonne Mitterrand died in January 1936 at the age of fifty-eight.

Her sister Antoinette (known as Mamie), the mother of Pierre and Lolotte, then shared in the upbringing of the young Mitterrands at Touvent. With a schoolteachers' guide, she taught them spelling and grammar. As even-tempered as Maman Yvonne was passionate, Mamie complained all her life of weak health but managed to live to the age of ninety-four.

Of the children, young François was not the most self-effacing, but he was the most obstinate, solitary, and private. If his brothers and sisters decided to go to a party together, he would say: "You go on ahead. I'll join you there." If they wanted to put on a play, he would agree to take part only on condition that he be given the role of his choice and put in charge of the production. If the children were forbidden to touch an object on the table, he would challenge authority, train his eyes on some distant point, and bring his finger to within a hair of the forbidden object. "François, didn't you hear?" Maman Mamie would scold. "But I'm not touching it," the boy would reply with all the confidence of a man sure of his rights. "Ah, François, if you put your intelligence to the service of your ambition, you'll go far," his grandmother would grumble, pretending to be annoyed.

If, as punishment, he was confined to his room with nothing but bread and water, François would soon wander out, impassive, as if nothing had happened. For the punishment to be effective, his clothes would have to be confiscated. At Jarnac, the ultimate pun-

ishment was to tie up the offender's arm with a long string affixed
to the huge laundry cupboard. When tied up like this, the children
actually had a lot of fun—except François, who would be the only
one to make an effort to free himself. His cousin Lolotte puts it
this way: "He accepted neither authority nor advice. For him, his
own ideas were law."

He did not like losing at games. When Papa Jules beat him at
chess after a fierce, protracted game, François would stay up all
night plotting revenge. But his competitiveness stopped short at the
Monopoly board, that symbol of financial greed. "I hated the idea
of wasting my time haggling over money. I didn't have any liking
for commerce and still don't. I found [other games] much more
exciting. The law of chance has the somber attraction of philosophy.
I took great delight in watching that throw of the dice decide for
me; it sends you to the dungeon, to hell, or, when journey's end is
in view, suddenly brings you back to zero, with the entire distance
to be covered again, or it takes you past ambushes as if it had eyes
to see them. In all honesty I have to admit I did not imagine it
could betray my hopes, whatever misfortune befell me. My trust
in it derived from the faith I had in myself."[36] Is this not one of
the keys to the president's secret garden?

As a dreamy, secretive child, François found his greatest pleasures in books. He would disappear for hours on end: "When I
entered the little loft in which my parents, twenty years earlier,
had stored the complete works of long-forgotten authors who
wrote about the Crusades, the Church, the Girondins, the wars
of the First Empire, the smell of dust and musty paper stirred my
imagination and a great wave of happiness came over me. My
personal madeleine is to be found in that special dust that is like
no other, with a vague clinging smell of maize (the grain that
used to be kept in the loft in the winter) and poplar (the floor
on which I lay to read was made of that wood), a smell fed on
literature."[37]

Although he was not the boldest of the children when it came
to taking the plunge and learning to swim, he proved to be
the one who bore pain most stoically. His mother marveled that
he never once complained during an attack of peritonitis that,
at the age of eleven, kept him bedridden for over four months

(he endured an operation that left him with a deep scar in the groin).

Young François made up for his somewhat inflexible character with an immense charm, growing up well aware that if he used it skillfully it was irresistible.

2

THE IMPRINT

THE "FIGHTING WOMEN" OF THE SOCIALIST PARTY WILL
long remember August 4, 1982. It was on that day they learned
that compensation for maternity leave, so long demanded and so
long promised, was to be postponed indefinitely. Was it the result
of some unexpected hitch in the economy? Not at all. "It's merely
a question of ethics," murmured Pierre Bérégovoy, who had just
been made minister for social affairs, as he left the Elysée Palace.

"The government is trying to refuse women the right to dispose
of their own bodies as they wish," stormed the French Women's
Liberation movement. "There is a limit to women's patience,"
fumed Mme Simone If, chair of the family planning commission
and technical adviser to Yvette Roudy, minister for women's affairs.[1] To make matters worse, Roudy could not even intervene at
the time to appease her comrades' anger. A Cleopatra of modern
times, she lay on her sickbed, recovering from what is commonly
known as a nose job.

The Socialist party executive committee was astonished by the
affair. The following Thursday at a ritual breakfast, Mitterrand's
hierarchs at the Elysée sputtered with indignation as they attacked
their warm croissants: "What are our women members and voters,

our wives, daughters, mistresses going to say? . . . How can Béré[2] cut out the sixtieth of the 110 propositions that, from the beginning of the presidential campaign, have served as our table of the law. Shame on him!'"

The sovereign master's equivocal silence ought to have alerted his guests. The president was in one of those meditative moods his close friends know very well. A few hours later, the heavens would crash down on the heads of the croissant eaters. An interministerial rumor suggested the postponement of the issue had come from the head of state himself. In one of those strange and unpredictable changes of mind typical of him, François Mitterrand had listened to his conscience. The stalwart Catholic—the part of him that had always been against abortion—simply contradicted the part of him that had written the Socialist platform, that had taken such care not to forget women's rights.[3] The party man gave way to the moralist. Women's rights were suspended.

But only for a time. A few days later, faced with what seemed like millions of French women up in arms, the Catholic beat a hasty retreat. Passing off the change as part of the debate process, Pierre Bérégovoy announced triumphantly that "maternity leave would be compensated." The president had made up his mind, although his equivocations in the process had confused many. Indeed, the whole process was incomprehensible to anyone who did not appreciate the effect of Mitterrand's religious upbringing.

THE SCHOOLTEACHERS OF the Socialist party will long remember December 1982 . . . and even more, the summer of 1984. In December 1982, after eighteen months of patient consultation, Alain Savary, minister of education, decided at last to draw up a plan to revamp the French schools into a long-promised single, public, secular educational system. Delight surged through the Socialist benches in Parliament and in all the state teachers' training colleges. Since May 10 of that year, there had been a great deal of apprehension. Many had even begun doubting it would ever happen, so pusillanimous had the minister in the rue de Grenelle shown himself to be. If that call for reform had not been answered, little could be hoped for from this government. After all, had not the Socialist candidate's victory been largely due to those battalions of schoolteachers, assistant lecturers, and lecturers who had offered their services to the party and labored long, tedious hours in gray, smoke-filled rooms to build the dream of a secular society?

What the anticlerical Socialist reformers had failed to take into account was the determination of parents with children in private schools and leaders of Catholic education. No sooner had the minister revealed his plan than enormous, angry demonstrations broke out throughout the country, province after province, like some latter-day crusade.

The surprising thing was that such a plan was presented three months before the municipal elections. Had the prudent Alain Savary lost his head? At the New Year, a time when calm traditionally reigned in the chamber, the Left had gone and put a cat among the pigeons. Once again, François Mitterrand had to repair the damage. In a January 2, 1983, interview from his mountain retreat at Latché, he solemnly buried the hatchet. The president declared he would respect parents' free choice: "I want no constraints, especially in an area of such vital importance. My deepest personal philosophy, which I shall keep to my dying day, is respect for conscience."

But the war was not over. The words of January 2 promised no more than a delay. Alain Savary was soon back at work and rushing things. "We must get this business over with," the government began saying. "We must get the law passed!" The president had promised nothing would be imposed—everything would be open to discussion. Yet there they were, refusing the people's representatives the right to amend the bill and accepting, in a final shady deal with the Socialist deputies, changes that even stiffened the bill a little more. As a result, the government now had on its hands perhaps the greatest demonstration of popular opposition France had ever seen. The archbishop of Paris, Msgr. Lustiger, accused the government of going back on its word, and two million parents, teachers, and young people invaded the capital. Nevertheless, the Socialist parliamentary benches and teachers' training colleges were resolved, and the government's determination seemed unshakable. A few words from the president, sniffing the country air in Georges Pompidou's Cantal or Valéry Giscard d'Estaing's Puy-de-Dôme, suggested he fully approved of his ministers (beginning with the prime minister) and was even encouraging them.

Hardly a week had passed, when, on July 12, the French nation, busy packing for the holidays, learned from the lips of their president that he had decided to withdraw the catastrophic Savary law. In the process, the disowned minister, hearing the news on television like everyone else, decided to resign; the prime minister soon wanted to do likewise.

The teachers' training colleges, empty for summer holidays, were effectively silent; a stupor silenced the Socialist deputies, now deprived of their summer holidays because they would need to address new school laws. Meanwhile, it was announced that the new minister of education of the new Fabius government, Jean-Pierre Chevènement, would concoct, in due course, a new bill that *might* be put to a national referendum.

Soon everything changed again. Why put the bill to a referendum when the new measures announced by the new minister were more or less acceptable to the advocates of the private sector and did not upset the public? Eventually the entire battle fizzled out. On the beaches, hills, and woods, French men and women who sensed the importance of the event began to wonder. How could such comings and goings, such changes in direction be explained? Only the astute reader would have been able to find an answer in François Mitterrand's writings or speeches.

There could be no doubt that the public man was inclined to support a unified secular educational system in which private and religious schools would have to submit to norms laid down for all. But the private man, the man who wanted his two sons educated as he was, in private, religious schools (the Ecole Bossuet and the Ecole Alsacienne, in particular), was less sure of what was right and proper. The president replied to a congratulatory letter sent by the pupils' association of his own alma mater, the Collège Saint-Paul at Angoulême, "Neither time nor divergent paths can erase the memory of years spent together nor break the links that bind us to our institution. You may be assured—indeed, no one can be in any doubt—that there will be no question of challenging the principle, so dear to us, of freedom in education. If certain developments prove necessary, I shall make sure that they are carried out only after long, thorough discussion, and in such a way as to respect the interests and opinions of those concerned."

On receiving this august missive, the teachers at the Collège Saint-Paul—led by Canon Coudreau, who had been decorated in December 1982 with the Légion d'honneur at the instigation of the Elysée—concluded, logically enough, that nothing too damaging would be attempted by their former pupil. In fact, however, though it allowed for every possible hope, the fine, ambiguous wording of the letter did nothing to banish anyone's fears.

The fact that Mitterrand can espouse contradictory truths with equal sincerity is illustrated by another incident. On an official visit to the southwest in May 1982, he made a brief excursion to the Creuse to visit Jean Védrine, a friend from the Resistance (decorated in 1982). The philosopher Jean Guitton, whose family owns a house nearby, was invited to the festivities and greeted in more or less these terms: "M. l'académicien, you attended state schools and today you are proselytizing for the Church. I was educated in a religious school, and I have distanced myself from it. How do you explain this paradox?" The conversation then centered on the book the famous writer had devoted to his mother.[4] In it, he explained how his mother, a convinced Catholic, anxious for him to avoid any temptation to reject his faith, had wanted her son to have a full secular education. The question of the future of private schools then naturally cropped up, and François Mitterrand exclaimed, with sudden vehemence, as if to convince himelf: "Admit that the private schools are the schools of money, schools for bourgeois!"[5]

The gap between the positions of the political leader and the feelings of the ex-boarder at a Catholic school seems in fact to reflect not so much his opinions on private education as his feelings toward the Church itself. "Private education has become a weapon in the hands of conservative power, and the leaders of private education use it. They are our inveterate enemies. We can expect nothing from them. There is a clear identification between Catholic education and its parents' associations with the conservative parties," Mitterrand declared at a conference organized in Paris between Socialist believers and nonbelievers in November 1977.

"The Church is cut off from the working masses. To have administrative power against one is bad enough. But to have spiritual power (or what is supposed to be such) against one when one is poor is worse! . . . With Christ obscured and the Church in collusion with power, the only outcome left is a hand-to-hand struggle for victory here and now that will deliver you from slavery, poverty, or humiliation. . . . There is more charity in the heart of Louise Michel than in the Communion of Saints of the Roman church," wrote Mitterrand, with all the unhappy bitterness of one disappointed in love.[6]

Where are the roots of such rancor, such disapproval, to be found? In the eight years spent at the Collège Saint-Paul? "François Mitterrand could not have been shocked by his teachers' attitudes," his former schoolfellows declare unanimously. The Collège Saint-Paul of Angoulême was run by diocesan priests. It differed very little from hundreds of boarding schools whose images are preserved in a whole literature, and in which generations of boys destined to become—God willing—the elite of the region were nourished on a classical and profoundly religious culture.

At Saint-Paul, where, one is assured, selection is not based on social grounds, the children admitted were children of good Catholics. The sons of rich cognac merchants or paper manufacturers (the paper mills were the town's biggest employer), of shopkeepers, physicians, and lawyers mingled with children of penniless aristocrats and modest clerks without, everybody agrees, the teachers showing any special consideration for the better-off. Yet social differences were not entirely erased. There is nothing like a little inequality to stimulate amour propre or creative rivalries. So a distinction was drawn between the "excellent families"—the four Mitterrand sons belonged to this group—the "well-off," and the "interesting cases." These gradations naturally meant that parents and teachers regarded and treated one another in subtly different ways. The notions of caste, milieu, and class were of great interest to the parents. "What does his father do? Do you know if he's related to the X's or the Y's?"—such were ritual questions when boys visited one another during the holidays. For the children, however, such matters were of less importance. They all wore the same uniform: blue in winter with gold roses (already!) embroidered on the lapels; gray in summer with silver roses. This was because the school badge itself incorporated four roses, together with the motto *In graciam veritate* (In grace there is truth).

Discipline, though less severe than in the Jesuit college of Sarlat in the nearby Dordogne (François's volatile brother Jacques was threatened several times with exile there), was nevertheless, by today's standards, on the harsh side. The pupils rose at 5:45 A.M. "Even now a morning spent lazily in bed seems to me a rather immoral luxury," Mitterrand later confessed. They washed in cold water—very quickly in winter—and attended mass in the chapel, where the combination of incense and the unspeakable smell of damp stone made many an empty stomach rebel. Then followed study time, breakfast, recreation, class, study time, recreation, class, and so on until dinnertime. After evening prayers and preparations for the night, lights went out at 8:00 P.M.

"Your heart, my God, is less inflexible than the rules." Opening the school year for 1933, Canon Bouchaud,[7] no doubt anxious to rekindle cooling embers, wrote in the school magazine: "Learn to smile when at work, look on the bright side of work and of discipline, too! It isn't there to thwart you, but to sustain and protect you. And the teachers? See your relations with them on the bright side, too. They are fond of you, they want nothing but the best for you, even when they scold you—perhaps especially when they scold you. Look on the bright side of life!'"

The Abbé Maes, the master responsible for discipline, had his own views of life and a unique way of expressing them. "You must always practice exquisite politeness among yourselves," he preached. "Politeness is like chocolates: there are ordinary ones and there are exquisite ones." This story is perhaps less frivolous than it might seem. The lessons of this saintly gourmet bore their fruit, for when François Mitterrand is in an attentive mood, his politeness becomes so smooth as to be almost sickly sweet.

Morality weighed even more heavily on the schoolboys than the rigors of the timetable. Nowadays this morality would seem narrow-minded or finicky: the slightest breach of discipline—a collar opened at vespers, for instance—and the boys would be sent home for a week. A look exchanged with a girl during some excursion incurred a month's banishment. A letter from a girl meant expulsion.

What does it profit a man to gain the whole world and lose his soul? Apart from the compulsory daily mass, Sunday vespers, and various pious exercises on feast days, the pupils were supposed to go to confession each week. Each semester they attended a retreat under the direction of a Jesuit in a religious community at La Coquille, in the Dordogne. So strict was this way of life that, in later years, many pupils were put off practicing their religion and sometimes even lost their faith. François Mitterrand was not, it seems, put off. All his life he has loved religious rituals. One of his sisters-in-law remembers: "As soon as Danielle left with the children for the Christmas holidays in the mountains, he came with us to midnight mass." Jean-Noël de Lipkowski remembers visiting Cologne Cathedral with Mitterrand in 1956 and finding him prostrated in prayer, in the darkness, kneeling on the stone floor behind a column. The future president of the Republic was also very fond of stained glass windows and, before being elected, was planning to write on the subject.

In that tiny closed world of three hundred pupils and fifty teachers, François Mitterrand stood out. Even today, his old school friends feel a certain loyalty to him, though they do not all share his opinions or vote for him. No doubt his accession to power made him greater in their eyes, but all remember him as an outstanding pupil. "He never lost his nerve. For me he has always been an example," says Dr. L'Hoiry of Aubeterre. "He was likable and rather religious," comments Jean Rocheboitaud. "He was sensitive and very friendly. He had a good sense of humor and was very witty," reports Pierre Chiron. General de Bénouville, an altar boy with Mitterrand, notes: "He was a pious boy, filled with a great hunger for love and thirst for knowledge."

Yet from a scholastic point of view, François was not outstanding. Robert Mitterrand, his senior by thirteen months, was far more successful: Robert graduated from school at fifteen, excelled in every subject as well as in sports, and carried off all the prizes. To top it off, he won a place at the Ecole Polytechnique at an exceptionally early age, becoming "the youngest successful candidate since Marshal Foch," according to local rumor. In a letter that went down in family history, Robert announced his academic successes to his parents and added: "François is sixth. I asked him if he intended making an effort next month to get closer to the top of

the class and he replied that he was quite happy where he was."
A reply only to be expected, perhaps, from a proud younger brother
to an excessively brilliant older one, but a response nevertheless
very much in character.

François' peers regarded him as very intelligent, but his reputation scarcely went beyond that of an above-average pupil. He
was excellent in subjects that interested him: history, geography
(he called it "my passion, my poetry," which might explain his
distinct liking for presidential travel), French, Latin prosody, and
religious instruction. In these he carried off the first prizes. On the
other hand, he was poor in subjects he found uninteresting and
these, rather than risk a poor result, he preferred to give up altogether: "At school, I was hopeless at math. In the lower classes,
the math teacher, who rejoiced in the symbolic name of Trinques
[one of the meanings of the French verb *trinquer* is "to get the
worst of it," "to cop it"], left me after the first two terms to what
he called my daydreams."[8] And in language learning—the young
Mitterrands all spent part of the holidays each year in Great Britain
with English friends—François does not seem to have benefited as
much as he perhaps should have: he admits he seldom took part
in conversation. Rather than speak less than well, he preferred a
haughty silence. As a result, the English language did not come
naturally to his lips and he extended his opprobrium to the English
nation as a whole, to its pomp and circumstance. At table, he
resolutely refused to handle his knife and fork in the British way;
to this day, his peas are always consumed in the French manner.

The young François made his mark not so much by academic
success as by his manner. He affected an arrogant strangeness, an
almost romantic style. Though sociable and capable of friendship,
he often kept his distance, and, though a loner, he was quite capable
of joining in when he wanted to, taking part in team games if he
had any chance of shining. Indeed, there were occasions when he
threw himself into sports with the greatest enthusiasm. In 1932,
with Pierre Chiron, he carried off the school championship in Basque
pelota. In football, he was goalkeeper. His love of sports seemed
to bring out a tendency to literary hyperbole. In March 1933, he
described a cycling race and the victory of one of the pupils, a boy
of African origin, for the school magazine: "Tigori, the winner, was

reminiscent of those proud heroes of antiquity who outrun the goddesses."[9]

Sometimes he could be open, sometimes entirely closed, as if he had battened down invisible defenses; woe betide anybody who tried to breach them. He usually spent the recreation period alone under the pink-flowering chestnut tree, reading or simply lost in thought. It would come as no surprise to see him enter the chapel and take Communion every day. Indeed, some even thought they detected in him the special radiance that is the mark of the chosen. His philosophy teacher, Msgr. Jobit, was to refer to "the deep contemplative life of François Mitterrand" in the school magazine for 1935. No one would have been very surprised if he had chosen a career in the Church, provided he could hope to occupy a position worthy of him.

According to Mitterrand, he did not find it easy to take part in the communal life of the school. His arrival had been delayed for twenty-four hours by a cold, so he missed the official opening of the school year. This is how he relates the incident fifty years later: "It was weeks before I really felt part of a society whose structures had been decided the day before. By that I mean the desk you occupied in class, your bed in the dormitory, your row during prep, your position in games, your memberships in the various coteries that formed in the recreation periods. It took me weeks to move from the outer periphery at which I believed an unjust fate had left me through the concentric circles separating me from the innermost group of boys who had been there before me, as if, in twenty-four hours, the wall of habits had been built and the tight circle of friendship closed."[10]

It is possible this bookish youngster, hitherto unacquainted with any other society than his family, experienced this feeling of temporary exclusion more keenly than others. For sensitive souls, the first day in a boarding school inaugurates a long, hard apprenticeship from which one emerges with a coat of armor, ready for life's ruthless struggles.

The experience was all the harsher in that he was a shy boy, which explains why he twice failed his oral in the first part of his *baccalauréat*. "The oral of my first *bac* still haunts my dreams. There I am opposite the examiner, in the hall of the Faculty of

Letters at Poitiers, which smells pleasantly of summer dust. Words
are dancing inside my head, but won't get beyond my larynx. And
the little that ever gets out doesn't obey grammatical norms. It was
a sorry business. In my dreams, I still relive that examination, which
I failed because I was incapable of uttering a clearly articulated
sound. Even today, when I have to speak in public, a sort of refusal
wells up inside me."[11]

Yet François Mitterrand was capable of surprising everybody.
One day he asked his mother for money without wanting to tell
her what it was for. Mme Mitterrand knew her son was not a
spendthrift (at school, he erased the pages of his exercise books in
order to use them again)[12] and gave in. The next day she learned
he had bought a railway ticket and gone to Bordeaux to compete
with young orators of the region. A public speaking competition
had been organized by the League for the Rights of Religious Ex-
servicemen, and young François had carried off first prize for the
Aquitaine region. This was in 1934. Secretive as ever, he waited
until he knew he had won before informing his family.

Although he accepted discipline, this well-behaved pupil was not
averse to defying authority on occasion. One teacher, the Abbé
Perrinot, having forbidden his pupils to use their pens to take notes
during lessons, was surprised to see François quietly writing under
his very nose, flouting his order. "What is the meaning of this?"
the priest demanded furiously.

"But you forbade us to use a pen, and, as you can see, I am
using a pencil; you made no mention of pencils," François replied.
The affair caused quite a stir and was eventually taken up by the
master in charge of discipline, who came down on the side of the
rebel.

On another occasion, irritated by the school's lack of a sports
field, François decided to take the matter up with the supervisor.
The young pupil expatiated to the dumbstruck supervisor on the
importance of physical education in schools. "There is no freedom
without means," he concluded proudly. Prophetic words!

Such outbursts brought him a certain prestige as well as great
notoriety. He was regarded as a character. In a class photograph
from 1931, one can see, in the middle of the upper row dominating
his comrades, a good-looking youth with regular features and a

haughty curl to the lips; Mitterrand was fifteen at the time. The photograph brings to mind Alain's words: "In judging a young man, estimating his potential, and guessing his future, one should look not at his forehead, or even at the shape of the nose, but at the thrust of the chin, which indicates obstinacy—a quality without which the other gifts will be dissipated and which, with patience and perseverance, can make up for almost all of them."

If he himself is to be believed, François Mitterrand already sensed what his future held. "If you asked me if I ever saw myself as a king or pope, then I would have to reply that if such an idea ever crossed my mind, it could not have lasted more than a summer. But I did have the intolerable sensation of bearing the whole world, of which I only knew ten villages in a single province, on my shoulders. I thought so much about it that I almost had a sense of being its creator. In short, I was closer to myself and others at fifteen than I am at nearly sixty!" he writes, with commendable candor.

The calling would seem, then, to have come early. Some of his school friends even claim to have heard him announce it: "Later, I shall be president and my train shall stop at Jarnac." The story is perhaps too good to be true, but man's most audacious deeds often spring from childhood fantasies. In 1975, Mitterrand admitted: "In any city, I feel I am emperor or architect—I make decisions, I settle disputes." Emperor? No less.

In the early 1930s, the tumults of the century began to pervade the walls of that tiny privileged enclosure, the Collège Saint-Paul. The economic crisis was spreading and lines of the unemployed were growing longer. Schoolboys were still learning that France covered an area of 6.8 million square miles, had 80 million inhabitants, and formed over the surface of the globe that constellation of pink patches called the Empire.

But everyone sensed the world hung in the balance. As in every school for boys in France, arguments raged elsewhere. To the fury of the teachers, a modest local publication was being secretly passed from hand to hand; as its name suggests, *L'Action angoumoise* moved in the orbit of Action française, which had been condemned by the pope.

At Saint-Paul in the thirties, there was also, it seems, a handful

of left-wingers with ready slogans on the class struggle. In the midst
of this minor tumult, where barricades were built of words, François
Mitterrand remained silent. Lost in daydreams, it seems he was
not even aware of what was going on around him. "My school did
not train me in the Marxist disciplines. Marx and Engles were, I
suppose, taboo in latitude 46 degrees north. I passed my *baccalauréat* without hearing their names mentioned,"[13] he wrote fifty
years later, to the great surprise of some of his comrades.

Young François was regarded by his teachers as a pupil whose
main interests were literary, a boy for whom politics held no interest
whatsoever. He was of a religious turn of mind, devoted to the
cause of the humble, and easily moved to pity: "At seventeen, I
discovered Gide, Martin du Gard, Claudel, Jouhandeau, and became fanatically devoted to Paul Valéry. Through Dostoevsky and
Tolstoy I discovered a whole new world of sensation and thought—
in other words, the wretchedness of the world."[14] And perhaps this
young Catholic was beginning to identify one of the principal causes
of that wretchedness: money. In 1934, he wrote about his Easter
holidays in the school magazine: "Holidays, sun, gaiety, why should
one abandon all that? Mardi Gras has fled like a vulgar banker
with his fine clothes and his festive airs." Early on, the bankers
were put in their place.

When the four Mitterrand brothers remember their years at Saint-
Paul, they recall with nostalgia arriving at the station and walking
up the steep street, which soon got them out of breath. They remember their Sundays far from home in the big house belonging
to their good *"correspondantes,"*[15] Mmes Girardel and Guetta,
mother and daughter, both wig-sporting war widows. The two
women carried out their mission by getting the Mitterrands to tran-
scribe books into Braille for the blind while their one-armed cook
stuffed them with cakes.

When grown, all four visited the school often—François more
than the others. In *L'Abeille et l'architecte,* this is how he describes
that period: "The Bible had nourished my childhood. Eight years
in a religious school had trained me in the disciplines of the mind.
They have never left me. I have kept my ties, my tastes, and the
memory of my kindly, mild-mannered masters. Nobody washed
my brain. I emerged free enough to exercise my freedom." It is a

favorable enough account of an education that, if he is to be believed, developed his personality without ever narrowing his consciousness. There is nothing in these tender memories that might have disposed him to butcher the whole concept of religious education. Nothing, that is, except a party program.

3

WHO AM I?

ON SEPTEMBER 27, 1982, ON AN OFFICIAL VISIT TO GASCONY and Aquitaine, President François Mitterrand stopped at Figeac, a small township in the Lot. Since the press office at the Elysée had trumpeted abroad the news that he would be making an important speech there (though for months he had said nothing), the press, the government, and the Left came and held their breath. They were not to be disappointed, but many were surprised.

"What I have called socialism is not my Bible," the former leader of the Socialist party declared out of the blue. From that day on, the word *socialism* disappeared from Mitterrand's vocabulary for two years.[1] But the head of state continued after that opening blast, "It is my duty to express the wishes of the whole nation. Ah! How firmly I hold to that diversity, to that pluralism! And how I want France to remain profoundly diverse and different, without being divided. How I love those who challenge me,[2] providing I share with them the common language of those who love France and wish to serve her. Nothing will ever be done under my authority that can in any way alter that diversity."

The political commentators were amazed, ordinary French citizens perplexed, and there were stirrings among Socialist party members. What did it all mean? Little more than conjecture emerged. When all was said and done, the man who had spoken so piously of pluralism and ecumenism was also the president who said he was determined to transform the France of the free economy into a thoroughly socialist society. He was the victorious candidate determined to apply to the letter a very broad program of nationalization of enterprises, hearts, and minds—a "socialist project," which would replace the world of bourgeois archaism with a future of logic, science, and rationality. He was the fearless strategist determined to advance democracy and willing to share power with a few Communist potentates toward that end.

To double the confusion, François Mitterrand added: "I am determined that each of you, man and woman, be in a position to assume responsibility, to see his or her share of it increase. I want you all to be able to make use of your opportunities so you will never be held back or stifled by the organization of society. I believe in the value of the individual." The irony was that the new head of state brought with him a vast increase in the number of civil servants, the publication of innumerable detailed regulations, and state control over private enterprise, individual initiative, and competition.

But what of his words? Had he undergone a sudden conversion? Would there be a reverse march in his seven-year term? Were his words only double-talk, a mask for some Machiavellian maneuver? Or was the consummate politician spreading a very wide political net?

To answer these questions, it is important to establish just how deeply socialism runs in Mitterrand's being. Surely his words were no cry of the heart; he had known nothing of socialism in his school days.

The young François who had traveled from Angoulême and now found himself, on an October afternoon in 1934, on the platform of the Gare d'Austerlitz, was no Eugène de Rastignac of Balzac lore. That he felt a certain legitimate desire to succeed in life, that he had some ambition—of that there could be little doubt. If it ever occurred to him to throw down Rastignac's challenge to the capital—"It's now between the two of us!"—Mitterrand had no notion of courting the rich, getting introductions to the powerful, or marrying into money. Nor was his first act of defiance to go and dine at the house of some Mme de Nucingen, though he did have in his pocket four letters of recommendation from his family to influential people, including François Mauriac, a friend of his uncle's; General Guillaumat,[3] a distant relation of his grandfather Lorrain; the prefect Joinot des Yvelines, the brother of Madeleine Joinot, a friend of his mother's; and Maurice Marcilhacy, a barrister at the Conseil d'Etat and conseiller général for Jarnac.[4] Of his visits to these people Mitterrand was later to say: "Only the first—François Mauriac, as it happens—spoke to me about myself and my future. The other three waxed eloquent about themselves, so I only went back to see the first."

This shy youth, with his pale skin and profile of a proud Hidalgo, already had a penetrating gaze. Mitterrand seemed keen to measure himself against others, anxious to test his own worth. But what did he know at eighteen of life and the world? He knew the eternal order of fields; the names of trees, plants, and birds; the smells of undergrowth. He could tell time by the light of the sky.[5] He had spent his life in quiet, prosperous small towns. Nothing could be more alien to him than the world of factories and desolate suburbs. He felt no temptation to rebel against his background, his culture, and the morals he had imbibed. He had, as one used to say then, a "social conscience," but he was mainly a bookish young man, for he had read a great deal and books were his dearest companions.

François Mauriac guessed this better than anybody. "He had been a Christian boy, like me, living in the provinces. He wanted what I had wanted as he looked out to the hillsides and forests of the Guyenne and the Saintonge rising up before him. He had been that Barrésian child, clenching his fists in a desire to dominate life. He decided to sacrifice everything for that domination."[6]

Unlike so many provincials, disoriented by the harsh ways of the Paris jungle and sordid accommodations that awaited them, François Mitterrand did not have to defend himself against temptation or vice. He was to have the privilege of learning freedom under the gentle protection of a milieu that was to be an extension of the family cocoon and the world of his school at Angoulême. At 104, rue de Vaugirard, he found food and lodging assured. The school was an establishment run by Marist priests.[7] Some hundred provincial students shared his happy lot. All came from "good families," all were Catholic and middle class. "We weren't the cream of society," said one former boarder, "*they* tended to go to the *jèzes* [the Jesuits]." François Mitterrand had one advantage over most of his fellow boarders: the good fathers were positively disposed toward him. After all, he was the nephew of Robert Lorrain, one of their most beloved ex-boarders, who had died young and whom François Mauriac had described as "an angelic boy, one of those whom Maeterlinck calls the forewarned, because they have a sense that God will take them before life has sullied them." This relative, which made young François particularly welcome, was also no doubt a standard to be lived up to.

All those who stayed at "104," as they called it, have fond memories of the place. At the beginning of the academic year of 1934, Henri Lacombe, chairman of the students' committee, welcomed the newcomers and defined the atmosphere in this way: "You will never feel alone here. This old house has preserved the traditions of urbanity and charm peculiar to French life, of polite society at the best periods. Here the term *student* will never be used by anybody in a pejorative sense. Politeness and consideration for others have created this atmosphere, which you will come to love and in which friendship will flourish."

Every Wednesday evening, lecturers—preferably well known and fashionable—came to broaden the young men's intellectual horizons. Daniel Rops came to speak about God; François Mauriac, an old boarder at "104," about literature; Jean Guitton, also a former boarder, about philosophy; Henri de Taste, a deputy for Paris, about a journey to Tahiti; Canon Thellier de Poncheville, about Jacques Cartier and his mission to Canada; economist Gaëtan Pirou, about the crisis in capitalism, concluding: "There is no reason to believe it is about to collapse."

Passionate arguments were common, and in them temperaments found expression and convictions were forged. These students of law, the humanities, or medicine, candidates or students at the *grandes écoles*, were all conscious of their privileges. Their "104" was a mere fifteen-minute walk from the Sorbonne, Law Faculty, Ecole des Science politiques ("Sciences po"), and other prestigious establishments, and a short walk from the legendary Montparnasse and heart of the Latin Quarter.

The rooms at "104" were simple and still lacked running water

(although showers had just been installed on each floor when François Mitterrand arrived from Jarnac). François's room was soberly
furnished with a table, wardrobe, bed, and shelves for his books,
which included, among others, Jules Romains's *Les Hommes de
bonne volonté* and Dostoevsky's *The Brothers Karamazov*. Of the
characters in the latter Mitterrand was later to say, "They are not
just characters in a novel, but human beings who plumb themselves
as in real life." One thing is clear: François Mitterrand scarcely
seems to have suffered from the lack of luxury there. He did not
have, nor was ever to have, a need for opulence. He did not have,
nor was ever to have, even a sense of luxury,[8] even if it is all too
apparent he has a liking for pomp and circumstance.

François would never—as did his brother Robert—have thrown
his shirts furiously at the laundry maid at Jarnac because they did
not have enough starch. Nor would he, as did his brother Jacques,
have spent hours looking for a rare piece of furniture. Only the
prospect of finding some long-coveted book could inspire such
patience in François. (When he left for the army, his last words to
his young sister were, "Look after my books.") His clothes, often
regarded by friends as erring on the light side, did not make him
a trendsetter. Indeed, until quite recently, the first secretary of the
Socialist party seemed to be lacking in good advice about his appearance.

On the other hand, he must have appreciated the fact that "104"
had a garden, a tennis court, facilities for table tennis and billiards,
a music room, and a huge library, where boarders could work in
silence and read the newspapers (except, of course, for *L'Action
française* and *L'Humanité*).

Thanks to the diligent bursar, Abbé Haour, the food was good
and plentiful. The lay sisters added a kindly note: if one of the
students happened to be sick, Mother Marc would tirelessly climb
the stairs with vegetable broth. The constraints were not harsh:
one had to be punctual at meals (latecomers had to come and bow
before the superior as a sign of contrition); after dinner, everyone
was asked to meditate for a few minutes in the basement chapel
("there is only one interesting thing in the world, and that is becoming a saint," the father superior, the Abbé Plazenet, would
often repeat). The students, who perhaps didn't agree with him,

could go out in the evening on condition they not abuse their leave and come back at an acceptable hour (11:30 P. M.), when the janitor would be waiting.

Because his interest in politics soon became greater than that of his fellow boarders, and because he handled words with a virtuosity that was rare for a boy his age, François Mitterrand soon made his mark at "104." "He was certainly one of most brilliant students," said Father Rey-Herme, then a young seminarian. "He could be sarcastic, but never hurtful. He hated triviality and familiarity," said one former boarder, Bernard Warenghien de Flory. Mitterrand was to make a lasting impression on his contemporaries there. He went on seeing them; every year, they met for dinner in a Latin Quarter restaurant, but politics was strictly banned from the friendly gatherings. After May 1981, all those faithful friends were to be decorated with the Légion d'honneur.[9]

Mitterrand's love of writing suggested earlier on that he might take it up professionally. He often wrote for the review *Montalembert*. He loved unusual words and rare turns of phrase. His friends tend to make fun of this, though not without a touch of admiration. But this somewhat precious, slightly pedantic young man was not the Narcissus one might think. In that small religious world, his zeal and self-denial were noticed. François Mitterrand belonged to the Saint-Vincent-de-Paul Conference, a charitable association to which about thirty other boarders at "104" also belonged. Mitterrand was consistent in his support: every Saturday afternoon, he went off to visit his "families." He would take with him, as well as fine words, a pair of worn shoes that still had life in them or a coal ticket. In 1937, he became the association's president at "104," as his father was in the Charente. Father O'Reilly comments: "He carried out his tasks with firmness, for he is an authoritarian, severely reprimanding those of his comrades who did not regularly perform the duties for which they had volunteered." In October 1937, again in the review *Montalembert*, Mitterrand himself said of his acts of charity: "We went off each week to bring help to those people, feeling, deep down, we were making a great sacrifice. In exchange for our paltry gifts, they showed us their poverty and taught us that sacrifice was merely the opposite of penitence. If we learned nothing else, that lesson was a valuable one."

This young Mitterrand, so devoutly Christian, won the admiration of his masters at Angoulême. In the school magazine, Father Jobit notes in March 1935: "In his letter, François Mitterrand moves with great virtuosity from politics to economics, from the social to the religious. . . . He attended, and not only as a spectator, the recent incidents at the university and his family were not a little surprised to find in a leading newspaper, in the front row of the demonstrating students, the face of friend François. . . . He has served soup to the unemployed—'truly magnificent work,' he tells us. . . . He still remains a faithful *jéciste* [a young Christian student activist] and is keen to tell us so."

Another letter sent in March 1935 to his old school in Angoulême says a great deal about Mitterrand's state of mind at the time. As a student of "Sciences po," he describes the climate in the rue Saint-Guillaume thus:

> It's a right-wing school. Politics is of such prime importance here that religious matters often seem to take second place. The "Sciences po" student is usually Catholic, but not militant. He has not yet understood that the present crisis is not of a political order, but is profoundly dependent upon the moral order. He has not understood that it is not institutions that govern a society, but each individual's moral worth that constitutes his strength and governs the institutions themselves. That is why there is still a great deal of work to be done at "Sciences po." A whole mentality must be changed. Of course one finds a great many former pupils of Catholic schools who have preserved their faith intact and who practice their religion conscientiously. But how many seem to live it in the depths of their hearts? I know there are some, but I also know there are not many. How are we to remedy this state of affairs? It is a very delicate question to resolve. One would have to be able to replace the present aspirations of our young people with nobler, truer aspirations, or rather, direct the ideal that animates them with a different, stronger ideal. Christian action does not exclude political action—it complements it. But political action must not take precedence over Christian action, or it goes beyond its true role. This, unfortunately, is what is happening—hence, the imbalance in the forces for renewal.

The content of an action cannot be saved by its form. If one presents oneself as a champion of the cause of Catholic action, one is not met with sarcasm, but one does not rally those who believe they are living their Christian life.

What role, then, is one to play in such circumstances? I believe there is only one: do not Popes Leo XIII and Pius XI tell us to bring into the political groupings to which one must belong, and which are accepted by the Church,[10] the directives and principles of our faith?

Through social action, combined with political action (and the two are ever more closely bound up together), one must teach those around one that only Christianity is capable of undertaking a total renewal. Examples of the inner Christian life are indispensable, but they will count for nothing until examples of Christian action have been achieved.

Not yet nineteen when he wrote this letter, Mitterrand clearly considered himself a part-time missionary ready to devote himself to convincing the heretics. This moralizing side to his character was most apparent decades later when he tried to bring the sheep that had gone astray into the Socialist fold. The question here is whether all the great principles and fine sentiments he expresses are not primarily intended to bring reassurance to his former masters, and nothing more. Although they attest to his commitment, his friends from "104" do not remember him as an exceptionally devout Christian—far from it. He went to mass every Sunday, going to a different church each time. But there was nothing very remarkable about this regular practice. What was more rare was his taking Communion every Sunday.

"I remember a conversation over dinner when François Mitterrand assumed rather Voltairian airs, but perhaps he was just playing a part," says Father Rey-Herme. "He was, in fact, superficially Voltairian, above all, I think, because he didn't want to appear too conformist," Jacques Benet retorts. François Dalle, Mitterrand's closest friend, adds: "He was a practicing Catholic, but did not seem to be crucified by the problems of the faith."

In any case, as a youth, François Mitterrand already seemed to be imbued with the notion that in order to change events, one must

first change men. Can this be seen as a presentiment of some
political mission to come? Of course not—the time was not ripe.
"Lawyer, journalist, politician—what would François become later
on? We had no idea and neither did he. We were certain only of
one thing: he would never run the family vinegar factory," says
François Dalle. Yet Marie-Louise Terrasse, François' first fiancée
(of whom we shall hear more later), very clearly remembers him
saying: "Later, when I have a voice in the chapter, I shall decide
this or that."

THE PROTECTED WORLD of "104" passed judgment on the troubles of the day. While François Mitterrand continued with his university studies (a law degree and "Sciences po"), dark clouds loomed
on the horizon: the world economic crisis, the rise of fascism, the re-
armament of Germany, the Spanish Civil War, the war in Ethiopia,
the great Moscow trials, the *Anschluss*, and Munich. France was
split into antagonistic blocs and riven with furious polemics. Right-
wing organizations recruited more and more members and were
on the march. Scuffles broke out in the streets. Scandals deepened
an antiparliamentarian atmosphere. The rise of the Left, followed
by the victory of the Popular Front, terrified the bourgeoisie. "At
'104' our students were very conservative, very hostile to the Popular Front. Though some had hoped for a victory of the Left, there
were not many, and François Mitterrand was not one of them,"
Father O'Reilly, who succeeded Father Plazenet, remembers.

At this time, as many witnesses testify, Mitterrand was even an
overt supporter of Croix-de-Feu.[11] "He was my national volunteer
leader," Henri Thieullent, now a notary in Le Havre, explains. "He
didn't hide the fact," Jacques Benet adds. "For that reason, I even
had to warn him one day that the Communists wanted to smash
his face in," remembers Pierre Chiron, a friend from Angoulême
also studying in the capital at the time.

In the review *Montalembert*, the house's internal magazine, Jacques
Marot, a future journalist in the Agence France-Presse and a friend
of Mitterrand, had this to say of him when writing up accounts of
the lectures given in 1935: "François Mitterrand had a solution for
other problems that were just as serious: that solution was the
Croix-de-Feu. It showed us an ideal, a soundly based ideal—very

human because it was social, accessible because it was widely understood, great because it was French. Above all, Mitterrand is to be congratulated in managing to keep the tone of a perfectly honest man in a discussion that might have turned in the direction of pure politics, an area in which the most sensible people become stupid and lose their tempers without knowing why. This stems, no doubt, from a perfectly admirable calm, strengthened in him by a wise, philosophical slowness." And this is François Mitterrand at nineteen.

Indeed, on May 16, 1935, Colonel de La Rocque was invited to give a lecture at "104," in which he declared, among other things, "We must reestablish the nation in French tradition and, to achieve this, must destroy the maleficent influence of Freemasonry in finance and industry. I shall soon give orders for a mobilization against the revolution of Messrs. Blum, Daladier, Cachin, and their ilk." Nowhere is it said (nor does anyone remember it being said) that François Mitterrand had any hand in organizing that lecture, or that he behaved as a zealous member of the Croix-de-Feu.

The colonel was then at the zenith of his influence, embodying a nostalgia for order, the desire for state reform, and a certain awareness of social problems, all tinged with paternalism. Later, Marshal Pétain was to draw ideas and slogans from the colonel's program (Work, Family, Nation). Although he dreamed of a strong executive power, the colonel did not intend to override the laws of the Republic. He liked authority, but not adventure. During the demonstrations of February 6, 1934, in which the Croix-de-Feu showed its strength, it prevented a confrontation and a march on the National Assembly. Some people even claim that if the Third Republic did not collapse on that day, it was thanks to the Croix-de-Feu.

Colonel de La Rocque's supporters, who were generally of middle-class origin, were conservatives, if not reactionaries. But, contrary to the image so often propagated by his detractors, there was nothing fascistic about de La Rocque. He was much more a unifying conciliator in the manner of de Gaulle's Rally of the French People (RPF) of 1947 than a fascist in the Mussolini mold. He was more impulsive than dynamic. Although his young supporters marched around in uniform, this paramilitary style was not a monopoly of the Right. Even the Young Socialists sported scarves, berets, and arm bands (Hitler had not yet put parties off uniforms forever).

Despite his denials, rumor has it that François Mitterrand was tempted by Action française. Yet there is no evidence he joined the movement. His fellow students—and Father O'Reilly with them—believed that, for a few months at least, Mitterrand was attracted (at least intellectually) by the movement. In fact, like many students, he admired Maurras's literary style and turn of mind, which almost concealed what had become his more familiar beliefs. In 1937, in an article entitled "The Hunt for the Great Man," written again for the review *Montalembert*, Mitterrand wrote: "So often the elite is no more than talent put to the service of cowardice and stupidity. Men like Anatole France, who bang their fists on tables at public meetings and, in the evenings, put on their woolen socks, tell us nothing worth saying! Not one of them, except perhaps Maurras, goes any way toward fulfilling our impatient expectations. . . . We see nothing but sculptors of smoke trailing behind manufacturers of doctrine." That "except perhaps Maurras" reveals the respect Mitterrand felt at the time for the editorial writer of *L'Action française* and the circumspection a young Catholic like himself had to show toward him, at least publicly.[12]

"I was a student member of Action française and regarded François Mitterrand as definitely belonging to the same family as myself," declares Maître Jean-Baptiste Biaggi, who was for a long time an activist of the extreme right. He goes further: "All my comrades in Action française considered him at the time to be a Cagoulard.[13] They even claimed Mitterrand had taken the oath."

There is nothing to support this theory except Mitterrand's personal friendship, which he has never hidden, with several leaders of the mysterious Cagoule—first and foremost, with Jean-Marie Bouvyer. Bouvyer's family, like Mitterrand's, was from the Charente region and used to spend the summer holidays at Rouillac, nine miles from Jarnac. Mitterrand describes this family as "very entertaining, very excitable, and utterly devoted to Action française." The oldest of the boys, Jean-Marie, "a great friend of François," came to a bad end. A member of the Cagoule (no. 219), he was involved in the murder of the two Rosselli brothers, Carlo and Nello, both Italian professors (one of economics, the other of history) and socialists famous for their opposition to Mussolini and fascism. It was Jean-Marie Bouvyer who tracked down the victims to Bagnoles-de-L'Orne, where they were taking the waters, and observed their movements. Later, while doing his military service in the Third Regiment of the Africa Corps at Constantine, he was arrested by the police, and in the spring of 1938, was jailed. François Mitterrand, who does not abandon his friends in distress, visited him several times at the Santé; his fiancée at the time, Marie-Louise Terrasse, clearly remembers going there with him.

After that first encounter with the movement, Mitterrand—and many of those who know him well have confirmed it—became a very close friend of François Méténier. According to the Elysée, Mitterrand did not know Méténier until after the war, and then only slightly. It seems that in 1949 Mitterrand's eldest sister, Colette Landry, brought to his attention the distress of an imprisoned man suffering from advanced cancer. Mitterrand, then a young minister, intervened to get the man's sentence reduced and have him removed from prison. Did he carry his concern so far as to go and remove him himself, as some of his friends have suggested? Mitterrand himself does not remember doing so. Later, Mitterrand attended his funeral, as Pierre de Bénouville, among others, can testify.

Others believe these links were much older and closer. Michel de Camaret,[14] a friend of Méténier's, remembers a picturesque incident. In 1950, accompanied by Méténier, Camaret called on Mitterrand, then the young minister for France overseas and the man responsible for the former colonies. Méténier, who had a playful sense of humor, turned to Mitterrand and said: "Let me sit in your chair. I'd like to know how it feels to be a minister." As they left, Michel de Camaret claims Méténier turned to him and said: "Ask Mitterrand for anything in my name and it shall be given you."

In any case, this "diabolical individual, this fearless epicurean,"[15] was more of a troublesome acquaintance. Méténier had taken part in all the major actions of the Secret Committee for Revolutionary Action. He was, in a sense, the foreign minister of Eugène Deloncle, boss of the Cagoule, and as such had made contacts with those around Mussolini and Franco. At the time of the Cagoule trial, Colonel Emmanuele Santo, who was in charge of Italian counterespionage during the fascist period, recounted how Méténier had come to see the Italian leaders and told them: "Your duce is and will be our model and we agree with him entirely that fascism will become a norm of political life throughout Europe. France must, in our opinion, draw inspiration from the Italian fascist regime and apply it to its own situation."

It was agreed that, as a reward for the physical liquidation of the Rosselli brothers, the Cagoule would receive a hundred Beretta semiautomatic rifles from the Italians.[16]

Similarly, Méténier's implication in the attack on the CGPF (the ancestor of the CNPF) at 4, rue de Presbourg, which caused two deaths (two policemen on sentry duty) in June 1937, brought him a twenty-year prison sentence and loss of civil rights for life at the Cagoule trial in October 1948. A former leader of the Cagoule interprets this double attack in this way: "The purpose was, by blaming the attack on the Communists, to rid the country of the Popular Front, and at the same time get new credit from backers."[17]

François Méténier had joined Vichy in 1940 at the request of Raphaël Alibert, Marshal Pétain's minister of justice and himself a Cagoulard. As such, he was among those around Colonel Groussard, who ran the protection groups and arrested Pierre Laval, then head of the government, on December 13, 1940.

Méténier, a former industrialist from Chamalières, was said to be "a lover of good food, with an unbounded admiration for the fair sex, who lived in lavish style."[18] Du Moulin de la Barthète described Méténier as "a good fellow . . . slightly cracked, with a strangler's hand and the heart of a whore. A funny sort of thug."

Without wishing to implicate François Mitterrand in that secret organization, it must nevertheless be noted that Méténier was not his only friend who belonged to it. Mitterrand was also close to Gabriel Jeantet,[19] a former president of the student's section of Action française, who was responsible for providing the Secret Committee for Revolutionary Action with weapons. He was also later to be close to Marshal Pétain at Vichy and a propagandist of the national revolution. Mitterrand even wrote an article for Jeantet's review, *France: Revue de l'état nouveau*. The writer Jacques Laurent, Eugène Deloncle's nephew and a friend of Gabriel Jeantet (with whom he published a very anti-Gaullist work, *L'Année 40*), claims Mitterrand and Jeantet were "extremely close." "But," he adds, "Jeantet was very pro-Resistance and was deported by the Germans for that reason."

In his book *Hitler contre Pétain*, Jeantet tells how he was the marshal's contact with German officers who were plotting against the führer and how he worked tirelessly with envoys from the Resistance movement to prepare ground for a reconciliation between Pétain and the Gaullists at the Liberation. In a memorandum to the examining magistrate investigating his trial, Bernard Ménétrel, a confidant of the marshal, confirmed that Jeantet had worked for both Pétain and himself as an intermediary between them and the "secret army."[20]

It is clear, nevertheless, that Mitterrand's milieu and networks of friendships pushed the future leader of the Left far more toward the sulfurous banks of the extreme Right than to the side of the Socialist chimeras.

As the product of a disturbed and dangerous period, François Mitterrand was anxious, and must have questioned himself as he looked around. Did he really know as early as 1936, as he declared in 1969[21] (when he was beginning to dream of embodying the Union of the Left), "on which side right and justice were to be found" (the side of the Popular Front)? Those who knew him at the time certainly did not think so. Were it not that he was interested in a great variety of things, one would have every reason to doubt his words when, at the seventieth anniversary of Jaurès' death, Mitterrand declared[22] that, arriving in Paris in 1934, he rushed to the Café du Croissant to pay his respects.

Out of curiosity, Mitterrand paid several visits to the National Assembly, accompanied by the deputy for the Meuse, Canon Angèle Polimann, a man who belonged to the right-wing Independent Republicans for Social Action and lived at "104." This giant of a man was a good speaker, as he often demonstrated to the students. He had been chosen by the voters of Bar-le-Duc in 1933 on a platform denouncing "the sorry record of the left-wing majority" and advocated a "return to healthy traditions." At Vichy, he was to be among Pétain's closest colleagues.

Nevertheless, as he listened avidly at the Palais-Bourbon, François Mitterrand was moved by the intellectual distinction and moving eloquence of Léon Blum ("whereas I didn't appreciate it at all," admits Henri Thieullent, who was with him that day). Mitterrand was already sensitive to the quality and inspiration of words, from whatever source they came.

Another speech that left its mark was one by Paul Reynaud, the most brilliant and competent of the hopefuls on the parliamentary Right, who argued for the virtues of devaluation to the great detriment of the Left. Reynaud's reasoning so impressed the "Sciences po" student that he communicated the experience to his teachers in Angoulême. "He heard Paul Reynaud speak about devaluation," Father Jobit relates in the school magazine.

His brothers remember how surprised they were when, one day over lunch in Jarnac, François, who had become a disciple of the rising star of the liberals—what we would now call "free marketeers"—spoke out in advocacy of a change in the exchange rate of the franc. His family was greatly impressed by such unexpected, very Parisian erudition. It proves at least that he could be attracted by other points of view than those of the extreme Right. Provided it was modern in spirit and expressed itself intelligently, the liberal Right, too, found an echo in him.

In a battle that raged through the university at the time, Mitterrand stood solidly with the moderate Left: he supported Professor Jeze, the defender of Haile Selassie and international law against the policy of force being implemented in Ethiopia by Mussolini's Italy. Fighting had broken out in the lecture halls and the right-wing students wanted to prevent the professor from giving his lecture. The Left turned Jeze into a symbolic figure of the courage and independence of intellectuals when faced with the threat of fascism: "François and I were for Professor Jeze," Henri Thieullent confirms.

Was this a sign of a shift in the young Mitterrand's political thinking? No, for a little later, the Spanish Civil War, which was to play such a large part in the politics and literature of the time, hardly held his attention, even though he was to write in 1969: "I felt an instinctive horror for Franco, his band and his bandera."[23] At the time, in fact, François Mitterrand, as president of the students' literature section, wrote for *L'Echo de Paris*, a newspaper that was rather favorable to General Franco and hostile to the Left in general.

In the Latin Quarter of the time, where *camelots du roi*[24] and left-wing students exchanged blows as a matter of course, there was also a great deal of lighthearted banter at the expense of politicians and political institutions. Much fun was had by all. The politicized students tended to know one another, since the student population was much smaller then: in 1937 there were only about thirty thousand university students in Paris, as opposed to three hundred thousand today. Just for a laugh, Mitterrand appointed himself Ferdinand Lop's prime minister (a mere minister would not have been enough). Lop—the eternal buffoon of the Latin Quarter, the unconventional candidate of every election who, at each campaign, proposed extending the boulevard Saint-Michel to the sea—had found, for a brief entertaining moment, a disciple who would go far.

François Mitterrand was not one of those students who spend the whole day bent over their desks. He wandered the streets, observing what was happening in the world. At the Mutualité, he went to listen to the great intellectuals of the time: André Chamson; André Malraux, the bard of antifascism; and Julien Benda, the fiery rationalist. But he also listened to Maurice Thorez, the future leader of the Communist party, and Jacques Doriot. "We didn't see very much of [François] at lectures," Jean-Baptiste Biaggi remarks.

Nevertheless, his inseparable friend, François Dalle, tells us: "In the morning, we would go to the Law Faculty library, where the climate was ultrareactionary, and, in the afternoon, we'd be off to the Sorbonne library, where anybody who was not a Marxist was regarded as a fool."

Fifty years later, François Mitterrand remembers: "At the university, I was intimidated by my socialist friends. Having been initiated into scholastic philosophy, but finding the new vocabulary unfamiliar, it took me some time to recognize their dialectic as the medieval recipes I had been taught. . . . It bothered me to hear the Marxist Left speak a French translated from German. Words ending in *ion* and *isme*[25] rasped my ears. I flattered myself that I possessed a classicism that seemed to me to be revolutionary in a superior way."

The admiration of the young student was not easily won. He recognized no intellectual master. In him were combined a critical spirit and the wish to shock. In an article entitled "La Chasse au grand homme,"[26] Mitterrand wrote:

> Subject of meditation on the many ways in which stupid people can be taken in: the parties, our masters, have reached rock bottom; their stall displays nothing but calves' heads with tongues hanging out, because they have nothing more to say—they have just gilded the horns to make them look smarter.
>
> On the Left, among others, we find Romain Rolland, quite surprised at suddenly seeing himself so particularly appreciated, and with good reason, by those who have never opened a single one of his books. André Gide, who, knowing the gate to be strait, has chosen the ninth passage, the one that leads to Moscow. Oh! Nathanaël thou art translated. . . . Sometimes a blackbird thinks it's a thrush. . . . Thus the blackbirds Chamson, Cassou, Guéhenno, and Aragon have admired their plumage in the pool of their illusions and declared themselves extremely satisfied. Among them, only Julien Benda cannot possibly believe it is true.

Mitterrand's taste in literature revealed a mature critical sense. To a questionnaire put to the boarders of "104" concerning their favorite authors he replied: "Valéry, Baudelaire, Mauriac, and Claudel." In answer to the question "What is the role of literature?" Mitterrand wrote: "An indispensable and dangerous one: it makes one run the risk of thinking and feeling only as a writer." He cited Pascal's *Pensées* and Rabelais's *L'Abbaye de Thélème* as the books he would take with him in his knapsack if he were going to war. Paul Valéry's *Eupalinos*, François Mauriac's *Dieu et Mammon*, Montherlant's *Aux fontaines du désir*,[27] and Paul Claudel's *Le Soulier de satin* were the ones he said he would take if he were going on a long journey.

This selection reveals a sure sense of literary quality and a sophisticated liking for those who take a haughty view of life. In Montherlant's *Service inutile* there is a sentence Mitterrand seems to have made his own: "The only crowns that are worth anything are those that one gives oneself." He was not to be remiss in weaving those crowns.

Mitterrand's concerns and ideals may in large measure be explained by the climate of the period. "We felt war was inevitable, and that if Hitler invaded France we would not be ready," François Dalle remembers. "I remember a visit to Germany during which we first became aware of the German army, with its panzers and its athletes diving by the thousands into the Rhine at the sound of a whistle. We saw twenty thousand soldiers march past, and their obvious superiority made us very anxious indeed."

François Mitterrand never liked the army and its hierarchy, despite its constant presence in his family. He did not pass his PMS (préparation militaire supérieure) and was therefore to do his military service as a private. François Dalle notes: "Learning the soldier's handbook by heart struck him as utterly stupid. When I myself failed, François sent me a letter of congratulations: 'Bravo, I see you're no cleverer than I am.' "28

But it was 1938, the year of the *Anschluss*. Germany invaded Austria and Hitler entered Vienna in triumph. The great democracies did not do anything in response. François Mitterrand did. In a curious article entitled "Jusqu'ici, mais pas plus loin" ("This Far, But No Further") in the review *Montalembert*, he wrote:

France, England, and Italy have commented on the *Anschluss* in more or less curt terms. They have, effectively, acquiesced in it. What they are saying is, "That is enough—keep your hands off the rest of Europe. That is enough blackmail—our armies are being equipped and our peoples are beginning to lose their tempers. Be careful, you've come this far, but no further." This is a display of temper, but temper is not the same as anger. . . . It may well be true that France would be insane to risk war in order to save a lost peace: the death of one man is no doubt more serious than the destruction of a state. Yet, behind all these arguments, I still feel a certain unease. . . . Seeing the triumphal arrival of the god of Bayreuth on Mozart's native soil, I know what sacrilege is being planned and, in spite of myself, I feel a sort of shame, as if I were personally responsible.

Earlier in the article, he had written: "In politics, only two postures are tenable: either total abandonment or absolute force. Abandonment, if motivated by sacrifice, would be the finest testimony of a people's greatness. Individuals are capable of sacrificing themselves; why should nations not be capable of doing so? Is such heroism beyond the reach of that shifting, living mass of individuals that make up that fiction called a state?"

This thinking is certainly ambiguous. What Mitterrand seems to be saying is, more or less, "let's feel shame, but let's not do anything." It is a typical reaction of the time: half pacifist, half patriotic.

EVEN WHEN THE CLOUDS darken, even when danger is imminent, it is not possible to devote oneself morning, noon, and night to trying to tackle the world's problems. In the late 1930s, if one was twenty, in good health, and fairly talented, one found relaxation in sport. François Mitterrand showed a clear preference for games like tennis and table tennis—games played one on one. Even in team sports at Angoulême, he was goalkeeper, the most individual position on a football team. Later, he played golf.

At "104" Mitterrand was as much admired as teased for his competitive spirit on the court. Henri Thieullent remembers, with some amusement, "He only lost his temper when his doubles partner played badly." For a small aluminum cup, the pitiful trophy awarded at the end of the tournament, François did not hesitate to run the risk of sunburn or muscle strain. One victory is described as follows by Jacques Marot: "Huffing and puffing, a determined Mitterrand beat Perney 6-4, 3-6, 6-4. He certainly had our congratulations!"[29] There may not have been much style to Mitterrand's game, but no one could deny he was a fighter.

After sport came music. It was never to be the future president's first love, but his friend Jean Roy got him to like Erik Satie and Chopin. Louis Gabriel Clayeux, another boarder at "104" and also a music lover, got François Mauriac to share his love of Mozart and even, on one memorable occasion, took Mitterrand off to a concert with the famous writer. With Henri Thieullent, who had a superb collection of records in his room at "104," Mitterrand discovered New Orleans jazz.

He would also go dancing at the Cercle Interallié and Boeuf-sur-le-toit. Mitterrand has a good sense of rhythm, it is said, and loves to dance with his sisters, cousins, and women friends.

Then, of course, there was love. At twenty, shy men are often awkward with girls. "*He* was very aggressive with them," claims Jacques Benet.

Aggressive? Only until the day Cupid's arrow hit. It happened one January evening in 1938 at the annual ball of the Ecole Normale Supérieure, an occasion of great pomp, presided over by Head of State Albert Lebrun in the full ceremonial dress of the Légion d'honneur. In the crowd appeared a young beauty, chaperoned by her older brother, who turned out to be a student at "Normale Sup," and an elderly aunt. She was fair-haired, radiant, and wore a pink organdy dress that she had recently worn as a bridesmaid.

François Mitterrand, "still a bit spotty," did not hesitate. "Will you dance, Mademoiselle?" he asked.

The young lady agreed. Together they danced a waltz, fox-trot, tango, and Charleston. All evening she remained his prisoner, as he complimented her, amused her, teased her, and strutted about. In short, he jealously monopolized her until the aunt came and announced that Cinderella's coach was waiting. Just as in the fairy story, Prince Charming knew nothing of his new love.

"What is your name?" he inquired.

"Maman forbade me to tell anyone," she replied.

"Then you will be my Beatrice," he rejoined in a perhaps over-learned reference to Dante's heroine, the symbol of eternal love and chastity. "How old are you?"

"Sixteen," she said. This was not true: she was not yet quite fifteen.

"And what do you do?" Mitterrand continued.

"I'm studying for my *bac* at the Lycée Fénelon," she replied. This was another untruth—she was only in her fourth year.

"And where do you live?" he asked.

"Avenue d'Orléans"—now the avenue du Général Leclerc—"near the Luxembourg."

"Can I see you again?" Mitterrand pressed.

"Maman has forbidden me to see boys," the young lady replied.

But the enamored youth had enough clues there to track down the beautiful stranger. Every day, as classes ended at the lycée, he searched the Latin Quarter. One day, on the boulevard Saint-Michel, in front of the Biarritz crêperie, he found her, just as fair and radiant as before, with a friend.

"There! Watch how I get on with that girl!" the lovesick youth said with false boldness to François Dalle, neglecting to tell him this was his Beatrice.

Thus began an idyll with Marie-Louise Terrasse, whom the whole of France later came to know as Catherine Langeais, the television celebrity. The liaison was as passionate (at least for Mitterrand) as it was platonic. They met each day and he wrote her letters, all numbered.[30] François Dalle, and later Georges Dayan—a friend who was to play an increasingly important role in Mitterrand's life—acted as postmen.

François was madly in love. Often in the evening he took his friends to where she lived, gazed up at her window, and whispered: "She lives there. She sleeps there."

For six months the meetings continued, with crossed hearts and kisses stolen and given. One day, on the boulevard Saint-Michel, Marie-Louise saw François coming. He was particularly smartly dressed, though he was not noted for his foppishness, wearing a navy-blue suit, an Eden hat with turned-up rim (the uniform of "Sciences po"), and yellow gloves. He was holding a rose.

"What are you doing disguised like that?" Marie-Louise asked.

"You'll know soon enough," François replied mysteriously.

Trembling with curiosity, the girl was to find out when she got home. Her mother was quite flabbergasted: "Just imagine, a young man was here just now asking for your hand. So I told him, 'My daughter is much too young. She's only sixteen.' He replied: 'Two of my sisters, Antoinette and Colette, married at sixteen.' I pointed out to him that he had not yet done his military service. He only said: 'Very well, I shall do it then.' "

So François Mitterrand gave up his student's deferment. In 1938, just after the Munich Accords had been signed, he found himself at the fortress of Ivry, in the Twenty-third Colonial Infantry Regiment, as a private.

Meanwhile, the families began gathering information about each other. The backgrounds were compatible. M. Terrasse, a university professor, was general secretary of the Democratic Alliance, the Center-Right group led by Pierre-Etienne Flandrin. The family was well-to-do, holding its place in one of the small Parisian worlds just as the Mitterrands enjoyed an honorable reputation in their province. François and Marie-Louise were, therefore, allowed to meet officially. They became engaged during the "Phony War," on March 3, 1940.

Out of love for his betrothed, the student from Jarnac who cared little for military hierarchy was to experience the discipline of the barracks firsthand. For a young, cultured, middle-class individualist to find himself at the bottom of the military ladder must have been sheer torture. He had to learn to salute without ever being saluted in return, to get up at five in the morning to the sound of the bugle, then to spend the rest of the day wasting time, awaiting orders and counterorders, only to be suddenly called to perform tasks with the utmost urgency, to submit to the arrogance of stupid sergeants all too happy to exert their authority over the recruits from the world of privilege. He had to exhaust himself performing pointless tasks or on marches with no destination, to learn the army handbook by heart, to regard the so-called fields of maneuver as future burial places. The everyday lot of Private Mitterrand was grim indeed. Often, unable to bear it any longer, he went over the wall and, running the risk of severe punishment, jumped on the moped that had been lent him by François Dalle, who was still at university, flying off in the direction of the Luxembourg.

It was a sad time. It is easy enough to imagine his state of mind, frayed with passion for Marie-Louise and furious at having become so ignominious. His need to see his fiancée was all the stronger for having no other emotional outlet. His mother had died in January of 1936;[31] his Grandfather Lorrain, in 1937. François Mitterrand's youth was over.

4

TO BREAK AND TO SOW

THAT PIERRE JOXE, THE FORMER PRESIDENT OF THE SO-cialist group in the National Assembly who became minister of the interior, is a difficult man to get on with, most of his political friends would concur. People of the most divergent views agree on this point. All the leading figures in the Socialist party can recount how, during his period as president of the parliamentary group, Joxe would berate deputies and ordinary party workers alike, and how he pursued Pierre Mauroy, the first prime minister of Mitterrand's presidency, with rancor and vindictiveness. In the end, he even succeeded in irritating Mitterrand himself, who had always treated him with the utmost indulgence, as he has since by appointing Joxe one of his ministers. But the following affair created quite a stir in the little court at the time. Indeed, it deprived a few deputies of their rarest and most envied privilege: the ritual Thursday breakfast at the Elysée.

The story goes back to October 21, 1982. The National Assembly was about to debate a bill likely to arouse a great deal of passion and resentment. The bill in question would give amnesty (restore pensions and even decorations) to soldiers who had been compromised in putschs and plots in Algeria. The bill was Mitterrand's idea. He had promised it during his 1981 campaign, wanting to forget the past and reconcile the national community. But for a great many Socialist deputies, it was too bitter a pill to swallow. They had entered politics during the Algerian War and not, of course, on the side of those traitors, Raoul Salan and Edmond Jouhaux.[1] In order to get the deputies to show such indulgence and get the bill passed, their parliamentary leaders—and, above all, Joxe, the president of their group—would have to display a good deal of skill and understanding.

The breakfast on October 21 was specifically intended to pave the way for the maneuver. All the guests had arrived at the Elysée treading on thin ice, to say the least. They were prepared to pass the bill because the president of the Republic wanted it—but to pass it was to forget Pierre Joxe. Scarcely had Joxe swallowed his first sip of tea than he exploded in characteristic fashion, "Give these traitors their rights back? Why don't we bring back Pétain's remains to Douaumont and rehabilitate him while we're at it?"

"Yes, why not? We should think about it!" replied the president icily, not uttering a word more for the rest of the meeting.

The following week, the Elysée let it be known that the president would be taking his coffee alone until further notice. No invitation cards were issued the following week, nor the week after: his lordship was still sulking. In the end everyone had to accept that the ritual had been suspended. Pierre Joxe had stuck in the presidential throat like a fishbone. Pierre Mauroy, Lionel Jospin, Jean Poperen, Louis Mermaz, Paul Quilès, Pierre Bérégovoy, and several others then discovered that the president's feelings toward the Vichy regime were perhaps more complex than they had thought.[2]

The years of the war, Occupation, and Liberation played a crucial role in François Mitterrand's life. Though the same could be said of many of his generation's public figures, it was true to a much greater extent in his case. Those years brought with them a break with a certain background, milieu, and social order. Mitterrand's hopes in love had been shattered; he had given up practicing his religion; he had made the first major decisions in his life, escaping from the prisoner-of-war camp and joining the Resistance; and he had experienced his first political snubs, the most important from General Charles de Gaulle himself. Not all these events left immediate traces, for some were to have a delayed effect. But they all affected him deeply. The time to break was also a time to sow.

At the end of this period, for him richer in adventures than for many other people, François Mitterrand was still a long way from finding his socialist vocation, but was already dreaming of a great destiny. He could see that the fantasies of his childhood and adolescence were not so wild after all; he was now among the leaders of men and, perhaps, among the great ones of this world. The ambition to play the leading role would not leave him.

CAPTIVITY

In 1939 at the fortress of Ivry, Mitterrand was a young middle-class intellectual desperate to get married, performing his military service with little enthusiasm. That same year he moved on to the Lourcine barracks, in the boulevard de Port-Royal. Thanks to his friend Georges Dayan, Mitterrand had been able to get himself posted as private secretary to the commanding officer. He carried out his meticulous administrative duties conscientiously, the monotony being broken from time to time by a game of chess with his boss. The exhausting marches and exercises were over. Sergeant Mitterrand—for he had now been promoted—found a way of life much more to his taste. Indeed, he admits, "my civilian nights made up for my days."[3]

He had rented an attic flat, which he shared with Dayan, who was to remain his closest friend, through thick and thin, until he died in 1979. Dayan, too, was something of a character. Tall, handsome, refined-looking, always one for a good time, this North African Jew from Oran possessed a rare virtue: the ability to take an interest in others, but above all, in François Mitterrand. He seemed born to be his confidant, his liege man. This discreet man was certainly the only person with an intimate knowledge of all the twists and turns of the future president's private and public life. He never confided to his other friends more than a small part of what he knew. In order to preserve the freedom so precious to him, Mitterrand gave each of his friends the key to only one secret drawer. Georges Dayan, however, had the keys to all.

Ever a man behind the scenes of the political world, making

contacts and intriguing when necessary, Dayan kept up links with many different circles. He kept an eye out for any trouble that might be brewing for his friend and dared, when necessary, to tactfully whisper in his ear what those around him were bursting to say, but never had the courage to.[4]

Was he ever a socialist, this lawyer, briefly deputy for the Gard, later senator for Paris? That is another question. His commitment to François Mitterrand was always more personal than partisan. If his friend had remained among the enlightened conservatives, one can be fairly certain Georges Dayan would scarcely have minded. He gave his friendship, never went back on it, and never regretted it.

In 1939, despite the dangers that loomed, the life of these two young privileged soldiers was not too harsh. More or less every evening, François Mitterrand met his beautiful, fair-haired fiancée. And when, in summer, the Terrasse family went off to their country house at Valmondois, near L'Isle-Adam, the younger soldier was as assiduous in his courtship as ever. That is, until Thursday, September 4. On the previous Friday, the German army had crossed the Polish frontier. The day before, at 11:00 A.M., Britain had declared war on Germany; six hours later, France had done the same. That Monday, when Sergeant Mitterrand, his hair all disheveled, returned to the barracks on his friend's moped, his fellow soldiers were preparing for war. He hastily packed his things and reached the railway station at Pantin just in time. The regiment was on its way to Alsace. Those who thought they were going to fight soon learned to wait.

The "Phony War" had begun. In the cold and damp, the soldiers dug antitank trenches in the mud, uncoiled miles of barbed wire in the rain, got bored, and sometimes marched: in January 1940, the regiment was deployed between Sedan and Malmédy.

In the March gloom of that suspended war, François' engagement to Marie-Louise was at least a promise of happiness. It was a fragile promise, for by May tanks were rolling and bombs dropping. The waiting was over and the offensive began through Belgium. But the regiment had to fall back to Stenay, near Verdun. The Germans turned up on June 14 at a place called Le Mort Homme, a name that evoked sinister but glorious memories for the veterans of 1916.

François Mitterrand was wounded by shrapnel from a Minnewer-fer.[5] This wound was rewarded with the croix de guerre. Evacuated to Vittel, then to Bruyères, he was taken prisoner at Lunéville. Later, he remembered those battles: "I saw officers of my regiment who would die bravely in May playing poker in April without caring anything about their troops—for them, they were the price that had to be paid for the Popular Front. They did not like Germany, but they admired the Third Reich. They loved France, but not the French. They were nothing more than the residue of a society moving quickly to its end."[6]

During the summer François Mitterrand became no. 27716, at Stalag IX A, near Kassel. It was a situation he found almost unbearable. Three times he tried to escape. The first, in March 1941, he set off with a priest, the Abbé Leclerc, walked some 370 miles through snow and cold for twenty-two days, only to be caught a few miles from the Swiss border. "My poor friend had pneumonia. I hardly sneezed—that gave me a certain confidence in my powers of resistance. It was no small matter. . . . Later, I learned that inner strength comes from a long maturing process," he explained in a 1973 interview with Pierre Desgraupes of Le Point. The second time, he managed to get on a train and reach Metz, but was given away by the manageress of the hotel at which he was imprudent enough to stay.[7] On the third try—December 10, 1941—he pulled it off.

Once? Twice? A third time? These three attempts will surprise no one who knew the defiant young François. He had never been able to accept fetters or failure. (When, in 1980, someone expressed surprise that he was entering the presidential race again, he replied: "I only escaped on the third try." He also said: "In refusing to give up one refuses death.")

But his determination to escape cannot be explained by patriotic motives alone. Worrying letters confirmed that his most cherished ties were threatened. It was a version, set in modern wartime conditions, of La Fontaine's fable of the two pigeons: the temptation to fly away is more likely to affect the one who is at liberty to do so. François's escape was, above all, to reconquer Marie-Louise, whose feelings seemed to be wavering.

"I, too, escaped in order to be with the girl I loved, and when I got to Paris, she'd dropped me for a guy called Plat," recounts Patrice Pelat, with a touch of humor. Pelat was one of Mitterrand's closest friends in captivity—a colorful character, once an ordinary worker in Paris who had taken part in the 1936 strikes for holidays with pay, a former member of the Communist party, who was to become Colonel Patrice in the Resistance and, after the war, an industrialist.

THOSE EIGHTEEN MONTHS of captivity, from June 1940 to December 1941, seem to represent a decisive period in François Mitterrand's life, one worth considering in greater detail.

First, there was the setting, or rather, the moral climate, of the camps. Before they had time to understand what was happening, the men had been captured, piled pell-mell into trucks, and thrown into the camps. Their whole world had been shattered, the country had fallen apart, the army had collapsed, and all links, especially those that bound them to their families, had been severed. They numbered 1.8 million—almost all of them between twenty and forty years of age, and constituting one-third of the working male population, according to the 1936 census. They were entering the closed worlds of stalags (noncommissioned officers and privates) and oflags (officers). Of these 1.8 million, 51,000 never returned.

The first reaction was one of stupor; the second, of anger. Someone had been responsible. Far from home, the prisoners began indiscriminate accusations against the politicians, the Popular Front, the army high command. "On several occasions," recounts Jean Védrine, a friend of François Mitterrand's and one of the "men of trust"[8] in Stalag VIII C, "French generals had to be protected in our camp from the threats to which they might have been exposed from ordinary prisoners."[9]

In the camps, as in the country as a whole, examining one's conscience was the order of the day. Soon, the common thinking was that if France had been defeated, it was her own fault (which each Frenchman soon translated as my neighbor's fault). Weygand used the singular when delivering this great national *mea culpa* during a cabinet meeting at Bordeaux in June 1940. "France," he said, "has deserved her defeat. She has been defeated because, for half a century, her governments have chased God from the schools."

Pétain took up the theme. "Our defeat," he declared on June 28, "stems from our own slackness." And many others spoke in a similar vein. Félix Gaillard, a future Radical-Socialist[10] prime minister, wrote in 1941: "We have lost the war because we wanted to wage a national struggle with a government of parties. In a democratic government, a man becomes a man of his party before being a man of his country." In January 1942, seventeen leaders of the Centre d'Action des Prisonniers de Guerre Repatriés wrote: "The prisoners admit that the defeat was deserved, that it was not an unforeseeable accident. The military defeat merely hastened a process of breakdown that was already far-gone, but had not yet completely destroyed the fabric of French society. In a sense, it brought the process to a happy end."[11]

In addition to those feelings of self-recrimination, the prisoners felt great anxiety. News from their families was haphazard and belated. French towns had been bombed, the exodus had turned out onto the roads, in indescribable disorder, thousands of civilians left to their own devices. Because they knew so little, the prisoners thought a great deal was being hidden from them.

"I saw comrades weep for sorrow or powerlessness," says Jean Védrine, "imagining what was happening to their families, learning that one of their children was sick or had died, or that their wives or girlfriends were being unfaithful to them."

During the first few months, the soldiers had believed they would soon be set free because an armistice had been signed. Then they fell into despair and bitterness. They felt that now that France was at peace again and could enjoy the simple joys of everyday life, they would be forgotten. Doubt spread insidiously among them: after all, were they not an irresistible tool for German blackmail, to be used to force the French government to give in to German demands until the Third Reich won its ultimate victory?

The only consolation was that they were all in the same boat, and this feeling created a new sense of solidarity. Small clubs were set up with new rules in which the old hierarchies were irrelevant. Old divisions disappeared. For many, whole ideologies were rethought. Tepid Catholics became fervent for the first time in their lives; previously pious men began to doubt their faith. There was intense intellectual activity. The future was discussed and dreamed about, and the political and social institutions of a new France were imagined. The principles that seemed to govern Marshal Pétain's National Revolution—the cult of the nation, the glorification and protection of the family, the communal spirit, respect for work, regionalism, a return to the land—were accepted on the whole. Pétain was the object of almost universal respect. No one realized his advanced age had seriously undermined his ability and authority, if not his ambition. The defeat was not his fault—he kept up the image of a conqueror, a leader who had cared for his men— his "children," as he used to call them. In 1940 he won the hearts of the French army in captivity—the prisoners felt he alone had tried to negotiate their liberation and show concern for them. "If ordinary life had improved at all, it was thanks to the 'Pétain parcels.' Our stomachs, at least, were grateful," notes the Abbé Florin, who was one of the "men of trust" in Stalag IX A. Lastly, it was under cover of the marshal's person and before his effigy that the prisoners were able to bear witness to their patriotism in the presence of their German guards. To pay homage to the victor of Verdun was a way of reminding the enemy that it, too, had once been defeated, and that a new defeat was always possible.

"There were few political divisions in the camps: the great majority was for Pétain and regarded him not only as the head of state, but also as a grandfather and protector; there were Gaullists, whose numbers increased with the victories of the Allies; Giraudists[12] and many others who managed to divide their allegiance between Pétain and de Gaulle. There was also a tiny minority of pro-Nazis who were beyond the pale," Jean Védrine remembers. Gilbert Forestier writes: "Some prisoners even believed, at least up until 1942, that de Gaulle and Pétain were in collusion."[13] Védrine notes (and this is important): "Once they had been freed, a lot of prisoners remembered that de Gaulle had hardly given them a thought, and that they had heard nothing from him when they were in the camps."

It would seem that, at the time, François Mitterrand shared his companions' feelings. But above all, he discovered a world of which he had been entirely unaware. Until his captivity, he had led a life protected from financial worries and plebeian vulgarity. He had encountered poverty only through the distorting lenses of charity or literature. Behind the barbed wire he discovered privation, moral and physical pain, the inevitable lack of privacy that came hard to an individualist. What struck him most, even more than the privations, was the roughness of social relations. This is how he describes life in that first camp:

> At noon, the Germans brought in pans of rutabaga soup and small, round loaves of bread. They then left us to get on with it for the rest of the day. At first it was the law of the jungle: the knife ruled. Those who got hold of the soup pans helped themselves first and the others had to depend on their kindness for a little salty water to survive. How did the mass of ordinary prisoners overcome that absolute power? After all, a knife is a knife, and gives unchallenged power to whomever is prepared to use it. One has to have seen the new delegates—nobody quite knew how they had been appointed—dividing up the black bread into six slices, equal to the nearest hundredth of an inch, under the wide-eyed supervision of universal suffrage. It was a rare and instructive sight. I was assisting at the birth of the Social Contract. I shall not be telling anyone anything new if I observe that the natural hierarchy of courage and uprightness, which had just emerged as more powerful than the knife, was only distantly related, in the world of the camps, to the old hierarchy, the old social and moral order. What a mockery! The old order had not withstood rutabaga soup.[14]

What François Mitterrand, to his immense surprise, discovered above all in the stalag was the existence of other people. For the first time he met reprobates and lowlifes, but he also met left-wing workers, trade unionists, and indigent priests.[15]

In adversity, uneducated men sometimes prove stronger, more energetic, more courageous, and altogether more admirable than men from more comfortable circumstances. A whole system of values was oscillating in the prisoner's head.[16] He was not the only one who was confused. Many priests and religious men—as educated as he, as firm in their convictions and prejudices—experienced a similar shock of discovery, one that would contribute a great deal to the development of the French church after 1945. A great Jesuit, Father Dillard, who sneaked himself into Germany with those sent to perform forced labor, has described his astonishment at the time: "The workers' judgments on men and events ran quite counter to ours, often to a shocking degree. But, on reflection, we came to see that they were more imbued with Christian feeling than the others. Our way of life, our ceremonies, our concern with protocol, our literary, artistic, and philosophical culture were tinged with capitalism, bound up with a bourgeois form of civilization."

"Tell me about your life again. I may have something to teach you, but you have more to teach me," François Mitterrand would say to his companion Patrice Pelat, who had started work at the Renault factory at the age of fifteen.

Then there was Bernard Finifter, a Jew who had only just emigrated to France as a result of persecution. Mitterrand taught him French and was always curious to know of his traditions and the world from which he had come.[17]

He questioned others; he questioned himself. Captivity, loneliness, and an utterly artificial way of life were conducive to doubt. Take property: In his lecture of May 16, 1947, at the Théâtre Marigny, he told of a prisoner who received a food parcel addressed to him personally and suddenly rediscovered all the proprietary reflexes, becoming less sharing and less courageous:

> Rediscovered proprietary reflexes. . . . Each Frenchman carries within himself the concerns of the petty proprietor; all those who are not, dream of being one; all those who are, intend to remain one. . . . In the stalags, each person brought his own belongings at first and then, when he got his first parcels, kept what he could. He immediately registered whatever was edible, but whatever wasn't, he kept. It was a sort of supplementary prison, in which one could, with some object in view, remember earlier times or recapture the sensation of owning. One already had a world of one's own, but it was also a burden; how many of us never tried to escape because we became creatures of habit.

Again we return to relationships between men: after his first attempt to escape, François Mitterrand was confined to a section of the camp where prisoners reputed to be intellectuals—priests, teachers, lawyers, students—were kept under vigilant guard. He was amazed, he says, by the degree of consensus among them. Much later, in 1969, he wrote: "Cut off from the world, we set about building our own society. . . . The order of the earliest months had rested on the domination of the knife and on the hierarchy of the jungle. It was soon swept away and the knife, because it divided up the loaves of bread into equal parts, became the very instrument of justice. Neither my life in Paris nor the upbringing I had been given in my native Saintonge had prepared me for such experiences. I had traveled little. I think I learned more from that commando unit closed in upon itself than from the teachers in my youth. I am not saying we built the ideal phalanstery, but I have never known a more balanced community than that one."[18] The imprint was so strong that, forty years later, one of his closest friends said with affectionate irony: "François believed the stalag model could be transposed, and that French society might draw inspiration from it."

But one must be wary of attributing to the young prisoner all the feelings and ambitions of the Socialist candidate of later years. In 1947, his vision of the camp was much less idyllic. Time, dreams, and opportunity had not yet transformed it. He had not yet drawn from the camp the lessons—real or supposed—the man who dreamed of embodying the Union of the Left would find. Indeed, in the May 1947 lecture, Mitterrand took up a formula that was much revered at the time among prisoners of war: the spirit of the camps:

> I wondered and I still wonder what form the spirit of the camps would have taken were it suddenly to take on flesh. The spirit of the camps, the spirituality of the camps—yes, of course, that did exist, but not only in one direction; one might even go so far as to say the spirit of the camps was not only sharing bread, but also stealing bread.
>
> We should not overidealize the phenomena of captivity and believe those who went through that period have been made perfect by calamity, have had their faults eradicated, and, on contact with harsh reality, have come to repent their past and are ready to construct an ideal future.

Captivity was a daily war, not only with the enemy, but usually with one's neighbor, for it is much more difficult to live with those whom one loves than with those whom one hates; it is much more difficult to live with those whom circumstances happen to have brought to your door than with those whom one knows to be opponents. That, too, was one of the lessons of captivity.

Rather than the camp spirit, it was a matter of team spirit— one might almost say, gang spirit: a community of thirty to thirty-five men, subdivided into hundreds of communities of seven or eight, among whom total solidarity existed: sharing of parcels, tasks, work—yes, that division of labor that enables each individual to use his own strength more thriftily and for the common good!

And sometimes, too, for the benefit of a single man. The seed sown in the stalags was, in fact, to grow only very slowly, after thirty years of experience and trials. But the hope for a new society was all the stronger then because those "intellectual" prisoners felt a world had just collapsed: "What I had seen of the last days of the Third Republic had taught me there was nothing left in it to love, and nothing to be hoped from it. It fed on its own decline and drew enough strength from it for one to believe it was eternal. The day will come, I thought, when it will collapse of its own accord—exhausted, undermined from within. But when?"[19] These men did not regret the passing of that world. François Mitterrand believed this army of prisoners would form a postwar political force welded together by shared suffering—one any new state would have to reckon with.

Patrice Pelat remembers: "He said to me, 'You'll see, the politicians will have to listen to us when the war's over. We will do a lot of things together.'" Another prisoner, the left-wing Gaullist Philippe Dechartre, who would not meet Mitterrand until after he was free and working in the Resistance, had the same impression: "He was already becoming a champion of electoralism. He had calculated what political leverage the prisoners of war might have."

In 1940 or 1941, to hope for a new society was not necessarily to be on the Left. After all, at Vichy there was talk of the National

Revolution, and in Paris, of the National-Socialist Revolution. The
François Mitterrand of those years was regarded by his comrades
as a man of the Right. "Quite definitely on the Right," Maître Biget,
a notary in the Vendée and native of Angoulême, emphasizes. "He
was a Royalist," Marcel Pierron of Bordeaux declares. "He never
stopped talking about his monarchy."

In an editorial in *L'Ephémère*, the camp newspaper, prisoner
Mitterrand launched into an attack on socialism and collectivism:
"The social spirit is in fashion. We are not spared its exhortations
in articles, studies, and books. Everybody paraphrases in his own
way the words of the Gospel: love one another. But usually we
don't get beyond paraphrase. Who has not read to the point of
saturation such solemn, sometimes equivocal terms as statism, collectivism, socialism, and so on? In fact, they are merely various
ways of considering the same problem: how to stop a man from
biting his neighbor (or, perhaps, how to encourage him to do so)?
Words ending in *ism* solve nothing."

In another editorial in *L'Ephémère*, on November 15, 1941 (just
prior to his third, this time successful, escape attempt), he returned
to the themes of responsibility and atonement, which had been
worked to death in speeches and propaganda emanating from
Vichy:

Let no one imagine we are rebels, ready to submit our claims.
We know only too well the shortcomings of the complaints system. If we have been given the bitter task of representing before
history the generation that squandered the wealth and treasure
of more splendid centuries, then at least let our wounded, suffering nation, which, despite its pain and fear, has refused to
die, be able to depend on the support of her exiled sons. When,
in June 1940, the split occurred that separated us, to the East
and North, from France, which of us did not feel the weight of
his personal responsibility? No, we are not rebels, for, in some
vague way, we are awaiting the bill for that old account that
should have been paid then.

These themes of the sins committed by the French and the need
to atone were certainly the ritual refrains of Marshal Pétain's speeches,

the homilies of most priests and almost all bishops, including Msgr. Baudrillart, who, before the war, was listened to attentively at 104, rue de Vaugirard.

Paul Delouvrier, Robert Mitterrand's friend, explains the feelings of the young imprisoned François: "I often had news of him through Robert, and I remember very well that the general tone of his letters was very Pétainist. For a *petit bourgeois* like him, the marshal was defending familiar values."

And what of de Gaulle? In 1971, François Mitterrand wrote: "It was at Lunéville, in the camp where we were waiting to be transferred to Germany, that I first heard the name Charles de Gaulle. One of my friends, a talented young actor who dabbled in astrology, told me there was an unknown general who had refused to accept the defeat; then he added, 'What a fine name for a good story.' I agreed, and wondered what it portended."[20] A few lines later, referring to Schaala, the camp he had been sent to after his second escape, Mitterrand goes on: "We were able to pick up General de Gaulle's voice. It was the old nation, the old adventure, the old future. That voice presaged the spring with new love. It demanded effort and a determination to be strong. I had no difficulty understanding that what it was saying to me and the others was as simple as honey, milk, and bread. . . . That is why, although I have never been a Gaullist, I have always refused to be an anti-Gaullist."

These words may come as a surprise from someone who tirelessly harassed de Gaulle, the accursed adversary. But it must be remembered that when François Mitterrand wrote those lines, his old enemy had been dead for over a year. As long as he was an immutable obstacle, it was right to attack him. Once in the grave, he became worthy of praise; Mitterrand can be proud that in the end, he judged him more fairly. Indeed, two years earlier, in late 1968, after the general's authority had been challenged and the mystical link that bound him to the French seemed broken, François Mitterrand saw that the statue would be knocked off its pedestal and began to doctor his memories somewhat (without, however, completely abandoning all animosity, since the end had not yet come). He wrote: "Seen from Germany, Pétain and de Gaulle did not embody two contradictory policies. It was 1941. The voices from London scarcely reached our sheds. But the romanticism of passion was on the rebel general's side and I was twenty-five years old. That was enough for me. But my decisions were not affected by the general. He was a long way off, talked a great deal, and was a general. France seemed closer and greater than he. I admired him, but I was as proud of our deeds as of his. I hope I will be forgiven that youthful sin."

Let us return to the camp and to 1941. Behind the barbed wire, men's characters, as well as political and social ideas, were being forged. The future party leader did not pass unnoticed by his comrades. They regarded him as "courteous, but never familiar," "haughty and private," "insolent and rather pretentious."[21] Many have described the "fiery look" in his eyes. All recognize the hold he already exerted over others, his determination to be first. "I think he already believed in his destiny," says the Abbé Florin. And Maître Biget tells how "one day, a fellow in a khaki jacket, with oddly bright eyes, came up to me and said: 'We are both from the Charente, we are going to start a literary academy, and I shall be chancellor of it.' " As in all the camps, in conformity with the Geneva Convention, cultural activities were allowed by the Germans, who thought them—providing they did not assume too much importance—useful for morale and, therefore, for discipline. Thus the ZUT (Zigenheim Université temporaire) was started at Stalag IX A at Zigenheim. Among the founding members were Yves Brainville, the future actor; Robert Gaillard, who, in the 1950s, was to publish best-selling adventure and love stories; Albert Baron, Mayol's nephew and employee at the Folies-Bergères; and Bernard Monsour, Maurras's ex-secretary. "Mitterrand gave us lectures on Voltaire or Rousseau, or on the life of the Latin Quarter," François Château, a notary at Vichy, now remembers. "He sat down and talked for three hours without notes. We found that very impressive."

ZUT published a pamphlet bringing together cartoons of its honorable members (about fifty), each accompanied by an epigraph in verse. Mitterrand appears with his forehead crowned with bay— it is the profile of a Roman emperor. His epigraph, written by Maître Biget, is as follows:

Haughty, sensitive, and peremptory
Unchallenged temple of the mind

He has a brow circled with glory
One could say he is a Dante Alighieri.

ZUT also published the newspaper *L'Ephémère*. Naturally, Mitterrand was its editor, which satisfied his love for writing and power. He was, however, a permissive editor. On September 1, 1941, he allowed a prisoner, who signed himself Asmodée, to publish a strangely penetrating portrait of him:

Like Vautrin, François Mitterrand is a man who takes many forms. Indeed, he has a gift for ubiquity, and I strongly suspect he may know something of the fearsome secret of double personality. Like some Janus, we see him here, the elegant editor of the newspaper, a stylish writer, a perspicacious, subtle philosopher; then we see him there, in the infirmary, a punctual, hardworking, devoted servant of the oath of Hippocrates. . . . It must not be forgotten that Mitterrand has a private cult of aristocracy—that is to say, he is constantly consumed by the devouring flames of lyricism, beauty, elevation of thought. Physically, he is a simple, quiet creature, who, like Marianne [the symbol of the French Republic], looks as if he were preserved in honey. We must not be taken in: like the bee, he has both nectar and sting. He has a sharp mind and a tender heart, . . . which allow [him] to go through life with rose-colored spectacles. . . . But Mitterrand is a skeptical sage who could never have the degrading abnegation of the slave Epictetus and, even through rose-colored spectacles, his dark eyes look on the dark side. However, how well he agrees with the Latin elegiac: "I am gently bound by a mass of fair hair and delicate arms."

Let us make one final allusion to Marie-Louise. Mitterrand never stopped praising her charms. "Isn't she beautiful?" he would ask, showing her photograph to anyone willing to look. So surprising an attitude in this most reserved of men is no doubt explainable by a secret, troubling anxiety. He needed reassurance. On August 15, 1941, he wrote an article steeped in bitterness. It was called "Melancholy": "A year has gone by. . . . Autumn, winter, spring, summer, the wheat, the rye, and the barley are ripe again, and with them, all the things subject to the law of the seasons and passing time. A year and those we love grow up, grow older, far from us; a year, and the work of every day is done without us; a year, and oblivion begins to creep over our joys and our loves."

He would have to wait four months more—four long, interminable months—to escape.

VICHY

Mitterrand managed to escape from Stalag IX A, despite the barbed wire, searchlights, and sentries. He was caught at Metz. From there, he was sent to a sorting camp for escapees near Boulay. The Germans intended to send him off to Poland to teach him respect for the rules. But it was from the sorting camp that Mitterrand escaped. He was picked up by two old ladies who ran a café-tabac and who put him in touch with an escape line run by a nun, Sister Hélène. He found himself back at Metz. There, in a church, he joined up with two other escapees. They caught the train that ran along the frontier (Lorraine had been annexed by the Third Reich), knowing that, nine miles away, work on the track would be so heavy the train would be forced to slow down. They would then be able to jump and run. In the black of night, in the middle of a storm, they found themselves again in the occupied zone of France. The three separated. In mid-December, François Mitterrand entered the free zone through the Jura, near Chamblay.[22]

He was not there by accident. He knocked on the familiar door of his cousins by marriage, the Sarrazins, who lived at Mantry, near Lons-le-Saunier. With open arms they welcomed the renegade, who looked like a "bird fallen from its nest." They gave him big spoonfuls of *cancoilotte*, the local cream cheese. He greedily made up for lost sleep. Later, in the persons of two cousins of his own age, he rediscovered the delights of female company. He strongly advised one of them, Guitte (who was later to marry his Resistance friend, a former boarder at "104," Jacques Benet), to buy Zoé Oldenbourg's *Argile et Cendres*. A few months later, he wrote to her: "I now feel capable of leading men."

He was back in Jarnac with his father and sisters for the New Year celebrations. The entire family awaited a Homeric account of his adventures and exploits, but he said nothing. The war and camp had certainly changed him. In his 1947 lecture Mitterrand explained: "Freedom at that moment was also the knowledge that one had much to say to oneself; it was the silence that takes hold of you because it all seems too vast, because it all goes beyond the consciousness of a single man, and because freedom is, perhaps, in the final analysis, for each individual, little more than the simple possession of silence."

So his memory of that moment is a bittersweet one. He was happy to see his family again, but irritated by the gap of incomprehension that separated prisoners from free men: "The prisoners will understand me," he wrote three years later, "if I remember the sort of irritation I felt at the outpourings of my family when, after eighteen months, we were reunited. What I needed was a very simple truth, and what I was given were too many words, too many gestures."[23]

Perhaps, too, he was at an age when relations between parents and children become exasperating. Above all, he was very unhappy: during his absence, Marie-Louise had fallen in love with a Polish count.

But he had to go on living. To begin with, he had to find a legal existence once more: to get food, he needed a ration card, and to get that, he needed an identity card, a residence certificate, and a demobilization certificate. Anyone without papers was presumed a criminal and ran great risks. François Mitterrand set about getting papers and work.

When approached for the necessary papers, the conservative mayor of Jarnac refused Mitterrand—out of cowardice. This merely confirmed the low opinion the young prisoner had had for some time of his country's leaders. But everything was sorted out in the end. Thanks to Major Le Corbeiller, an army officer and close friend of General Giraud's son, who was, in turn, an army friend and contemporary of François's brother-in-law Pierre Landry, Mitterrand finally got a job with the General Commissariat for Prisoners of War in the rue Hubert-Colombier at Vichy. It was a modest job, as was the pay: 2,100 francs a month.

Should we be surprised—or shocked—that he accepted such a job? Probably not, for his feelings, as we have seen, were rather Pétainist, he scarcely had any choice, and not all those who worked

for the Vichy government were fervent supporters of the National
Revolution. Joseph Mitterrand at least was delighted as he accompanied his son to Vichy: the banker Jean Bréaud, a native of Jarnac,
clearly remembers meeting them that day in the street. The young
escapee rented a room at 20, rue Nationale, and placed on the
room's chest of drawers a portrait of Marie-Louise, who now loved
another man.

As he entered the spa town that had become a pseudocapital,
young François must have felt he was entering into his personal
pantheon for the first time: many of the intellectual elite still continued to support the marshal. Of course, François Mauriac no
longer showed the same enthusiasm for the man of destiny as he
had in June and July 1940. Neither did Claudel. But others were
still intoning praise: André Gide, Saint-Exupéry, Giono, Paul Mo-
rand, Jacques Chardonne, Drieu La Rochelle, and, of course, Maurras—all men whose talents had dazzled Mitterrand before the war.
Later, General de Gaulle was to remark with bitter humor: "All
the best people were for Vichy. We had only the Jews, the negroes,
and hunchbacks—the poor specimens and the bad lots."[24]

Being an employee at the General Commissariat for Prisoners
did not yet have anything very compromising about it. Mitterrand's
first boss, Maurice Pinot (a former prisoner, of course), was a
member of the upper bourgeoisie. Pinot's mother's maiden name
was Talleyrand-Périgord. His father, one of the founders of the
Comité des Forges, the powerful steel bosses' federation, was the
father-in-law of the ambassador André François-Poncet. As an
economics journalist, Pinot had also worked in the office of the
president of the employers' federation, C. J. Gignoux. Once free,
young Pinot, "whose temperament was more social than Socialist,"[25] went on a campaign to assist his comrades who were still in
captivity or had been repatriated. "In France, where people had
got used to the idea of living without them, their distress was
underestimated," he explained. "When they did come back, they
were all too often received as embarrassing intruders, with whom
one would have to share few jobs and inadequate supplies. They
were regarded either as unlucky or as not clever enough to escape.
They did not see themselves as heroes, but the prisoners found it
hard to take when they were made fun of by those who had hidden

or deserted their units, or who had been lucky enough to elude the enemy's grip."[26]

Specialized centers were needed to assist them. In order to plead their cause, Maurice Pinot had gone to Vichy, accompanied by Pierre Join-Lambert of the Council of State and Henri Guérin, both ex-prisoners like himself. Pinot gives his own account of those early days: "We were surprised by what we saw in the free zone. We seemed to be submerged under waves of flags, marches, and military music. In the town, generals and colonels swarmed the streets, strutting around quite shamelessly as if they had won the war. All political activism took place in a few hotels, a few houses, and even a few bars. For someone used to the order of the ministries in Paris, the spectacle of these senior civil servants, sitting around in hotel rooms, assisted by collaborators handling files in bathrooms, was somewhat disconcerting. Such a setting gave a precarious and derisory character to our talks."[27] But the mission bore fruit: in September 1941, Maurice Pinot was appointed commissioner for the rehabilitation of prisoners.

These senior civil servants, hostile to the occupying power and to the marshal's regime (if not to the marshal himself), were not the only ones to accept or even to claim a role in the institutions of Vichy in order to serve the cause of their compatriots. Maurice Pinot, among others, feared that those prisoners who had been freed or who had escaped would be used by the collaborationist movements; it was rumored that Pierre Laval, who had come back to power in April 1942, was thinking of organizing the repatriated men as a group devoted to himself.

It was in this context that François Mitterrand joined the General Commissariat for Prisoners. He soon found his own niche. On his office wall he stuck up a French Railways poster depicting Vézelay.[28] He was in charge of a modest sector, but one he knew well: information on the action of the commissariat and its branches, the prisoners' hostels, and the mutual aid centers throughout the territory. But, from the earliest days, his activity had a hidden side.

Indeed, soon after his arrival, he was working with André Magne manufacturing false papers. "It was a veritable factory. We made false identity cards and false food cards," remembers Georges Baud, then director of the commissariat in the southern zone and founder

of the Pétain circles in the stalags and oflags. "Manufacturing false
papers may not have been very heroic, but it showed his state of
mind," says Jean Védrine. Mitterrand was also involved in planning
escape lines.

It was by no means odd for a Resistance activity to develop within
a Vichy organization. Elsewhere, in the army of the armistice, the
youth camps, and so on, others struggled as best they could against
the Germans, although they continued to adhere to the marshal.
The earliest Resistance newspapers often revealed the same duality.
But the gap between the Resistance and Vichy was widening slowly—
above all, after the occupation of the southern zone on November
11, 1942. "We were fighting against the Germans, but nobody was
overtly against the Vichy regime," says Pierre Coursol, a member
of the General Commissariat for Prisoners.

For his part, François Mitterrand dreamed of playing a more
active role in the Resistance. During the summer of 1942, he went
to Montmaur, in the upper Alps, where, thanks to subsidies from
Vichy, a maquis was set up, perhaps the first maquis in France.

Antoine Mauduit (who later died in deportation), a former officer
and prisoner, a Catholic and mystic, a man with a dynamic personality, established a working party in Montmaur for escapees and
those in hiding. There Mitterrand met escapees from Lyon: Etienne
Gagnaire (future mayor of Villeurbanne), Jacques de Montjoye,
and the journalist Marcel Haedrich. Haedrich recounts:

> Montmaur was the fiefdom of a funny, fascinating character,
> Mauduit—a slightly cracked young industrialist from northern
> France. Before the war, while still in his early thirties, he had
> left his business and family and signed up in the Foreign Legion,
> in order, he explained, to rediscover man. A passionate admirer
> of Léon Bloy and highly religious, he had made the last few yards
> of the pilgrimage to Notre-Dame-de-la-Salette on his knees.
> Mauduit, like me, had been through an oflag. He had been lib-
> erated by volunteering to fight the British and Gaullists in Syria.
> On his arrival in France, he hastily forgot his commitments, of
> course, and opened a reception center where escapees would pick
> themselves up. When he considered them worthy enough, Mau-
> duit enrolled them in his chivalric order, which he called "the

Chain." The knights of Montmaur were to form the chain for national recovery and victory.[29]

In Vichy at about the same time, François Mitterrand met Suzy Borel (the future Mme Bidault, then a civil servant in the Ministry of Foreign Affairs), who organized passports for men to escape into Spain. He also met another diplomat, Bernard de Chalvron (a member of Pétain's private office), who was beginning to set up on behalf of the Resistance an infiltration network into government bodies. He also brought together three former boarders at "104": André Bettencourt, Pol Pilven, and Jacques Benet.

Was this as a cover? Or was it loyalty? At the same time, Mitterrand often saw others who were close to Marshal Pétain— Gabriel Jeantet in particular. Formerly an influential member of the Cagoule, Jeantet had opted for Pétain at the time of the armistice, just as François Méténier had done. Summoned to Vichy by Raphaël Alibert, also an ex-Cagoulard and then keeper of the seals, Jeantet had become a leading member of the marshal's office. Violently anti-German and overtly anti-Gaullist, Jeantet was a fervent supporter of the theses of the National Revolution. For the purpose of propagating them, he had founded the Association of France, intended to bring together all Nationalists likely to be receptive to the Pétainist ideology. In June 1942, he founded *France: Revue de l' état nouveau*, a periodical whose cover was decorated unequivocally with a *francisque* (or Frankish battle-ax), the Pétainist symbol.

Politically, Gabriel Jeantet was not a subtle thinker. His first editorial, in June 1942, is extremely explicit:

Thrown into war in the camp of the capitalist democracies through the inexplicable fault of a gang of international financiers, Talmudist prophets, Communists in Stalin's pay, and incompetent politicians; ill-prepared for the shock by years of anarchic deliquescence, riven by its social struggles, and ill-defended by leaders lacking any human worth, character, or honesty, our country has been subjected to the greatest military catastrophe in its history. And it is amid the terror of this defeat, through the moving voice of the marshal, that there suddenly has been

revealed—raised by the instinct for self-preservation that lives
in the people as well as in individuals—the doctrine of revolutionary salvation, opposed to liberalism and communism alike.
We were afraid—why hide the fact—of certain suspect alliances:
with that stiff-jointed bourgeoisie that was perfectly well aware
that the success of the National Revolution would mean the end
of its rule. We will say nothing of its fierce selfishness, the un-
scrupulousness with which it organized the subjection of the
factories, completed the ruin of the artisan class, and plunged
the peasantry, despoiled of everything it had, into mortal despair. . . . But among those who did not hesitate to follow their
interests of the moment, to flatter the Communists, to wear the
masons' apron, or to marry off their daughters to Jews, we know
of many who today declare themselves fervent disciples of the
marshal. But it is to them the marshal has declared: "I shall
resume against a blind, selfish capitalism the struggle the sov-
ereigns of France waged and won against feudalism. I intend for
our country to be rid of the most wretched of all yokes: that of
money."

The struggle against money, liberalism, communism, and the
bourgeoisie—these are themes dear to Catholicism. There was a
great deal there to attract young Catholics of the 1940s who had
been altered by their experiences—men such as François Mitterrand.

Mitterrand not only had links with a number of Vichy men
through friendship, but also through a certain community of ideas.
Eugène Claudius-Petit, who after the war joined Mitterrand's party,
the Democratic and Socialist Union of the Resistance (UDSR), relates: "In 1943, I met François Mitterrand on the banks of the
Rhône on behalf of the United Movements of the Resistance; he
explained to me that the Vichy corporatist laws were extremely
interesting. I remember responding, with some vehemence, that
they led to fascism."

Mitterrand was to take up all these themes after the Liberation
in the repatriated men's newspaper, L'Homme libre (and in articles
that were rather indulgent toward Marshal Pétain).

Money

On October 26, 1944, Mitterrand wrote: "You have expelled monarchs, some of whom were good men. But you have not understood that the most powerful of them still despise you. Money! King Money. . . . It is no use writing about democracy and tolerance, solidarity and fraternity—all that will fall to dust if we cannot see beneath those words the enemy lying in wait for us, the international of money." This text foreshadows in a most striking way the speech he delivered in December 1972 at the national congress for the signing of the Common Program of the Left at the Porte de Versailles: "We do not need monopolies, we do not need the masters of money, the new lords, the masters of armaments, the masters of the computer, the masters of pharmaceutical products, the masters of electricity and telecommunications. . . . We shall not demand much for the misfortune of so many centuries. But, as far as money is concerned, always money—well, yes, this world must change!" And on April 30, 1974, during the presidential campaign, Mitterrand was to recall in a television address the ancient hostility of the Catholic church to lending on interest (even though today the Vatican lives off exactly that).

The Bourgeoisie

"On the last day of the rising, we reviewed some of our patriotic groups. Ill-dressed, badly equipped, dirty, they bore the mark of astonishing nobility, but lived in Courbevoie, Pantin, Bobigny, Montrouge [working-class suburbs of Paris]. The others, or, to be more precise, the other—the bourgeoisie—were waiting for someone else to do the job for them," Mitterrand wrote on September 8, 1944. He had forgotten that most of his friends in the Resistance had not come from the working class—far from it. But then, one had to comply with the climate of the period.

The Parties

In November 1944, the future first secretary of the Socialist party attacked the party mentality: "Whenever division is introduced, the party mentality has already been there. This is because the party mentality has destroyed our unity and constructed the very misfortunes against which the prisoners of war strove so hard to preserve their own unity."

In his book *Eglise contre bourgeoisie*,[30] historian and sociologist Emile Poulat has shown how the "swing to the Left" of a section of French Catholicism in the 1960s had a precursor in the nineteenth century: then the Church had been fiercely against liberalism, political democracy, money, and pluralism (philosophical or political), and to the bourgeoisie, that had brought about the Revolution. The posture was considered ultrareactionary and counterrevolutionary. But in the twentieth century, the Left took up the same themes and dressed them in new clothes. François Mitterrand's writings show the extent to which he adhered to the nineteenth-century view of things. And the development of his thinking can never be understood if that link is ignored.

Indeed, in 1942, in an article in the same review, *France*, Mitterrand did not hesitate to place himself in the counterrevolutionary line or to describe post-Revolutionary history as "150 years of mistakes."[31] This article, entitled "Pilgrimage to Thuringia,"[32] evoked the feelings of the prisoner in the train that had taken him to Germany:

> Our miserable convoy struck me as symbolic. In its tragic reality, it marked the consequences of a gradual abandonment of reality. In nourishing Europe with its fraternal ambitions, by imposing its warlike ardor, by spreading its blood outside its frontiers (and for impossible frontiers), France had exhausted itself; it occurred to me that we, the heirs of 150 years of mistakes, were hardly responsible for it. I resented the triumphal history that inevitably preceded that slow movement of a generation in cattle trucks. I discerned the logic of events and asked myself if it were just that our misery should be the payment for misunderstood glory—or, to be more precise, if it were just that our decline should be imputed to us, because although we had abandoned our weapons, everything else had previously been taken from us. I thought of the judgments that would condemn our collapse. The corrupt regime, incompetent men, and institutions emptied of their substance would be all incriminated—and rightly so. Would the glorious mistakes of the past also be condemned?

Perhaps. But two other articles in the same issue are embarrassing in their proximity. Under the title "The Science of Man," Dr. Alexis Carrel, who was highly fashionable at the time, makes some more than ambiguous statements about the specificity of the French race: "Less than two years after the most complete defeat in its history, France is affirming not only her determination to rise again, but also that of developing to the greatest possible extent the hereditary qualities that are still intact, though they lie slumbering in her population. We must tackle the problem of the molding of personality through chemical, physical, and psychological factors of the environment!" And under the title "The Condition of the Jews in Rome under the Papacy," a certain Gérin-Ricard writes coldly: "Few examples in history provide a more accurate idea of the Semite peril than the way Rome had to treat the Jews—who encouraged prostitution, gambling, the receiving of stolen goods, and homosexuality—which was exactly the way they would treat a bull emanating from Pope Clement VIII."

The friends of the president of the Republic retort that such occasional excesses in *France: Revue de l'état nouveau* were a stratagem and that in those troubled times, in order to work for the Resistance in the evening, one had to put on a more conformist garb during the day. No doubt. But very few members of the Resistance wrote such texts—especially in such a context.

The celebrated episode of the *francisque* has given rise to even more polemic, especially as François Mitterrand has exposed himself to the blows of his opponents by refusing to face up to them.

One fact is certain: the *francisque* was awarded to him, he claims, in December 1943, together with the vague title of "representative of the students" (which does not appear to correspond to any post occupied by him at that time or before). What precisely did the *francisque* represent, and in what circumstances was it given to him?

Originally, the *francisque* had no legal existence. Designed by a lapidary working for Van Cleef's, a certain Ehret who was a former cavalry officer in Philippe Pétain's propaganda department, this little symbol was given by the old marshal as the mood struck him to those he happened to meet and like. Many (who were later to repent it) were quite willing to indulge in the boldest and basest activities to obtain the right to sport it in their buttonholes. So widespread did the practice become that its wearing had to be regulated; this was done by a decree of August 25, 1942. An order was founded run by a council whose first task was to draw up its statutes. This council, presided over by General Bricard, comprised—apart from members of the marshal's civil and military offices—various individuals, including Gabriel Jeantet and the journalist Simon Arbellot.[33] It met each month to decide on awards. There were two conditions: to have acted before the war in a "national and social manner," and to have demonstrated since an active devotion to the person and work of Philippe Pétain. Simon Arbellot has left an amusing account[34] of the meetings of that council, in which Admiral Platon, "a rigid Protestant with short-cropped hair and an intransigent-looking monocle" who had been defeated at Dunkirk on June 4, 1940, rejected nine out of ten applicants as "Gaullists," whereas André Lavagne and Jean Jardel, members of Pétain's civil office, rejected all those proposed by the admiral, saying, " 'He's a collaborator, I vote against.' "

According to Arbellot, "incredible as it may seem, the wearing of the *francisque* was the equivalent in Vichy of a sort of Resistance medal." We do not have to concede quite so much, but the small tricolor badge did distinguish those faithful to Pétain from those faithful to Pierre Laval.

Was François Mitterrand among Pétain's faithful followers? Indeed he was. "All those working for the commissariat were given the *francisque*," Georges Baud explains. "The marshal, who loved the prisoners, wanted to thank us for what we were doing for them. It would have been dangerous to refuse it. But there was never any official conferring of the badge, or any reception in our honor. It was given to me at the same time as to Henri Guérin, Pierre Join-Lambert, Van Batten, Laffond, Pierre Coursol, and even Maurice Pinot, who was highly embarrassed by the fact." (This last point is not entirely certain, since Pinot joined the Council of the Order of the *Francisque* in person.) But this is not the most important point. What is important is that Georges Baud and his friends were decorated before Maurice Pinot's resignation, which occurred in January 1943, whereas François Mitterrand, Pierre Chigot, and Jean Védrine were decorated afterward, at the end of the same year, when the southern zone had long been occupied, the Vichy regime was tottering, and equivocation was no longer possible.

"I never found out who exactly proposed me for the *francisque*," Jean Védrine now says. "I didn't ask for it, I was never consulted, no oath or commitment was demanded of me, and I never knew if I had a sponsor. The most likely hypothesis is that Dr. Ménétrel wanted, by that decoration, to show his hostility to Laval's policies." It is true that Dr. Ménétrel had helped out Jean Védrine and Pierre Chigot in early 1943, when they found themselves out of work after resigning from the General Commissariat for Prisoners.[35]

François Mitterrand also resigned, but he did have sponsors for the *francisque*: his old friend Jeantet and Simon Arbellot. Arbellot, who presents Mitterrand as an ardent member of the Resistance, writes: "He was aware of the patriotism, to the point of sacrifice, that animated the marshal and his friends; he was aware of the daily drama that was being played out in Pierre Laval's group, of the different, but constant, resistance of both men. One day he asked me—or rather, me and Gabriel Jeantet, who was in charge of the youth movements—to offer his candidacy for the *francisque*. It was accepted unanimously by the Council of the Order under the approving monocle of Admiral Platon."[36]

Mitterrand does not deny the sponsorship[37] of a man who, even in 1966, continued to regard Pierre Laval as a resister. But he declares that the *francisque* was never given to him, for the very good reason that he was then in London. In any case, it is true that he was no longer in the official employment of Vichy and was devoting most of his time to Resistance activities—while maintaining close personal ties with several members of the marshal's entourage. Was this a way of covering himself? The Communist Robert Paumier, who knew him well (and, like so many others, who was decorated with the Légion d'honneur in 1982 and then, like some, invited to accompany the president on an official visit to the USSR in June 1984), declares: "Mitterrand wavered between Vichy legality and the Resistance." Philippe Dechartre goes further: "Mitterrand was a Vichyite, anti-German, very brave, and utterly committed to the war." The future president of the Republic was later to carry his *francisque* like a cross. He always evaded the question, thus helping to create, and then to increase, the malaise.

The first station in this way of the cross was in April 1945, during the constitutive congress of the National Federation of Prisoners of War, a meeting in which Mitterrand played a decisive role. Rereading the verbatim reports of those congress sessions, one is struck by his professionalism and ability to manipulate the debate. From the opening of the session, the Communist Pierre Verrier, decorated with the Légion d'honneur in 1983, addressed him thus: " 'I see M. Mitterrand on the platform. I would be happy to see the lifting of the moral obliquy that still hangs over a comrade who, during the Vichy period, was given the marshal's *francisque* d'honneur. . . . M. Mitterrand may have had his reasons, but I demand that everybody in a similar situation go before a purging commission so that there will no longer be any doubt about them.' " François Mitterrand replied: " 'I was appointed by General de Gaulle, who must have been a good enough judge of men to entrust me with the post of secretary-general to the prisoners of war, because it was I who created the Resistance movement. . . . On the level of pedigree, Verrier, we might argue our respective cases. When the general appointed me—at a very difficult moment when great risks were involved, because, when I flew to Algiers in November 1943 and crossed the Channel in my little boat in February 1944, it cannot be said that such missions were very easy—he knew what he was saying.' " This was certainly a good way of answering without answering by making considerable use of an umbrella called de Gaulle.

Ten years later, in December 1954, François Mitterrand was minister of the interior. He was attacked by the Gaullist deputy for the Sarthe, Raymond Dronne: " 'The great republican you claim to be has too dubious a past to inspire feelings that cannot be produced to order, that instinctive outpouring called trust. I do not reproach you with wearing in turn the fleur-de-lys and the *francisque* d'honneur.' " Mitterrand replied: " 'That is untrue.' "

Dronne countered: " 'It *is* true, and you know it. I have watched your shifts and changes—you have always known how to trim your sail to the prevailing wind. I am convinced you were far less interested in France than in the career of M. Mitterrand.' "

On that occasion, once again, the young minister refused to clear up the matter. It is true he has never worn the fleur-de-lys. Did he ever wear the *francisque*? He could have confounded his detractors by throwing light on the conditions in which it had been awarded to him. But he never did. Was this due to pride, embarrassment, excessive skill, love of secrecy, haughty indifference, or excessive prudence? If nothing else, surely it was due to misguided calculation.

What is certain is that he was not immune to the political leanings of Vichy and the attractions of Marshal Pétain, so much so that in 1944, in the first issue of *L' Homme libre* (the newspaper of former prisoners in the Resistance), Mitterrand's companions had to ask him to tone down an article revealing too much indulgence toward the old marshal.[38]

Sent to cover the Pétain trial for the same newspaper a year later, Mitterrand wrote ironic articles contemptuous of almost everybody—judges, procurators, and witnesses—with the exception of one individual: the defendant.

THE RESISTANCE

At the time when the *francisque* was awarded to him, François Mitterrand had been a member of the Resistance under the name of Morland for almost a year. The occupation of the southern zone on November 11, 1942, seems to have played a decisive role in that decision. All his hesitations were now overcome.

Laval, entangled in the politics of collaboration, then tried to use the repatriated prisoners. Maurice Pinot refused to lend his name to such maneuvers and lose the respect the former prisoners had for him. So in January 1943 he was sacked (according to many witnesses, Marshal Pétain was not informed of the fact). Laval appointed André Masson, who was more docile, to replace Pinot. Out of solidarity with Pinot, all the upper echelons—fourteen in all—of the commissariat in Paris and in Vichy resigned. It was an almost unique example of the rebellion of a whole organization. Georges Baud, Jean Védrine, André Magne, Marcel Guénault, Pierre Chigot, Van Batten, and François Mitterrand promptly disappeared.

Two weeks later, in early February 1943, six of them met at Saint-Sylvain-de-Bellegarde (Creuse) in a house owned by Pierre

Chigot. There Magne, Mitterrand, and Védrine talked for hours about what they were going to do. How could they infiltrate the commissariat, now run by Masson? How could they oppose Laval? They drew up plans and thought up structures. The POW Resistance was born. It was later to adopt the name National Rally of Prisoners of War; former boarders at "104," including André Bettencourt, François Dalle, and Jacques Benet (Mitterrand already knew how to rally his faithful), were to join the team from the outset. "We were all on an equal footing," Benet recounts. "There was no leader. The key man, the main organizer of the action, was Maurice Pinot. Though discreet out of prudence and not very talkative out of shyness, his credit and influence were considerable. It was he who obtained from General Revers[39] the finance necessary to set many of us up. Our first equipment and weapons came from the Army Resistance Organization."

"François Mitterrand and Jacques Benet were the two motivating forces of a team that eschewed any hierarchy," says Maurice Pinot. "Each member contributed what he could, according to his means, character, own methods, and area of influence."

But Mitterrand was not slow to impose his preeminence. "I find it hard today to analyze exactly how François, in a few months, became the most important of us," says Jean Védrine. "I have no memory of the title of president that has sometimes been attributed to him in later accounts, but it was from him that I received information, directives, and, later, funds. He strove with great tenacity to maintain networks of friendship with the repatriates' associations in the departments—which were to prove, when it came to important decisions, stronger and more effective than the links between parties. He had political ambition, in the noble sense of the term, for himself and for us." Indeed, Mitterrand irritated more than one person. "He showed too much self-assurance, cynicism, and sometimes offhandedness," Védrine admits. "He was thought to be cold and individualistic, but what irritated and disturbed his friends most was his frequent lateness at meetings, though it is true this misled his opponents."

Nevertheless, François Mitterrand was emerging. He was becoming a leader; certainly he was behaving like one. The times were propitious. The resisters, all volunteers, knew no other hierarchy than the one they created, no ranks but those they assumed. Promotion could be extremely rapid. War always deals the cards again—underground war even more so. Opportunities occur every morning to a young, impatient man whose horizons are so far-reaching. "He was already a potential politician, while his friends had no particular ambitions," says Philippe Dechartre. "The fact that Pinot was more a contemplative type than a man of action was also a great opportunity for him."

The techniques that were to develop into the Mitterrand manner began to become evident. He got himself known, made contacts widely with Resistance groups such as the Combat movement. He began a systematic inspection of the provinces. He gave heart to the troops and summoned his faithful friends, met up again with Pol Pilven and such camp comrades as Patrice Pelat, Jean Munier, and Bernard Finifter. Later, in the UDSR, in the Convention des institutions républicaines, and, finally, in the Socialist party, François Mitterrand would always establish his authority by relying on a cohort of utterly devoted supporters. Indeed, former prisoners would be well represented among them.

Charles de Gaulle was another leader surrounded by companions. But François Mitterrand had *friends*, bound to him more by personal affection than by a community of ideas. "They all know the frontiers that keep friendship from turning into intimacy."[40]

There was a risk-taking element to Mitterrand's temperament that is still there. He has always had a sense and a liking for spectacular acts of brilliance that may seem like acts of defiance. In July 1943, he got past the screening mechanisms set up by the authorities and slipped into the Salle Wagram in Paris for a meeting organized by André Masson, the new commissioner for prisoners. Lost in the crowd, Mitterrand addressed officials on the platform: "You have no right to speak on behalf of the prisoners." The hall gave him an ovation and those around him protected his retreat. This courageous act did much to enhance his prestige among his comrades. Some time later, Maurice Schuman, the spokesman of Free France, praised this brave deed on the radio from London.[41]

Mitterrand's greatest act of prowess, which was to secure his place among his comrades, would also be decisive for his future: he appointed himself envoy of the movement to General de Gaulle.

Indeed, some weeks after their collective resignation, Maurice Pinot
and his friends realized they would have to become known and
recognized by the head of Free France. Maurice Pinot explains:

In May 1943, we learned of the establishment of the National
Council of the Resistance (CNR), led by Jean Moulin. The CNR
and various Resistance movements brought together all the political parties and trade unionists hostile to Vichy. We decided
that if the POW groups were not represented in that body, it
would run the risk, at Liberation, of being undervalued, forgotten, and excluded. And, in any case, continuing the struggle
against the occupying forces meant we needed means only General de Gaulle and his men could provide. So it was of the utmost
importance to make contact as soon as possible with the various
tendencies within the CNR.

That is why Maurice Pinot, alone or accompanied by François
Mitterrand (or Morland, as he was known) or Jacques Benet, met
several leaders of the CNR: Claude Bourdet, Emmanuel d'Astier
de La Vigerie, Jacques Baumel, and Eugène Claudius-Petit. These
men did not conceal the fact that General de Gaulle was not entirely
well disposed toward the prisoners of war. The general had many
grievances against them and could not understand why the escapees
or repatriated men wanted to form a group of their own instead of
joining the various Resistance movements on an individual basis.

"Anxious to establish his authority, the general mistrusted these
corporatisms, and indeed all factions that might challenge his power,"
Philippe Dechartre now comments. Like many other Frenchmen,
the general knew little of the conditions and consequences of captivity. His own detention during the war had left him with a deep
sense of bitterness. He believed that most prisoners of war had
surrendered without fighting. In his day, a prisoner who was not
wounded went before a court martial after his liberation. When
Pierre de Bénouville pointed out the resistance of the prisoners of
war, de Gaulle chuckled: "But there is no insurrection among sheep."
Maurice Pinot comments: "The general openly despised us and
regarded the oflags and stalags as so many despicable Vichys. He
believed we had bet on Giraud, whereas for us Giraud was merely

a famous general who had escaped with some panache. He didn't know we admired him for his military clear-sightedness, his non-conformity, and his audacity. Curiously, he did not realize what an asset the prisoners of war could be for him. Instead of winning them over by showing concern, he proudly ignored them, believing them to be in the service of the enemy."

To this handicap was added another: the existence of a rival movement (the MNPGD), which had also originated in the stalags and was led by both Philippe Dechartre and de Gaulle's own nephew, Michel Caillau (the son of Marie-Agnès de Gaulle). Caillau, who in the Resistance called himself Michel Charrette or Michel Chambre, obviously had no difficulty in his relations with Free France. But although Charles de Gaulle and the CNR already found it difficult to understand what use would be served by a specific Resistance organization of the POWs, it was even more impossible for them to recognize several. The National Rally of Prisoners of War, led by Pinot and Mitterrand, very soon realized the two movements would have to be merged. Mitterrand and Benet met Michel Caillau and talks began.[42] There was much mistrust on both sides.

Philippe Dechartre explains:

Between François Mitterrand's movement and ours was a fundamental difference of outlook. For us Gaullists, captivity represented failure and, to expiate that sin, we wanted to take part in military action. On the other hand, for the men of the National Rally of Prisoners of War, whom we regarded as Pétainists, defeat represented a sort of judgment of God—they felt the unfortunate prisoners had paid for the others and therefore had a mission to purify the country, enabling it to rise again. We found them a rather sentimental lot and didn't show much interest in what they called the "prisoner mystique."

The rally leaders realized their image ran the risk of being definitively compromised in the eyes of General de Gaulle, who was becoming increasingly recognized as the sole leader of the French Resistance. Maurice Pinot then thought of sending the journalist Marcel Haedrich as an envoy to Algiers, only to learn that François Mitterrand had appointed himself for this mission. "In November,"

Pinot says soberly, "François Mitterrand took the initiative to go to Algiers. We knew nothing about that journey until his return on February 26, 1944."

Mitterrand had been planning it since the summer of 1943. He had had sent from London, though nobody knew quite how, information signed "Morland" making him known to both the Central Bureau for Information of Free France and General de Gaulle. De Gaulle was later to write in his *Mémoires de guerre*: "The relations that were established for us by our envoys traveling between Algiers and mainland France—Guillain de Bénouville, Bourgès-Maunoury, Gaston Deferre, Emile Laffon, François Mitterrand, my nephew Michel Caillau, and so on—kept us sufficiently in touch."

All that remained was to find a way of getting to Algiers. It was not easy, especially since the Germans were beginning to search actively for the so-called Morland. On November 11, 1943, the youngest member of Mitterrand's team, Pol Pilven, who had spent the night at Vichy in Mitterrand's former room, was arrested in the early morning by the gestapo and taken away with the landlord, M. Renaud. Both were deported to Buchenwald; the unfortunate landlord never came back. François Mitterrand had had a close shave. Later on several occasions he was narrowly to escape the German net.

"In October 1943, Mitterrand told me to make contact with the Army Resistance Organization," Pol Pilven remembers. It did not take long. "In November," says André Bettencourt, "I went with him to a secret airfield near Angers, where he was to embark for London. He had had several secret meetings previously in my presence, especially with General Revers, then chief of the secret army, whom he saw several times." As in almost all such cases, the plane was a Lysander. Mitterrand also took with him General Deleplace, one of the chiefs of the Army Resistance Organization.[43]

It was not a very glorious arrival. "I knew London and the French services of the Algiers Committee," wrote Mitterrand.[44] "I was handed a register for my signature that enrolled me in Free France. Since I balked, I was left in a room without doors or windows [*sic*], with my boots still caked from the mud of Angers and a shirt I had worn for three weeks." In other words, he was left to cool his heels.

After a few detours, Mitterrand finally landed at Algiers. Thanks to Henri Frenay,[45] who had just been appointed commissioner (that is, minister) for the prisoners, Morland was received by the head of Free France in early December at the Villa des Glycines.

A friendship, or at least mutual affection, might have begun at that moment between two men who had similar family backgrounds and many affinities: the same love of books, a Barrésian sense of nation, a very profound Catholicism—and therefore an inbred animosity toward or suspicion of the bourgeoisie and money. The emotions of the young resister (Mitterrand was only twenty-seven) about to meet the leader and symbol of Free France can be easily imagined. His purposes can also be surmised: to make known the merits of his movement and, even more, to have his own merits recognized. François Mitterrand had gone to Algiers expecting to be dubbed by the lord and made his valiant knight. Arriving tired and expecting understanding, he instead received a slap in the face. The general proved reticent, haughty, imperious, scarcely even courteous.

Mitterrand has twice described the interview, in an almost serene way in 1971 (after the general's death) and more bitingly in 1969 (when the general was still in power). The 1971 version, from *La Paille et le grain*, reads:

There he was in front of me with his funny head, which looked small for his tall body, that face of a *condottiere* knocked into shape at some Catholic school, . . . the man I had so much imagined. . . . He was pleasant enough, though his first remark, delivered half in earnest, half in jest, seemed preposterous: "They tell me you came in an English plane."[46] As he spoke to me, his fine, rather soft hand swung backwards and forwards, as if to the rhythm of some cradle song. He questioned me about the state of the Resistance, its methods and mood. But although his voice remained unemphatic, there was a hardening of tone when we got to the main point of the meeting. He attached great importance to propaganda in the camps and work among the escaped prisoners in France. . . . He wanted the dispersal of rival networks to cease immediately. After their merger, which he expected to be carried out under the direction of a certain Michel Charrette, his own nephew, they would get weapons and money—

not before. What objection could I raise to rules obviously necessary to national discipline? I replied that, useful as such discipline was, the Resistance had its own laws and could not be
reduced to simply carrying out orders coming from outside—
that, as far as the networks in question were concerned, his
instructions remained inapplicable. The interview was brought
to an end.

The 1969 version[47] describes a very different atmosphere:

As I hesitated to agree to merging the three POW organizations
into a single formation under the authority of one of his nephews,
as he had ordered, he coldly took leave of me. Afterwards I had
some difficulty getting back to France. . . . Much later I learned
from a document that, during my stay in Algiers, it had been
suggested to General de Gaulle I be sent to the front in
Italy. . . . I shall never know whether I owe avoiding that twist of
destiny to the kindness of the head of Free France or to my haste
in rejoining my comrades in the Resistance at home.[48] I learned
from the adventure that it was best to keep quiet if one was
within reach of the special services at Algiers and declared that
Resistance and Gaullism were not exactly the same thing. Despite
praiseworthy efforts, I was never able to overcome his distrust.
Thus began an incompatibility of temperament that still survives.

After a quarter of a century, the wound to amour propre had not
healed.

Mitterrand did not at all care for de Gaulle's rough treatment.
That unsuccessful meeting set two very difficult men against one
another. Its failure also stemmed from the lack of mutual understanding that often separated resisters inside and outside the country (Jean Moulin noted this separation in many of his reports).
Mitterrand writes as if he alone were the spokesman, the mandated
representative, of the people inside: "I regarded our Resistance in
the country, constantly subjected to torture and death, as quite
different in nature from the Resistance outside, and did not believe
the latter enjoyed the preeminence it claimed. I questioned whether
the word *Resistance* could be applied to struggles being waged from

London or Algiers, which were more like episodes in a traditional war. I admired the handful of men who, around Charles de Gaulle, affirmed the French presence on every front. . . . But I felt different, and took pride in a struggle whose glory, I believed, belonged to my people."

Difficulties, however, were almost a matter of course. The disfavor Mitterrand complained of was not limited to him personally. General de Gaulle's abrupt manner with people stemmed from his temperament. René Pleven remembers him saying: "There are two ways of putting things: the pleasant, and the repellent. I can't help it—I always use the second." In fact, he didn't always have a choice: if de Gaulle had not affirmed his preeminence in such an abrupt way, he would have been bogged down in rivalries, maneuvers, and the plottings of his own friends, who were divided into antagonistic clans.

As far as Charles de Gaulle was concerned, François Mitterrand had another defect: he belonged to a defeated army for which the head of Free France had little time.

Maurice Pinot has a few indirect memories of the unsuccessful meeting between the two:

> When I saw François Mitterrand again in March, he told me of the difficulties of his trip. He brought back General de Gaulle's agreement, countersigned by General Giraud: we were recognized, and we were going to get funds and weapons. But Mitterrand told me the general had received him badly, heaping scorn on the demand of former POWs to be grouped into a specific Resistance movement. "Why not the hairdressers and cooks?" de Gaulle reportedly asked. Nevertheless, before bringing the meeting to an end, the general said: "We will help you, but you must have a single organization. It will comprise yours, the Communists', and Charrette's. You will regroup under Charrette's orders."

This was the other reason for the ill-feeling between Mitterrand and de Gaulle: Charrette, the nom de guerre of Michel Caillau, was de Gaulle's nephew. Caillau distrusted Mitterrand. In a letter of

December 1943 (a document provided by Pierre Bloch, who received the mail at Algiers), he warned his uncle about him:

MRPGD

MIX/N°   12/8/43

. . .Miteran [*sic*], after a brilliant war, was one of the leaders of the Pétain circle in his camp in Germany; he worked on his stalag newspaper and escaped. On his return to France, he joined the Commissariat for Prisoners of War, where he was in charge of propaganda. For whom, you can imagine. At that time he was a dynamic member of the legion. He belonged to a small group of close friends of Armand Petitjean, who was very Action française. Two months after Laval's return, he resigned with Pinot, worked for a time with us, but regarded the information services as useless fools, and the Resistance as mere childishness. Hence the split. Miteran's ideas then began to evolve slowly; he gradually adopted, to all appearances at least, all, or almost all, our ideas, and set about with Pinot trying to put them into practice. I wonder who got him over to London.

VERGENNES (Michel Charrette)

This unjust, mischievous epistle was, quite obviously, not a letter of recommendation. To make matters worse, the general's entourage suspected Mitterrand of Giraudist sympathies.

Did François Mitterrand commit this crime of *lèse-majesté*—did he, after his return, meet General Giraud before General de Gaulle? Many Gaullists at Algiers thought so, and many people still believe it today. There are a number of clues supporting this view. Jacques Mitterrand, then a lieutenant in a bombing unit based in Morocco, was to learn of his brother's arrival at Algiers in a telegram signed by Giraud.[49] Many witnesses attest to François Mitterrand's genuine sympathy for General Giraud. One of his companions, Jacques de Montjoye, remembers Mitterrand saying: "We do not receive instructions from London: the National Rally of Prisoners of War is of Giraudist obedience—we must remain independent."

In fact, the whole affair is probably quite simple. Two men met and didn't take to each other, victims of that mysterious alchemy crystallizing likes or dislikes between people from the very begin-

ning. Twice in the next two years they were to meet again, but
never grew any closer.

AFTER THAT BITTER FIRST meeting, Charles de Gaulle was not
to make François Mitterrand's return to France any easier. "When
he expressed his wish to get back to the mainland to the appropriate
services, he realized they were not enthusiastic about it," Jean
Védrine explains.[50] "They would have preferred to keep him away
from the Resistance inland." In the end, through a friend of his
mother's, Major de La Chenelière—who, as chance would have it,
was a member of General Giraud's staff—Mitterrand managed to
get a seat in a military transport plane bound for Marrakesh. From
there, with the help of Josephine Baker, a volunteer in the Free
French forces, he was able to get to London in General Montgom-
ery's plane. He spent several weeks in the British capital before
being allowed to rejoin his comrades.

Mitterrand took advantage of this forced stay to meet various
important people, beginning with Colonel Passy, boss of the Central
Bureau for Information of Free France, who saw practically all the
resisters coming through London. The two men became close enough
to play bridge together with a French couple, M. and Mme Mamy.
Another meeting, which was to prove very useful twenty years later,
was with the Communist Waldeck Rochet, who gave Mitterrand
information on the National Committee of Prisoners of War.

"When I saw François again," says his friend Jacques Benet, "he
talked a lot about Waldeck Rochet, with whom he got on very well.
Rochet had even given him a letter to post to his mother. François
was very surprised that a Communist could be the sort of person
one would want to visit. I had always thought this friendship played
a part in the Communists' 1965 decision to support Mitterrand in
the presidential election."

Mitterrand was finally able to leave England on February 24,
1944. At Dartmouth, in Devon, he went on board a Vedette boat
commanded by Captain David Birkin, Jane Birkin's (the actress's)
father. He landed without incident on the Brittany coast, at Be-
can-Fry near Guimaec, where he was met by Louis Mercier (decorated with the Légion d'honneur in 1982) and his wife, Philomène.
"We didn't know who he was," Philomène Mercier recounts. "But

the next day, when my husband took him to catch the train at Morlaix station, he thought he was driving someone important. On the road they crossed two Germans on a motorbike, who took a good look at them before continuing on their way. 'If those two only knew who just escaped them,' François Mitterrand said with an important air."[51]

Mitterrand did not go back empty-handed. In his comrades' eyes, his meetings in Algiers and London had considerably increased his authority. "Because of his political intelligence and meetings with the general and others, he had gained in stature and credit," explains Maurice Pinot. "My decision to withdraw also helped his ascent, as did his making up for the absence of several other leaders." War is often generous toward the ambitious.

With Mitterrand's return, the merging of the POW movements, which the general had specifically ordered and everybody felt the need of, came about. But de Gaulle's nephew, Michel Caillau, was not the mastermind behind it. "Of his own accord," says Philippe Dechartre, "Caillau dropped out. He never agreed to merge our movement with the Pétainists and Giraudists." Nevertheless, on March 12, 1944, the National Movement of Prisoners of War and Deportees (MRPGD) saw the light of day in a smoke-filled drawing room at 44, rue Notre-Dame-des-Champs. This meeting brought together the National Rally of Prisoners of War, led by Maurice Pinot and François Mitterrand;[52] the MRPGD, led by Philippe Dechartre, Charles Moulin, and Michel Caillau; and the National Committee of Prisoners of War, criticized by Maurice Pinot as "a tactical and belated creation of the Communist party, anxious to be represented in every area of activity."

The merger had not come about easily. Some leaders of the MRPGD found it difficult to become allies of the Communists (the memory of the German-Soviet pact of 1939 was still very much alive). The Communist Robert Paumier (decorated in 1983) remembers very clearly the clashes that erupted throughout the talks. "Mitterrand was violently anti-Communist and I was violently anti-Pétainist. 'Who are you? Who is financing you?' Mitterrand asked, adding, 'One can never be sure with people like you.' And, since I am not so easygoing myself, I retorted: 'And who are you? We might compare our curricula vitae to advantage.' All this took place in the presence of Philippe Dechartre and Antoine Avinin (the founder of *Franc-Tireur*), who represented the CNR. They both kept score."

In his memoirs, Henri Frenay, who, it must be remembered, was not in France at the time but at Algiers, gives a quite different version of the affair: "On his return to France, François Mitterrand claimed he had received instructions from Algiers to bring into the merged movement a very small group whose very existence I had hitherto ignored and which was quite simply an emanation of the French Communist party. Faced with this demand, which was presented as coming from the Committee for National Liberation, his comrades acceded. This initiative, of which I was unaware until after the war, made possible the infiltration of prisoners and deportees, and was to have serious consequences." Later, Frenay suggests that Mitterrand acted in this way to thwart his own plans: "Indeed," he writes, "chance had put me in a position that might have had great importance politically." This thesis is contradicted, however, by all the other evidence. In any case, two Communists were to sit on the five-man executive committee of the United Prisoners' Movement. "Once the merger had come about," says Robert Paumier, "Mitterrand always acted in a loyal way. We never feared any underhanded moves. Indeed, at that time, I wrote on a bit of paper: 'Mitterrand will play a leading role later.' And, in any case, the merger benefited all of us. The CNR gave five hundred thousand francs to Dechartre, a million to Mitterrand, and two million to us, the Communists."[53]

Shortly afterward, François Mitterrand was officially appointed secretary-general of the prisoners of war. "When I proposed his name during a cabinet meeting at Algiers, General de Gaulle had absolutely nothing to say against it," says Henri Frenay. So, at twenty-seven, Mitterrand became the official responsible to the Ministry for Prisoners of War (or, rather, the interim minister). It was an ephemeral post, of course, but one that indicates the importance he had acquired. In the end, therefore, the meeting at Algiers, difficult though it had been, was to his benefit.

THE LIBERATION

The Liberation, the decisive moment for anyone dreaming of power, was approaching. As the Allied troops, together with those of Free

France, closed in on the capital, the insurrection spread. On August 15, 1944, the Germans began evacuating their administrative services. The former prisoners (now resisters) were impatient. One of them, André Pernin, recounts:

> We had freed the General Commissariat for Prisoners in the rue Mayerbeer on August 18.[54] François Mitterrand led our group. When we burst into the office of Robert Moreau [the successor to André Masson, who had been forced out in January 1944], Moreau, ever the polite civil servant, stood up and asked what we wanted. "For you to get out," Mitterrand replied. Apparently very much in control of himself, the commissioner tried in a most civil way to talk matters over. But there was no time. Mitterrand interrupted, "There is no time to argue, Monsieur—you must get out. This is revolution and we are making the revolution." Shortly afterwards, a group of six FFI (French Forces of the Interior), armed to the teeth—I hardly knew any of them—took up position in the entrance hall on the ground floor, revolvers in hand, checking all visitors. On the first floor were two boxes of Molotov cocktails. Later we realized the insurrection in Paris had been started too early, on the insistence of the Communists.

François Mitterrand became the undisputed boss on the premises, and was to remain so until Henri Frenay's arrival on September 1, 1944. His first task was to regroup the prisoners' movements and mutual-aid centers of France and Navarre. He had only one message: "We must unite and mobilize to receive the million and a half comrades still held behind barbed wire." What could be better than a conference to bring about a proper federation? Plans had to be made.

Mitterrand was to expend even more energy bringing the prisoners together upon finding himself more or less without work. Indeed, he refused the job offered by Henri Frenay of secretary-general of the Ministry for Prisoners of War. "I suggested he stay with me as secretary-general," Frenay writes, "that is to say, in a post of the utmost responsibility, overseeing the whole of my department and coordinating the work of six sections. It was to place him at the highest level of the civil service hierarchy. The offer, it seemed to me, was a tempting one, almost unhoped-for for a man of his age and background. Nevertheless, it was declined, for François Mitterrand's ambitions lay elsewhere and were greater still."[55]

Was he dreaming of becoming a minister at once? It is unclear. In any case, François Mitterrand would not accept becoming number two in a place he had been number one, even if only temporarily. Others would not have shown his reservations: at about the same time, a young unknown called Jacques Chaban-Delmas was to become secretary-general at the Ministry of Information.

Entry into the Consultative Assembly, which Mitterrand had long coveted, also eluded him. The four seats reserved for the prisoners of war were given to Jacques Benet, Etienne Gagnaire, the Communist Pierre Bugeaud, and Philippe Dechartre, who recounts: "It had been a good battle. Mitterrand had been had. Failing to become a minister, he would have liked to have been a deputy, for a civil service post meant nothing to him."

There remained the leadership of the prisoners' movement. In October 1944, François Mitterrand was elected president of the National Movement of Prisoners of War and Deportees. Jean Védrine recounts: "From October 1944, François devoted himself entirely to the movement and its newspaper, *L'Homme libre*. While the comrades were concerned above all with questions of everyday life and the claims of repatriated prisoners, he was preoccupied with options and programs—that is to say, with the future and role of former POWs in the nation."

Mitterrand wanted to accelerate the unification of the departmental associations. He traveled a great deal in the Paris region and provinces (his knowledge of political geography and local politicians began there). Did he want to make this movement a political party, as some of his comrades from that time think? Ever since his captivity, he had been convinced that the former POWs might constitute a force with which politicians would have to reckon. And when he was in London, awaiting an opportunity to return to France, he had sent a telegram to Félix Gouin, president of the Consultative Assembly at Algiers, protesting against "any attempt to eliminate the prisoners of war still in captivity from a first popular election." (There were plans at the time to proceed to municipal elections immediately after the Liberation, without waiting for prisoners to return.) But this may well have been simply an attempt to protect his comrades' rights so they would not feel forgotten or excluded by the nation.

At the prisoners' congress in April 1945, Mitterrand adopted somewhat contradictory positions. On the one hand, he asked those representatives of the prisoners' federations who were tempted by political action "to swear on their honor they would never represent the prisoners as such in political organizations." On the other, he declared: "We must represent the interests of the prisoners of war in every sector of national reconstruction. We represent 1.8 million Frenchmen—we must make their presence felt. We must advise on fiscal and monetary reforms; we must give our opinions—we who have suffered from the absence of the nation—on the defense of the rights and greatness of that nation."

In fact, what he wanted was perhaps not so much the formation of a new political party as the establishment of a network of influence. He wanted the POWs to impose their viewpoint, get themselves heard within the various political parties—to be, in effect, what is now called a pressure group.

This hope, shared by many resisters, was not to be realized. "Within the traditional parties, the generation of the Resistance might have played a determining role, imposed its own view of society, modernized the methods of action and political information. It preferred to flow into the molds set by the established leadership and please the bigwigs," he was to deplore twenty-five years later.

Whose fault was this? Was it a lack of character, trust, or ambition on the parts of all those men who emerged from their ordeal? François Mitterrand's reply in 1968 was that it was de Gaulle's fault. "Once he was back in Paris," he writes, "the general set out to remove systematically the leaders of the home Resistance, regarded by him as undependable, because they had loved and served their country outside his control and without his permission. In his eyes, there was nothing more dangerous than patriotism that was not stamped by the cross of Lorraine."[56]

Ex-prisoner Mitterrand may be attributing too many of his own aspirations to his friends. At the time, most former prisoners were more concerned with resuming a peaceful civilian life than taking up politics. And, in any case, the prisoners' movement had been widely infiltrated by the Communists. Mitterrand soon drew the following conclusion: he would have to enter the field in the traditional way of election at the earliest opportunity.

BUT AS 1944 CAME TO an end and 1945 began, the major task of the president of the prisoners' movement and his friends was still to prepare for the return of a million and a half comrades still in the camps. They began to come back in March, as the Allies advanced, the flood reaching its maximum point in late spring 1945 and ending in early summer.

These returns presented enormous problems: reception, housing, feeding, clothing, identity papers, money. Most prisoners went through Paris, up to fifteen thousand arriving every day. In a France destroyed and ruined, the material difficulties were enormous. "What the prisoners found most difficult to accept," explains Jean Cornuau, a POW officer responsible for the Paris region, "was not being given a suit, a pair of shoes, and a small gratuity upon arrival. It was very difficult calming them; there was a general lack of understanding." Another version comes from the minister, Frenay: "The discontent of the prisoners was largely fueled by the Communists, who awaited them as they got off the train. As if by chance there was always a Communist to get into the trucks with them, take them to the repatriation centers, and provoke them to anger."

In any case, the Communists planned to use this force. One of them, Pierre Verrier (decorated in 1983), reveals: "To put pressure on the government and alert public opinion, I thought of organizing a great demonstration: all the departmental POW associations would meet together at the Salle de la Mutualité and we would invite the minister, Henri Frenay, to come and explain his actions."

Appointed to organize the gathering, which was fixed for June 5, 1945, Jean Cornuau (decorated in 1983) recounts:

I went to invite the minister, but, despite my insistence, he refused to come. Then I went to the prefect of police, Luizet, to ask permission to set up loudspeakers outside the hall and march to the Arc de Triomphe to lay a wreath. We agreed the demonstration would break up in the Bois de Boulogne after passing the Ministry for the Prisoners of War, which was situated at the bottom of the avenue Foch. We expected twenty thousand comrades; at least fifty thousand came. When the minister learned this, he let it be known during the meeting, through his assistant Jean d'Arcy, that he was ready to come see us. I admit I consulted my comrades in a rather tendentious manner. And when I put the question to the crowd, through the microphone, they replied: "No, no question of letting Frenay come." Then the procession formed with Jean Bertin, François Mitterrand, myself, and a few others at its head.

Pierre Verrier comments: "François Mitterrand put himself at the head of the procession, though he was not one of the demonstration organizers. He shouldn't have been there, but you know what he's like—he always has to put himself at the front!"

"We set out for the Etoile," Jean Cornuau continued. "As we were laying the wreath, I turned round and I saw there were comrades still well beyond the Concorde. Then we arrived in front of the ministry. At first everything passed off quietly, but soon hostile shouts broke out."

The Communist Pierre Bugeaud acknowledges that his party comrades did their best to provoke these outbursts by shouting "Frenay to the scaffold!" Others even burned his effigy in front of the ministry gates.

"Mitterrand was white with rage," Verrier remembers. "He said to me: 'We won't be able to control the situation. It's quite out of control.'" He adds:

At the time, his sister-in-law, Christine Gouze-Renal, was the private secretary to the minister, Henri Frenay, and all this commotion put him in a very bad position. Then I suggested, "Since Frenay won't see us, we must be received by General de Gaulle." "Get up onto the roof of my car and tell your comrades I'm going to take you as part of a delegation to the general," the prefect, Luizet, who had followed the demonstration, then suggested. I did. The tumult calmed down at once, and we set off for the rue Saint-Dominique. There were five of us: François Mitterrand, Jean Cornuau, Georges Thévenin (of the Communist party), Jean

Bertin, and myself. When we got to the Ministry of Defense, where de Gaulle worked, we were looked at askance and kept waiting. After twenty-five minutes Mitterrand got up and said, exasperated, "I'm going. My dignity will not allow me to wait any longer."[57] So I said to him, "To see de Gaulle, I'd wait twenty-four hours here." Then he sat down. A few minutes later, Admiral Ortoli informed us we would be received at a later time.

Only three days later General de Gaulle received Jean Cornuau, Georges Thévenin, and François Mitterrand. "And not me!" Pierre Verrier still laments. "Mitterrand took my place."

Since their meeting in Algiers, Mitterrand and de Gaulle had met face-to-face only once—in September 1944, when the provisional secretaries-general of the ministries were presented to the head of Free France. "You again!" de Gaulle is said to have exclaimed on seeing Mitterrand, who was aggrieved at the remark. But on June 5, 1945, the general was furious: he thought Mitterrand had led the demonstration. It was at this point de Gaulle remarked (René Pleven remembers): "Mitterrand? But he's a Communist!"

Jean Cornuau observes: "The prisoners' demonstration had so exasperated the head of the provisional government that he wrote an account of our interview that was incorrect, partial, and in bad faith." Indeed, in his *War Memoirs*, the general writes:

The ceremonies inspired by the return of the prisoners, particularly the men deported for resistance activities, were so many opportunities for the "Movement" to call out its noisy gangs. In Paris itself, parades were formed, filing down the boulevards . . . under the windows of the Ministry of Prisoners, marching to cries of "Down with Frenay!" . . . The instigators hoped that the government would turn the police against the demonstrators and excite popular indignation, or else yield to the threat and sacrifice the vilified minister . . . Nevertheless, the matter was soon settled. I summoned the leaders of the "Movement" to my office. "What is happening," I told them, "is intolerable. I demand that it come to an end . . . Public order must be maintained. Either you are impotent to deal with your own men, and in that case you must indicate the fact to me in writing at once and announce your resignation; or you are really the leaders, in which case you will give me your formal promise that all agitation will stop from today. If, before you leave this building, I have not received either the letter of resignation or the promise, you will be arrested as you leave my room. I can give you only three minutes in which to decide." The leaders conferred in the window niche and returned at once. "We will do as you say. We guarantee that the demonstrations will cease." Which seemed to be the case from that very day.[58]

It should be noted that the general mentions no names.

Jean Cornuau has a quite different memory of the meeting, though he confirms that the atmosphere was very tense and the general very cutting:

From the outset he launched into François Mitterrand and accused him of "pissing vinegar" in his editorials for the newspaper *L'Homme libre* on a minister who did not deserve it. Without wishing to hear our reasons, he criticized us for not allowing the minister to speak at the Mutualité. And when I pointed out that he himself had not thought fit to invite Henri Frenay to this meeting, he said nothing. When we tried to explain the difficulties of the POWs, he replied by talking about the greatness of France and the need for all French people to tighten their belts. When we suggested that since he himself had been a prisoner, he ought to show more understanding, he got angry. But the general never asked us for a commitment in writing and never threatened us with arrest. When he writes, "From that day, the demonstrations ceased," I reply: "False, they went on." You only have to read the newspapers of the time. And yet, the day after the meeting, François Mitterrand launched an appeal on the radio for them to stop. I'd even go so far as to say that our meeting was fruitful, since, a few days later, the minister released the necessary funds.

Cornuau concludes: "I left his office feeling very annoyed. In November 1942, I had lost my Pétainist illusions. On June 5, 1945, my admiration and confidence in de Gaulle vanished forever."

Curiously enough, François Mitterrand nowhere refers at length to this interview, though it would seem to finalize the psychological break between the two men. But in political circles, the story endured, especially among the Gaullists, in a version that reportedly came from the general, through Michel Droit.[59] It is as follows:

> I summoned Mitterrand to the rue Saint-Dominique, where he arrived flanked by two acolytes. I said to him, "What's all this? Commotion on the public highway in time of war, for, although hostilities have ended in Europe, they are still continuing in the Far East! Do you realize what that means?" He replied, "I do not approve of these men, *mon général*, I went with them to make sure they didn't do anything silly." I said to him, "Well, you will dissociate yourself from them, you will write that down. Here's a piece of paper, a table, a pen—go ahead." He said, "That requires reflection, *mon général*." I replied, "Quite right— if you have not written or signed anything in three minutes, you will leave this room and immediately be arrested." He then rose with his two acolytes, walked over to the window, said a few words to them, and came back. "We understand, I'll sign," he said. That is the kind of man Mitterrand is.

This version of the facts, related by Michel Droit, was confirmed by Henri Frenay: "Perhaps it was the day after, the general told me about the meeting in some detail. I remember it perfectly: he told me he had demanded they dissociate themselves from the demonstrations of the Federation, otherwise they would be arrested. They did as they were told, the general said."

General de Boissieu, de Gaulle's son-in-law, also repeats this version of the facts in his memoirs:[60]

> There were sometimes entertaining moments in General de Gaulle's office. One day . . . the usher announced the prefect of police, Luizet. He entered, absolutely furious, informing Gaston Palewski that a demonstration against the government, in favor of the deportees, who, they said, had not been properly received, was taking place in the streets. It was led by a number of civil servants from the ministry, including a very senior one. . . . Gaston Palewski went off at once to inform the general, who

ordered the prefect of police to apprehend the senior civil servant and his assistants and bring them at once to the ministry where he would tell them what he thought of their behavior. A few minutes later, I saw some young men, looking rather pale, go up the stairs. I returned to my work. Later, I was called up by Gaston Palewski on some matter and saw, in the room next to his, the leader of the demonstrators writing on a sheet of paper words that, it seems, had been literally dictated by the general under threat of arrest.

Like de Gaulle, General de Boissieu does not give the names of the demonstrators. But in private, he claims de Gaulle would not have wanted to allow the publication of that "piece of writing" by François Mitterrand in case it contained spelling mistakes.

Among the former prisoners, this version produces shrieks of indignation, and it is pointed out that such an arrest following an audience had neither precedent nor any legal basis.

In any case, the break was well and truly consummated. After that, "François Mitterrand and I were barred from the list of Compagnons de la Libération by General de Gaulle, whereas Henri Frenay had put us at the top of the list; François was extremely upset," Patrice Pelat confides. But Frenay hardly remembers the affair.

Of their third, decisive meeting, the two men drew the following conclusions: General de Gaulle was now convinced he could not trust young Mitterrand, and François Mitterrand now knew that he could hope for nothing from General de Gaulle.

DANIELLE

Despite the ambitions, passion, and furies of public life, private life continued. François Mitterrand had escaped with hopes of reconquering Marie-Louise. While in the camps, he had often dreamed of finding her again, talking to her, and holding her in his arms, and had frequently spoken of her to his companions.

As soon as he was back in France and had recovered his strength, he had lost no time in getting to the capital. He was prudent enough, however, not to go and ring on his fiancée's door. On that Christmas Eve of 1941, he knew where he could see her: after midnight mass in the church of Saint-Dominique, in the rue de la Tombe-Issoire, where the Terrasse family usually worshipped. He still hoped the shock of such an unexpected reunion would revive their love—especially since it was Christmas Eve. But at the first glance, and after the first words exchanged, François realized he had been living a dream. Marie-Louise no longer loved him.

The break was formally made in early January, after a quick lunch in a restaurant on the Champs-Elysées. After a long, exhausting, and tense walk through the streets of the capital, a tired Marie-Louise, whose feet hurt, told François she had irremediably fallen out of love with him. Words, she said, could not explain it—all one could do was understand.

When engagements are broken off, well brought-up young ladies return their rings, which is what she did. At that moment, the two young people were walking along the banks of the Seine. Legend has it François Mitterrand threw the diamond ring into the dark waters of the river before rushing off, desperate and brokenhearted. Those close to him, however, say he still had the ring at the bottom of his pocket when he landed at Algiers.

All his friends, though, agree on the main point: it took him several months to get over the break. But the rejected fiancé was never to show any rancor toward the unfaithful beloved. At the time of the Resistance, François Mitterrand's friends partly explained his courage, fearlessness, and occasional apparent unawareness of danger by his disappointment in love.

Pierre Ordioni, in captivity a friend of Marie-Louise's brother, gives a surprisingly literary conclusion to the episode: "Early in 1941, I had just escaped and was spending most of my time with Marie-Louise Terrasse, who read me short stories she had written in order to pass the time. Those stories were so good that for a long time I hoped she would go further than Colette. 'My fiancé,' she said, 'is an exceptional person. He demands as much of me as he does of himself. He isn't religious, but he's of a mystical turn of mind. The sense he has of God and of the mission each of us has place him quite outside the run of ordinary men.' "[61] Ordioni goes on:

Marie-Louise Terrasse is also an exceptional person. I was to see her again nearly thirty years later when my concierge asked me

into her office to watch some political event on television. That
screen was truly a strange window on the world. Suddenly I saw
Marie-Louise's fresh young face, which Catherine Langeais's
makeup could not hide. "And now," she said with that charming
smile, which had not altered one jot over the years, "as part of
our programs for the presidential election you will hear M. François Mitterrand." Then her face slowly vanished to be replaced
by that of General de Gaulle's rival. Reflections on the sleeping
waters of a stilled current of life. . . .

How did François Mitterrand pass from Marie-Louise Terrasse
to Danielle Gouze? Their meeting might have come from the pages
of a romantic novel. In the pious biography, *Danielle Mitterrand*,
published with the subject's approval, journalists Michel Picar and
Julie Montagard recount the first meeting in great detail. It took
place in the spring of 1944. François Mitterrand had just come
back from London and was meeting up again with his friends.
Among them was Patrice Pelat, who was assiduously courting a
splendid young girl called Madeleine Gouze (later to be known as
Christine Gouze-Renal).

There were four or five of them who met at Christine's on that
March day in 1944—Patrice, of course, but also Bernard Finifter,
Jean Munier, and François Mitterrand. As they were talking with
Christine, François went up to a cabinet on which stood the
photograph of a girl.
"Who's this?" Mitterrand asked.
"My sister."
"She's quite ravishing. I'll marry her."
This conversation, as reported by Christine, has now gone
down in history. It is recited like well-known lines from a sonnet
or the final dialogue in a play. Caught between the attraction
she felt for Morland [Mitterrand] and what he had just said about
her sister, Christine was cut to the quick. A Pygmalion for those
she loved, a theatrical producer before she had any idea she
would become one, she wrote to her young sister: "I have a fiancé
for you. . . . The Easter holidays are not far off—come spend
them here and meet him." When Christine met her young sister

at the station, she realized what a distance would have to be covered before the young provincial girl became a presentable fiancée.

Danielle was wearing short white socks and a pleated skirt like she always wore.

"You can't turn up to meet him wearing socks! This afternoon we'll go and buy you some stockings."

Danielle had no intention of giving in. Why should she be made to play a character? If he liked her, he would have to like her as she really was. . . . A clash was only just avoided. Danielle did as she was told, but, the next day, went back to her socks.

The meeting was arranged to take place at the restaurant Chez Beulemans, in the boulevard Saint-Germain. The two sisters slipped to the back of the restaurant. From there they kept their eyes riveted on the revolving doors. They were early. Christine, who seemed more excited than Danielle, suggested: "If it's love at first sight, give me a little sign of approval. If you don't like him, pull a face." Suddenly Christine gave Danielle a nudge. There he was!

He was wearing a big, soft felt hat that dwarfed his face; his mustache blurred the lines of his mouth like a spelling mistake; and he was enveloped in a tan coat.

"He looked very South American," says Danielle, as if one could already glimpse her love—and François'—for that part of the world and its civilization.

"At that time, François looked like a tango dancer," Patrice Pelat was to say.

Danielle pulled a face, eloquently conveying her disapproval to Christine. Love at first sight was to be postponed! They talked about this and that. François' interest in Danielle was obvious, but she was irritated by his way of showing it. No, really, she didn't like him. That rather sharp form of wit, which rubbed people the wrong way while charming them at the same time, irritated her. What was the point of talking about her *bac* when it wouldn't be happening for another two months? What did that double-edged humor mean? Danielle did not feel equipped to answer. When she was alone with Christine again, she explained: "I can't be in love with him because he's a man."

Christine did not understand. "What I like," Danielle explained, "are boys!"

This story was not made up. Six months later, on October 28, 1944, at the church of Saint-Séverin in Paris,[62] Danielle Gouze took François Mitterrand for her husband on her twentieth birthday.

The true story of this marriage, which, rumor agreed, was not without its trials and tribulations, belongs to the president and first lady of France alone. Yet Roger Gouze, Danielle's brother, has stated publicly that it was also a battle. He writes:

I don't know why public life so seldom works well with private life. It was not long before I wondered how my younger sister, whose somewhat wild character I could surmise—a country girl rather than a girl of the city (the finest example of a Rousseau-type education, her husband once told me)—adapted herself to so fragmented a life. Love often unites quite dissimilar people. It is a source of many storms and immense joys. Only difficulty enriches: "What is done easily is done without us," Valéry says. I had the impression that in their case, nothing would be done without them. . . . Where does the perfection of a couple lie? In shared, uninterrupted serenity, or in the storms of a passion that can neither unite nor separate?[63]

This rather somber diagnosis by Roger Gouze notwithstanding, what matters is that the Catholic bourgeois from Jarnac encountered in Danielle's family a milieu diametrically opposed to his own, one that symbolized precisely what, thirty years later, the very heart of his electorate was to be.

"Let me introduce you to my anticlerical, Republican fiancée," the once-pious young man was fond of saying. "My son-in-law is very churchy," his father-in-law often joked.

Antoine and Renée Gouze, Danielle's parents, were both schoolteachers and anticlerical—he was even a Freemason. "With them, being atheists and anticlerical was a matter of principle. The schools had to be public, secular, and compulsory," writes their son Roger. He explains: "We thought that as long as there were two kinds of schools, and therefore two cultures, there would be two classes— one of which would oppress the other. In our opinion, the private schools were for children who were abnormal, either by some supposed superiority of caste, or because of the obvious inferiority of their intellects."[64]

The favorite maxim of François Mitterrand's father-in-law was: "When faced with money, the army, and the Church, the people will always have a revolution to make." Mitterrand's brother-in-law, Roger Gouze (also a teacher), remembers the Popular Front:

> I belonged to the left-wing of the Socialist party, which was first to hold out the hand to the Communists. For the people of the Left of my generation, 1936 was to remain the high point of their lives. What a new dawn! . . . On October 1, 1936, I arrived as a young teacher at Chambéry. I immediately started the first *maison de la culture* in the provinces with a few colleagues and the support of the municipal council. People had to be helped to occupy the leisure they had just won. . . . I experienced joys that even today prevent me from despairing completely of men. I taught an old building worker to write—and then worked with him on Sundays digging the foundations of a youth hostel. I discovered the mysteries of fishing in the Lac du Bourget with a zinc worker, whom a colleague of mine, a science teacher, was initiating into the mysteries of life, those which stir in matter to light up the soul in man. . . . I felt I was a cog in an immense machine for producing happiness.

"For producing happiness"—these are words that might have been used in slogans by militants of the Socialist party in the heyday of 1981.

In *Miroirs parallèles*, Roger Gouze remembers meeting his brother-in-law for the first time:

> My guts belonged to the people and my heart was on the Left. I don't think it was the same for him. He was better at sifting his opinions, being no doubt more selective than I, with his remarkably well-balanced mind. . . . I remember telling him early on (and was certainly one of the first to do so) that in

France there could be no solution of the Left without the Communists: "You have to take them as they are, knowing what they are, with their enormous defects and their equally great qualities." Much later, I wrote to him: "I have always told you there is no solution of the Left without the Communists. It may be there isn't one with them, either. . . ."

It seems nothing is simple on the Left.

François Mitterrand had fond memories of his religious education. In contrast, Danielle and Roger were, they themselves claimed, virtually martyred by Catholics. "When my grandmother sent me to Saint-Jean-des-Vignes, I was four years old," says Roger Gouze. "She had said nothing of my parents—or rather, of the secular competition they practiced. How did the nuns find out? We have never been able to explain in any other way how those angels with white coronets became transformed into tormenting phantoms. The starched beaks of their collars became threatening. I was constantly criticized for badly washed hands and dirty fingernails, and my ears hurt for hours after being pulled and turned back for inquisitorial examinations."[65]

Similarly, Danielle was to endure incredible ill-treatment at the lycée at Dinan, where the headmistress, "utterly secure in her faith," seems to have made her pay very dearly for the anticlerical feelings of her father, then principal of the boys' school. Danielle recounts how she was systematically given poor marks, despite being an excellent pupil; how she was not allowed to eat because she couldn't recite the grace; and how her name was not put on the honors board. In the end she became ill and had a nervous breakdown. And because Antoine Gouze had turned the chapel into a gymnasium, an attempt was even made, it seems, to burn down his school. "Don't send your sons to Dinan, on pain of mortal sin," people would whisper outside Breton churches on Sundays.[66]

"Ever since for Danielle, whenever anything bad happens it's always the fault of the priests," one of François' sisters now laughs.

Such persecution may have led the first secretary of the Socialist party to write: "Have you any idea what the life of the secular schoolteachers was like at the time when the intolerance of the Church reigned? That they tended to erect secularization into a dogma to combat another dogma I am quite willing to concede. But what they were defending was freedom of thought. If secularism seems to some to belong to another age, is it not because it had to resist the workings of another age?"[67]

Antoine and Renée Gouze were to undergo many other very real misfortunes. Roger Gouze recounts:

> My father was dismissed by Vichy in 1940. As a Freemason and idealist, sickened by Vichy's vindictiveness, he refused to fill up the forms on which he was supposed to list the Jews (pupils and teachers) in his establishment. The inspector then discovered a dirty comb on a bedside table and lavatories that needed cleaning. My father was dismissed for failing in his professional duties and was forced to retire to his house at Cluny. "For weeks," my mother told me, "I thought your father was going mad". . . . Then began the life of a half-pay officer, of republican, anticlerical views under a semifascist, staunchly pro-Catholic regime. Things got more and more difficult for them. . . . Then, one day in March 1943, History, with a capital *H*, knocked on the door, as they say. Léonce Clément, one of my friends and a teacher like myself, asked my parents if they could take in Henri Frenay, his boss in the Resistance, who could no longer live at Lyon because the German and French police were making it impossible for him to carry on with his activities and were even putting his life in danger. Frenay's closest collaborator, Bertie Albrecht, had already been arrested once and owed his salvation only to his courage in simulating madness: he was interned in a psychiatric hospital, where his friends managed to get him out.

Michel Picar and Julie Montagard note: "The month prior to his arrival at Cluny, Frenay had attended a meeting with a man who was trying to bring all escaped prisoners of war into a single Resistance movement. The man was called Morland. As you may know, this was François Mitterrand. That accumulation of signs, that elaborate weaving of the Fates in secret, was to tell Danielle their meeting was inevitable."

The Gouze family, then, had suffered much injustice from Catholics and right-wing politicians. They had known poverty, cold, and, above all, a terrible feeling of exclusion. How could they fail to harbor feelings of animosity, and even a desire for revenge?

Did Danielle Mitterrand push her husband to the Left, as some of her friends believe? Can a husband who sometimes feels guilty grant his wife concessions—even ideological ones—he would grant to no other woman? In any case, the first secretary of the Socialist party has said several times that Danielle was further to the Left than he was: "She considers me much too moderate in my political life," he confided to Hélène Vida in 1972.[68]

5

THE FOURTH REPUBLIC: A CAREER

"'THE STRENGTH AND TRANQUILLITY WITHIN ME HAVE NOT changed, because nothing deep down has ever changed inside me." So said the president of the Republic on June 28, 1983, when he received three journalists from television station Europe 1—Philippe Bauchard, Gérard Carreyrou, and Ivan Levaï—for a broadcast breakfast at the Elysée. When Levaï asked Mitterrand if he felt as strong, untroubled, and serene as before his ascension to the supreme office, the head of state replied by claiming that, having explored the difficulties and interest of his office, he felt a sense of both unity and peace.

The gilded setting of the Elysée Palace did not, of course, encourage metaphysical doubts. But why not believe the president of the Republic when he displays such serenity?

Since he has been in the Elysée, whatever obstacles and disillusionments have awaited him, François Mitterrand has always appeared to be a man very pleased with himself, one who refuses to be upset by everyday worries or circumstantial obstacles. He seems to take equal pleasure and ever renewed interest in laying wreaths, decorating meritorious citizens, visiting the provinces, or looking leading world figures—who, since 1981, have at last been his peers—in the eye.

In opposition, he always reminded one of a pouting Roman bust expecting to become a full-blown statue someday. In power, he seems to float on air. One might even be tempted to think he is capable of walking on water. François Mitterrand seems to live his mandate as an assumption. The state of grace, dissipated for others, lives on in him: how could his victory be other than sheer happiness, since he lives it as his personal fulfillment? He is at last where he should always have been. And he will stay there, God willing, until the final second granted by the executioner known as universal suffrage.

The first secretary of the Socialist party has always felt ready to assume the trappings of a sovereign: he has always had a certain vision of himself, which he has successfully communicated to his faithful followers. Yet the serenity he affects today is certainly of recent origin. For a long time his successes were tinged with bitterness and resentment—even when he seemed to be one of the most favored up-and-coming young men in politics.

During the twelve years of the Fourth Republic, from 1946 to 1958, the deputy for the Nièvre began a unique ascent that was to mark his destiny: rapid progress along the paths of power that bristled with traps and ambushes.

Eleven times minister, in ever more important posts (including the interior and justice, which, according to the canons of Republican hierarchy, are the ultimate steps leading to the prime ministership). Nevertheless, Mitterrand never got his feet on that final step. Men of his generation, no more gifted than he and to whom he certainly did not feel inferior—Maurice Bourgès-Maunoury and Félix Gaillard, for example—were to get there, but not he. He was regarded as less of a statesman than Mendès France, less startling than Edgar Faure, less promising than Félix Gaillard, less representative than Guy Mollet. Above all, he seemed less dependable than any of them—instinctively, he was mistrusted.

Whereas some politicians, as if protected by divine grace, leap from success to success without hindrance from any enemy, Mitterrand always had to almost apologize for achieving his ambition. "He will be the man who succeeds without pleasing, progresses without charming, makes a place for himself without ever being quite accepted. He is seen to have more precocity than grace; his impatience is admired more than his authority."[1]

It is not that he leaves people indifferent: from the outset, he made faithful friends who were not to desert him. But from the beginning he aroused mistrust and suspicion—and there were always those who abominated him—no doubt because he is so private and secretive. His rivals and enemies tend to explain his behavior as overweening ambition; those who like him describe him as a man in search of inner unity, a project, or an idea.

People know he is clever (perhaps too clever?) and adroit (perhaps too adroit?). His colleagues know only too well the agility he displayed in taking control of the UDSR, the linchpin of every majority at the time. This seizing of power strangely prefigures, though on a smaller scale, his final takeover of the Socialist party.

The François Mitterrand of the Fourth Republic was merely a hint of what was to come. Was he a man of the Left? Of course not—his trajectory oscillated between Center-Right and Center-Left with one constant: a deep-seated, virulent anti-communism. Sometimes he foresaw the movements of history, as his African policy showed. Yet he did not set out to be ahead of his time, as his declarations on "French Algeria" proved. He brought no ideology, carried no majority with him. No one regards him as a charismatic leader, even if nobody questioned his sense of authority and fairly disputative temperament. Mitterrand is a public speaker of acknowledged talent, a lawyer whose quibbles have often surprised and disconcerted his opponents. But, during the period of national reconstruction, he made no contribution to the economic debate. All in all, he was regarded at the time as a very good supporting actor.

He was a supporting actor very fond of high society and its games, feeling very much at home in white tie and tails and very quickly becoming drunk with Parisian successes. During the Cannes Film Festival Mitterrand was seen with starlets at the Milord l'Arsouille Cabaret, at the wedding of Prince Rainier of Monaco and Grace Kelly, and at the Villa Varamista in Florence, the home of Violet Trefusis[2] (the illegitimate daughter of George V, in whose house, Mitterrand was to say later, "intellectual Europe was rebuilt").

Weekends were spent at the home of Pierre Lazareff, owner of the
Paris newspaper *France-Soir*, or at the home of Marcel Bleustein-
Blanchet.[3] There he met *Tout Paris* society. "It was a time when
Danielle wore the clothes of great couturiers and François talked
of his handicap in golf," notes Françoise Giroud. Under the admiring gaze of the ladies, this Mitterrand looked like a butterfly
dazzled by artificial lights. He had not yet emerged from his chry-
salis.

THE TAKEOFF

What was he to be? A journalist? A lawyer (but he had not yet
passed the law certificate,[4] which would allow him to practice at
the bar)? François Mitterrand had the qualifications to take up
either profession. He had a love of words and the biting wit of a
polemicist; he liked to play the righter of wrongs or defender of
the oppressed; he knew he was capable of organizing his grip on
others. So he took his place among the new elite that emerged after
the Liberation.

At twenty-eight, he had just occupied the (temporary) post of
secretary-general for the prisoners. He had made a name for himself
within the all-powerful National Federation of Prisoners of War.
He was not, therefore, an unknown in the new ruling class. It may
well be that from 1945 he had secretly opted for a career in politics.
For the time being, though, the journalist he then was was noted
more for the vigorous tone of his editorials than an interest in the
distribution of the *Libres* newspaper (which, for lack of efficient
management and sufficient readers, was soon to die a fine death,
like most of the publications to emerge from the Resistance).

While he waited for a political opening—an appointment or a
constituency—this young husband (soon to be the father of a little
Pascal, who was to die at the age of three months) had to support
his family. At the time, they lived in an apartment bordering the
racetrack at Auteuil. Danielle didn't like it. "I felt I was neither in
Paris nor in the country," she said later.[5]

Eugène Schoeller, founder of the L'Oréal perfume and cosmetics
firm, a man whose political sympathies were always staunchly on
the Right,[6] offered Mitterrand the job of president and managing

director of the Editions du Rond-Point, one of whose publications was the women's magazine *Votre beauté*. Max Brusset, who ran the group's advertising at the time, remembers: "He was given an office, salary, car, and chauffeur."

François Mitterrand had hoped, on joining the group, to launch a proper political newspaper. But the climate of the Liberation and Eugène Schoeller's personal troubles meant the project was postponed. Lover of literature that he was, Mitterrand would have liked to have given *Votre beauté* a more cultural tone,[7] but this was not the magazine's purpose. The young journalist's plans led nowhere. However, this was no more than a minor disappointment.

A few months later, on June 2, 1946, arrangements were made for the legislative elections. Deputies were to be elected to a second Constituent Assembly, which would then draw up a draft constitution.[8] Mitterrand was a candidate in the fifth constituency of the Seine (Neuilly, Asnières, Saint-Ouen, Clichy, Courbevoie, Levallois, Puteaux) under the label of the Assembly of the Republican Left (RGR, Rassemblement des gauches républicaines).

Under this firmly left-wing and certainly ambitious name were grouped several small parties, what was left of the great prewar groups. Hiding under its colors above all was the old Radical party, still afraid of its own shadow—the party of the two Edouards, Daladier and Herriot.

The RGR set out to bring together all the enemies of Marxism, the Socialist-Communist majority, and the clerical parties—in other words, all those who wanted to be neither of the Left nor of the popular republican movement, the MRP (Mouvement républicain populaire).[9] It comprised, together with the old Radicals, former members of Pierre Etienne Flandrin's Alliance Democratique (Flandrin had been a prewar prime minister, then Vichy's foreign minister); the Parti de la réconciliation française, which brought together what was left of Colonel de La Rocque's French Parti social; and, lastly, the Parti socialiste démocratique, composed of the friends of Paul Faure, secretary-general of the SFIO[10] before Vichy, whose pacifism had led him to Pétain. Philip Williams, in his *Politics in Postwar France*, notes that the major objective of most of these groups was to put back into the driver's seat leaders whose career had been interrupted by the law of ineligibility that affected those parliamentarians who, on July 10, 1940, had voted full powers to the marshal.

It was a curious choice for the François Mitterrand who had so strongly criticized the prewar parties and pleaded for a generation of new men to come to power. A year earlier, he did not have words harsh enough for Daladier and Herriot:

> Herriot has one rare merit: he was the author of that famous definition, the "average Frenchman." How could the French not be grateful to him for that? Average Frenchmen, average France. Such a notion makes no demand on the mind or the muscles. . . . Of course, we had learned in the history books that France was a great country. Now, there's a very tiresome word. Great? How can we expect M. Herriot to feel at home in a period in which people are talking of greatness all the time? By dint of living an honest, average sort of life, the French went to Munich with the other Edouard, the little one. . . . And Vichy was the bitter reward of all those who, because they had refused greatness, were to be the first victims of the demands of baseness. . . . And so, after so many average stupidities, which led to so many great catastrophes, words of greatness have now come to us. De Gaulle, Bertie Albrecht, Narbonne, Mederic, and all those who, in their prisons, in their camps, were able to reconquer the very soul of our people and become our only friends, our only masters.[11]

This was a fine spate of words, but a very rapid about-face.

This first act of commitment, which is more like a minor disavowal, may be explained in various ways. François Mitterrand does not care for secondary roles, and probably did not want to be swamped in a party too rich in major personalities. He was, of course, not left-wing enough to think of joining the SFIO. And the MRP, the new Christian-democratic group, which welcomed the generation of the Resistance and allowed a coexistence of outlook ranging from the Center-Left to the traditional Right, was certainly too structured (and also too encumbered with leaders) for his taste. Lastly, he felt no sympathy whatsoever for the stormy, unnatural, tripartite alliance between the SFIO, MRP, and Communist party.

The elections took place under a system of proportional representation, with multimember constituencies. The RGR came fifth, after the Communist party, MRP, SFIO, and the Parti républicain de la liberté, a right-wing group led by Edmond Barrachin. Though his vote was quite respectable (21,511), François Mitterrand did not receive a sufficiently high percentage to capture a seat. In that rather left-wing constituency, with a few enclaves belonging to the traditional Right, the RGR was not fighting on the most favorable terrain. But this first entry into the political arena at least shows under what colors François Mitterrand was fighting: he was, without any doubt, on the Right at this time.

Six months later were elections to the first National Assembly. (In the meantime the French had adopted, without enthusiasm, the constitution of the Fourth Republic.) This time, François Mitterrand ran in the Nièvre. But he had no ties with the region. He was brought in two weeks before the elections. The local prefect even questioned the legality of this impromptu candidacy, Mitterrand had not changed his colors, but this time he fought his campaign under the vague name of "Republican Action and Unity."

His appearance in this department, which was once reputed to be very Catholic and which comprised "three dukes and peers" (the wondering words of the current Socialist leader himself), was brought about by the immensely rich Marquis de Roualle, boss of the Olida food concern. "On several occasions," René Pleven recounts, "the marquis told me how he had been approached by Edmond Barrachin. 'There's a hyperactive young man in my department running all over my land,' said the marquis. 'I'd be very much obliged if you could find him some viable affiliation.' "

Alain de Roualle, the marquis' son, confirms this: "My father, who had always taken an interest in the political life of the department, was looking for a right-wing candidate to confront the tripartite alliance. On the advice of his friend Edmond Barrachin, he was to make contact with a respectable Catholic young man named François Mitterrand. I saw him at the house at least fifty times. My father helped him a great deal financially and introduced him to all the right people. For us, he was an ideal candidate, very much our type."

"Then François got a lot of support from Emile Boutemy, secretary-general of the Employers' Confederation,[12] and from his colleague Brulefer, president of the Federation of Chemical Manufacturers and mayor of Clamecy (in Nièvre). François was very close to both of them," Max Brusset remembers.

When the Socialist leader was later to recount his political beginnings in the Morvan, he omitted to mention, curiously enough, the considerable help he had been given by the marquis and those two captains of industry. On the other hand, he expatiated at length on the support given him by Henri Queuille, a minister during the Third Republic who had joined General de Gaulle at Algiers before becoming a permanent member of the Fourth Republic governments. "I introduced myself to the deputation in the Nièvre in 1946. Good Dr. Queuille had sent me with his blessing: 'We are giving you this opportunity because it isn't one—go all the same. You'll pull it off if you listen to everybody, but take nobody's advice.' "[13]

The newcomer made a favorable impression, and not only in the châteaux. The clergy of Nevers were just as pleased by his arrival, as Léon Noël, Gaullist ex-ambassador and ex-president of the Constitutional Council, remembers: "When we were campaigning in the 1951 elections and were hoping to get the support of the Church and the faithful for our candidate, Canon Andriot of Nevers replied: 'But we have François Mitterrand. He's such a pious, fervent young man. We are very satisifed with him. He defends our ideas.' "

Showered with such blessings, the intruder felt much at home in this provincial setting and this time did extremely well: his list came second, with 25.5 percent of the vote, behind that of the Communists (33.7), but ahead of the Socialists of the SFIO, whose local leader, the deputy Dagain, swore eternal hatred (many parliamentarians of the time remember) for François Mitterrand. Mitterrand's profession of faith, the document that every candidate must send to each elector, is worth quoting in full. One could have sworn it came from a member of the current right-wing opposition[14]:

> You will say *no* to the budget deficit and inflation. *No* to this bastardized electoral law. *No* to economic collapse: the government has borrowed 650 million dollars, our total annual expenditure amounts to 140 billion francs, the entire national income is swallowed up by the budget. *No* to administrative

waste: 276,000 civil-service jobs have been created. *No* to hasty and costly nationalization, which further burdens our expenditures. *No* to power sharing with the Communist party, the party Léon Blum called a foreign Nationalist party.

To bring an end to disorder, we must:

• Defend all our liberties and, above all, liberty in education, for the child belongs to his parents, not to the state.

• Fight to bring about the country's economic recovery, encouraging production by the abolition of regulations impeding people's freedoms; demanding the return to sound methods of budgeting; struggling against state monopoly, which is replacing private initiative everywhere; fighting for the abolition of useless jobs.

• Insist that rights of ownership no longer be subject to legislators' whims, that they be respected in their entirety.

• Demand that religious peace be maintained in an atmosphere devoid of all sectarianism.

And so on.[15] These words have a highly contemporary ring to them and, as will be seen, were well received by local bigwigs.

Elected in 1946 on a Center-Right ticket, François Mitterrand took up the same political position at the elections of 1951. The young deputy for the Nièvre (who had already been a member of the government several times) headed the list of the Union démocratique et républicaine des indépendants, which brought together the UDSR (the small centrist party to which he belonged), the Radical party, the PGR, and the PRL. At this time Mitterrand enjoyed the friendship of such men as Michel Clemenceau (PRL) René Pleven (UDSR), Paul Reynaud and Roger Duchet (both Indépendants—that is, conservatives), and Martinaud-Deplat (a Radical).

This was certainly a Center-Right coalition, with a left-wing fringe (the Radicals) and a right-wing fringe (the Indépendants). Above all, it was a forced alliance, directed against both the two great parties of the Left (which had become bitter enemies) and General de Gaulle's RPF, whose rise was disturbing Mitterrand and his friends. They were not wrong: when the votes were counted, the RPF came second, behind the Communist party but ahead of Mitterrand's list.

In his profession of faith that year, the young minister played up his activity in government and the services he had rendered to the department. Above all, he flattered himself that he had belonged to the Ramadier and Schuman governments, which "were marked by the eviction of the Communists (May 1947) and by the firm struggle against the political strikes." Compared with some of his friends in the UDSR, François Mitterrand sometimes seemed rather moderate. In the Loire, the Bidault, Pinay, and Claudius-Petit list asked the electors the following question: "Do you or do you not want France to become a Soviet state?"

As for the RPF, Mitterrand denounced it with these words: "You will say *no* to government by a single, fanatic military party." He was situated, therefore, right at the heart of what was called the "third force" (a chaotic alliance of the SFIO, the MRP, and the small Center groups), which was fighting on two fronts at once: against the Communist party and the RPF.

Meanwhile, the outsider of 1946, anxious to establish permanent roots in the region, got himself elected a municipal councillor for Nevers (which he was to remain until 1959). He also became, in 1949, general councillor of Montsauche, a shrine of the Resistance, by beating the Communist (a certain Bigot). Journalist Robert Danger described the electoral campaign—which seems to have been rather picturesque—in the March 19, 1949, *France-Soir*:

In these public meetings, M. Mitterrand, who hates equivocation [we are assured!] begins by describing the situation: "I am presenting myself in a very difficult canton, I know, but I have chosen it in order to fight a Communist. I hope to win, because that will make one less. . . .

The young candidate displays a very sporty mentality, since he doesn't hesitate to provoke to a duel (at table tennis) a Communist militant, said to be the best player in the village. Under the fascinated gaze of the people of the Morvan, François Mitterrand took off his jacket and crushed the local champion, who, good sportsman that he is, concluded: "I shan't vote for you, but you're no fool."

By that triple victory—as general councillor, municipal councillor, and deputy—Mitterrand set up for himself a bastion he was never to neglect. He was always fond of returning to the reassuring customs of the provinces, where one tends to be received with little delicacies, where conversations are conducted in a rather formal way on matters of no great import, where rumors from the city play a greater role than fashionable ideas. There he was to enjoy long walks in the misty forest and relaxed, natural contacts with the electors, which were a pleasant change from the tinsel and glitter of Paris life.

His electors were still to remain faithful to him in 1956.[16] For them, he was now *"le beau François."* This flattering appellation had some basis in fact: when readers of the women's magazine *Elle* were asked in October 1951 to name the fourteen most attractive men in French public life (actors excluded), the young minister rated a good position on their list (where he was surrounded, in particular, by Maurice Druon, Louison Bobet, Jacques Chaban-Delmas, Albert Camus, Hubert de Givenchy, and Hervé Alphand).

FRANÇOIS MITTERRAND, ANTI-COMMUNIST

When François Mitterrand took up politics, the Communist party, with 26 percent of the electorate, was the largest in France and loudly proclaimed the fact. With the romanticism of the Resistance still so close, the Party, which prided itself on losing seventy-five thousand members in the struggle (untrue), was at the height of its prestige, fascinating a great many intellectuals. The great polemics of the gulag, Stalin's bloody purges, and the great risings in Eastern European countries had not yet sullied its image. Nevertheless, the Party aroused fear by the very fact of its power and infiltration into the workings of the state. It was feared for its organizational ability, mystery, suspected secret activities, intolerance, spirit of revenge, and links with the Soviet Union. It was also feared for its sudden reversals and (who knew?) attempts to provoke a revolution, which some Party leaders advocated at the Liberation.

Every politician had to make up his mind whether to be for or against it. And François Mitterrand did not hesitate for a moment: he was among its most determined adversaries—and not only in his electoral declarations. He was to show this as minister for war veterans, his first ministerial post. When he started working there (at the age of just thirty), he did not find a very easy situation:

> When I entered my ministry, the staff were on strike, because the Communists didn't want to give it up.[17] I was alone, except for one colleague [Georges Beauchamp] who was allowed to enter the premises. The secretary, the daughter of the Communist deputy Demusois, was sleeping in the minister's office. Zilbermann, the chief union representative and inspector general of the ministry, also a Communist, had taken over the offices. I couldn't make a telephone call, except under Communist surveillance, so for three days I remained their prisoner. Fortunately, I was able to get my friend out and publish under my signature a decree dismissing all senior civil servants in the ministry who were on strike and appointing in their place presidents of the prisoners' associations.[18]

There can be no doubt this was a difficult situation.

Pierre Nicolaÿ, current vice president of the Council of State, who belonged to all Mitterrand's ministerial offices, is still flabbergasted by the situation then existing: "Zilbermann had such power that when he arrived at a ministry staff meeting, everybody stood up as if he were the minister. It was very impressive."

From the outset, then, François Mitterrand proved he was not a man to be intimidated by the Communist party. The sacking and replacement of the senior civil servants created a few storms. In the Communist ranks, there was astonishment and horror. Tempers rose. Zilbermann went so far as to tell the minister quite simply that there was no question of giving in. The minister retorted curtly: "I will not be spoken to in that way. You may leave."

Realistic as ever, the Communist party gave in. In exchange for a resumption of work and its cooperation, it managed to get some of the dismissals quashed. But later, Mitterrand managed to eliminate the most influential Communists in his ministry one by one. And he recounts with scarcely concealed satisfaction: "When I saw my colleague Maurice Thorez [general secretary of the Communist party] again at the cabinet meeting of February 5, 1947, he came up to me and said most affably: 'I understand. There are things you have to do when you're a minister. You were quite right.' "[19]

At the end of that same year, the first confrontations of the Cold War became increasingly visible. In France, the Communist party, excluded from the government in May (Mitterrand had unhesitatingly supported this decision of Prime Minister Ramadier), organized strike after strike. The factories were submerged beneath a wave of violence and sabotage. Several times clashes with the police were narrowly avoided. To face up to the situation once and for all, Robert Schuman, the MRP leader who had since become prime minister, decided to recall eighty thousand conscripts. He put before the National Assembly a bill that would guarantee the right to work against strike pickets. François Mitterrand approved it warmly. When, in the cabinet, a heated argument broke out between the advocates of conciliation and firmness, he placed himself unequivocally in the latter camp. While certain Socialist ministers hesitated to use such strong-arm tactics, Mitterrand turned to Daniel Mayer, the SFIO minister of labor [now president of the Constitutional Council] and asked: "Can you see any other way of achieving the same result?" It was Vincent Auriol who reported the words of the youngest government minister in his diary. The next day, when Robert Schuman announced the measures ordered by the Council of Ministers to the National Assembly, he was strongly attacked by the Communists, beginning with their leader, Jacques Duclos: "The government is lying. The prime minister is a former German officer, he's a Boche. . . . He's a fawning dog, a filthy swine." Floribond Bonte was hardly more agreeable: "Hitler didn't manage to smash us and nobody else will." This was the prevailing tone. It is understandable that Mitterrand would rush to the defense of the prime minister and accuse the extreme Left of coming out with nothing but insults. On May 1, 1948, during a public meeting in the Nièvre, he called for a union of all Republicans to block the road to communism.

Mitterrand's views were quite unchanged when he became the minister responsible for information in the government led by Radical André Marie—the changes of cabinet were continuing, at an accelerated rate. During the debate of a budget bill concerning broadcasting in July 1949, François Mitterrand clashed with the Communist deputy from Nice, Virgile Barel:

VIRGILE BAREL: The editorial direction of the radio news programs is under the direct orders of M. Dayan, a member of M. Mitterrand's office, is it not, M. le Ministre? . . . One of the chief news editors is at present a member of the minister of the interior's office. . . . Another is an RPF sympathizer. All this represents a resolutely violently anti-Communist management, hostile to the working class. This became quite clear during the miners' strike, when the radio poured out the most hate-filled, lying diatribes against the workers struggling for their security and their children's bread.

FRANÇOIS MITTERRAND: For some months now, I have had to take great care, M. Barel, lest a certain amount of news material find its way into our broadcasts—material slanted in a direction that would have pleased you more and that, up till now, was capable of being produced in the shadows in a way I personally regard as pernicious. But I am not aware you complained then. You will forgive me if I congratulate myself on what is the very object of your criticism. . . . Indeed, I am striving to the utmost to keep the propaganda of the Communist party off the air. I agree it is not always easy, but in any case I am trying.

VIRGILE BAREL: You've admitted it—you are forced to conceal the truth in order not to make Communist propaganda.

FRANÇOIS MITTERRAND: I believe this propaganda, yours in particular, is harmful to the interests of my country. I have therefore no reason to encourage it. . . . French radio must have a policy— a national policy for the defense of France's interests. It must choose between several themes, several tendencies, and the government considers itself, logically enough, the qualified representative of the French nation since it has the confidence of the majority of the National Assembly; it is therefore its duty to express the will of the nation.

MARC DUPUIS (Communist party): You are vomited by the country and you know it.

FRANÇOIS MITTERRAND: Among those who have the authority to speak to the country and world it is quite normal, is it not, that the first should be those who represent our democratic institutions? That is why I say the government, whenever the interests of the country are at stake, is perfectly in its right to tell the radio what direction it is proposing to the French nation as a whole. That, at least, is how I see it—it is up to the National Assembly to express its opinion on the matter.

MAURICE KRIEGEL-VALRIMOND (Communist party): You have clearly admitted that the radio is not the national radio, but the government radio.[20]

In this matter, François Mitterrand was not solely responsible for his actions. He and several others had been given the strictest instructions from Vincent Auriol, who notes in his diary entry of October 9, 1947: "As far as the radio is concerned, I have asked Mitterrand to get rid of the Communists running the news programs. And to cut out the 'Tribune Libre' [an open current affairs discussion program]. And to organize daily propaganda on the government's activities." The "Tribune Libre" was cut out, and such Communist journalists as Francis Crémieux, former chief editor of the news programs, were dismissed.

After the strike of November 11, 1947, at the broadcasting station, Vincent Auriol asked his assembled ministers at a cabinet meeting: " 'What would happen in time of war or social upheaval if the Communist technicians prevented the radio from functioning? We would have to plug the interministerial telephone exchange into a secret broadcasting station, otherwise it would be impossible for the prime minister and his ministers to communicate with the country.' Mitterrand nodded and said: 'Quite right. This is a serious matter. I'll look into it.' "

But Vincent Auriol's hopes were not to be fulfilled. Indeed, in a discussion shortly afterwards with the prime minister, then Henri Queuille, on the question of finances, Auriol returned to the problem: "I told him: 'Public opinion is disorientated because it doesn't know what the government is doing. You have no government newspaper; nobody tries to orient public opinion. We ought to bring in André Marie, who has a sense of publicity, instead of Mitterrand, who seems overloaded in his little ministry.' "

Overloaded or not, François Mitterrand did not change his mind: he remained invincibly opposed to the party of Maurice Thorez and was to remain so as long as the Fourth Republic lasted. Anticommunism was one of the dogmas of the UDSR. In 1952, it published a pamphlet stating: "The UDSR intends to wage a struggle against communism on every front—to unmask its lies mercilessly, to use the existing laws against it, and if necessary, to extend them. In particular, we should make membership in the Communist party incompatible with exercising administrative functions involving responsibility and security."

This, then, was the atmosphere inside the parliamentary group of the UDSR, of which François Mitterrand was then president. The most zealous members of this group even considered trying to get incompatibility between membership in the Communist party and responsible posts in the civil service included in the constitution.[21]

Personally, François Mitterrand did not lag far behind. Pleading in 1950 for the adoption of a new electoral law, with a majority list and a single ballot, he declared (the argument seeming to him conclusive): "If it were adopted, we could ask everybody without exception to unite against the Communist party and it would be difficult for anybody not to respond favorably to our appeal." For him the important thing was to arrange matters so that the French Communist party could "no longer hold up the workings of our institutions." In 1954, the UDSR was to take the initiative in setting up a national committee for the return to balloting by arrondissement (since the Liberation, France had voted on lists proposed for each department, with proportional representation); this system was to be installed under the presidency of François Mitterrand.

On this point at least, he has been consistent. On November 2, 1955, during a debate on the reform of the electoral system, he took Prime Minister Edgar Faure to task with the same arguments: "If what you want is to lend a helping hand to the Communist party and enable it to emerge at last from its isolation, as M. Barrachin so rightly feared, then go ahead."

In his political column in L'Express, Mitterrand made regular pleas for ballot by arrondissement. On November 23, 1955, he wrote: "We know why the government is hostile to ballot by arrondissement—after all, one can see why: what would become of M. Edgar Faure without the devoted and persistent help of the MRP?[22] Nevertheless, the question of dividing up constituencies according to a national quotient seems to some so impossibly complicated it must be given up. . . .[23] Since balloting by arrondissement has appeared on the scene, a noble concern for justice seems to trouble the conscience of these gentlemen—they are now proposing to divide up France by slide rule. . . ."

Two days later, he returned to the subject: "The Communist party and the MRP have found a common area of agreement: electoral reform. Both are in favor of proportional representation and are combining their efforts to bring about this form of ballot. This is because ballot by arrondissement has one major inconvenience for them: it allows the electorate to choose their representatives freely. . . ."

François Mitterrand's anti-Communist declarations could be quoted endlessly. He published one, however, at the end of the Fourth Republic (in June 1958, to be precise) in his newspaper, *Le Courrier de la Nièvre*, that sums them all up: "I have always fought communism. I can say categorically—and the people of the Nièvre will attest to this—that I have driven it back in this department. I shall struggle unflaggingly to spare France the horrors of a collectivist dictatorship."

This inveterate anti-communism is not, however, without its subtle distinctions. There can be no doubt that François Mitterrand finds the Communist ideology, methods, and apparatus utterly repellent.[24] But this does not mean he holds up to public obliquy the millions of electors who possess such precious votes. In 1954, in an article in the newspaper *Combat*, he wrote: "We do not confuse the anti-Communist struggle with constant victimization. We do not consider the millions of people who vote Communist definitively lost to the nation. The Communist party has lost support when action has been taken in social matters. Communism must be fought on both the ideological and the practical planes."

Three years later he declared to Georgette Elgey: "The Communist party is of the Left if one considers the five million electors who vote for it; it is not if one takes into account its methods of action, refusal of free discussion, and authoritarian sectarianism. Without the Communist electors, there is no left-wing majority." In other words, well before the new constitution and the electoral system forced Mitterrand into an alliance with the Communist party, he refused to regard Communist electors as beyond the pale.

If he is to be believed, it was even the possibility of an alliance with the Communists that prevented René Coty from making him prime minister: "At the time of the 1958 crisis, René Coty called me and asked me: 'Would you accept Communist votes?' I replied: 'Of course, and if that were not enough, I would ask for them.' He then said to me: 'That is impossible.' "[25]

Is this simply a way of reconstructing one's past with hindsight and thus appearing as a pioneer of the Union of the Left? Perhaps, but it is also a way of transgressing a taboo: there were not many politicians willing to count the votes of Communist deputies in their majority in the last years of the Fourth Republic (during the debate on his investiture, Pierre Mendès France had refused in advance to take the vote of Communist deputies into account). If he is to be believed, François Mitterrand, so very ardently anti-Communist, found himself totally transformed at the end of the Fourth Republic, since for him it was no longer a question of accepting the votes of electors, but of Communist deputies representing a hated apparatus.

AMBITION

The young deputy for the Nièvre who took up his seat in the National Assembly on November 12, 1946, was really in doubt about nothing. And what cause for doubt could there be for this Byronic hero? Mitterrand had barely been in the new chamber a few weeks when, on January 15, 1947, he joined the government (its youngest member) as minister for war veterans. Scarcely had he had time to get used to the assembly than he was set up in an official palace in the rue de Bellechasse, donning the uniform of a minister, which he was to wear unremittingly for twelve years, weekends included: navy-blue suit, white shirt, and black tie. A photographer, wanting to take a more relaxed picture of the young politician, asked him to change his clothes. He refused. Mitterrand's election posters showed him wearing nothing but white shirts and black ties. Is this a frivolous detail? Marcel Haedrich recounts: "Vincent Auriol remembered as one of the great achievements of his seven-year term making a tie obligatory at the Elysée. The first time he received them, the 'new gentlemen' appeared as *maqui-*

sards, dressed any old way, with (it was the fashion) the collar outside the jacket."[26]

In any case, fate proved favorable to Mitterrand: happy events followed one another at an intoxicating rate. At the time, the war veterans was a relatively prestigious ministry. But above all, this beginner had entered a very exclusive club: that of the fifty or so deputies of ministerial caliber who, throughout the twelve years of the Fourth Republic, constantly shared power with one another, succeeding or replacing each other. They formed a magic circle almost inaccessible to the common run of deputies and senators, an armada of some eight hundred aspiring politicians who harbored hopes, almost always disappointed, of one day being accepted into the club.

For François Mitterrand, things could not have been easier: after the short-lived Léon Blum government (December 1946) and the election of Vincent Auriol as first president of the new Republic, the Socialist Paul Ramadier, famous for his goatee, Hellenic culture, and simple tastes, was asked by the new head of state to form his first government.

Eugène Claudius-Petit recounts: "My friend Ramadier called me in and offered me the Ministry for War Veterans. I didn't want it— I wasn't interested in laying wreaths of chrysanthemums. What I was passionately interested in was reconstruction, everything concerned with the future; I had no wish to settle past accounts. So I told Ramadier that, for a portfolio like that, he would do better to ask a man who knew the shady world of former prisoners and deportees from the inside. As it happened, there was in the UDSR a young member of our parliamentary group who had just been elected in the Nièvre. He would do very well, I told Ramadier."

Paul Ramadier had in mind another candidate for the job, a Freemason and Socialist like himself: his friend Albert Forcinal. But Eugène Claudius-Petit proved a persuasive advocate for his man. And, in any case, the UDSR was indispensable to the coalition. So the matter was settled in record time: "I even drove François Mitterrand to the Elysée myself," Claudius-Petit now admits. "To think that I bear that responsibility before history!" he adds with a sigh.

Georges Beauchamp gives a different version of the affair: "If

François became a minister, it was thanks to a group of young SFIO resisters, of which I was one. We went to Ramadier and told him: 'Mitterrand is the man you want.' And I still remember that when I called him to tell him he had been made a minister, he refused to believe me."

In any case, the young deputy for the Nièvre joined the government. True to form, he pretended to find this promotion quite natural. Nevertheless, he wrote to Eugène Claudius-Petit announcing, by way of thanks for such effective work on his behalf, that he had decided to join the UDSR officially.

Scarcely had he got his foot in the stirrups than the new minister for war veterans, following his natural inclination, set about surrounding himself with faithful followers and displaying his family spirit. He appointed to his office his older brother Robert, who for a time was to be its head, and such old friends from the Resistance as Georges Beauchamp and Jean Védrine, who were to remain important members of his entourage. Once again, he demonstrated his love of reigning over a friendly tribe.

"Every evening or so, former prisoners of war visited him in his office," Pierre Nicolaÿ remembers. It was not only out of comradeship or friendship. François Mitterrand was beginning to apply a system he had denounced two months before from the platform of the war veterans' congress at Clermont-Ferrand on November 15, 1946. He had just been elected in the Nièvre, and said: "The political party that holds, has held, or will hold the Ministry for War Veterans and War Victims has a considerable advantage in infiltrating the federation. . . . Now, as I have said before, our association must defend itself. If we do not take defensive measures, we shall soon see the association belonging to whomever has the ministry, whichever side he may be on, be it the side of the man there today or the side of those who will come later. . . . It is quite normal if someone accuses me of wanting to take it over. Only the future can judge."

Premonitory words—indeed, the future has judged. Two months later, François Mitterrand, now minister for war veterans, applied the lesson he had given himself, conscientiously setting about infiltrating the federation with his own men at all its nerve points. Later, he called on this reserve group whenever he needed reinforcements in his takeover of the UDSR leadership. And the same men came to his aid when he was about to take over the Socialist party. But if he succeeded in getting his former POW comrades to work for him, he also worked on their behalf. He got through the assembly an official statute defining their rights and privileges and managed to get pension increases for them "of between 72 and 78 percent," as he boasted during the legislative campaign of 1951. He seems to have been a good minister, if one defines a good minister as one who looks after the interests of his subjects.

Only the women deportees have bad memories of Mitterrand in the rue de Bellechasse. Even today they criticize him for playing the cuckoo and occupying their nest. It is a very curious story, which several of them (notably Germaine Tillion, Anise Postel-Vinay, and Geneviève de Gaulle) have told. When the deportees returned in 1945, they managed to requisition for their association several stories in a luxurious building overlooking the Jardins du Luxembourg, at 4, rue Guynemer. During the war, it had been occupied by the German army's "gray mice," as the women soldiers were known. In late 1946, the women deportees learned that the businessman representing the property interests of the Vatican in Paris (the Holy See owned the building) was planning to evict them and rent the apartments for the highest possible amounts. Horrified at the idea of being evicted, thus losing a hostel and an occupational rehabilitation workshop, they began seeking help wherever they could find it. Journalist Alain Vernay (who married the sister of Simone Veil, also a former deportee) remembers going to get help from Léon Blum, briefly prime minister in December 1946. François Mitterrand, then a minister, was also approached, but in vain. The inflexible Vatican agent managed to recover the premises, and the women deportees had to pack their bags. But they were very surprised indeed (to say the least) when they learned a few weeks later that among the lucky tenants of their former premises were two former ministers for war veterans: Henri Frenay and François Mitterrand (who was to remain in the building for many years). The satirical magazine, *Le Canard enchaîné*, took great delight in pointing out the coincidence.

It is true, however, that the young minister thought of others: when in power, he wanted his family, friends, and subordinates to share the benefits. In fact, this tendency to nepotism has increased over the years.

Journalist and novelist Marcel Haedrich recounts:

When François became minister of information, we were brought closer together. The radio was already making problems for him. He would get a telephone call from the Matignon [the prime minister's office] saying: "It's a scandal!" He was summoned before the Council of the Republic—that amused him to no end.

"What can I do for you?" he asked me.

"Nothing, absolutely nothing." What could a minister do for the editor-in-chief of *Samedi soir*?

"A car, perhaps?" he suggested.

I used to drive around in a prewar, patched-up black Citroën, which had cost me a fortune to get. Production had just started up at Citroën and Mitterrand gave me a voucher for a spanking new car—a splendid metallic-gray job, which I bought at the fixed price (half of what I'd paid for my old jalopy) and then resold at a profit. Such were the benefits of poverty and politics.[27]

On the other hand, the new minister could prove unamenable to pressure, as he recounts here:

When I was minister of information, a friend called on me one day, accompanied by Baron Ténard, who was, I believe, a very important individual at Saint-Gobin. He was also the owner of the newspapers *Le Bien public* at Dijon and *Paris-Centre* in the Nièvre. During our conversation, Baron Ténard adopted a very imperious tone: "You are now minister of information. We need your signature—your career depends on it. You have forty-eight hours." I shall not tell you what ensued. I would never see either of them again. I was deeply hurt. How could someone speak to the representative of the state in this way? Again, while I was at the Ministry of Information, I learned of the *France-Soir* affair— and the unpleasant adventure, which, under the auspices of Robert Salmon, had put the newspaper of the Resistance in the hands of a financial group. I also signed the permission to allow *Paris-Match* to appear. But after an edifying conversation with

Jean Prouvost, I was gradually led to the conviction that big capital acted in France as if in a conquered country.[28]

Nevertheless, under the Republic that had been so kind to him, François Mitterrand was very concerned about his own destiny. The leading lights of the Fourth Republic always smoothed his way. Not a government was formed without him being offered a post in it.

Thus in 1948 (when he was just thirty-two), the prime minister, Robert Schuman, thought of making him minister of the interior. The president of the Republic, Vincent Auriol, was in favor. In his diary Auriol is full of praise for the young minister: "The interior is a job fraught with difficulties. . . . Schuman mentioned Mitterrand; I told him it was an excellent choice, for he is serious and intelligent." Unfortunately, though flattering, the post was too exposed to unpopularity in that year of the violent strikes fomented by the Communist party. Moreover, the UDSR would not hear of it. There could be no question of one of its members bearing the burden of decisions whose consequences might be fearsome.

"Mitterrand accepted," Vincent Auriol confirms, "but, learning of it, the UDSR refused. It is to be hoped that the Gaullist newspapers will launch into a great attack on the tyranny of the parties over men. It is quite pitiful! The Radicals don't want it. Nor does the MRP. Why? Because they fear social conflict and want to leave the job to the Socialists. . . . I tried to persuade Mitterrand, who initially accepted the post, but he had to refuse, against his will, on instructions from his party. If he had stuck with his initial decision, as he wanted to, he would have been threatened with expulsion. So he came with demands for unacceptable guarantees."

All was not lost, however: the offer was a flattering one, in view of the circumstances. That he was offered the post at all, given the explosive situation, says much for his reputation for a cool head and strong will.

Much stranger today seems the suggestion made by Léon Blum— the pope of socialism, who had the ear of the Elysée during the formation of the next government—of Radical Henri Queuille. Blum was thinking of the UDSR's hope of getting a very important portfolio—finance—but one equally fraught with danger. Vincent Auriol reports: "After Queuille's departure, Léon Blum came to see me. He said he doubted whether Queuille would succeed with Mendès at finance, though it would be a very good appointment and assist Socialist participation. 'One might try Mitterrand,' he suggested. 'After all, Barthou and Poincaré were hardly older than he.' "

So the stock of the deputy for the Nièvre was still rising. For it was clearly not his experience of financial and budgetary matters, nor his interest in them (in the twelve years of the Fourth Republic, he never took part in a single major economic debate) that justified Léon Blum's support. But the political significance of this proposal is worth noting: although classed in the Center-Right and elected as such by the people of the Nièvre, Mitterrand was valued by such prestigious Socialists as Léon Blum and the president of the Republic, Vincent Auriol. However, Auriol once confided to Marcel Haedrich: "Your friend Mitterrand intervenes all the time at cabinet meetings. I have to say to him: 'M. Mitterrand, you will speak when I ask you to do so.' "

Others no doubt would have been dazzled by such success, but not François Mitterrand: his eyes were already fixed on higher things, on more distant horizons. He was to write: "At the level of the politician there is only one ambition: to govern. Those whose only ambition is to become under secretary of state display a shopkeeper mentality—they are not true politicians." It was a time when he was fond of repeating to his friends: "Any fool can be prime minister at fifty; I intend to be prime minister at forty. . . ." Did such remarks spring solely from a love of provocation, a desire to shock? No doubt. But there was nothing absurd about them. Having been offered the Ministries of Interior and Finance at the age of thirty, Mitterrand was quite legitimate in thinking the prime ministership could not be far off.

The trouble was that under the Republic it was not enough to be thought highly of by certain leading figures; one also had to take into account the party organizations, which did not always have the same criteria. Anyone who wanted to become head of government not only had to be recognized by the institutional hierarchs as suitable material, but also (and this was more difficult) had to cross the obstacles erected by the competing apparatchiks.

These days President Mitterrand has forgotten none of the feelings he felt at that time: "It made me furious to think I would be prime minister when others wanted me to be and that I would have to go when they decided."[29] At this time, then, he was in favor of a strong presidency without knowing it.

To a journalist who was also one of his women friends, he confided some years later: "During the legislative campaign of 1956, everybody thought I was tired, perhaps even ill.[30] In fact, I was stifling my rage at not yet being prime minister." In 1956, François Mitterrand was just forty and had lost his bet. Nevertheless, he had not spared his efforts. Knowing he had to depend on others, the young minister had done what he could to increase his chances and had patiently cultivated those in powerful positions within the UDSR.

THE CONQUEST OF THE UDSR

The UDSR emerged just after the war at the instigation of several former members of the Resistance who dreamed of bringing a breath of fresh air into politics. They did not want to fall back into the Right-Left cleavages, which were absurd in their eyes and which they considered responsible for the collapse of 1940. They wanted to exorcise the demons of sterile quarrels—the endless struggle between clericals and anticlericals over education, the class struggle, and so on—that had torn France apart. They wanted to avoid the resuscitation of parties discredited because they had prostrated themselves before Marshal Pétain. Lastly, they wanted to bring together in a "French-style laborism" a generation of new men open to ideas of progress, often Socialists, but anti-Marxist.

These were the hopes of the UDSR founders. Reality soon disappointed them. Immediately after the Liberation, the traditional political formations reappeared and a powerful new competitor appeared: the MRP, founded by Christian democrats and social Catholics led by Georges Bidault. Bidault had predicted: "With the women, the bishops, and the Holy Ghost, we will have at least a hundred deputies." If there was any milieu in which the new UDSR hoped to recruit support, it was there, in the new Catholic generation. The growth of the MRP stopped those hopes short. Further to the Left, the Communist party was attracting many men who had emerged from the Resistance; the old SFIO, still anticlerical, rejected the support of the new forces.

For want of being large enough itself, the UDSR then formed an alliance with the SFIO, whose general direction was more or less in line with UDSR laborist dreams. "We must struggle," it was said in UDSR ranks, "against the Radicals, advocates of the status quo." Benefiting from this alliance, the UDSR won twenty-seven seats, to which were to be added four associate members, in the first Constituent Assembly. At the beginning of its parliamentarian life, it sat in the Center-Left. The great men of the movement were René Pleven, General de Gaulle's minister of finance in 1945; Eugène Claudius-Petit; Jacques Soustelle; René Capitant; Jacques Baumel; and even an escapee from the Third Republic, Maurice Delom-Sorbé, one of twenty-four parliamentarians who had refused to vote plenary powers to Marshal Pétain (Delom-Sorbé was to be decorated with the Légion d'honneur in 1981 by President François Mitterrand).

Very soon in that assembly, in which the deputies of the three great parties—the Communist, Socialist, and MRP—moved like disciplined troopers, the UDSR acquired an originality it was always to preserve. This originality stemmed from the juxtaposition of a mosaic of individuals with very independent outlooks who were resistant to the discipline of the big parties.

But harsh electoral realities forced them to moderate their ambitions with each passing day. A few months later, in the elections of June 1956, the SFIO, which mistrusted this small ally, tried to limit its number of seats. As a result, the UDSR was forced to make an alliance with the Radical party and the nebulous RGR (which, only a few months earlier, it had pretended to despise so much). Only two men took sufficient offense at this alliance to leave the party: Henri Frenay, former boss of the Combat movement, and Léo Hamon.

It was at these elections, as we have seen, that François Mitterrand made his entry into political life. When he linked up with the UDSR, it was more of a loose structure than a real party. Its leaders, especially René Pleven, whose right to leadership no one then challenged, wanted to turn it into a real party. But things were still in too fluctuating a state. It was, therefore, a good place for someone who wanted to establish himself, to carve out a place in the sun, providing he had ambition, determination, and skill—three qualities François Mitterrand was not lacking.

Nevertheless, his joining the UDSR surprised his masters in Angoulême. At an inauguration at the Collège Saint-Paul in spring 1947, the Abbé Perrinot asked the young minister: "What exactly do the letters UDSR stand for?"

"Union démocratique et socialiste de la Résistance," the new minister replied proudly.

The priest gave a start: "What? You? Socialist?"

François Mitterrand reassured him: "Don't worry, Father, I chose the most right-wing group I could find in the National Assembly."[31]

It was a joke, of course, but the priests at Angoulême were not the only ones to be surprised. The Socialists in the National Assembly were, too, as René Pleven attests: "When François Mitterrand joined the UDSR, certain deputies from the SFIO came to me and said: 'You're crazy to accept him—he's on the extreme Right!' "

There is a paradox here: the dominant feeling of the UDSR was then strongly Gaullist. There were a great many unconditional supporters of the general in the group: René Capitant, Jacques Vendroux (de Gaulle's brother-in-law), Pierre Clostermann, Jacques Soustelle, Michel Debré, and Jacques Baumel. Others had retained a deep admiration for the head of Free France: René Pleven, Eugène Claudius-Petit, Pierre Bourdan, Pierre Chevalier. François Mitterrand, reticent as ever, seemed fairly isolated.

Yet in only seven years, he was to take control of the party. This operation was spread over three phases. First, he was to expel the Gaullists. No one would have bet much on his chances of succeeding, but three years and the tactical errors of the parties in question made it possible.

General de Gaulle's return to the political scene on April 7, 1947, triggered the first hostilities. When he addressed the French nation on the day the RPF was launched at Strasbourg, people noticed he was flanked by eminent members of the UDSR: René Capitant, Jacques Soustelle, Antoine Avinin, and Eugène Claudius-Petit. A week later, the political bureau of the party decided unanimously to allow dual membership in the UDSR and RPF: members of the UDSR could join the RPF, but strictly on an individual basis. This unanimity in fact concealed three well-defined tendencies: some people were ready to follow the general faithfully; others expressed their devotion to him while entertaining doubts as to the purity of his intentions and determination to respect the constitution; still others, who had as their spokesman François Mitterrand, were frankly opposed to an initiative that to them seemed "seditious."

In the months that followed, René Pleven, a born conciliator, tried to bring about an alliance between the "third force" (the Socialist party and MRP) then in power and General de Gaulle, in order to confront the Communist peril (it has been said that, in France, the Cold War took the form of violent clashes and serious strikes). Various emissaries and intermediaries were at work, but their proposals were haughtily rejected by the charismatic leader of the RPF, who did not intend to negotiate with parties that, as he put it, "cook their little soup on their little fire." And the general did not change his mind. As a result, at the 1948 party conference, René Capitant, representing the most Gaullist members of the UDSR, proposed a radical measure: nothing less than a parliamentary strike by the UDSR deputies to force the National Assembly to dissolve.[32]

François Mitterrand, of course, did not see things in this way and assumed leadership of the internal opposition. He even became the defender of the existing regime, which had succeeded in "re-establishing Republican order." He threw out a challenge to the Gaullists: "If things had been settled earlier with more mastery,[33] we would not be having so much trouble putting things back in place." And, turning to the Gaullists, he added: "We are told: 'You don't want to give up your seats.' That may be true, but I would say rather: 'You are in quite a hurry to take ours.' " All in all, he concluded, "The Fourth Republic is nevertheless a fine edifice to construct."

As usual, René Pleven tried hard to bring the antagonistic points of view together, but in vain. Of course, he was reelected leader unopposed, which shows that none of the conflicting tendencies had yet won the day. The arch-Gaullist René Capitant became vice president, so his position in the party was not marginal. But Joseph Perrin, a faithful supporter of François Mitterrand, was also made vice president. This schoolteacher, ex-president of the National

Movement of Prisoners of War and Deportees, was still editor of the former prisoners' newspaper, *Le PG*.

René Capitant's provocative initiative (he is well known for this kind of thing) was to light the fuse. François Mitterrand was at last able to launch an offensive in grand style and get the better of the Gaullists in the UDSR. Indeed, on December 9, 1948, Capitant decided to set up a Gaullist parliamentary group distinct from the UDSR, which he called Action démocratique et sociale. Thirteen deputies of the UDSR (about half its number) followed him. The UDSR itself, reduced to thirteen members, now lost for a time any autonomous administrative life. (Fourteen deputies were required at the time to constitute a parliamentary group.) The UDSR then had to link itself to the Radical group (the supreme humiliation) in order to preserve its representation in the assembly commissions (until the happy day when the UDSR was joined by a deputy from Constantine, Cadi Abdel Kader, allowing it to regain its independence). In other words, the defection of the Gaullists very nearly killed off the UDSR parliamentary group.

Things did not bode well for the 1949 congress. An already serious situation was made all the more difficult by the group statutes, which were imprecise on a number of points. Could one claim allegiance to a party while belonging to a parliamentary group not the parliamentary expression of that group? Of course, what was to dominate the debates was not so much the legal matter as the political problem.

The leader of the dissident group, René Capitant (then forty-eight), decided to attack first, believing, as a faithful disciple of Charles de Gaulle, this to be the best defense. He accused François Mitterrand (then thirty-three) of making the break inevitable by his intransigence: "Our comrade Mitterrand," he said, "has defined his position perfectly clearly. It consists of making his prime political objective the struggle against the RPF and even against General de Gaulle himself. He believes (and has said as much) the general represents the danger of fascism.[34] From the moment Mitterrand decided the RPF was doomed by its leaders as well as its methods, it was clear our duty to loyalty and honesty forced us to part."

René Capitant delivered a warning to those who wanted to stay inside the UDSR: "You are destined to be absorbed by the Mitterrand tendency and to merge with the Radical party."[35] (Capitant was right on the first point, wrong on the second.)

Faithful to himself, René Pleven still tried to hold the Gaullists. Believing the break both necessary and desirable, François Mitterrand, on the other hand, helped them on their way. And wanting to reassure those who would remain with him, he exclaimed: "It is not a question of winner or loser, but of a majority tendency determined that the party discipline will be respected. We would be able to work with reduced numbers if we were certain there would no longer be the discord or ambiguity that till now has prevented us from knowing exactly where friend and enemy stand."

The Gaullists were out. In spite of all he had said, François Mitterrand certainly seemed the victor. He had got what he wanted. And René Pleven, who had failed to maintain unity, was in difficulties.

The second stage of Mitterrand's seizing of UDSR control began with the Marseille congress, in October 1951. Since August, René Pleven had been the new prime minister. But François Mitterrand, who had been minister of France overseas in the first Pleven cabinet, was not included in the government team this time. "The MRP was opposed to his presence," Pleven explains, "criticizing him for an African policy too favorable to the Rassemblement démocratique africain." The RDA, led by Félix Houphouët-Boigny and the Guinean Sékou Touré, was regarded as too sympathetic to Marxism by Georges Bidault's friends, who preferred Léopold Sedar Senghor's Indépendants d'outre-mer.

Of course, François Mitterrand did not at all like being excluded. Indeed, this widened the gap between he and René Pleven, strengthening Mitterrand's determination to wrest control of the party from him. "From the moment he felt excluded from Pleven's team, he felt he no longer owed him anything," Georges Beauchamp now confirms.

The young deputy for the Nièvre, who had never acknowledged any political boss or intellectual leader, had made up his mind this time to play his own card. Indeed, according to Louis Deteix, a former POW and one of François Mitterrand's long-standing friends, the maneuvers had begun the year before: "It was just before the

Lyon congress, in 1950. We had met at François's house at Cluny. There were seven or eight of us, and for two days he explained how we were to take over the party by getting former prisoners in the federations to join. 'This is how we are going to get them into the UDSR,' he explained. We had a good laugh together over the trick we were going to play on the 'old men' [René Pleven and Eugène Claudius-Petit]."

In fact, in 1950, over a third of the members of the outgoing executive committee were not reelected, but were replaced by former POWs. The following year, over 35 percent of the outgoing members suffered the same fate. In this way the Mitterrandists became the majority. And Joseph Lanet, the party general secretary, deplored at the congress rostrum that "many new members of the executive committee are neophytes who have only recently joined the party."

François Mitterrand was not to abandon so effective a device too soon. His faithful henchmen, Joseph Perrin and Louis Deteix, were to use the membership lists of the former National Movement of Prisoners of War and Deportees to form departmental federations; Mitterrand himself, the day before one congress, was to urge a former Vichy POW, Pierre Coursol,[36] to join the party, even going so far as offering to pay his membership fee. "We call these new federations 'directory federations,' for we suspect the names of members were taken from directories," explained René Pleven, still somewhat aggrieved. The ex-treasurer of the party, Pierre Raynal, now president and managing director of Presse-Océan, sighs: "Since the membership fees were paid and we had no means of checking them, we could hardly oppose them."

François Mitterrand, who had long dreamed of supplanting the "old men" (in 1947 remarking to Edouard Bonnefous, "We are not going to serve as a stepping-stone for those gentlemen"), distanced himself from René Pleven on all the great issues—Indochina, the European Defense Community, the religious schools. This led to Mitterrand being regarded as the leader of the left wing of the UDSR. That René Pleven failed to obtain the participation of the Socialists in his government at the very time he was excluding François Mitterrand was a coincidence the deputy for the Nièvre was quick to turn to his own advantage: "The vocation of the UDSR is to bring together the socialist forces," Mitterrand said at the time. "Under no circumstances can the representatives of our party agree even to talks with the RPF. We are ready to come to an agreement with Republicans who refuse to abolish at a stroke the conquests of the Liberation." Yet the very man who, in the congresses, preached the coming together of socialist forces had, to the astonishment of members, just had himself reelected in the Nièvre with the votes of the PRL.

The 1951 congress enabled him to make his mark. René Pleven was, of course, unanimously reelected chairman of the executive committee. But this time François Mitterrand managed to get his friend Joseph Perrin made general secretary. It is worth pointing out that a former prisoner of war thus succeeded Joseph Lanet at the head of the party machine. It is not simply gossip to stress that Joseph Perrin's secretary was the daughter of a former POW. This young lady was called Paule Moreau, later to become Mme Decraene (and now one of President Mitterrand's private secretaries at the Elysée).

The political bureau itself took on a distinctly Mitterrandist color. Georges Dayan, Mitterrand's closest friend, was elected assistant general secretary, and two of the four vice presidents were former companions of the National Movement of Prisoners of War and Deportees: Bastien Leccia (decorated in 1982), and Louis Deteix (decorated in 1947 by Mitterrand, who was to give him the rosette in 1981; Deteix took part from the very beginning in the annual pilgrimage to Solutré). "From that time on, I directed the discussions in the executive committee or congress the way François wanted," Deteix notes.

So that nobody would be in any doubt as to his newly won power, François Mitterrand demanded a vote on some minor question at the first meeting of the executive committee following the congress. The "Plevenists" had to concede at once: Mitterrand's majority was overwhelming.

All accounts of the official meetings of the UDSR of this period show that nothing was done in the party without him: when he was away, decisions were postponed. The deputy for the Nièvre was already displaying his political skills: the leader of the UDSR was the first secretary of the Socialist party in embryo.[37]

Already at the time it was (still) the schools' question that preoccupied the parties. The congress reaffirmed the UDSR's position favoring freedom of education and hostility to any monopoly, while it condemned (notably in the person of Jacques Baumel, future general secretary of the UNR) the principle of state subsidy of private education. A month before, however, no doubt out of fidelity to Prime Minister René Pleven, the party deputies had voted in favor of the bills proposed by Marie and Barangé providing for certain kinds of assistance to the families of pupils in private education. Joseph Lanet and François Mitterrand had not taken part in the vote. But when Joseph Lanet went to the congress demanding the abrogation of the Barangé law, Mitterrand's attitude was "conciliatory and appeasing"[38]—though only up to a certain point. For at the same time, the deputy for the Nièvre was criticizing the MRP for reviving a quarrel by proposing the Barangé law, which he regarded as "outdated." "In order to pay for the helping hand given by an article in the *Osservatore romano*,"[39] he said, "the MRP has sown disarray in French political life for many years to come and taken up its position on the Right."

This was obviously not the feeling of a man like René Pleven. But the founding father of the UDSR certainly realized he had lost hold of his party. He no longer felt master in his own house. He did not accept the criticisms of the new general secretary, who deplored the participation of his party in the right-wing governments of Antoine Pinay and René Mayer (to which, coincidentally, François Mitterrand did not belong).

Above all, René Pleven deplored having been deserted over Indochina. Up until the 1953 congress, the UDSR had consistently supported French policy in Indochina and had always congratulated René Pleven, the more or less immovable minister of defense, for his action at the head of his ministry. But the deterioration of the situation in that arena had gradually led the party to question its position and François Mitterrand to distance himself from it. At the 1953 congress, therefore, Mitterrand came out in favor of disengagement and a ceasefire in Indochina, thus implicitly condemning the actions of René Pleven he had until then supported. This shift may be seen as the new mark of a political evolution that was to take place in the last years of the Fourth Republic,

from the Center-Right to the Center-Left. It may also be seen as
an illustration of Mitterrand's rejection of compulsory loyalties (unpopularity soon submerged the former prime minister). This attitude was to play an important role in the mistrust aroused by
François Mitterrand among his colleagues in government.

He inspired a good deal of mistrust. A former minister of the
Fourth Republic sums up Mitterrand's behavior as follows:

> I noted that as soon as Mitterrand left the government and re-
> turned to the back benches, he immediately demolished all the
> bills with which one knew he was in fundamental agreement.
> The reason is simple enough: he could not accept such bills being
> presented by a government stupid enough to do without him. At
> the end of his interventions, in which he often gave proof of a
> fearsome Machiavellianism, the bill and the man defending it
> had to be demolished. He had no peer in seizing upon some
> detail, exaggerating it, caricaturing it—and thus ruining the whole
> structure. If someone remarked that he had shown no hostility
> toward the bill in question while in power, he then retorted, not
> in the least put out: "It is not the bill I am attacking, but its
> application."

This ruthless technique was to be denounced by the then prime
minister, Edgar Faure, in the National Assembly on November 29,
1955: "Obviously, one always looks forward with interest, and
some degree of apprehension, to M. Mitterrand's interventions.
This is not only because of his talent and the interest of what
he says, but also because of the particular choice of dates on
which his interventions occur." This was a subtle and mocking
way of stressing that François Mitterrand fired his arrows as
soon as the government seemed vulnerable: he was always in
on the kill.

In his profession of faith for the elections of January 1956, François Mitterrand, who had been minister three times and held some
of the highest offices in the outgoing legislature, dared to write:
"What I am fighting is a majority that has governed France. I am
in no way associated with the record of this legislature, which I
unreservedly condemn."

Such an attitude did nothing to improve his image, of course. One day, while advising Edouard Bonnefous not to join a government Mitterrand himself had not been invited to join, Bonnefous retorted: "It's all so simple with you: when you're in the government, the UDSR must be in the majority; but as soon as you leave the government, the party has to go into opposition." Today René Pleven comments: "Mitterrand was a man with whom one would not go on a tiger hunt alone." And André Monteil, former MRP minister of the navy and a friend of Mitterrand's, remarks: "Under the Fourth Republic, François Mitterrand had against him the fools, the ambitious, and the overcredulous—the fools because he was intelligent, the ambitious because they always found him in their way, and the credulous because with him one never knew where one was."

François Mitterrand's disagreement with the European Defense Community had even more serious consequences, involving the complete takeover of the UDSR. The takeover idea had been launched by Jean Monnet and Robert Schuman and was supported by René Pleven himself in 1950; the UDSR had supported the plan to create an integrated European army.

Up until 1953, François Mitterrand, a great advocate of Europe in general, had voted for all the motions approving this plan that divided the political class and the French nation as a whole, bringing about surprising convergences and cleavages between parties and within parties. Even at the UDSR congress in autumn 1952, Mitterrand declared: "I am still waiting to hear a single argument, a single point, a single judgment that would lead me to think, on the smallest, narrowest, least important aspect of general policy what the real danger is in joining a defense community that would disappear without that community."

Some months later, in January 1953, during the debate for the investiture of René Mayer, Mitterrand declared, in much the same vein:

A political authority with precedence over any European institution—that would have been preferable; it is still preferable. Whatever may be done to give precedence to those political institutions over fragmentary institutions will also be preferable.

But one has to begin at the beginning, respond to certain threats, move forward, move forward at a faster rate than the advocates of Europe first wished.

Nevertheless, I allow myself to point out to you, Monsieur le président de Conseil, that if a political authority must lead the European army, the same argument would have applied in the case of the coal and steel pool.

Despite these unequivocal declarations, parliamentarians and civil servants very hostile to the European Defense Community, who were brought together under the Action for National Independence Committee (which included Michel Debré, Jacques Chaban-Delmas, and Léo Hamon), have always said that on this question at least, François Mitterrand was on their side. Was it a case of double-talk? "Even if we did not see much of him," Jacques Chaban-Delmas notes, "François Mitterrand made it clear to us he thought as we did. He always promised to come to our meetings—but in fact, never came." Jacques Bloch-Morhange says, however: "In fact, Mitterrand did not cease hesitating as to which attitude he would adopt on the inevitable day when the choice about the European army would finally come before parliament."[40]

This quarrel was to die down when, under the Mendès France government, the National Assembly supported a motion that the question be indefinitely postponed. The government refused to accept responsibility for the plan and made the bill (which in fact divided it internally) a question of confidence (an almost routine procedure at the time). Eugène Claudius-Petit, UDSR minister of labor, criticized Pierre Mendès France for this and resigned rather noisily. François Mitterrand, minister of the interior, did not flinch, on the grounds that "the European Defense Community does not justify the fall of a government that has so much to do."

Exhausted by so much criticism and disagreement, René Pleven stepped down at the Nantes congress in 1953, even refusing the honorary presidency of the party. François Mitterrand had carried out the third phase of his seizing of power. He was elected president of the UDSR by fifty votes. There were eleven abstentions and no votes against. He had won at the age of thirty-seven. (When René

Pleven and Eugène Claudius-Petit, having lost the battle, went to see Mitterrand at party headquarters in the rue du Mont-Thabor to borrow a few typewriters until they sorted themselves out, Mitterrand curtly refused their request: "Out of the question. *I* am the UDSR.")

So he was now officially head of a party and the mind behind a parliamentary group that was indispensable to any coalition. He could legitimately believe he had arrived at a decisive point on the road to power. Mitterrand made no attempt to expand the UDSR: in 1952 it had 13,097 members and, in 1957, scarcely 14,000. This very modest expansion led René Pleven to remark, at a banquet given at the end of the 1957 congress: "President Mitterrand, you have allowed the UDSR to fulfill the dream of every woman: to grow old without getting fatter."

It was at this congress that François Mitterrand was to come out in favor of a regrouping of the Center parties "between a conservative Right and a Left sometimes led to make promises it cannot fulfill."

MITTERRAND THE AFRICAN

In becoming minister of France overseas in July 1950, François Mitterrand won his first great portfolio. At thirty-three, he ruled over black Africa, Madagascar, the Comoro Islands, the establishments in Oceania, and Saint-Pierre-et-Miquelon.[41]

The Cold War was at its height; the Korean conflict had just erupted; and France was fighting in Indochina. Open to the influence of many different tendencies and exposed to a ferment of instability, black Africa was becoming a serious cause for concern. In France itself, most parliamentarians and political groups did not have the faintest idea what was happening there.

The Communist party was in favor of separatism, an attitude François Mitterrand did not fail to denounce: "A primitive nationalism deprived of any historical context was emerging and developing, fed by disappointment and bitterness (sometimes by hatred), maintained by a latent racism, and aroused by Communist propaganda."[42] The other parties, including the Socialists, reacted instinctively, advocating unflinching repression.

The UDSR's attitude was more original: having been responsible for the colonies in General de Gaulle's provisional government, René Pleven had proposed, at the Brazzaville conference, "the advent of a new era in relations between France and her African possessions." From that time he had remained open-minded to African realities, which General de Gaulle in 1947 had defined (and at the same time limited) as follows:

> In French Africa, as in all the territories where men live under our flag, there would be no progress if men on their own soil did not benefit from it morally and materially, if they could not rise gradually to the level at which they would be capable of taking part in the running of their own affairs. It is the duty of France to act in such a way that this is made possible. . . . The purpose of the civilizing work carried out by France in the colonies rules out any idea of autonomy, any possibility of developing outside the French bloc of the Empire.

For once, François Mitterrand found no difficulty in following René Pleven, finding it easy enough to take on this policy, which he was to make his own (at least until 1958). After the vote on the outline bill proposed by Gaston Deferre in Guy Mollet's government, Mitterrand was to write in 1957: "Proposed in all willingness by the government, supported by the elected representatives of the overseas territories (and in particular by M. Houphouët-Boigny and the RDA, passed by a large majority, and applied loyally, this bill will at last fulfill the now thirteen-year-old promise of Brazzaville."[43]

And when, in the National Assembly on June 1, 1958, he was to express unambiguously his hostility to the return of General de Gaulle, Mitterrand nevertheless paid tribute to "the man of unique prestige, incomparable glory, exceptional services rendered—the man of Brazzaville, who more than any other represents by his very presence on this rostrum a hope for the peoples overseas."

It is true that a few years later Mitterrand was to change his mind: "It is an admirable irony of history," he was to exclaim, "that Gaullism was identified with the liberation of the colonized peoples, since from the Brazzaville conference to the 'Vive l' Algérie française' of Mostaganem he has been the advocate of the Empire against decolonization. At Brazzaville, this was to forbid forever any hope of unfettered self-government."[44] (This was true up to 1958, untrue thereafter.) De Gaulle's return to power by means François Mitterrand disapproved of was enough, in his eyes, to tinge with opprobrium all the general's subsequent acts. But in 1953 that stage had not yet been reached, and François Mitterrand was to do all he could to anticipate—and even to benefit from— the policy defined at Brazzaville.

During the full year he spent in the Ministry of France Overseas in the rue Oudinot,[45] François Mitterrand had opportunities to display every facet of his character:

Ambition
Unlike his predecessor, Alfred Coste-Floret, Mitterrand was not content just to administer and back up the initiatives or inertia of the local governors. He wanted to influence French colonial policy and leave his mark on it.

Individualism
Even if his policy was inspired by the prime minister (with the encouragement of President Auriol), Mitterrand found it quite normal that he should be its first beneficiary.

The Ability to Manipulate
Thanks to the support of the African deputies of the RDA, whose loyalty he was able to win, Mitterrand increased his influence within the UDSR.

Authoritarianism
Those who resisted him were replaced.

Pragmatism
Mitterrand intended to encourage developments, on condition that he kept full control over events, by acting on the results of elections, if necessary.

Liberalism

Despite angry pressure from the local colonists and governors, he
supported the African leaders struggling for the emancipation of
their peoples.

But François Mitterrand was not to prove to be a great visionary
(in the current sense of the term). Not for a moment was he to
imagine the rapid progress of the African states toward independence (though very few politicians, it is true, and not even General
de Gaulle, foresaw this).

Mitterrand expressed his beliefs as follows:

Paris is the authentic, necessary capital of the French Union.
The African world will have no center of gravity if it confines
itself to its geographical frontiers. It will become divided, fragmented, repeat for itself our own most unhappy experiences.
There is already talk of nationalism. We still remember irreducible racism. Bound to France in its political, economic, and
spiritual totality, the African world will cross four centuries at a
stroke and fully carry out its modern role, which is both original
and complementary. From Flanders to the Congo, the "third
continent" will be balanced around our metropolis.[46]

This view was not the result of a sudden, recent conversion.
Mitterrand had always been attracted to Africa and sensitive to its
difficulties and contradictions. Even before his first long tour there,
his ideas of the continent were not simple. Thus, on June 24, 1945,
he wrote in *Libres*, the newspaper of former POWs:

It is no doubt very ambitious to claim to bring to the so-called
backward peoples what we still call our civilization. It is usually
thought that to build roads, carry out vaccinations, set up factories, and rationalize production are major signs of progress in
peoples. We ought to know from experience that the material
benefits of science lead with disappointing regularity to providing
men with additional ways of killing one another. . . .

One can only give what one has. . . . The French worship the
universal, but they have forgotten to ask the opinion of those
concerned. And, after all, why should they exchange their dates

and donkeys for factory smoke? There's no accounting for tastes. This said, let us try to see the facts as they are: looked at from the appalling point of view of utilitarianism, our colonies are necessary to us. To abandon them would be to abandon ourselves. If our methods are unpleasant, let us change them. But let us avoid the eternal inferiority complex. Let us not praise our virtues excessively, but let us not be forever jeering at our faults. Our work is imperfect—a mixture of good and bad, heroism and cupidity, generosity and stupidity. But who has done any better?

There is perhaps more caution in this article than in any of those he was to write subsequently. In fact, François Mitterrand was to discover this continent only in August 1949. Invited by the High Commissioner of French Equatorial Africa, Bernard Cornut-Gentille, the young minister of information paid a visit to Radio Brazzaville. He took the opportunity to make a long journey through the Congo, Gabon, Chad, and the Sudan, returning to Paris via Cairo, Damascus, Jerusalem, and Athens. He was accompanied by Danielle Mitterrand; Claude de Kemoularia, Paul Reynaud's young cabinet chief (now ambassador to the United Nations); and Pierre Chevalier, UDSR deputy for Orléans (who was to be murdered the following year by his wife in a fit of jealousy).

Mitterrand was to write of these experiences in *Ma part de vérité*:

I returned from that journey burning with a desire to act. I had seen an administration that was easygoing but closed to new ideas, outdated, and obsessed with ready-made formulas learned from Gallieni and Lyautey. I had seen the colonial pact flourishing after its abolition. . . . I had seen Africa plundered, its raw materials exploited and sent off to be processed elsewhere. I had seen humiliated, or still-resigned men. . . . Yet, despite all this, I had seen that France was loved. . . . I felt something like fear at the prospect of the nation collapsing under the debris of its empire if it proved incapable of confronting the new times fast enough. But I felt independence would come only at the end of a long process. It seemed to me that in the immediate future, black Africa would fragment; that it possessed neither the structures nor the political elite capable of forming and holding states together; that its territories, whose frontiers had been traced in the chancelleries of Europe with ruler and compass, had no ethnic or geographical reality.

Shortly afterward, as minister of France overseas and a colonizer without illusions, he confided to his friend Jean Roy (then subprefect of Montbard and a former boarder at "104"): "Peoples are like children: they grow up, then they must be gradually given their freedom."

Those who were with Mitterrand on that long African journey noted not only the young minister's thoughtful interest in the continent and, perhaps, his fascination with it (he went on his first big game hunt), but also his regal temperament. Mitterrand insisted that everyone's timetable be subjected to his own will and whims.

As Alain de Boissieu, General de Gaulle's son-in-law, who was at Pointe-Noire at the time, recounts in his memoirs:

In August we had a visit from the minister of France overseas, François Mitterrand. He was supposed to be at the Jockey Club at a certain time. When, after a half-hour wait, the minister had not appeared, nor any message been received, the club president decided to start the proceedings. . . . The high commissioner's office later let it be known that the minister would be coming in the evening, but in a private capacity. The next day, François Mitterrand arrived at Pointe-Noire in the high commissioner's train, but unaccompanied by M. Cornut-Gentille. We learned that when the convoy had left the plain, it had stopped, though no incident had taken place. In the end, the train arrived an hour late, which the troops who were to present arms on their arrival did not appreciate at all, for it is extremely hot in full sun at noon at the equator. It was soon learned that the delay had been due to a game of cards that had lasted longer than expected. . . . That day it seemed to the inhabitants of Pointe-Noire that if punctuality is the politeness of kings, it was not that of certain representatives of the Fourth Republic.[47]

Another story was very much in the news at the time. For the fiftieth anniversary of Chad, the governor, Henri de Mauduit, had planned festivities to which had been invited all those (industrialists, civil servants, journalists) who had helped or might help the development of the territory. Quite obviously the minister would preside over the ceremony. François Mitterrand accepted the invitation, saying he would come accompanied by some fifty friends.

There was amazement and consternation at Fort-Lamy, where the small local budget and available accommodations did not allow such liberality. But the heavens were on the side of the Territorial Assembly: a particularly heavy rainy season had damaged the airport. So, using the defective state of the runway as an excuse, the governor got out of the awkward situation and canceled the festivities without offending the minister—or so he hoped. In fact, the minister *was* offended and turned up unannounced from Madagascar, where he had been on a tour of inspection, to check whether landing and takeoff had really been affected. Having landed on terra firma and seen through the subterfuge, Mitterrand immediately took sanctions. The governor, Mauduit, was replaced within twenty-four hours by a certain Hanin. A chain reaction of sanctions proceeded through the lower echelons.[48] One civil servant named Tailleur was so outraged by these measures that ten years later he ran against François Mitterrand in the Nièvre in the hope of making him pay for that abuse of power—but in vain.

But what François Mitterrand is remembered for during his time at the Ministry of France Overseas goes well beyond mere anecdote. His contemporaries freely acknowledge his merits. He definitely avoided a colonial war, they say, and removed the African deputies belonging to the RDA from Communist influence. The future leader of the Union of the Left was already proving expert in the art of embarrassing the Communist party. The affair is worth examining in detail.

When François Mitterrand arrived at the ministry, French Africa was in a sorry plight. Disturbances had broken out in various parts. Harsh steps had to be taken. The worst was to be feared, including a bloodbath: "Battalions of troops were sent to the sensitive spots, garrisons were doubled, prisons filled. But our consciences were clean. In voices charged with emotion, we deplored the situation and put the blame on agitators whom, it was said, were in the pay of foreign powers. The African world, the colonists repeated (and most of the governors echoed them), would only regain trust in France if France ceased to show weakness."[49]

The native population, whose status remained unenviable, had a few deputies in the French National Assembly. The young, above all, were becoming increasingly restive with the domination of the colonists, the last survivals of forced labor, and the paternalism of the missionaries. Although it is true that the colonial administration did its best to propagate education and improve hygiene and the local infrastructures, almost all whites in Africa still regarded blacks as children and the African peoples as vassals of France. The natives of the French Union were expected to obey; argument was out of the question.

In this context, the RDA, which brought together some of the more radical African deputies, was a thorn in the flesh of most political parties. It was suspected of wanting to win autonomy through disorder and violence. This inter-African party, which held its first congress at Bamako in 1946, simply demanded more freedom, new rights, and a share in the country's affairs. But it had committed a capital crime: 6 African deputies had allied themselves with the Communist group (which then comprised 183 deputies). They were heavily criticized for this. Yet François Mitterrand notes: "At the time of its parliamentary link with the Communist group, Maurice Thorez was deputy prime minister and a full participant in the majority. Was it not illogical to require African deputies, who were entering our assemblies for the first time, to display a discernment and discrimination singularly lacking in parties and men perfectly apprised of the danger presented to France and democracy by the Stalinist presence at the controls?"[50]

In actual fact, the responsibility for the links between the Communist party and RDA fell squarely on the clumsiness of the other political parties, who had failed to give a proper welcome to the new African deputies, just as they had failed to send observers to their first congress. The party of Maurice Thorez, showing more skill, welcomed the first black deputies with open arms. Its members had taken the deputies on a tour of the capital and initiated them into the intricacies of the Palais-Bourbon and home civil service. Later, when the Communist ministers had been removed from the government, the RDA found itself thrown into opposition with the Communist party.

Its unchallenged leader, Félix Houphouët-Boigny, deputy for the Ivory Coast and a Catholic doctor from a family of tribal chiefs, was not remotely Marxist. In the National Assembly, he had initially been noted for a measured, but firm and insistent, speech on the civil liberties demanded by his people. In the atmosphere of the time, there were those who immediately saw this as a declaration of revolutionary war. In the Socialist party, the MRP, and among the Gaullists, there were many who believed that the RDA was "the advance guard of the Soviet Fifth Column" in Africa.

When violent incidents broke out in the Ivory Coast, Félix Houphouët-Boigny found himself facing charges in the law courts. Several members of his party were locked up. He himself was forbidden, in principle, to remain in Paris, though it was perfectly well known he was not looking for a confrontation.

Upon arrival at the Hôtel Matignon, René Pleven, who was well acquainted with African problems, realized that if bloodshed was to be avoided, it would be best to make contact with the RDA and sound out its true intentions. "As soon as he was appointed," Eugène Claudius-Petit recounts, "Pleven sent for me and said: 'We must think about it—it's absolutely essential we get closer to the RDA.' "

René Pleven knew perfectly well it was with Félix Houphouët-Boigny that the dialogue had to be established. In the assembly, the deputy for the Ivory Coast had been nicknamed "the African Thorez." But the new prime minister had long realized this nickname was not justified. "After hearing him speak several times in the assembly, I knew perfectly well he was not a Communist," he said in a private conversation.

While René Pleven was seeking dialogue, the deputy for the Ivory Coast, a man of moderation and wisdom, was moving in the same direction. Houphouët-Boigny had come to realize the Communist party was using the RDA more than helping it. He knew that in order to achieve the means for a gradual emancipation, he would have to resume relations with the "third force" government.

When an emissary from the prime minister's office discreetly sounded out Félix Houphouët-Boigny, he was given a positive welcome. A meeting was arranged at the Hôtel Matignon for mid-August 1950. Paul Henri Siriex, a member of René Pleven's private office who attended the interview, describes it as follows:

For over an hour Houphouët-Boigny pleaded his cause before an attentive, silent René Pleven. At the end of the meeting, the prime minister's religion was determined. As I led the Ivory Coast deputy out, the prime minister said to me: "Call Mitterrand immediately on the interministerial. Tell him I have just seen Houphouët-Boigny and will inform him of what took place at the meeting. Above all, lose no time—he's as sensitive as an actress of the Comédie-Française."

In fact, Mitterrand didn't seem to know how to take it, for I was received more than coolly. "Who are you, anyway?" he greeted me. "You never introduced yourself to me. Today the prime minister receives Houphouët-Boigny; tomorrow, no doubt, it will be the president of the Republic. So what is the point of having a minister of France overseas?" I tried in vain to explain that it had been impossible for the prime minister to call him himself at that particular juncture, and that I regarded myself as too minor a figure to ask for an audience from him. But I couldn't get through to him. In any case, he had hung up. He was only thirty-four.

All this struck me as very petty, and such behavior did not fit the reputation for courtesy and charm François Mitterrand already enjoyed. . . . René Pleven knew how interested Mitterrand was in Africa, where, in 1949, he had undertaken a long journey. We knew that the maintenance of the colonial status quo would not satisfy him. His declared hostility to the Communist party was as well known as his opposition to General de Gaulle. We also knew how fond he was of the ins and outs of politics, and as a result, most people were very wary of him. . . .[51]

Displeased by the events, Mitterrand nevertheless followed the prime minister's instructions and made contact with Félix Houphouët-Boigny: "He was rather downcast, rather emotional. I treated him rather roughly. I warned him I was going to double the garrisons in Africa and would hold him responsible for any disturbances. I explained that human, social, and economic demands would have my full support if they were justified, but that I could not allow them to assume a political character. It was premature to speak of independence."[52]

In fact, it would not seem that François Mitterrand had acted so threateningly, for in accepting the meeting, the leader of the African Democratic Rally had already accepted the principle of compromise.

Two of Mitterrand's assistants, Pierre Nicolaÿ and Georges Beauchamp, attended that first meeting between the rebel leader and the young minister of the Fourth Republic. The demands of the black leader struck them, from the beginning, as being quite reasonable. "They concerned three points," Pierre Nicolaÿ recounts. "A labor code was to be drawn up and respected by the French trade unions; the blacks were to be allowed to assume elected office in their towns or villages; and, lastly, the sales of the European or Lebanese intermediaries who bought the blacks' crops were to be checked by the Weights and Measures Department, for it was universally recognized that the rate for coffee varied with the color of the seller's skin."

François Mitterrand assumed personal responsibility for accepting these requests on condition that calm returned to Africa. At the end of tough bargaining, Houphouët-Boigny signed a pact. "He agreed, in a two-page text, to act henceforth within the framework of the French Union. François Mitterrand was to keep this document in a drawer instead of issuing it to the press. Thus, Mitterrand did not seem to have dictated his conditions, but he kept a secret advantage over the black politicians."[53] Pierre Nicolaÿ, who attended the meeting, noted: "It was really by this sign that I saw he was a statesman."

Félix Houphouët-Boigny immediately sent off a letter to the leading members of the RDA at home, asking them to cease the open struggle against the colonial administration. This was a calculated risk on the part of the black leader, who put all his authority and reputation on the line. At the same time, it is true, several leaders of the movement were freed on orders from the minister. Shortly afterward, the RDA broke its links with the Communist party and, as a token of gratitude, joined the UDSR. Six African deputies[54] were to discover with some surprise how common fierce personal rivalries were in their new group. Félix Houphouët-Boigny, who was not without wit, commented: "The UDSR was the only place where blacks could watch whites eating one another."

Once the way had been paved by René Pleven, François Mitterrand was able, with his usual skill, to turn confrontation into cooperation. This development was not to everyone's taste, however:

It goes without saying that in both the home country and certain European circles in Africa, this policy immediately aroused lively reaction. Those less in favor heaped scorn on the minister's naïveté; those who were most hostile declared that the government had betrayed them. The criticism was often voiced that we were handing Africa over to communism and separatism, and there were endless questions in the National Assembly. A vehement, abusive press warned the public (to the benefit of agitators, whom any healthy, balanced, and strong regime would have condemned to prison or death) of the abominable plot that meant the end of the French presence.[55]

Seven years later, Mitterrand's view was to alter perceptibly. He then wrote:

As minister of France overseas, I tried to initiate a new policy, but the Gaullist deputies suffocated it indignantly. To extend a hand to the outcasts, to free those in prison, to spare the ringleaders prosecution in the courts was to be the accomplice of anti-France. Deputies Bayrou, Malbrant, and Castellani, Gaullists of strict observance, came to the rue Oudinot and begged me not to persist in my folly. Ah, how bravely they embodied the nation! According to them, I was eliminating the French presence—I was protecting the Stalinist contagion.[56]

Once again, after 1958, François Mitterrand concentrated all his blows on the Gaullists, forgetting to attack those members of the MRP who were no longer his prime enemies. It is true that the RPF was hostile to his liberal policy, and that it was not until General de Gaulle's private visit to Africa in 1953 that members of the Ivory Coast section of the RPF (hitherto inveterate enemies of the RDA and Félix Houphouët-Boigny) listened to counsels of prudence. The RPF was not the only enemy of that policy, however. In 1951, as if to lend emphasis to his plans, the minister of

France overseas was to take the African deputies of the RDA (but, with wise precaution, not in the same plane) to the inauguration of the new port of Abidjan—to the horror, needless to say, of local colonial society ("the same society that, a few months later, was to call Houphouët-Boigny 'dear Félix'," Georges Beauchamp comments).

The minister was displaying his authority. The event has been recounted by Paul Henri Siriex:

> This journey in the grand style was in many ways very different from the usual ministerial visits. A young minister, flanked by his secretary of state, M. Coffin (a Socialist schoolteacher from the Berry), and an elegant, liberal-minded *grand bourgeois*, Jean Fourcade (president of the assembly of the French Union), was accompanied by two veterans: General Legentilhomme (who was hardly suspected of progressive ideas) and the governor, Pierre Chauvet—neither of whom was likely to arouse the mistrust or antipathy of the Europeans of Abidjan, who still harbored nostalgic feelings toward Vichy. There was also a judge; the son of a great tribal chief of the Baoulé region, Alphonse Boni, who was one of François Mitterrand's former fellow pupils at the Collège d'Angoulême and whom he had taken into his private office. . . . Mitterrand had sent strict instructions before leaving Paris: there was to be no ostracism of the RDA deputies, the very same who had triggered a campaign of insubordination.
>
> A considerable crowd had gathered around the aerodrome. Incidents were inevitable in the climate of tension and surprise created by such an innovation; however, order was maintained. The minister (whose youth was itself a sort of provocation) and the chief (wearing an old-fashioned colonial helmet) were received by the whites as coldly as was Félix Houphouët-Boigny, but I think the minister must have felt secretly pleased. . . . The governor, Péchoux, having tried to prevent the return of the RDA deputies and assumed responsibility for severe repression, could not be the one to preside over a reconciliation between colonists and blacks. So François Mitterrand appointed him to his private office. . . . But all that had to be done, as we now say. And it was done.

As a realist, Mitterrand realized that this agreement with the RDA could not be allowed to strengthen the movement's influence. Neither parliamentary opinion at home nor the African colonists were ready for such a development. The elections of 1951 gave him the opportunity to calm the troubled waters: "One lends only to the rich and, in the circumstances, the proverb was not disproved in imputing to M. Mitterrand clever maneuvers tending to make the success of the RDA as modest as possible in order to make its entry into African political life as smooth as possible. In any event, strict instructions were not necessary. . . . To guide the votes of the electors in the bush, he could trust his governors, who were naturally concerned with stability."[57]

Pierre Nicolaÿ, director of Mitterrand's private office at the time, now declares: "The minister had quite simply given instructions to the governors to limit the success of the RDA." Put crudely, François Mitterrand had the elections rigged. As a result, a few leaders of the RDA were made to bite the dust. That was how things were done then.

Another episode (which is more than picturesque) was to confirm the image right-wing parliamentarians had of an ambiguous Mitterrand. This episode aroused in the young minister a lively sense of injustice that became important later.

At first glance, however, the affair does not seem very important. In early 1951, Paul Bechard, high commissioner in French West Africa and a former Socialist deputy, prosecuted two white priests at Dakar: Father Paternos, procurator-general of his congregation, and Father Rummelhardt. The priests' newspaper, the influential *Afrique nouvelle* (which was later to move in a very liberal direction and whose allies were to change accordingly), gave a highly uncomplimentary account of a defamation trial involving the high commissioner and those questioning his integrity. The two priests were symbolically sentenced to a suspended fine of fifty francs.

There was a scandal in the small colonial society. Paris was immediately informed. The MRP rose up in indignation. The Catholic hierarchy became involved. But François Mitterrand backed the senior civil servant, whose reaction struck him as quite legitimate.

There were storms on the Right during a vote on the budget of the France Overseas department on April 4, 1951. As a retaliatory measure, the Indépendant (conservative) deputy Edouard Frédéric-Dupont proposed an amendment in which the minister's salary would be reduced by a thousand francs, a way of blaming the governor who, "out of Socialist sectarianism, has had two white priests sentenced in court." The amendment was adopted in a 241-175 vote. Mitterrand threatened to resign. The government opposed the adoption of the whole of the ministry's budget, thus amended. The adoption of the budget was postponed until three weeks later. This time it was the Communists who wanted to reduce the minister's salary on the grounds of repression in Africa. In the end, the budget was passed and the minister kept his full salary.

It seemed that the affair had ended there. But in fact, François Mitterrand was suspected by the Right. He had already been criticized for his defeatist mentality. Now he was practically counted among the enemies of the Church, with the aggravating circumstances of treachery: how could this former pupil of a good Catholic school so abase himself as to throw two priests, "even for a few minutes, into the dock, where thieves, swindlers, and prostitutes usually stand?" Edouard Frédéric-Dupont demanded in irrepressible fury.

Neither the episcopate nor the MRP was to forget the incident—especially since the latter was always on the best of terms with the overseas Indépendants, rivals of the RDA on the black continent. They were to use their combined influence with René Pleven, once again prime minister in August 1951, to remove François Mitterrand from the ministry in the rue Oudinot.

As René Pleven admits: "I needed the MRP to form my ministry, and the *sine qua non* of their participation was the removal of Mitterrand."

Mitterrand himself felt great bitterness and a strong sense of injustice at the time (a feeling that in him always seems acute, especially when he is the victim).

According to Georges Beauchamp, there is no doubt that two of Mitterrand's psychological breaks date from this undeserved exclusion. He describes the first: "The Catholic hierarchy's unjust and cold dismissal of him distanced Mitterrand from the institutional Church." Since Mitterrand's religious feelings were already beginning to cool, this denial of justice only sharpened his mistrust of the clericals. Beauchamp describes the second break as follows: "Simultaneously, his departure from the government freed him from any sense of deference toward René Pleven. Nothing now prevented him from seeking the presidency of the UDSR."

In fact, as we have seen, François Mitterrand had already been engaged for nearly two years in the struggle to win the party leadership. But from that point on, he could pursue his ambitions in an unfettered way. Where he had once proceeded obliquely, he could now prepare a frontal attack. In sacrificing him to the MRP, René Pleven allowed him to become his official challenger.

Whether he had planned it this way or not, François Mitterrand left the Ministry of France Overseas by a side door. On the left. He then found himself in a paradoxical and uncomfortable situation. The Right was never to abandon its mistrust of a man who, it could be said, was a decolonizer within colonization.[58] On the other hand, the decolonizing faction of the Left regarded with suspicion this all-too-clever minister, whom it viewed as guilty of wanting to perpetuate the Empire.

Mitterrand himself was to admit twenty years later: "I was wrong to wish to reconcile opposites. There is colonial emancipation only as there is social revolution—worldwide and irreducible."[59]

As the current president now knows only too well, reconciling opposites is a risky and thankless exercise, even when one's personal temperament inclines one to it. In proving too advanced for some and too prudent for others, one runs the risk of losing the support of both.

The minister of France overseas had shown himself to be a perfectly acceptable administrator, but he was penalized as a politician. It was a lesson the future Socialist leader would not forget. Indeed, the Algerian affair and Suez expedition were to find him much more conformist.

One benefit, however, came his way (and it was not a negligible one): the Africans of the RDA were grateful to him and were to remain faithful. Jean de Lipkowski, then a young UDSR deputy, still remembers how dazzled he was at the Bamako congress in September 1957, to which he had been invited along with Roland Dumas, another young UDSR deputy, by Mitterrand: "I saw all those Africans pay him personal, emotional homage," he recounts. "It was very impressive. Although they applauded Pleven, they loved Mitterrand."

THE BREAK: FRANÇOIS MITTERRAND LEAVES THE LANIEL GOVERNMENT

Morocco and Tunisia, two French protectorates, posed serious problems to the government of the Republic in 1953. Since Liberation, relations with both states had been fairly good despite certain incidents, but, to say the least, successive French governments had shown little political imagination in their regard. And as soon as the first disturbances broke out, the classic hesitation between the instinct to repress and the desire to move with the times surfaced.

François Mitterrand was caught up in precisely this conflict and was even, it could be argued, a perfect illustration of it. He realized (and said as much) that changes were necessary. But he conceived changes, as did almost all his peers, only to bind the associated states even more closely to the home country. He was ruthless in his criticisms of successive ministers at the Quai d'Orsay, who were responsible for the protectorates, for not knowing where they wanted to go. Though temperamentally a Jacobin, he realized the importance of a more innovative approach. But he was no emancipator— merely an advocate of evolution. It was not enough to make him, in this area, a man of the Left, but it was going too far to place him among the ranks of the conservatives. He seemed rather like an enlightened centrist, skillful in using others' mishandlings and shortsightedness to demonstrate his own perspicacity.

As a minister of state in the first Edgar Faure government (which only lasted from January 20 to March 8, 1952—not even three months), the deputy for the Nièvre was preparing, at the prime minister's request, a report on the development of Franco-Tunisian relations. Pragmatist that he was, Mitterrand proposed a return to the ancient treaty of Bardo (1881), which gave France responsibility for the defense, diplomatic representation, and equipment of Tunisia.

Apart from these three areas, everything seemed to him negotiable. Thus, he was bringing into question the Convention of La Marsa (June 8, 1883), in which France had taken over direct administration of Tunisia, leaving to the local authorities no more than a ceremonial role. Without using the term, he was advocating internal autonomy—on condition, of course, that the interests of the French living in the country were safeguarded. There was no question of independence, therefore, but instead of reforms that were far-reaching enough to arouse hope of avoiding it. François Mitterrand expounded this line in the assembly in June 1953 as follows:[60] "Which of you would agree that the presence of France in North Africa should be open to debate? . . . We must stay there." This was then the position of many so-called liberals and of most of the Left. It was also, more or less, to be that of Pierre Mendès France, who in his speech at Carthage, after becoming prime minister in 1956, proposed "internal sovereignty" to Tunisia. It was still not a question of independence, which was to come only two years later under the government of Socialist Guy Mollet, partly as a consequence of the Moroccan crisis. (François Mitterrand, a member of that government, was to approve this decision, but felt the affair to be an inevitable failure. If the differences between the two countries had been tackled earlier and with greater flair, the French might have been able to remain in Tunisia. This was then both his conviction and that of a large number of liberals.)

This rejection of passivity, of a policy without prospects, of the weakness of a government, which its proconsuls on the other side of the Mediterranean all too often presented as a fait accompli, provoked Mitterrand's first real break: he dramatically left the Laniel government, formed in June 1953, in which he served as minister to the Council of Europe. Undermined by the war in Indochina and the accumulating difficulties in North Africa, the Fourth Republic was then entering its final agony. The government of Joseph Laniel, a conservative peasant, nicknamed by François Mauriac "the dictatorship by calf's head," was largely made up of the MRP, the Radicals, and the Right; despite difficulties of all kinds, it was to hold on for almost a year, the defeat of Dien Bien Phu delivering it the coup de grâce.

The Moroccan affair caused François Mitterrand's resignation. Disturbances broke out in that country, and the resident-general of France, Hautecloque, supported by the army, the overwhelming majority of the European notables, and some Moroccan notables (such as the Glaoui, pasha of Marrakesh), took advantage of the situation to depose Sultan Mohammed V, replacing him with an honorable old man chosen for his docility, Moulay Ben Arafa. The foreign minister, Georges Bidault, and the prime minister, Laniel, virtually faced with a fait accompli, gave their approval to the operation.

François Mitterrand, who was offended (even shocked), later explained his position at the time:

> Thus the deposition of the sultan was organized by the resident-general and local civil servants with the complicity of two ministers, without the government being informed. The new sultan had already taken possession of the throne when his name was still being looked up at the Elysée. . . . In short, the state was no longer the state and the French were learning with each passing day to love their Republic a little less. . . . I resigned. A leading morning newspaper heralded this departure with the headline: "Mitterrand deserts the sinking ship."[61]

The next day, the ex-minister gave a long interview to *L'Express*, then a very new weekly paper: "I believe in the virtues of firmness and prestige, but they must be put at the service of an evolution that will not work against us if not carried out with us." The matter was quite clear: François Mitterrand had left the government because he could accept neither its weakness nor its conservatism. This resignation was to strengthen his image as a determined advocate of reform in the eyes of the UDSR membership and the public.

Yet it has still not been explained why Mitterrand, who had so ridiculed René Pleven for his participation in the right-wing governments of René Mayer and Antoine Pinay, had agreed to join with the same René Pleven the Laniel government, which was certainly no further to the Left and neither particularly prestigious nor popular. This compromise was all the more paradoxical in that, according to the UDSR executive committee records of June 22, 1953, the conditions laid down by François Mitterrand to Joseph

Laniel (two ministries and a secretariat of state) were not entirely satisfied since the UDSR was not given a secretariat of state. As for assurances of a more liberal, more coherent policy in the French Union, these were very vague and were not respected. Did Mitterrand agree to join the government simply in order to leave it?

Some of his enemies are certain he did, first and foremost among them René Pleven, who was minister of defense in the Laniel cabinet and remained there to the end. "Mitterrand," he says, "resigned because he had realized that Mendès' time had come." Indeed it had, but only ten months later: on June 12, 1954, the fall of Dien Bien Phu brought down the government. During the subsequent debate, Pierre Mendès France had drawn up a list of charges many saw as a "premature investiture statement."[62] In any case, Mendès France effectively became prime minister. During the previous months, it seems, he had had many contacts with François Mitterrand.

Jacques Bloch-Morhange has recounted the role played by Mitterrand in the fall of the Laniel government:

On that June day in 1954, we found ourselves in a small restaurant at lunchtime in the rue Surcouf where we usually met. At three o'clock, a debate would begin in parliament, the outcome of which would determine the survival or death of the Laniel government. . . . Sitting around the table were Robert Buron (MRP); Robert Lacoste (SFIO); Jacques Chaban-Delmas, Michel Debré, François Mitterrand, Joseph Lanet, Jacques Kosciusko-Morizet (UDSR); Raymond Valabrègue; and Olivier de Pierrebourg. . . .

We had a sense that France had long since squandered its last card in the Far East. We also felt that the basic struggle against the European Defense Community vote would very soon be brought into the foreground—we knew the Americans would urge it, assisted by the Christian democrats. . . . We thought we should bring about the fall of Laniel at once, push forward Edgar Faure or Mendès (Mitterrand felt Mendès had the best chance of success), open up peace negotiations without leaving Indochina, and oppose the pressures that would inevitably be brought to bear in favor of the European Defense Community. Such was, apart from the delights of the menu, the order of the day for that meal.

The politicians around the table held the fate of the majority in their hands, since no governmental combination could be constructed or survive without their support. . . . It was necessary, therefore, to work out the arguments we would have to use to demand the immediate departure of the present government. Each of us proffered his ideas on the matter and Mitterrand jotted them down on the back of the menu. He then intervened: "If you agree, I'm quite willing to accept the risk of making such a speech in the name of us all." This was immediately greeted with unanimous approval. He then told us how, that afternoon, he would build up his intervention; how, moving from mere description, his speech would gradually turn into an indictment; and how he would entrap the prime minister in such a way that he could not escape without being defeated. This is precisely how things turned out on the afternoon of June 12. At that point, I understood Mitterrand's technique—it is still the same today. . . .

Arithmetically, a possible Mendès majority was short by five or six votes. Mitterrand set out to get them on the benches that, at the time, were regarded as more or less opposed to Mendès. He promised secretariats of state, got Mendès to give these on June 17, formed his government, and turned five opponents into five supporters. . . .

It cannot be denied that Mitterrand, our spokesman, managed to bring down Laniel, found Mendès enough support to form his government, and made possible the tragic but necessary diplomatic success of the peace in Indochina.[63]

THE MENDÉSIST TEMPTATION AND THE AFFAIR OF THE LEAKS

François Mitterrand never wanted to link his fate and name to anyone. In his youth, at an age when so many others look for mentors or directors of conscience, the boarder at 104, rue de Vaugirard, displayed, as we have seen, a lack of enthusiasm for the glorious names of the moment, as if he had found no sun bright enough to dazzle him.

At Vichy, in the Resistance, at the Liberation, no man—especially not de Gaulle—had enough sway over him to win his loyalty. Henri Frenay, it must be conceded, impressed him for a time, but not enough for Mitterrand to want to become his second. In the UDSR, he did not resign himself to accepting the leadership of René Pleven. Although he had cordial relations with President Vincent Auriol and such immovable and powerful men as Henri Queuille, Paul Ramadier, and Robert Schuman, he regarded none of them as his master.

In politics, Mitterrand sometimes treats his colleagues with cruelty, and never with indulgence. Compliments are not his specialty—when he tries to be pleasant, his style becomes heavy. Of course, he is quite capable of praising others; indeed, he does it quite well in the case of subordinates who are (or will soon become) useful to him. But he has never flattered his equals—such an exercise is repugnant to him.

There is only one exception to this rule: Pierre Mendès France. "It was the only time François Mitterrand ever showed reverence for a man," says Georges Beauchamp. All those who were close to him at the time confirm this. For the man known as P.M.F., François Mitterrand dropped his reserve, even indulging in praise.

This strange admiration was, it is true, part of a general movement: P.M.F. then embodied in a certain intellectual, liberal, middle-class milieu renewal and modernity, rigor and enthusiasm, vision and confidence. Since 1945, he had been noted, in the National Assembly, for his pitiless critique of current economic and financial policy, advocating straight talk, the reconciliation of imagination and knowledge, and the necessary alliance between the public and private sector. With his look of a melancholy owl, his tired, worried face, air of an absentminded professor, and growing intellectual prestige, he was a sort of father figure to the New Left. Two brilliant young journalists, Jean-Jacques Servan-Schreiber and Françoise Giroud, enthusiastically set about fostering his myth. Day after day P.M.F. became the hero of the saga in their new weekly, *L'Express*.

A wave of public opinion followed. The political class, which was beginning to discover what was now a personalization of power, liked it less. With his speedy decision making, the new prime minister brought back confidence to a country that had been confused and depressed by government weakness and colonial failures recently cruelly emphasized at Dien Bien Phu. "Relatively speaking," political writer Jacques Julliard wrote, "the service rendered by P.M.F. to his country in that summer of 1954 was of the same nature as the action of Charles de Gaulle on June 18, 1940: he saved it from humiliation, prevented it from despairing of itself."[64]

François Mitterrand did not wait until the summer of 1954 to sing the praises of P.M.F. Just after Mendès France's first attempt to form a government, in June 1953, Mitterrand wrote in *Combat*: "In his words, his attitude, his tone, the deputy for the Eure expressed so admirably the need for a renewal of our parliamentary practices that the climate of the crisis was transformed. His rejection of intrigues and his disdain for incompetence did the rest: French politics changed its style."

One act of politeness often begets another. P.M.F. was equally lavish in his compliments in the preface he wrote for Mitterrand's first political tract, *Aux frontières de l'union française* (published in 1953): "I would like to say how much I appreciate the lucidity and precision of your analysis of the great problems of the French Union," he wrote, "how much I admire the intellectual and political courage with which you seek solutions." But although François Mitterrand and Pierre Mendès France greatly esteemed one another, they were never friends. In his biography of P.M.F., Jean Lacouture notes:

> Their common collaboration in the forum of *L'Express* brought them together, though it did not make them close friends. Mendès found in his young colleague a parliamentary zoologist of incomparable skill. Nobody knew better than he the various deputies' talents, weaknesses, past performances, secret aspirations, and acquaintances. Mitterrand was not the sort of man, like P.M.F., to burst out, upon seeing a tall, gray-haired fellow move to the rostrum: "And who's this now? But it's Frédéric Dupont! The immovable deputy of the concierges of the seventh arrondissement!"

Paul Legatte, a former Mendésist in the service of François Mitterrand and now a member of the Constitutional Council, adds:

"Mendès was fascinated by the facility with which Mitterrand improvised and dispatched speeches. While he himself had to labor over a white page, weighing each word and going over his work repeatedly, Mitterrand juggled with words and phrases. I even believed Mendès was secretly fascinated by the young minister's reputed success with women."

Similarly, François Mitterrand always admired and envied P.M.F.'s authority and seriousness in economic matters. *Envied* is perhaps not entirely the right word: the future president never regarded economics or its experts as realities and authorities before which he had to capitulate. The IMF (International Monetary Fund), OECD (Organization for Economic Cooperation and Development), and INSEE (National Institute of Statistics and Economic Studies) were just so many acronyms he had to know and be able to reel off, but before which he did not have to kneel, while he regarded experts in budget balancing and money reserves with as much suspicion as Molière regarded physicians. "All the plans for reviving the economy I have known always end up by increasing the duty on tobacco," Mitterrand jokingly repeated for years.

In 1954, P.M.F. wanted to make use of the parliamentary skill of the deputy for the Nièvre. Conscious of his ignorance and innocence in such delicate matters, Mendès planned to use the talents of his junior (who had contributed so much, as we have seen, to the fall of the Laniel government, which had enabled Mendès to enter the Matignon): his knowledge of the tiny world of the Palais-Bourbon and of the workings of the assembly, and his capacity to shine at the rostrum.

On the night of June 18, 1954, P.M.F. summoned to his home in the rue du Conseiller-Collignon François Mitterrand, Edgar Faure (number two in the future government, to be in charge of the economy), and a few personal aides (Georges Boris and Paul Legatte, among others), for the purpose of drawing up the list of ministers. Work could not begin until after eleven at night since Mitterrand, because of his lack of punctuality, could not be found until that late hour of the evening. Françoise Giroud, who, with her journalist colleague Jean-Jacques Servan-Schreiber, was to be closely associated with all the ups and downs of that government of seven months and seventeen days, exclaimed (with a touch of exacerbation in her voice):

Ah, François Mitterrand and his punctuality! We always had to wait two or three hours for him. And when he finally turned up, he launched into a stream of excuses so complicated and far-fetched as to show quite clearly he was making them up. And the more contradictory his story became, the more irritated he got with our disbelief—he'd have done better, of course, not to bother with explanations at all. And if, by some chance, he happened to be on time—before going out to a lunch, for example—the idea of being punctual so disturbed him that he would immediately invent some urgent file he had to consult or some article he had to read, so as to be quite sure he'd arrive well after everybody else.

Among those who work for him, Mitterrand's inability to be punctual has become proverbial. A member of his office recounts how, some months later in the middle of the Algerian affair, Ferhat Abbas turned up at the Ministry of the Interior for an interview with the minister, only to be kept waiting. An hour went by, then an hour and a half. When the minister's embarrassed assistant put his head round his boss's door to remind him that his visitor had been waiting for a long time, he saw Mitterrand quietly reading the cartoons in *France-Soir*.

How is one to explain such an attitude, one that often impedes the smooth running of affairs of state and, at the very least, breaks the rules of elementary etiquette and Christian charity? Does it stem from a wish to challenge others? Reveal delight in testing the patience of subordinates? Demonstrate an irrepressible need to be master of passing time? Or exhibit incomparable pleasure at feeling one is the master timekeeper of one's own life? All too often Mitterrand seems to be saying to his victims, whether they are accepting or merely resigned, "I shall do as I please!"

But let us return to the rue du Conseiller-Collignon, to that June night in 1954 when P.M.F. was forming his government.

Thirty years later, it is very difficult to name those who, in that new team (the most prestigious of the Fourth Republic), owed the honor of being chosen to François Mitterrand. However, it is almost certain that the selection of André Bettencourt (a friend from "104") as secretary of state to the prime minister (with special responsibility for information[65]) and the appointment of three other UDSR

members were the result of Mitterrand's good offices. It seems that
the appointment of Jacques Chevalier, mayor of Algiers, to the
secretariat of state of defense was also due to him. Mitterrand
himself obtained, with the Ministry of the Interior, the most prestigious portfolio he was to get in that Republic. In any case, he was
regarded as number three in the government, behind P.M.F. himself
and Edgar Faure. But was he really the third man in a troika?

According to Jean Lacouture, who enjoyed the confidence of
P.M.F., Mitterrand should be regarded instead as the most brilliant
of the younger members, the one whom no one had any doubts
would be at the Matignon before long. But Mendès, who found it
so easy to confide in Edgar Faure, could not help mistrusting a
man whom, according to Jean Lacouture, he called that "too brilliant political animal."

In that brilliant cabinet, which also included well-known Gaullists (Jacques Chaban-Delmas, Christian Fouchet, and General Koenig), there were no Socialists. The veto came from Guy Mollet,
SFIO leader, who could not accept ministers being chosen without
his approval. This absence did not upset François Mitterrand very
much. At his party congress at Aix-les-Bains in October 1954, he
declared:

> The notions of Right and Left have lost much of their meaning;
> that old division has been blown away by the wind of history,
> because the talent and authority of the prime minister have made
> division the catalyst that makes it possible for scattered elements
> to come together. And if these elements, formerly separated in
> rival groups, are now to be found together, it is because they
> belong to the same political generation. . . . What is certain is
> that the Mendès government represents, ten years after the war,
> the youth of the Republic.

We are still, however, a long way from the lyrical praises that were
later to welcome the Union of the Left.

There should be no illusions about the fulsome praise with which
Mitterrand greeted the prime minister's speech of that October.
The state of grace between P.M.F. and François Mitterrand had
ceased to exist for some weeks—the affair of the leaks had put an
end to it.

Once again, at a moment when Mitterrand was entering a new stage of his political career, he had to face a severe test. The paradox in this affair derives from the fact that Mitterrand, the suspect, had every right to a clear conscience, whereas Mendès France, who suspected him, proved (to say the least) unjust, illustrating in his own way Cardinal de Retz's famous maxim: "One is more often taken in by mistrust than by trust."

This is what occurred.

In early summer 1954, a rumor was circulating in Paris. In the corridors of the Palais-Bourbon and the editorial offices, it was whispered that a traitor was working for the Committee of National Defense and had communicated secrets to the Communist party. The name of François Mitterrand was the one most often mentioned. Early in July, Christian Fouchet, minister for Moroccan and Tunisian affairs, was informed by one of his former companions in the RPF, Inspector Jean Dides, that one of the inspector's informants, who had infiltrated the Communist party, had revealed that the typed report of the Defense Committee's last meeting had been read in full by Jacques Duclos in the party political bureau.

Taking part in that meeting of the Defense Committee, under the chairmanship of René Coty, were the principal members of the government: Edgar Faure, General Koenig (defense), François Mitterrand (interior), several generals, and the secretary-general for defense, Jean Mons.

"In what direction do your suspicions lie?" Fouchet asked. Dides replied: "My informant thinks it was Edgar Faure, but personally, I think Mitterrand is a more likely candidate. That's why I didn't take the file to the Ministry of the Interior."

Christian Fouchet immediately alerted P.M.F., who refrained from informing Mitterrand. Fouchet confided the affair to André Pelabon, the head of his office, a man in whom he had every confidence and had known for twenty years. This former student of the Ecole Polytechnique had once been an assistant to Colonel Passy, with the free French secret service in London. Pelabon knew how to deal with this sort of question. It was not until September 8 that he asked Roger Whybot, head of internal security, to start an investigation.

Pierre Nicolaÿ, then head of François Mitterrand's office, recounts his version of the affair: "It was more or less about this time that I was warned by Jean Mairey, director of National Security [appointed to this post by François Mitterrand], that an ultrasecret investigation on the minister was being carried out in Internal Security. He asked me to say nothing about it to my boss, but as you can imagine, I informed him immediately, and he did not wait a second to question the prime minister."

P.M.F. was then on an official visit to London, and Mitterrand spoke to him on the telephone. But instead of the assurances and protestations of trust he expected, he had the unpleasant impression he was speaking to an embarrassed man unsure of his ground. In other words, P.M.F. was pondering the matter. He had doubted the story, and perhaps at that moment still doubted it, but his view of the statesman's duty meant he could reject no hypothesis.

The minister of the interior was mortified, all who knew him agree. "It was a great shock for him," says Pierre Nicolaÿ. Pierre Charpy, then a journalist on *Paris-Presse*, who was dining at the time with the minister after a session at the assembly, confirms this: "He was completely shaken by Mendès' desertion." Françoise Giroud has this to say: "That was how Mendès was. If he had been told his son had committed a robbery, his republican morality would have made him reply: 'Investigate the matter and tell me what you come up with.' Yet any other father would have begun by protesting his son's innocence. And, it must not be forgotten, Mitterrand was not one of Mendès' friends."

In fact, the affair was soon to be cleared up and the true culprit discovered and sentenced. The investigation revealed that the leaks could not have come from a member of the government, still less from François Mitterrand. The reports of the meetings of the Committee of National Defense that reached the Communist party were so detailed and so accurate in the chronology of the various interventions that no human memory, even the most remarkable one, could have been so faithful. The hypothesis of microphones concealed in the room was dismissed after checks had been made. It was then discovered that only one person at the meeting took notes: Jean Mons, the permanent secretary-general at the Ministry of Defense. But he was quite above suspicion: no one questioned his patriotism and probity. His aides, however, also had access to the texts. And two of them, René Turpin and Roger Labrusse, were in more or less continual contact with the journalist Baranès, who was none other than Inspector Dides' informant. As it happened, he was also on good terms with the Communist leaders. At that point, the scenario became clear to anyone willing to see. Those responsible for the leaks were the two civil servants, and Jean Mons had displayed a certain lack of vigilance. Chief Inspector Dides had wanted to use the affair to bring into disrepute a government he detested, since it was making peace in Indochina, and a minister of the interior whom he hated, because he had sacked him.

François Mitterrand was all the more innocent in that the leaks had begun under the previous government, and his functions had not given him access to the sources.

Nevertheless—and this is interesting in itself—it was on him that suspicion naturally fell. At the level of those involved, this is easy enough to understand: Prefect of Police Baylot and Chief Inspector Dides, both removed from their posts by François Mitterrand, spread the rumor that by getting rid of them, he had wanted to put an end to the struggle against international communism.

What is strange is that the rumor was regarded as plausible in political circles, even on the part of men of good faith. Not all were, of course, and there were some who were quite willing to use anything against Mitterrand. During the parliamentary debate on the affair, on December 5, 1954, the conservative deputy for the Oise, Jean Legendre, a fanatical anti-Communist, even went so far as to suggest that François Mitterrand's resignation from the Laniel government had in fact been forced upon him because he was suspected of treason. On the extreme-Right benches it was even whispered that the tragedy of Dien Bien Phu could partly be explained by information Mitterrand was supposed to have given to the friends of the Vietminh—a fabrication without a word of truth, but one that was believed by many people of good faith.

During the debate, François Mitterrand called on his former colleagues in the Laniel government to give testimony: had he resigned on his own initiative or had he been forced to do so?

"On his own initiative," Georges Bidault, ex–foreign minister, had to concede. But he did so in such mysterious terms as to leave a vague suspicion in the air. Edgar Faure, on the other hand, was categorical. He testified he had done his utmost, at the request of

Prime Minister Joseph Laniel, to keep François Mitterrand on the government team and dissuade him from resigning. Jacques Chaban-Delmas went to the Elysée to tell the president of the Republic he would testify to Mitterrand's innocence. "This fabrication is quite odious!" he added. To which René Coty replied: "But how *can* you testify?" Michel Debré even went so far as to lavish advice and encouragement on François Mitterrand.[66]

This, then, was the climate of the time. In that fantastic story, political passions—stemming from colonial convulsions, the Cold War, the clash of ambitions in a republic in which power was for the taking—meant normal rules were not respected. The predecessors of P.M.F. and François Mitterrand—Joseph Laniel, René Pleven (minister of defense), Martinaud-Deplat (minister of the interior)—who were nevertheless aware of the first leaks, had not thought fit to warn their successors on handing over office. It was a curious view of the continuity of the state, which merely had the effect of postponing the investigation and discovery of the culprits.

In his book, *La IVᵉ republique*, Jacques Fauvet sums up the affair as follows:

The plot collapsed, and with it, the honor of some men—but not that of M. Mitterrand. It had illustrated the lamentable state to which minds and morals had descended. That civil servants should have recopied secret reports and handed them over to political friends was a crime justice was to punish only late in the day. It is not the first time documents have been forged by high-ranking policemen and informants to dishonor a man, a government, and a policy—and more than one administrative or political career has ended prematurely as a result. But that politicians of good faith could allow themselves to put their trust in such "documents" and use them as weapons and "proof" to defeat their adversaries was a lapse that gave rise to serious questions.

That François Mitterrand should have found himself at the center of suspicion is understandable enough. To begin with, as we have said, his peers distrusted him. Secondly, in the opinion of certain fanatical right-wingers, he was already capable of handing over black Africa to communism through the RDA—and was, therefore, the natural ally of Marxist revolutionaries throughout the world. Mitterrand thus found himself labeled as very left-wing by the most extreme right wing. He was to be carried toward the Left without really wanting to be.

François Mauriac, a perceptive, farsighted observer, notes in his *L'Express* column: "His enemies, with their inexpiable hatred, view François Mitterrand as one of the leaders—there must be several—of a Left that will one day have to be reconstructed."

At the time, the future Socialist leader learned one lesson above all from the affair: one has very few friends in politics, and mistrust is therefore the rule. Pierre Mendès France did not take up the defense of his minister, using all his authority, until December 1954 (some three months later) in the assembly: "Never for a single day, for a single hour, have I regretted entrusting to François Mitterrand the post of responsibility and courage he occupies. I am proud of having such a colleague in my government. Alas, the list of politicians, especially on the Left, who have been attacked in their honor is a long one. I was not yet born when Clemenceau was being basely insulted. . . ." It was a fine speech and a superb defense. Unfortunately, the damage had been done. "One evening I remember seeing François Mitterrand arrive at my home, his eyes wet with tears," Françoise Giroud recounts.

Between P.M.F. and François Mitterrand, who had esteem but not affection for one another ("they were two souls that did not vibrate in unison," André Monteil once remarked with a touch of lyricism), something had now snapped. "From that time on, from being allies, they became rivals. On a dozen occasions, their interests clashed either overtly or obliquely," says Paul Legatte. "They always found themselves on the same side and never agreed," Claude Estier remarked recently.

And, in fact, there were frequent clashes. "For the investitures of the Republican Front[67] in the 1956 elections, "they behaved like haggling stall holders in the Casbah," André Rousselet remembers. "Mendès did nothing to encourage the UDSR, which lost a lot of deputies as a result."

In the presidential election of 1965, Pierre Mendès France refused to be a candidate, and it was François Mitterrand who put himself forward. The former prime minister gave him his support—he could scarcely have done otherwise—but from a distance. As Claude Estier recounts:

I remember how, between the two rounds of the election, we had thought of organizing a big meeting since Mitterrand's first results were encouraging. We called Mendès on the telephone. It was nearly midnight; he got dressed and came. Jean Daniel then explained to him how useful a big meeting would be in which he, Mendès, would call on people to vote for Mitterrand. The choice of dates was obviously limited, since the election day was not far off. We suggested that the meeting take place on Wednesday or Thursday. Mendès then calmly took out his diary and said, quite unmoved: "Ah! I'm terribly sorry, but I'm busy those two evenings." After he had gone, Mitterrand turned to us and said: "You see, you must never ask Mendès for anything."

Three years later it was 1968, with its barricades, its students occupying the universities, and its workers occupying the factories. François Mitterrand was again a candidate for the presidency and said that, if elected, he would form a government with Pierre Mendès France as prime minister. But Mendès had not been consulted and did not conceal his anger.

For his part, Mitterrand is always angered by the difference in the way the two of them are treated, both by public opinion and by their peers: he feels there is always a prejudice against him and in favor of Pierre Mendès France. Françoise Giroud says: "When Lily Mendès, P.M.F.'s first wife, was already very ill, Mendès went off for the weekend with friends to stay at the house of Marie-Claire de Fleurieu, who was to become his second wife. And everyone said: 'Poor Mendès, how hard it must be for him! He's really very unhappy.' To this, François Mitterrand's comment was: 'If I went off for the weekend to stay with a woman friend while my wife was dying, everyone would say: 'What a swine!' "

There was to be no letup in this tension, these mutual irritations between the two men. For the presidential elections in 1981, Pierre Mendès France still kept his reserve, refusing to share any meeting with Mitterrand. Of course, the Left was very moved by the tears shed by Pierre Mendès France, who was already very sick, at the time of Mitterrand's investiture in the salons of the Elysée. But were they tears of joy, after the long hoped-for victory of the Left? Or were they tears of regret for the twilight of a life richer in prestige and glory than in true power? In any case, they were surely not tears of joy that Mendès shed at the moment of triumph of a more obstinate rival, one more skillful than he at grasping his opportunity.

The Left was also moved by the fine homage paid by the Socialist president to the great man who had just died. Indeed, Mitterrand's speech was remarkable, a fine ceremony. But was the head of state's pallor caused by the frosty weather, fatigue, or emotion felt at the disappearance of a rival after thirty years of mutually admiring jealousy?

François Mitterrand's words in a conversation in 1983 seemed more sincere: "Mendès has always been turned into an untouchable statue. Jean Daniel once wrote an article entitled 'The Just Man and the Cavalier.' The just man was Mendès, of course. I was the politician, the gambler. But does one have to admire a politician, who, in a career spanning a quarter of a century, was incapable of staying in power longer than ten months? Mendès wasn't even capable of keeping the Radical party together. He made a lot of mistakes about men. . . ." After a brief silence, Mitterrand added: "And, of course, he betrayed me."

ALGERIA

In August 1972, in an interview published in *L'Expansion*, Mitterrand addressed the reasons for his hostility to General de Gaulle's return: "When de Gaulle came to power, thanks to the colonels in Algeria, I had long since taken up a position in favor of decolonization." This claim to precedence in adopting the policy of decolonization toys with history. Of course, the future president had shown himself to be prudently liberal and reformist toward Algeria, as he had been toward black Africa. Nevertheless, first as minister of the interior under Mendès France, then as Garde des Sceaux under Guy Mollet, he had to give priority to maintaining order. For Mitterrand, as for most people, Algeria was part of France. It had to stay that way, and troublemakers had to be kept in their place. The reestablishment of order had, of necessity, to precede any political development. There was no question of negotiating with "terrorists," no question of a federal solution (which, it was feared, would in the end lead to independence). The only tactic, therefore, was to repress opposition. As minister of the interior, Mitterrand repressed opposition without apparent qualms of conscience; as Garde des Sceaux, he made no public condemnation of torture.

If, from 1956 on, under pressure of events—and the UDSR—he was prepared to make noises about a solution like federalism (without, however, much apparent conviction, for he had earlier found such a solution repugnant), it was more a matter of realism than of doctrine or prophetic intuition. The future Socialist leader, like virtually the entire SFIO (beginning with its general secretary, Guy Mollet,[68] who had become prime minister), discovered the truth while moving forward very slowly indeed. And until General de Gaulle's return, he had expressed, at least publicly, only one aim: for Algeria to remain French.

With the formation of the Mendès France government, however, the deputy for the Nièvre had realized a new drama was threatening. "We must deal with Algeria very quickly," he told the prime minister, who was only half convinced. Although Pierre Mendès France had sensed where the Indochinese drama was inevitably leading well before many other politicians, he had not yet realized that history was about to reveal itself elsewhere. "At that time," Mendès admitted to Jean Lacouture, "when I did not think the situation so very urgent and in danger of exploding, Mitterrand did. He had sensed very early on it might turn out badly for us." It was for this reason, among others, that Mitterrand had appointed Jacques Chevalier, the liberal mayor of Algiers, to the post of secretary of state at the War Ministry.

Like Chevalier, Mitterrand realized something had to be done as a matter of urgency. But what? In 1954, the height of innovation and liberalism consisted for him (and for many other people) in implementing the statute drawn up in 1947 by Edouard Depreux, Socialist minister of the interior. This liberally inclined but never-applied text proposed a limited integration of the Algerian Muslims into the French Republic. It was limited, because the Algerian departments had a special status and because their inhabitants of North African origin did not enjoy equal rights with those of European origin. The Algerian departments formed distinct electoral colleges. Nevertheless, the text proposed granting the vote to women, electing Muslims to the most important posts in their communes, and instituting agrarian reform. These measures, which had twice .been put before the Algerian Assembly, had been rejected, as a result of fraudulent votes, at the instigation of the French notables in Algeria.

It might well seem courageous on the minister of the interior's part to advocate the effective application of a statute that had remained a dead letter, since the French colonists had done everything hitherto to prevent it (their implicit slogan was not "Equal, but separate," but "Unequal and separate").

In fact, François Mitterrand seemed rather legalistic in the matter, wanting to give no more than what was already enshrined in the statutes. Just as in the case of Tunisia he regarded the Bardo treaty (then seventy years old) as an excellent solution, in the case of Algeria he considered the 1947 statute still to be the best solution.

During his first visit to Algeria, he expressed his political philosophy before the Algerian Assembly as follows:

What is the French Republic? According to our constitution, it is the territory of metropolitan France, departments of Algeria, and departments and territories overseas. . . . Where is Algeria in that enormous complex? At the very center, where the forces are gathered. . . . More democracy must be established here and elsewhere, the greatest possible number must find more joy, more happiness, and more determination to share in the national community, without which what you or I say means nothing. Think of the masses who do not always know and who place their hopes in us.

At the time he was speaking in this way, the "events," as the rising was to be politely called, had not yet begun. Unfortunately, those "events" were to impose more drastic choices—and soon. Mitterrand had no sooner left Algeria, declaring, "I have found

three French departments in Algeria in a state of calm and prosperity; I leave filled with optimism," than the first assassinations
were committed on the night of October 31, 1954. Police stations
were attacked, bombs were exploded, ambushes were laid. In all
there were eight dead, about forty wounded, and considerable material damage. On All Saints' Day, the French of metropolitan
France discovered to their surprise that there were advocates of
independence and an Algeria opposed to the French presence. But.
they scarcely appreciated the significance of the event—nor did the
politicians.

The government's response was twofold: to punish the perpe-
trators of the crimes and to begin economic and social reforms.
Reinforcements were sent out immediately, beginning with sixteen
companies of riot police, followed by parachutists who had been
repatriated from Indochina and who, thirsting for revenge, began
by calling the fellaghas Viets. By the end of November, the balance
sheet stood at: 1,188 individuals arrested, 750 imprisoned; 42
rebels killed, 28 wounded; 490 explosive devices seized; 417 fire-
arms discovered. It was not much, compared with what was to
follow.

Before the National Assembly, Pierre Mendès France and his
minister of the interior made oddly similar speeches on November
12, 1954. The prime minister declared: "Repression must be limited, but applied unflinchingly. No one must expect us to be lenient
with sedition: there can be no compromise with it. One does not
negotiate when defending the nation's internal peace and the Republic's integrity. The departments of Algeria have long been French,
. . . not a foreign country we protect."

François Mitterrand declared:

The rumor had suddenly spread that Algeria had been put to
fire and sword, thus closing the gap of a circle embracing Tunisia
and Morocco. That will not be, because Algeria is part of France
and because, from Flanders to the Congo, there is the rule of
law. Although there are some differences in application, law rules
everywhere, and it is French law. A single nation, a single parliament—that is the constitution and our will. No one has the
right to believe the government has ever doubted that. The gov-

ernment is determined to preserve the French domain in Africa, as far as the sorry settlements of our affairs in Asia allows it.

There was a formula that was repeated over and over: "Algeria is part of France."

The week before, the minister of the interior had gained the cabinet's approval to dissolve the Mouvement pour le triomphe des libertés démocratiques (MTLD), the most advanced of the Algerian parties. As a result, when the debate opened, René Mayer (the usual spokesman of the colonists), on hearing such Jacobin words, congratulated François Mitterrand on "the promptness and energy of his reaction." But this prohibition, which so pleased the colonists, had an unfortunate result: the MTLD, led by Messali Hadj, had had nothing to do with the first acts of violence. Its members, now hounded and charged by the authorities, found themselves thrown into the camp of the National Liberation Front—in other words, into a more brutal opposition.

On February 4, 1955, only a few days after the fall of the Mendès France government, François Mitterrand repeated in the assembly: "This is the very dogma of our policy: Algeria is part of France." Nowadays it is common to criticize Mitterrand for his lack of foresight. But his view was widely shared, and a minister of the interior could not, at the time, seriously speak in any other vein without immediately being accused of selling off three French departments. In the dialogue, very few politicians of the time would look good. A left-wing intellectual, Jacques Julliard, has defined the atmosphere thus:

The authorities dealt only with the more urgent problems, anxious to save appearance by improvising solutions that owed nothing to experience. The best disposed, the most clear-sighted, were caught short by this whirlwind of decolonization. No sooner had the Indochinese problem been settled than the problem of Tunisia presented itself; scarcely had Tunisia regained its calm than disturbances broke out in Morocco; no sooner had Morocco achieved its independence than an uprising enveloped the whole of Algeria. Today nobody would be surprised at this contagion. But at the time, anyone who predicted it was accused of arousing it. A certain patriotism blackmailed people into refusing to see things clearly.

This was so much so that François Mitterrand, who actually proposed concentrating all forces necessary in the Maghreb to avoid a defeat comparable to that of Vietnam, was almost accused of practicing a policy of abandonment. What, then, did he do? Forty-eight billion francs were released for the construction of roads, dams, and waterworks. It was decided to open up the civil service (even senior posts) much more extensively to Algerians. Thus, a management school was set up to train cadres; the school's students might then serve not only in Algeria, but also in mainland France. There was also a program to increase low wages, to reduce gradually the gap in pay between Algeria and France itself. But when, on January 5, 1955, François Mitterrand proposed to the cabinet the actual implementation of the 1947 statute, his plan was received as a declaration of war. Two ministers, Jacques Chevalier (secretary of state at defense and a reputed liberal) and Henri Fouques Duparc (secretary of state at air) threatened to resign.

The French deputies from Algeria raged at the assembly rostrum. François Quilici (conservative deputy for Algiers) fumed: "It should have been realized that the population wishes to maintain mixed communes, and that it regards equality between Algerians and French much more as an economic and social problem than a political one." General Aumeran stormed "against the initiatives of the minister of the interior, a neophyte and reformer, ignorant of Algerian matters, who is bringing division to hearts and minds." Roger de Saivre (a former Vichyite, conservative deputy for Oran) maintained that "the fellaghas want bread and lodging, but will not play their part in local politics."

Another seemingly more technical reform also threatened to light the fuse. Perhaps alerted by the first articles appearing in the press denouncing repression, François Mitterrand put an end to the fusion of local and mainland police forces. The local police, who had until then been independent of mainland control, used more violent methods; its officers were heavily compromised with the most intransigent of the colonists, the most notable. Certain liberals in Algiers informed Paris of this fact. But the measure caused discontent on both sides: the French police did not want to go to Algeria, and the French Algerian police did not want to be sent to the mainland. For the deputies from Algeria, the effect was disastrous. It was a clear sign of the French government's weakness.

On the eve of the great debate that saw the fall of the Mendès government, the Radical Senator Henri Borgeaud informed the prime minister that if the plans were kept, he and his friends would vote against the government (which they did).

The reforms proposed by François Mitterrand played a considerable role, therefore, in the fall of the Mendès France government. Mitterrand was regarded by the "Ultras" of Algeria as an irresponsible liberal. Once again, as with the affair of the leaks, it was the extreme Right that, by labeling him left-wing, drove him in that direction. Nevertheless, a closer look at Mitterrand's policies shows he was still extremely orthodox: although he had understood the need for legal reform and for an improvement in the Muslims' social position, he was more determined than ever to keep Algeria as part of France and did not care at all for the federal solution advocated by his own friends in the UDSR (notably by Eugène Claudius-Petit). In July 1954, Mitterrand said quite unambiguously: "To propose a federal system to Algeria represents a danger, for tomorrow it might demand its own diplomatic representation and army." He repeated this on February 5, 1955: "In the midst of a world perfectly capable of understanding this movement toward federalism, Algeria must remain the central pivot on which the central power of the Republic rests. Those in Algeria who demand a movement toward federalism are in the opposition."

It was not until the UDSR congress of 1956 that he declared: "If we pull off in Algeria what was promised in Tunisia—that is, internal autonomy—and if we are sure it will go no further, then such a solution should be tried." The explanation for this apparent change of heart lies in the UDSR members' recent unanimous vote in favor of the federal thesis (that is, against their president). And for the first time since taking control of his party, François Mitterrand found himself in a minority: his views on Algeria were regarded as too right-wing by men who were nevertheless far from being extreme left-wing. However, he had been supported in this matter by the young deputy Roland Dumas, who had also rejected the federal formula. The future defender of the National Liberation Front's French members was warning the government against any capitulation to the extremists, but also, it is true, to those who wanted to do nothing: "We must put an end," Mitterrand said, "to the humiliation and inferiority complex of the Muslim populations."

In fact, up until the fall of the Fourth Republic, François Mitterrand's language on the Algerian affair was in harmony with the feelings of the time. With the sole exception of the Communists and a handful of left-wing or liberal politicians, intellectuals, and journalists (whose views failed to influence public opinion), everyone seemed to regard the notion that Algeria was part of France as a sort of dogma. Even the Communist party (as unaware as any other of the importance of the struggle that was beginning) did not, at first, dare contradict that dogma openly. François Mitterrand, then, fully shared the dominant feelings of the time.

The other aspect of his action was repression. In 1955, while still minister of the interior, he declared: "Everything will be concentrated so the strength of the nation wins in all circumstances. Our harshest repression must be directed toward the leaders, at those responsible. All those who, in one way or another, try to create disorder and advocate secession will have every means placed at our disposal by the law turned against them."

Since all reform presupposed the crushing of the National Liberation Front (FLN), François Mitterrand, having become Garde des Sceaux in the Guy Mollet government, signed (together with Maurice Bourgès-Maunoury, minister of defense, and Robert Lacoste, minister resident in Algeria) the decree (no. 56258), which dispossessed the government and gave full power to the army in legal matters. This was surprising on the part of a man constantly declaring himself to be fiercely hostile to exceptional measures. The decree, which allowed day and night searches of citizens' homes, is seen today by most historians as one of the sources of a drama that was to mark the national conscience during the whole of that war: the extent of the repression imputable to the French forces.

In any case, it was from this time that such repression was to increase. The battle was widening in scope, the enemy showing no respect for the laws of war (twenty-six hundred terrorist acts were recorded each month). The politicians were increasingly at a loss, and the repression became more and more brutal.

During the seventeen months of the Guy Mollet government, François Mitterrand, who cannot be suspected of wanting to conceal torture, nevertheless said nothing to condemn it (at least publicly). And his pen, usually so alert and prolific, suddenly ceased to flow. Did governmental solidarity compel this? Mitterrand could have resigned, but did not choose to do so.

Indeed, Gaston Deferre has attested that at cabinet meetings the Garde des Sceaux often spoke vehemently against such practices. Other ministers, including Jacques Chaban-Delmas, who has always been loyal to François Mitterrand, have no memory of this:

> Once, under Guy Mollet's government, René Coty asked his ministers for their opinions on the executions of Algerian militants[69]: guillotining men who, however appalling some of their acts may be, are fighting for the emancipation of their country, is a gesture that can only aggravate hatreds. Three ministers—Robert Lacoste, Max Lejeune, and Maurice Bourgès-Maunoury—felt the sentences should be applied. Pierre Mendès France, Alain Savary, and François Mitterrand spoke in favor of the pardon, which René Coty granted on that occasion. . . .[70]

Similarly, reservations were expressed in April 1957: General Jacques Paris de Bollardière, commanding a sector in Algeria, asked to be relieved of his functions. In a letter made public, he expressed his agreement with Jean-Jacques Servan-Schreiber, who had been found guilty of demoralizing the army by his articles on torture published in *L'Express*. At the next cabinet meeting, Gaston Deferre, minister of France overseas, maintained that the general's gesture, whether or not one approved of it, now symbolized a sector of public opinion that disapproved of the excessive repression being used in Algeria.

François Mitterrand supported the same point of view.[71] But he again limited his criticism to the extent of the excess: some days later, before the Justice Committee at the Palais-Bourbon, he stressed that although the reports of the procurators-general revealed very regrettable facts, these were far less numerous than a section of the press said. But he added that "he could speak only for what came within his own authority—civil justice." Was he washing his hands of the rest? Mitterrand seemed afraid of scandal even when speaking up against a violation of human rights.

Germaine Tillion,[72] a resister, deportee, and former member of Jacques Soustelle's office in Algiers who fought to obtain pardon for those condemned to death, declares: "I went to plead their cause with President Coty several times, but in vain. My friend Professor Louis Massignon went to see François Mitterrand and tell him, given the importance of his responsibilities, the effect his resignation would have under such circumstances. Quite obviously, the minister was not prepared to listen." It is true that the general political climate, and that of the National Assembly in particular, was such that if Mitterrand had resigned on that question, he would have condemned himself to remain outside the center of power for a long time. Eugène Claudius-Petit, who has not always been kind in his comments on his former colleague, adds: "Mitterrand was in favor of repression. I often went to see him to plead pardon for some poor fellow—he sent me packing."

In fact, at the time, almost everyone pretended not to hear. "Consenting or chloroformed, the nation had resigned itself to the systematic use of torture," notes Jacques Julliard.[73]

It was not until March 1958 that Mitterrand, no longer a minister, took up a public position on the matter—and even then with carefully chosen words. La Question, a book by Henri Alleg (former editor of the Communist newspaper Alger républicain), described the torture to which the parachutists had subjected him. For publishing an article by Jean-Paul Sartre commenting on the book, L'Express was seized. In the next issue, François Mitterrand wrote:

If France is at war, has each of us the right to write whatever he likes on that war? And as much as he wishes? Probably not, if, as one says, the morale of the nation might suffer from it. Yet it is difficult to determine whether that morale is more surely affected by the man who denounces or by he who tolerates, by he who rejects colonial exploitation or by he who accepts it. Has Sartre the right to comment on Alleg's La Question in his own way? Has Alleg the right to write La Question and thus publish a book that may affect the nation's morale? Judge for yourselves. The government seems to have made its choice: the freedom of the press is guilty.

François Mitterrand had also made his choice: the government was guilty. But it took him some time to reach that decision.

When, in June 1957, *Paris-Presse* asked him what policy he advocated in Algeria,[74] Mitterrand replied (prudently reformist as usual):

- The maintenance of the indissoluble links between France and Algeria.
- Real equality between the Muslims and French born on Algerian soil and the French born in Europe.
- The administration of common interests by a federal executive and legislature sitting in Paris.
- The autonomous administration of each of the states in indigenous institutions for those affairs that are solely of their own concern.
- Universal suffrage.

He had, therefore, rallied to the federalism of the UDSR but had not used the word *negotiation* once (which was becoming a leitmotiv of the non-Socialist Left and the Communists). And when asked what he thought of Raymond Aron's book, *La Tragédie algérienne*, which considered the independence of Algeria to be inevitable, François Mitterrand replied: "Personally, I find it too pessimistic and too skeptical as to the chances of a homogeneous Franco-Algerian political totality."

In March 1958, a few weeks after the collapse of the Fourth Republic, Mitterrand was still writing in *Le Courrier de la Nièvre*:

The Communist solution, dictated by Russian imperialism, is unacceptable. To abandon Algeria would be a crime. The integration, pure and simple, of Algeria, advocated by the Social Republicans, is utopian. What Frenchman would accept a parliament in which a quarter, perhaps even a third, of the deputies were Muslims? What Frenchman would agree to opening up the civil service to Africans in the same proportion? For their part, the Socialists are obstinately stuck in their cease-fire/election/ negotiation triptych. The UDSR, which accepts the presence of the army in Algeria when its mission is to protect the population, persons, and property, considers, on the other hand, the use of force meaningful only if France's political aims are clearly set forth, only if the end of the fighting will definitely lead to an improvement in the social, economic, and political climate.

Slightly more audacious than the SFIO, which was not very difficult on this question, Mitterrand turned out to be no more realistic and even less prophetic.

The reason for this prudence may be explained. In 1957, François Mitterrand had just attended the RDA congress at Bamako and was sure he had defused the African independence movements— hence his strengthened conviction that the future of Third World countries must take place within the framework of the great former imperial groups linked to the West, rather than in the utopia of rootless nationalism. It was a time when scorn was heaped on the "handful of nationalist ideologues." In *Présence française et abandon*, Mitterrand writes:

> From now on, black Africa, which is still preserved, and Algeria, which is still strife-ridden, will avoid disaster only if metropolitan France realizes that there are no more small measures, fragmentary reforms, temporary accommodations capable of dealing with the problems. To hesitate further between integration and federalism would be to opt for independence. A strongly structured central power in Paris, autonomous federated states and territories within an egalitarian and fraternal community whose frontiers will stretch from the plains of Flanders to the forests of the equator—this is the prospect we should spell out and propose, for without Africa there will be no history of France in the twenty-first century.

It was not until 1959 and General de Gaulle's accession to power that Mitterrand pronounced, prudently as always, the word *negotiation*. At the UDSR congress in Paris in 1959, he said:

When you want a policy to succeed, you don't place yourself in a situation that will lead you inevitably to do the opposite. We are witnessing a desire to resolve the conflict by applying little touches here and there; whatever M. Debré says, to want a cease-fire is to prepare the ground for political negotiations. One is no doubt right to want that, but in so doing, one must accept the hypothesis that one day one will negotiate with Ben Bella, deputy for Tlemcen or Sétif.

Having rallied in 1960 to the idea of a negotiated solution of the Algerian War, François Mitterrand did not, from then on, refrain from condemning the incoherence, contradictions, and sudden changes of the government's Algerian policy. In a debate in the senate, he declared: "How many variations in government decla-rations, how many formulas, how many hypotheses, how many hopes abandoned by the wayside—Francification, federation. . . ."

In November 1961, he even went so far as to accuse the gov-ernment of "seeking an agreement with the GPRA rather than with the French."[75] He explained after the fact (always easy) that if he had remained in power, he would no doubt have ended up giving Algeria its independence: "We failed because the time was not ripe. De Gaulle delayed the hour, but was present at the meeting. I shall not try to say I was right against the calendar. I shall simply add that one cannot judge 1954 on the known data of 1977 and say: 'How could men of the Left in power in 1954, such as Mendès or Mitterrand, not have declared the independence of Algeria at once?' This would be to ignore realities and cut short the maturation of history in an imprudent way."[76]

In any case, in 1961, independent Algeria and the dislocated African community still filled François Mitterrand with bitter regret and left him unconsoled: "There was a time when some imagined that if the government had conceived an African policy as a whole, from the Mediterranean to the Congo, it would have been possible to place the future development of Algeria in a lasting frame-work."[77]

Brought up in the cult of the Empire, like all children of the bourgeoisie, the man who aspired to become head of government certainly found in those vast spaces an ambition for France more worthy of his hopes than the frontiers of the European continent. It was an ambition worthy of the dreams of the schoolboy in An- goulême sitting in front of the globe or sleeping at night with Vidal- Lablache's *Grand Atlas* on his bedside rug.

In 1962, on the eve of the final referendum that was to give Algeria its independence, Mitterrand was still writing in *Le Courrier de la Nièvre*: "What Frenchman does not feel a terrible wrench? There are many today who, like me, feel almost acutely the pain of that great departure. . . . Yes, Algeria is leaving us. . . . May she spare us her reproaches if, for a moment, we turn away to hide from her eyes our pain."

THE SOCIALIST EXPERIENCE

Today, paradoxically, no Socialist worthy of the name dares praise the time of the Mollet government, which made at least one record under the Fourth Republic—that of longevity (lasting for seventeen months). Far from being regarded as a success, this record is seen as an ordeal, and many of François Mitterrand's friends openly regret that their hero did not himself (and very quickly, as did Pierre Mendès France) cease to have any part in such a compro- mising experience.

Indeed, the elections of January 1956 saw the victory of the Republican Front. It was a very relative victory: the rather disparate coalition formed around the deputy for the Eure obtained 170 seats (the Communist party had 151 deputies; the Right, under 200). Nevertheless, since 1946 public opinion had never been so clearly oriented toward the Left. The cartel formed by Guy Mollet's SFIO, the Mendésist Radicals, François Mitterrand's UDSR, and Jacques Chaban-Delmas's Social Republicans won its bet. It was largely the personal prestige of Pierre Mendès France that attracted a section of the French voters and created a movement of opinion around a flattering halo. The former prime minister was regarded as deter- mined: he had demonstrated his ability to settle thorny problems quickly; he had awoken the French people's regard for politics; and he embodied a certain form of modernism, a desire to see France live from then on with its own time.

But no sooner was this brief victory won than the ambiguities

were revealed for all to see. Pierre Mendès France's leadership was
certainly not accepted unreservedly by his allies—especially not by
Guy Mollet, leading a structured and still deeply rooted party, who
felt Mendès had left him unduly in the shade.

François Mitterrand himself was extremely vexed by a "success"
that sent him back to the National Assembly at the head of a
debilitated cohort of six mainland deputies (without the thirteen
overseas and African deputies, he would not have been able to form
a group). In the battle, he had lost most of his troops.

A single new deputy, Roland Dumas, attested by his very oddness
to the renewal of the UDSR. This brilliant young barrister, with
his lion's mane, was to become a close friend of Mitterrand's. His
curious political career went by fits and starts: he was always
elected, but never reelected. Over the years, he tried his luck suc-
cessively in the Haute-Vienne, the Corrèze, the Gironde, and, finally, in the Dordogne. Like a one-shot gun, Maître Dumas got
himself elected, only to be beaten at the next elections; rather than
try to win back his lost electors, he preferred to move on and try
his luck in some other department.

Georges Dayan, François Mitterrand's recruiter-in-chief, endlessly tried to persuade a few extra deputies to join the UDSR,
managing to convince the young Gaullist, Jean-Noël de Lipkowski
(who was very Mendésist) to join the group.[78]

The former minister of the interior criticized Pierre Mendès France
for his electoral decisions. More than once he had put up a candidate
of his own against Mitterrand's, often encouraging less justified
ambitions than those of the UDSR militants. Later, those around
Mendès France were to acknowledge that Mitterrand had some
reason to feel ill-treated in this preelectoral bargaining. Mendès
himself was to say: "Everything was really botched up; candidates
were chosen in a very improvised fashion. After the event, I was
not very proud of how things were done."[79] This became one more
grievance between the two men.

Should we view this as a retaliatory measure (the affair of the
leaks being not far behind)? When, after the election was over, the
UDSR had to choose between Guy Mollet and Pierre Mendès France
for the prime ministership, the leaders (Plevenists and Mitterrandists agreeing for once) unhesitatingly chose the general secretary

of the SFIO. Guy Mollet was called on by René Coty to form the
new government, and was invested by the assembly on January 27,
1956. Pierre Mendès France realized the majority was too slight
for its chances of success to be very great—and, in any case, he
did not like fighting. He would have accepted the portfolio of the
Quai d'Orsay. In the end, though, he had to be content with the
post of minister of state without portfolio, which merely made him
look sadder than ever.

François Mitterrand had lost seats, but was rewarded by promotion. Not yet forty, he became Garde des Sceaux—the second
most important member of the government, according to protocol.

Also on the team were Christian Pineau (SFIO) at foreign affairs,
Gaston Deferre (SFIO) at France overseas, Alain Savary (SFIO) at
Tunisian and Moroccan affairs, Jacques Chaban-Delmas at vet-
erans, and Maurice Bourgès-Maunoury (Radical) at defense.

This was a team oriented, in principle, to the Left. Several measures of social justice were adopted from the outset—in particular,
for old-age pensioners—and soon a third week's holiday with pay
was granted. But on most issues, the non-Communist Left was to
follow policies the Right would have had no difficulty approving
and that it was no doubt quite happy to see being carried out by
those who usually fought them. There was a paradox here: the Left,
which by nature wanted to be liberating, but which was also Jacobin, was to carry out an increasingly repressive policy in Algeria;
the Left, which for doctrinal reasons wanted to be respectful of law
and international morality, was to tolerate torture without much
difficulty and to "cover" for the seizing of a plane organized by
members of the forces (the most famous plane in history, that of
the Algerian rebel leader Ben Bella); the Left, pacifist by temperament, was to practice against Egypt, in collusion with the British
Conservative government of Anthony Eden, the politics of the gun-
boat. On each of these points, François Mitterrand, far from dis-
tancing himself, was to show the greatest solidarity.

Pierre Mendès France soon resigned on May 23 on the question
of Algerian policy, which was to enhance his image as a decolonizer.[80] Alain Savary slammed the door after the boarding of the
Moroccan plane carrying the leaders of the Algerian rebellion, which
enhanced his stature as an uncompromising man of the Left. Fran-

çois Mitterrand, on the other hand, remained till the end. In all these episodes, he proved himself more Molletist than Mendésist. As he explained in 1977: "I had resigned three years earlier from the Laniel government. I did not want to set myself up in the position of a perpetual resigner."[81] The affair deserves closer scrutiny.

From the time of his arrival in power, Guy Mollet gave priority to pacification over negotiation—that is, to repression over diplomacy. Yet both his friends and opponents expected a change of tack. During the electoral campaign, the Republican Front, though remaining fairly vague as to means, made its intentions perfectly clear: France must be restored to her rank as a great power and peace must be made in Algeria. However, although it was thought that the head of government was trying to make contact, it soon became clear that maintaining order and eradicating the National Liberation Front had become his priorities. And no one in France, except for a few intellectuals, really opposed that policy.

Nevertheless, the general secretary of the SFIO had begun his government by appointing General Catroux, an able and liberal soldier, as resident general in Algeria in place of the Gaullist Jacques Soustelle (who, after having preferred reformist ideas, had soon become converted—and with some passion—to the theses of French Algeria).

In the case of Guy Mollet, however, a few rotten apples and many catcalls had been enough to divert him from his original intentions. Jeered wherever he went during his first visit to Algiers by a small white community (just like his own electors in northern France) afraid of being abandoned, he made it clear he sympathized with their position and immediately replaced General Catroux with one of his own party members, Robert Lacoste, who set about warning the French against "the magical belief in negotiations."[82] It was the end of liberalism, and nobody protested. In the National Assembly, special civil and military powers were voted to Robert Lacoste by 450 deputies (Communists included). The Right had an agreeable surprise. In the Socialist party, there was no question of not approving a leader who ran the machine so efficiently, while, for once, the Communist party wanted to give the Left a chance.

No one yet imagined that the Socialist government would be associated with parachutists' in Algiers seizing of power. The only leading politician to protest, Pierre Mendès France, did not convince François Mitterrand to do likewise.

THE PIOUS BIOGRAPHIES of the president of the Republic are silent on another episode: the Suez expedition. In July 1956, Colonel Nasser nationalized the Suez Canal, which had until then been controlled by a company with French and British capital. In Paris, this was seen as a provocation—especially since the Egyptian leader, who constantly threatened Israel, declared on his radio his sympathy for the fellaghas. On October 16, the French navy even intercepted a boat off Oran, the *Athos*, loaded with weapons coming from Egypt. Cairo was not only helping the FLN with propaganda, but was also sending it Soviet arms to kill French soldiers. There were demands on all sides for the greatest possible firmness. In *Le Monde*, Maurice Duverger, the great conscience of the Left, wrote: "The example of 1933–39 is clear. In the face of the megalomania of a dictator, one must respond not with ineffective legal procedures that bring the law into disrepute, but with force."

The same martial tone is to be found in statements made on the subject by François Mitterrand, who compared "Nasserian Egypt's hold on the canal to that of Nazi Germany on Czechoslovakia" (in other words, the nationalization of a great capitalist company leads the future Socialist leader to compare a Third World leader to the Nazi dictator).

In early November 1956, when France and Great Britain jointly launched the Suez expedition (which had been planned for many weeks with the connivance of the Israelis), all of French public opinion and of the political class applauded (with the exception of the Communists and the Poujadists). At the same time as Guy Mollet was announcing the expedition to the National Assembly, François Mitterrand was defending it in vigorous terms before the Council of the Republic (now the Senate). The dropping of the parachutists over the canal was approved by a 289–19 vote.

The affair ended when, under pressure from the Soviet Union and above all from the United States, the two European powers

were forced to withdraw and pitifully declare a cease-fire. The fine
military escapade ended in an unglorious return journey for the
"soldiers of peace," as Guy Mollet had called them.[83]

In that sorry episode, overwhelmingly approved by the French
in the grip of a fever of chauvinistic exaltation, François Mitterrand
showed no inclination whatsoever to distance himself. As he said
at the Palais du Luxembourg: "To act quickly is to act in the
interests of France."

He showed the same (at least apparent) conformism in the celebrated affair regarding the boarding of the plane carrying the five
FLN leaders.

On October 22, 1956, the generals in Algiers ordered the French
pilot of the official Moroccan plane (carrying Ahmed Ben Bella;
Mohamed Khider, a former MTLD deputy; Hocin Ait Ahmed; Mohamed Boudiaf; and Mostafa Lacheraf) to land at Algiers. The
team crossed French airspace on its way from Rabat to Tunis, where
Habib Bourguiba was organizing a conference on Algeria. The sultan of Morocco (to the fury of the French) had insisted on taking
with his delegation (but in a plane other than the one in which he
was traveling) the main leaders of the FLN, who, to their astonishment, were arrested and incarcerated.

French public opinion was delighted by this trick, and the press
applauded. In the Arab capitals there was fury and consternation.
By way of retaliation, French stores were looted in Tunis, and at
Meknès some thirty Europeans were slaughtered.

France had humiliated two Muslim states to which she had just
given, willingly or no, independence; above all, she had violated
the most elementary international law. This logic of force put an
end to the first attempts at dialogue with the Algerian nationalists.
In fact, the French government had been confronted with a fait
accompli. But the minister, Robert Lacoste, and the prime minister
had secretly approved of the operation. Those ministers who criticized the action could always resign after the event. This is what
Alain Savary did: the secretary of state for Tunisian and Moroccan
affairs, scandalized by the operation (and, indeed, in permanent
conflict with Robert Lacoste), refused to lend his approval any
longer to a policy that offended all his convictions. Pierre de Leusse,
French ambassador in Tunis, also resigned.

François Mitterrand did not flinch—even though he found himself in exactly the same position as under the Laniel government,
when the sultan of Morocco had been deposed without the ministers
having been informed. On that earlier occasion he had lost his
temper and left the government. This time he remained and said
nothing.

As if by way of justification, he explained to his friends in the
UDSR some months later: "I prefer to work with democrats than
to practice a sterile opposition against people who would not listen
to me." This was a flimsy argument that deceived no one: had
Robert Lacoste and Guy Mollet behaved like democrats in the
affair? It is highly debatable, to say the least.

But in private, the Garde des Sceaux betrayed his unease. Pierre
Nicolaÿ, the head of Mitterrand's private office, noted: "He had
become taciturn—one could no longer speak to him. We should
have left."[84]

In that left-wing government, François Mitterrand may have felt
himself to be in an unstable position. This, in any case, is the opinion
of Claude Estier, then a journalist on the left-wing *France Observateur*: "It seemed to me he was ready to resign, and if he did not
do so after Mendès and Savary, it was because Guy Mollet begged
him to stay."[86] And Mitterrand above all wanted to avoid a break
with the indispensable boss of the SFIO: he was convinced his
chances of becoming prime minister were at last becoming more
definite, that his hour was close at hand. Jacques Kosciusko-
Morizet, then French representative at the United Nations and a
member of the UDSR, declares: "He was bubbling with impatience. He believed he was capable of solving the Algerian problem. He told me to keep myself in readiness, for if he were called
on to form the government, I was to join him at once to work
with him."

The Guy Mollet government did in fact fall. Those around the
minister of justice who were expecting his promotion waited day
after day for a sign of good news. Georges Dayan was as sardonic
as ever: "Let's go and inquire as to the august old gentleman's
[President Coty's] intentions," he remarked.[85]

In fact, the wheel of fortune continued to turn but never stopped
in front of Mitterrand. Maurice Bourgès-Maunoury, Félix Gaillard,

and Pierre Pflimlin followed one another at the Matignon at an increasing rate. Everyone sensed that the machine was breaking down, that the institutions of the Fourth Republic were too weak to settle so acute a problem. Everybody felt something might happen. But that something was not François Mitterrand's arrival at the Matignon. When, in spring of 1958, the president was trying to settle the formation of what was to be the Fourth Republic's final government, many of Mitterrand's rivals were summoned to the Elysée, but not him.

"He was barred by General Ganeval, the military adviser to the president of the Republic, who wanted to prepare the ground for the return of General de Gaulle," a very informed source, Jacques Kosciusko-Morizet, hazards. André Rousselet adds: "There were two clans among René Coty's colleagues: the pro-Mitterrand clan, led by Friol, and the antis, led by Ganeval." On the other hand, François de Baecque, who belonged to the president's team, notes: "President Coty was a big enough boy to choose his own prime minister. He did not need the permission of his advisers." And René Pleven goes further: "If René Coty did not call François Mitterrand, it was because he could not, in all conscience, bring himself to make him the man supremely responsible for the conduct of the French government."

Later, François Mitterrand preferred to believe it was Guy Mollet who had barred him, and he often repeated this to those around him. But he believed in his chances to the end. His friend Guitte reports: "When de Gaulle came back to power, François Mitterrand said to me: 'And to think I was about to become prime minister at last!' "

De Gaulle's resurfacing was inexcusable, merely adding to his resentment of the general. From then on, Mitterrand's disappointment and indignation increased. He was to give this epilogue to the affair:

On June 1, when René Coty received me in the company of Roger Duveau to ask me to accept General de Gaulle's investiture, as he was doing with all the representatives of every parliamentary group, he held my hand in his for a moment, then said with a great sigh: "Ah! I often wanted to call you to settle the crisis, but it was impossible. There would have been incidents at Algiers." It was May 31. The riot, sedition, and coup d'état were now a fortnight old. As far as the president of the Republic—the guardian of established society—was concerned, nothing had happened. For me, it had!

6

THE FIFTH REPUBLIC:
A DESTINY

WILL IT EVER BE SAID OFTEN ENOUGH? THE FIFTH REPUB-
lic was François Mitterrand's great opportunity. Without de Gaulle,
the ambitious young minister would no doubt finally have reached
the Matignon and become one of those ephemeral prime ministers
at the head of a disparate coalition doomed sooner rather than later
to break up. His political career could have turned out this way.

Because of Charles de Gaulle, however, François Mitterrand had
a far greater destiny. By saying no from the outset, by assuming
once and for all an attitude of uncompromising opposition (where
prudence and calculation might well have driven him in the opposite direction), Mitterrand made the right choice—and as a result,
entered history. He became first the champion, then the prophet,
and finally the pope of French-style socialism. He became first the
counterpresident, then the opposition leader, and finally the first
Socialist to be elected president by direct universal suffrage. He
will definitely have, he knows, a paragraph in the history books.

This opportunity, however, was not handed to him on a silver
platter. He won it through fierce struggle. "He led a dog's life,"
Jacques Chaban-Delmas notes admiringly. Mitterrand was to battle
on for twenty-three long years, at the same time protecting himself

on three fronts: against the right wing in power (de Gaulle and his successors); against the Socialist Left itself and its leaders (which he had to seduce, tame, and in the end, destroy); and against the Communists—the indispensable, dangerous allies (whom he would have to use while keeping a wary eye on them, and with whom a coalition remained a permanent struggle).

Just as under the Fourth Republic, Mitterrand's journey over that quarter century was to be a series of ups and downs. As this Christian himself wrote, all his life he was to pay for each success with a trial.

Let us list the "downs":

- 1958: Mitterrand's electors and supporters abandon him to follow a triumphant Gaullism.
- 1959: The Observatoire affair very nearly ruins his reputation forever.
- 1968: He is even rejected by those whom he has persuaded to gather round him.
- 1974: Victory eludes him again and everyone expects him to retire.
- 1977: Betrayal by the Communist party puts beyond his grasp a victory that seemed likely from the legislative elections of the following year, putting in question his authority within his own party.

On the other hand, there were the "ups":

- 1965: The first real encounter with popularity and the people of the Left.
- 1967: He becomes sole leader of the Left.
- 1971: He takes over the Socialist party, becoming the unchallenged boss of its membership.
- 1981: The ultimate triumph and supreme revenge of the eternal loser, who enters the Elysée at last.

Not everyone would have been capable of withstanding such a series of trials. Not many would have been capable of turning so many failures into successes. If François Mitterrand has succeeded in this, it is because he has a secret—or rather, two. First, he possesses an almost abnormal stubbornness; second, his character, formed by facing danger and tempered by confronting threats, challenges, or rivals, places him outside the common run. There was the threat from de Gaulle, who rejected him and from whom he had nothing more to expect or fear. There was the threat from Michel Debré, who tried, in the Observatoire affair, to ruin his career. There was the challenge from Pierre Stibbe, the conscience of the Left, who wanted to undermine confidence in him during his first candidacy for the presidency. There was the threat from his partners in the Federation of the Left, who found it difficult to accept his preeminence. Lastly, later, there was the rivalry of Michel Rocard, whom he accused of trying to reap the benefits of his ten years of work. In every case, the opponent awoke him, stimulated him, forced him to rise above himself. The capacity to respond in such a manner is rare. It distinguishes the ordinary politician from the one who has a destiny. And it marks him forever.

Yet the career of François Mitterrand under the Fifth Republic poses a serious question: that of his sincerity. His entry into socialism was belated. His conversion coincided, give or take a few months, with his assuming leadership of the non-Communist Left. It was as if the Left were worth not a mass, but a series of orations and invocations to the founding fathers of socialism. This man of intuition, sensibility, indignation, manipulation, cunning, and long-term strategy was to bear this doctrinal corset all the more readily in that it was indispensable to him in his relations with the Communist party, in the leadership of the Socialist party (which owes its recovery to him and him alone), and in his conquest of the "people of the Left."

But during Mitterrand's time in opposition, these doctrinal juggling acts had a very perverse effect upon him: he soon got into the habit of talking and writing without taking much account of realities, as if everything were possible, as if it were enough to say something for it to be. And when he finally arrived in power, he was to pay dearly—very dearly—for this.

THE NO TO THE GENERAL

"May is a mad month," the first secretary of the Socialist party remarked in one of his best-written pieces,[1] surely never imagining

this beautiful month was, a few years later, to be that of his con-
secration.

He was not only thinking of the madness of May 1968 (which
had found him so unprepared) and that of 1958 (which, for so
many years, had ruined his hopes and disturbed his best-laid plans).

But it is true May 1958 was very mad indeed—mad enough to
set many a head spinning. François Mitterrand had quite personal
reasons to remember it. After the fall of the Félix Gaillard government on April 15, he waited beside his telephone for a call from
the Elysée that would fulfill all his greatest hopes. All the rules of
the game had either been flouted or abolished, and there was nothing more depressing for someone who wanted to methodically build
up a great career.

For over a month France remained without a government—at
precisely the time she most needed one. Everything was falling
apart; the Fourth Republic was dying on its feet. No sooner was a
majority cobbled together than it crumbled. Power was for the
taking, but it no longer tempted many. President Coty was not, of
course, wasting his time: he went on consulting, sounding out opinion, testing the water's temperature. He summoned Georges Bidault
of the MRP and René Pleven of the UDSR—the eternal prime
ministers-in-waiting—but they were too cunning to take on a mission they regarded as utterly impossible. He even approached three
Radicals who had not yet been prime minister: René Billières, Fernand Berthouin, and, above all, the subtle Maurice Faure. The
proposition was flattering but the job dangerous, and none of them
accepted. The three hopefuls turned out to be as realistic as their
two seniors.

In short, it was total deadlock. Meanwhile, a man who was dying
to say yes, dreamed of trying his luck, but was not asked. The
telephone in the rue Guynemer remained silent—desperately silent.

This all-too-evident power vacuum could not but increase the
agitation of the Europeans and soldiers in Algeria (who were hostile
to any compromise with the Nationalists—indeed, to any dealings
with them whatsoever) and extend this agitation to mainland France.
Skillful and enterprising Gaullists like Léon Delbecque (a man from
the North with the physique of a cowboy), Jacques Chaban-Delmas
(a member of the office of the minister of defense), and other

individuals working for other ends were already conscientiously infiltrating the movements or civil groups that, legally or not, were striving both for a French Algeria and against the regime.

On April 24, in Algiers, an impressive demonstration let out a hue and cry (a cry above all) for the formation of a government of public safety. In Paris it was felt that this time a government must be formed or the situation would soon get out of control. The reports coming in from North Africa were increasingly alarming. At last, on May 8, a man said yes to President Coty: Pierre Pflimlin, of the MRP. He agreed to try to form a government. He had a reputation as a good minister, a fervent European, a skillful, open-minded administrator, and, above all, as a pragmatist. This last worried Algiers and the right wing of the National Assembly enormously. No sooner had the mayor of Strasbourg accepted than the rumor spread that this Christian democrat would be just another type of Mendésist—one who was a discreet advocate of negotiation with the Algerian rebels. The fury in Algiers increased when the Socialist Robert Lacoste gave credence to the rumor by denouncing, quite overtly, the "diplomatic Dien Bien Phu" now threatening them.

This time, all the activists who could be mobilized in the white city "smelling of goats and jasmine" appeared on the streets. The military leaders consulted one another and, in a collective warning to the head of state, referred to a "reaction of despair on the part of the army"—in other words, a rebellion.

The appointment of Pierre Pflimlin, which had arrived too late and under bad conditions, could no longer be anything more than a brake on the fury simmering in Algeria.

In his newspaper, *L'Écho d'Alger*, Alain de Sérigny, who, for two years (with the help of Jacques Soustelle and Michel Debré) had consorted a great deal with the Gaullists, launched a ringing appeal to General de Gaulle: "Speak, *mon général!*"

On May 13, as Pierre Pflimlin was being presented to the National Assembly, the crowd stormed the palace of the governor general of Algeria. A Committee of Public Safety was formed that evening under the chairmanship of the popular General Massu, the idol of the *pieds-noirs*, the European Algerians.

History hung in the balance. François Mitterrand, who did not know everything that was happening, was nevertheless aware that the fate of the regime was being played out. That same day, he went to Enghien, in the Paris suburbs, to lend a helping hand to his friend Jean-Noël de Lipkowski. During the meeting, Lipkowski remembers, a note was passed to the president of the UDSR. He went white and, turning to his neighbor on the platform, said: "Our place is in the National Assembly." Both men dashed to a car and drove to the Palais-Bourbon.

"If de Gaulle comes back to power, I shall join him," Lipkowski warned his friend. Mitterrand, furious, retorted without hesitation: "I shall never work with those people, never!" It was an instinctive reaction.

That night, the National Assembly invested Pierre Pflimlin by a 274–179 vote. The Communist party chose, as a result of the events in Algiers, to abstain, giving credence to the idea that Pierre Pflimlin was favorable to negotiation. Everyone realized this government was the Fourth Republic's last chance. Mitterrand consistently voted for the investiture—anything rather than de Gaulle.

On that crazy night, the Socialists agreed to take part in a government led by the MRP. Symbolically, Guy Mollet accepted the vice premiership; no less symbolically, Jules Moch, who, ever since he had brought the strikes of 1947 to an end and come into collision with the Gaullists of the RPF, had enjoyed the reputation of being a strong, energetic man, was back at the Ministry of the Interior; Albert Gazier took over information. François Mitterrand was not even invited to join the government: the MRP had him in their sights. But his old adversary René Pleven occupied one of the leading government posts. As it happened, it hardly mattered—it was too late. From Algiers, the military leaders (and soon the crowd) repeatedly called on de Gaulle to help them.

The man of Colombey, who was not deaf, hastened to publish a declaration, which he had held in reserve for several days: "Today," he said in his inimitable style, "before the trials that once more rise up toward it [the people], let it know that I hold myself in readiness to assume the powers of the Republic."

It was clear: like Offenbach's bearded king, the general was coming—with giant steps. The army had already gone over halfway to meet him, pushed rather than followed by the French of

Algeria. The government had lost control of the situation. The assembly might pass a motion calling for a three-month state of emergency, but the initiative had slipped from those in power.

On May 17, giving the slip to the surveillance under which he had been for some time by hiding in the trunk of a car, the Gaullist Jacques Soustelle managed to leave mainland France and get to Algiers. He immediately became adviser to General Salan. The symbolic juncture of soldiers and Gaullists was thus achieved.

On May 19, at the Palais d'Orsay, General de Gaulle gave a press conference at which he refused to condemn what the Left was calling the "military sedition" and concluded by launching a martial: "I shall now retire to my village and hold myself at the disposal of the country."

The general had moved; now he was on his way. Very soon, one after another, the most prestigious politicians came to pay him homage. When, on May 22, Antoine Pinay went to Colombey, everyone realized that the principal leaders of the Fourth Republic were beginning to rally to the general.

On May 24, parachutists from Algeria landed in Corsica, where the Committees of Public Safety had seized power. Riot police, urgently sent from mainland France to stop them, prudently allowed themselves to be disarmed and collaborated with the crack troops. The forces of order did not intend to resist these centurians.

Enthusiastically sustained by the Gaullists, rumors of a military coup d'état in mainland France circulated from Dunkirk to Marseille. Everywhere it was whispered that the parachutists were about to land. Some noisily rejoiced, but the French are well known for fearing, more than anything else, that the heavens will fall upon their heads. And they gradually became convinced that only one man could prevent such a natural catastrophe: de Gaulle.

On May 26, while Guy Mollet slyly suggested to Pierre Pflimlin that he make contact with the general (which the prime minister hastily did that very evening), the Socialist deputies declared (by a 117–3 vote), in voices more raucously Republican than ever, that never, under any circumstances, would they support a candidacy that was and would remain a "challenge to legality."

It did not matter what the flock thought. Guy Mollet, who had no love of travel, went to Colombey three days later and came back very pleased with himself, sighing: "I have lived through one of the greatest moments of my life."[2]

The Fourth Republic was not yet buried, but it was already dead. On May 28, Pierre Pflimlin, who nevertheless had a majority in the assembly that would have been the envy of his predecessors (except that it was no longer in the assembly that the important deliberations were taking place—in abusing their power for so long, the deputies had lost it), resigned. Everyone understood he intended to make way for the general.

That same day, a great demonstration of the Left stretched from the Bastille to the Nation, with endless repetitions of the cry: "Le fascisme ne passera pas" (fascism will not pass). But what was meant by the term *fascism*? The parachutists? The army? The general? The crowd numbered two or three hundred thousand. Its massive character meant that at least half the population of Paris approved of the initiatives. It was the same population that, a few months later, was to vote yes four to one. This can only mean that many of those who took part in the demonstration were not terribly hostile to de Gaulle.[3]

François Mitterrand was at the demonstration. He saw things rather differently—at least eleven months later:

During the procession from the Bastille to the Nation, I noticed the gloomy faces of the demonstrators. I was irritated by the poverty of the slogans. No one wept for the regime that had collapsed, and I did not weep for it either. I felt I was in debt to that abandoned people. I felt guilty for its indifference. Whose fault was it if it regarded the public execution of democracy as a spectacle that did not concern it, that concerned only the mandarins, their words, and empty promises? I had taken part in the enterprise, I had respected its practices, I had not shouted loudly enough to upset the ceremonial. Was I going to continue acting like so many others for whom the change of Republic mattered little, providing it guaranteed the immutability of structures, privileges, and benefits? When I went back to the Palais-Bourbon, my decision was made: to preserve one's honor was the only way. . . .[4]

The man who beat his breast so fervently was one of the leaders of the Fourth Republic. But this most intransigent of republicans, who was beginning to denounce the usurper's original sin, was not yet a socialist, scarcely a man of the Left. Mitterrand reacted as a lawyer and moralist. At least, that is what he wrote.

In any case, René Coty did not share these moods. The president of the Republic, though a highly experienced parliamentarian and stickler for form, realized that it was not a time for analyzing texts and quibbling over rules, but a time for change and even for risk. He did not hesitate to have a message read to the parliament that was very much like blackmail: if the assemblies did not call upon General de Gaulle to form a government, he would resign immediately. In fact, the president was not running any great risk—the dice were already rolling. General de Gaulle went to the Elysée and agreed to form a government. A communiqué stated that he would ask for exceptional, constituent powers. Thus the man of June 18 became the last prime minister of the Fourth Republic as he was preparing to found the Fifth.

The party leaders rushed to the Hôtel de la Trémoille, de Gaulle's Paris residence (where a few months earlier his faithful followers had so much difficulty attracting even a few visitors). François Mitterrand, president of the UDSR, was one of those summoned. He must have gone there with feet of lead. "I think I was the only one to say," he reports, "that I would not support that candidacy until de Gaulle publicly disowned the Committees of Public Safety and the military rising. . . . I also told him that a regime cannot be founded on the omnipotence of one man."[5]

His friend Roger Duveau, chairman of the UDSR parliamentary group in the assembly and deputy for Madagascar, accompanied him and left an account of the dialogue:

"You are here, *mon général*, as a result of a very unusual set of circumstances, but you might just as easily not be here. You might never have been born, or you might have died earlier."

"What do you mean, Mitterrand?" the general asked.

"You see, *mon général*, if you will allow me to continue, a short time ago we embarked on the strange and dangerous path of *pronunciamentos*, which have until now been the preserve of

South American republics. Now, according to you, our only recourse in confronting that kind of tragedy, which runs the risk
of bringing with it the ruin of France, is yourself, *mon général.*
But you are mortal."

"I know what you are trying to say," the general interrupted.
"You want my death. I am prepared for it."[6]

At this the general brought the meeting to an end and walked out.

It was certainly a surrealistic dialogue, what with, on the one
hand, the allegorical spirals of François Mitterrand confronting a
savior he was rejecting, and, on the other, the curt replies of the
man of June 18 to a junior who profoundly irritated him. Once
again, the meeting of the two men ended in a short circuit.

On June 1, 1958, before the National Assembly, de Gaulle laid
his cards on the table. He wanted plenary powers for six months
and a mandate from the assembly to propose to the country indispensable changes to the constitution.

François Mitterrand said no. But when examined more closely,
his speech sounds almost like a "no, but." First, the "no": "At a
time when the most illustrious of Frenchmen presents himself before us, I cannot forget that General de Gaulle was first and foremost
called by an undisciplined army. . . . By law, the general will hold
his powers this night from the national representation—but in fact,
he already holds them through force." Then, the "but": "Someone
has just said: 'After a while, will you rally to him?' Well, yes, ladies
and gentlemen, if General de Gaulle is the founder of a new form
of democracy, if General de Gaulle is the liberator of the African
people, if he maintains the presence of France everywhere beyond
the seas, if he is the restorer of national unity, if he gives France
the continuity and authority she needs, then I shall rally, but on
one condition. . . .

No one was ever to know what that condition was. At that moment, Mitterrand was interrupted, his words drowned by the noise
of his colleagues. He never finished his speech, the mystery of the
ultimate condition remaining unrevealed. From what he did say,
however, particularly memorable in the mass of preconditions (all,
in fact, acceptable to General de Gaulle) is that question in the
form of an ultimatum: "Will you be able to guarantee the presence

of France everywhere beyond the seas?" While it may have been
a democrat speaking, it was not a convinced advocate of negotiations in Algeria.

Does that "no, but," or that "not if," or even that "not unless"
mean that François Mitterrand was really in any doubt, that he
had weighed in his conscience the full implications of acceptance
or refusal? It would not seem so, and all his friends attest to this.
Mitterrand himself has written:

And so that afternoon of May 29, when I walked alone for long
hours along the quays of the Left Bank, it was a sunny day, clear
and fragile. The river glittered in the shifting light of the sky. I
pondered the matter anxiously. Did one have to defend a crazy
system, one incapable of giving back to France her true rank?
Or did one have to lend a hand to the conspiracy that was about
to destroy it? I sought in the teachings of former years the lesson
I needed. Everything urged me to consent to the liquidation of
the Fourth Republic, with its *rois fainéants* and its mayors of
the palace. That grayness suited an ebbing life. Yet everything
made me shun that dictatorship visible to the naked eye, beneath
its innocent-looking mask.[7]

A dictatorship—he had said it. From then on, he would never
cease lying in wait for it, fearing it, and denouncing it—even when
the regime had shown over and over again it was the reverse and
had been legitimated several times by universal suffrage.

Whereas Pierre Mendès France was divided between contradictory loyalties, Mitterrand's was an angry, petulant no. On Pierre
Mendès France's attitude, Jean Lacouture observes: "Quite as much
as a heartrending rejection, it was an appeal. He does not refer to
that time in his life without speaking of pain, without observing
that, although he voted against de Gaulle, he felt deep down that
he was infinitely closer to him than many of these men—Tixier-
Vignancourt, for example—who rallied to the strong man while
pulling him to pieces behind his back."

François Mitterrand shared neither Mendès France's doubts nor
his hesitations. Although in May 1958 they found themselves side
by side once more, it was not with the same feelings: Pierre Mendès

France retracted out of private anguish; Mitterrand was tensing himself as one bends a bow before letting fly a deadly arrow.

On June 1, 1958, the general became prime minister with a comfortable majority. He had waited for twelve years before returning to power. "What enabled him to stand up to the storms was his self-control," a for once admiring François Mitterrand admitted to Pierre Desgraupes.[8]

From that day on, the scene changed for Mitterrand. At forty-two, he went into opposition. His life was transformed. He bade farewell to the official palaces, guards of honor, ministerial offices, and troops of underlings. He was no longer one of the princes who governed, and knew it would be like that for ten years at least. "I must think about things, travel a bit, listen to great music," he declared, with simulated enthusiasm, to his faithful followers Georges Beauchamp, Georges Dayan, Louis Mermaz, Roland Dumas, and André Rousselet.

He did not approach this desert crossing with a light heart. Of the fourteen UDSR deputies, ten had rallied to de Gaulle (notably René Pleven, Edouard Bonnefous, and Eugène Claudius-Petit). He had lost control of his group. His only consolation was the aberrant case of Roland Dumas. In spring 1957, Dumas had gone with other young parliamentarians (including Valéry Giscard d'Estaing and Christian Bonnet) to ask René Coty to call on de Gaulle. But, having fulfilled his wish, Dumas did not vote for the investiture. He definitively chose François Mitterrand over the man of Colombey, for which he would always be given credit. (It is almost astonishing that this exemplary and brilliant companion has not yet reached, unless it was for this reason, the topmost rungs of the hierarchy.)

If parties and spiritual families, even the most highly structured ones, were shattered during that mad month, the French themselves were much less divided. On September 28, a referendum approved of the new institutions by 79.25 percent of the vote. It was poor consolation for Mitterrand that de Gaulle's proposal was approved in his Nièvre (where he had ventured to explain to the astonished people of the Morvan that a vote in favor would bring in a regime like those of the South American generals) by no more than 75 percent of the vote.

Thus, the former deputy (the assembly had been dissolved as a result of the referendum) was almost alone in opposition. Yet not entirely so: on the same side were his eternal opponents, the Communists. Mitterrand was not slow to work out the consequences of this fact.

THE DARK YEARS: THE TRAGICOMEDY OF THE OBSERVATOIRE

Everything was going badly. In November 1958 Mitterrand was beaten at the legislative elections. For the first time since 1946, his electors abandoned him. And the very man who had pleaded so much for the establishment of single-member constituencies with a two-round ballot was to be found among its most famous victims. Yet the Communist party, acknowledging his anti-Gaullism, transferred their votes to him at the second round (the Socialist held his own). But it wasn't enough; the wave carried him off and an anonymous Gaullist took his place.

The landslide of the Fifth Republic supporters swept away many eminent victims, notably Pierre Mendès France, Edgar Faure, and Gaston Deferre. A close colleague of General de Gaulle, Léon Noël (soon to become president of the Constitution Council) recounts how, on the eve of those elections, the general had asked him: "Which members of the opposition are most likely to be beaten?"

"Pierre Mendès France," he replied.

"That's a great pity," the general averred.

"François Mitterrand, too," the expert added.

"That's a different matter," muttered the man of June 18, almost with delight.

François Mitterrand now had to earn a living: he had to begin a new professional life (though, to be fair, it was not to last long— only about six years). Reluctantly leaving the political stage, he passed without enthusiasm from the Palais-Bourbon to the Palais de Justice. Having joined the bar in 1954, he had carried out his apprenticeship under very special conditions: first as minister of the interior, then as Garde des Sceaux, he had had to apologize every week, in writing, to the chairman of the bar council for repeated absences due to ministerial obligations. It was, as an amused Roland Dumas relates, a unique case.

At the time, adventure was not to the taste of the former minister. He had to apply himself to the law, organize his life, find causes and clients. He formed a partnership with Irène Dayan (the wife of his friend Georges), herself a barrister. She told Charles Moulin: "I prepared files for him in the traditional way, in terms of the procedure, the establishment of facts, and the juridical rules. I must admit, things were not always easy with him. He did not feel entirely at home. Nothing irritated him more than the stereotyped language of the courts, with its *considering thats* and *whereases*."[9]

On top of all that, the new barrister's first steps were to be met with an amused curiosity. The judges awaited the debut of this former minister (a minister of justice at that) with ironic interest: it was a rare occasion for a bit of fun, especially since the famous beginner could not have been familiar with all the semantic subtleties and all the liturgy of legal circles. Yet Mitterrand won more than one case in the civil courts (either alone or as an assistant, a very secondary role for him). In the criminal court, he defended Dr. Schwing, a well-known chiropractor accused of illegally practicing medicine. He also defended the Marceau film company and director Roger Vadim for their screen adaptation of a reputedly licentious work, Choderlos de Laclos's *Les Liaisons dangereuses*.

An admiring Irène Dayan believes that, if he had wanted to, Mitterrand could have had a great career as a barrister. This, however, was not François Mitterrand's intention. He knew the bar led to everything—providing one got out of it. And he wanted to get out of it as soon as possible. He had only one idea in his head: to get his political revenge. But how? And with whom?

Of course, he still had the UDSR, but it was in a sorry state. When, on January 31, 1959, his group held a congress, only twenty-seven federations and one tendency (his own—the others had joined the general) had survived. In that desert, he could count only on a handful of faithful followers, always the same: Louis Mermaz, Roland Dumas, Georges Dayan, Georges Beauchamp, and André Rousselet.

On that day he already predicted:

The time will come when, from the conservative Right to the Socialist Left—with all the betrayal and anger, with disappointed ambitions, mingling the pure with the impure—we will all have to gather around a program of action. Agreement is possible with those who are prepared to fight and who have made up their minds to fight against the undermining of the state.

I include in this term all republicans of action, will, decision—all those who have suffered since 1944 (yes, suffered—sometimes to the point of despair) at seeing France miss all her opportunities, and who feel a kind of rage at it. You will see the day, if things continue in the way that has been laid down—you who are faithful to the mingled notions of Christian civilization, freedom of thought, and the great revolution, you who have failed once again to live up to the destinies of men of action but remain anxious spectators—when communism will pick up the pieces and build its own house. . . . There are some who have tried to show you that after the shortcomings of the Fourth Republic, only one road remains: that of communism. It is this we wish, above all, to challenge.

True to himself, the future Socialist leader set about eloquently lambasting at the same time something to which he was not exactly alien (the Fourth Republic) and something that had come about without his participation (the Fifth Republic). As at the time of the "third force," he found equally angry words to denounce the evil forces that had been aroused by Gaullism and the equally perverse alternative represented by communism (hence the dream of a gathering of forces stretching from democratic socialism to the conservative Right).

Meanwhile, he had to begin his reconquest. No sooner had he lost his seat in the National Assembly than François Mitterrand obtained two seats for himself, one after the other. It was quite a remarkable coup under the circumstances. In March 1959, he was elected mayor of Château-Chinon, at the heart of that same constituency in the Nièvre he intended making his own again at the first opportunity. In April, benefiting from the work in his department he had patiently put in over the years, he entered the senate. He was in very good company. Never (except perhaps after 1981) did the upper chamber have such a brilliant membership. The illustrious, defeated veterans of the lower house—Gaston Deferre, Edgar Faure, and many others—were all there in large numbers.

François Mitterrand was to turn out to be a talented critic. At the time he defined his intransigence regarding the regime he abhorred in an article in *La Nef*, a fashionable intellectual review of mildly left-wing views edited by Lucy Faure (Edgar's wife). In the spring of 1959 he wrote:

> The history of the peoples' democracies shows quite clearly how the association in power of the Communist party and a scattering of democratic groups dooms the latter to annihilation. The future balance of democracy depends on creating a strongly structured union of socialist and republican forces.
>
> But you will not bring about such a union by forming pacts with the enemies of the people, with the profiteers of an outmoded social system, with the anachronistic ambitions of the technocratic or military cliques. Our task is to struggle tooth and nail with whoever will join us against those groups that seized power on May 13. The conspiracy of May 13 must know that its insolent triumph, its intolerance, its privileges, its greedy appetite for jobs and honors are setting against it—and will set against it even more—all democrats, republicans, and liberals. They are the opponents of the ideology and methods of communism, but are aware that the danger threatening liberty and progress at the present time comes from a different direction. Each day brings a new tribulation. Anything is to be welcomed that will bring an end to the heartless politico-economic coalition that currently governs us, holds the state in its claws, and lacks in true greatness.

In other words, since de Gaulle was the representative of the privileged, technocratic, and military cliques, anything was justified in bringing them down. If this meant allying himself with the Communist devil, François Mitterrand was prepared to do so. He did not have any illusions about the Communist party. But after the triumph of the Gaullists ("that insolent clique") he believed the power relations in the opposition would inevitably change. The Communist party had just been severely damaged (it now had no more than eleven deputies) by the birth of the Fifth Republic. If all republicans, whether socialists or not, could unite and organize, they would soon represent a sufficiently strong force to embark on dangerous ventures. It was a calculation the new senator was not to forget. When he thought of reconquering power, he saw the Communists as horses; his friends and himself, as riders.

Was he already thinking he would be the man to bring those socialist and republican forces together, leading them to victory? If so, he was a very long way indeed from such an outcome.

Of course, he was not entirely alone. After July 1958, a new opposition tried to organize itself on the Left. On June 10, François Mauriac had written in his column in *L'Express*: "The Left is yet to be reconstituted." Pierre Mendès France, the socialists Daniel Mayer and Edouard Depreux, and Gilles Martinet (a brilliant journalist on *France Observateur*) decided to come together to create the Union des forces démocratiques (UFD). François Mitterrand joined them with what was left of the UDSR, but played only a secondary role. Encouragement and support came from certain trade unions (especially the teachers' union) and from groups that had opposed the Algerian War. Those on the Left who would have nothing to do with communism and could not see themselves in an SFIO, which had been so devalued by its North African policy, found themselves there.

It has been said François Mitterrand looked like a poor relation at the feast. Used to being first in his own outfit, he now found himself almost last in a group founded by others. He was moving into unknown territory, even discovering some very strange people indeed: left-wing Christians, trade unionists, rigid left-wing socialists. Gilles Martinet, an attentive witness, observed him smiling, "trying to make links, explore the terrain, make new friends, discreetly lay the foundations of new networks." But the natural, unchallenged leader of the UFD was Pierre Mendès France. In that forum, the former prime minister felt quite at home. His ambition was to transform that tiny mosaic into a true party (on the condition that others look after the logistics). In it, François Mitterrand played only a marginal role. In short, the new senator had to get used to a new train, one for which he was not the engine. He had no choice; philosophically, he resigned himself to it.

This is how, ten years later, Mitterrand described himself at this time: "I worked, dreamed, idled away my time, learned once again to love things and people. I got to know the holly of the forest of the Landes that gives time its density, and nothing speaks more eloquently of mind and matter than summer sunlight at six o'clock in the afternoon through an oak wood. I traveled, too. I went to Mao Tse-tung's China and to Iran."[10]

Was Mitterrand as serene as he liked to make out? Françoise Giroud, who knows him well, believes he was: "He's an exceptional case," she says, "for in him ambition has not killed the taste for the good things of life."

In any case, this wise philosophy did not come to him easily. Jacques Kosciusko-Morizet remembers how during a meeting at the home of Jean-Jacques Servan-Schreiber during the summer of 1958, François Mitterrand exclaimed angrily: "There'll never be enough lampposts in the Place de la Concorde to hang all those usurpers!"

WHILE HE DREAMED, IDLED away his time, sometimes pleaded in the law courts, and sometimes wrote or gave speeches—while he enjoyed the (for him) almost unknown delights of semi-idleness, a storm was brewing that was to leave him hurt and humiliated. This was the Observatoire affair, which he was to carry with him like a millstone round his neck.

In the morning of Friday, October 16, 1959, the political class was in a great state of excitement. It had just been learned that, during the night, unknown men had tried to assassinate François Mitterrand, senator for the Nièvre and a former minister.

It is a strange story, one that surprised and even frightened many people at a time when the difficulties in Algeria exacerbated passions and stirred in some unsteady brains dreams of assassination. François Mitterrand said he had been followed in his car through the Luxembourg district where he lived. He was worried, and left his own vehicle, a dark blue Peugeot 403, in the rue Auguste-Comte (exactly where, long ago, he used to meet Marie-Louise Terrasse, alias Catherine Langeais, at the time of their first love). Sensing his followers did not wish him well, he managed to jump over the railings of the Observatoire gardens, which were over three feet high. His attackers then fired shots into his car. The evidence consisted of seven bullet marks in the right-hand door and one bullet lodged in the driver's seat. He had had a close shave. ("Probably only his presence of mind saved M. Mitterrand's life," wrote newspapers of every political tendency.) His attackers had then driven off at top speed. The former minister rang on the door of the concierge at 5, avenue de l'Observatoire, to telephone the police. However, neighbors, who had heard gunshots, had already done so. It was past midnight.

Inspector Clot, head of the criminal brigade, soon arrived on the scene. Unfortunately, François Mitterrand could give only very meager details: he had been followed by a small, dark-colored car; he thought there had been two or three men. And to the press, which had rushed up with its microphones on, the man who had just escaped from a hateful assassination attempt refused to give any more information: "I am, like my political friends, a patriot. I am simply trying to serve France. It is sad that campaigns should be whipped up to this extent, setting French people against French people."

Still apparently shaken, he refused to say anything more. With mingled indignation and commiseration, everyone admired the sobriety of his words. And since Mitterrand was now counted among the advocates of a liberal solution in Algeria, the Ultras of French Algeria, the extreme Right, and the counterterrorists were suspected.

A number of people linked this assassination attempt with mysterious statements made by Gaullist Lucien Neuwirth, deputy for the Loire. Had not Neuwirth, who had played a crucial role in Algiers in 1958 (and had kept acquaintances there, but was no longer *persona grata* on account of his fidelity to General de Gaulle), remarked in the corridors of the Palais-Bourbon: "Commandos of killers have crossed the Spanish frontier and a list of well-known people to be killed has been drawn up"?

On the Left, there was general and immediate indignation. The Communist party demanded the government "take immediate steps to place the plotters and terrorists out of harm's way." The Communist labor federation, the CGT, condemned "this indescribable act" and called on workers "to redouble their efforts so that talks may be begun at the earliest possible time with the aim of effecting a cease-fire in Algeria and the free exercise of the right of self-determination." The Communist newspaper *L'Humanité* bore the headline: "Demand the Dissolution of the Fascist Bands." The UFD, genuinely shocked, called on "all democrats to be doubly vigilant." The SFIO expressed its solidarity.

In the meantime, throughout the weekend François Mitterrand received hundreds of affectionate and moving messages from all over France. He was a hero.

On Monday evening, the committee of the UFD met at five o'clock to work out its political reply and orchestrate the protests. There, among others, were Pierre Mendès France, Daniel Mayer, Gilles Martinet, and Edouard Depreux. But at six, François Mitterrand had still not turned up. At half past six, his secretary was kind enough to telephone the committee to tell them her employer would unfortunately not be able to come. Nevertheless, the committee decided to organize a press conference for Wednesday and called on the trade unions to join in the protest. Everyone looked worried, fearing fascist operations. Pierre Mendès France, by temperament and because he always feared a tragic end for a regime born from the favor of a military uprising, was already suspecting the worst.

As expected, the press conference took place on Wednesday at five o'clock at the Hôtel Moderne in the Place de la République. There was a big crowd. As usual, François Mitterrand was late. At half past five, thunderous applause broke out at the back of the hall: he had arrived at last, he was there. In the general emotion, the hero hinted that the brains behind the attempt might well lie closer to those in power than to the ultras in Algiers.

Was this young former minister so fearsome an opponent of the regime, then? And was that regime in such a sorry state that it had been driven to such extremes? There was not much time to ask these questions, for on Friday, a bombshell burst.

A certain Robert Pesquet, who had been administrative secretary of the RPF in the National Assembly and a Poujadist deputy for the Loir-et-Cher—a gray, curious, and excitable individual who had not left much of an impression in the corridors of the Palais-Bourbon—published a sensational article in the extreme right-wing weekly *Rivarol*. The assassination attempt, he maintained, had been set up, solely and entirely, by François Mitterrand himself.

The next day, in the corridors of the assembly, Jean-Marie Le Pen had gone about saying they would soon see what they would see: a real bombshell. And a bombshell it was. Some laughed, some smiled, some expressed incredulity—everyone was stupefied. But this Pesquet (whom it was later learned had had more than one brush with the law) persisted in his story. At a press conference, he declared he had met François Mitterrand on three occasions to plan the scenario of the false assassination attempt. They had agreed on the itinerary and methods to be used.

Of course, everyone protested it was too incredible, too absurd. But then Pesquet put forward solid bits of evidence: a few hours before the false attack (the dates stamped on the letters prove this), he had addressed to himself two letters, one to his home, the other to a *poste restante* at Lisieux in the Calvados. They were opened by the clerk of the court and described, in detail, the whole plot. Everything had taken place as planned, Pesquet explained, except that he had had to go round the gardens three times in his Renault Dauphine due to the unexpected presence first of a couple of lovers, then of a taxi. Then, being sure Mitterrand had left his vehicle and hidden among the bushes as planned, Pesquet had ordered his gardener, Abel Dahuron, to fire, so there would be no doubt of an assassination attempt. And on Monday, October 22, at six o'clock (the very time his friends in the UFD were expecting him), François Mitterrand had come to thank him at the Cristal, a bar in the sixteenth arrondissement.

After this press conference, there was a flood of sniggers and sarcastic remarks. On the Left, many were embarrassed, even downcast. Doubt wormed its way into the minds of those best disposed toward the senator for the Nièvre: if he had not lied, he had at least concealed the most important aspects of the business.[11]

It was felt that Mitterrand should explain himself, justify his actions (if at all possible). When questioned by the police again, François Mitterrand admitted he had met Robert Pesquet before the assassination attempt. He declared that he had been approached by him on October 7 at the Palais de Justice, where he was with Roland Dumas. At Pesquet's pressing invitation, the two agreed to have a drink with him at the café opposite. They talked. Pesquet insisted on paying the bill. But, as soon as Roland Dumas had gone,

Pesquet told Mitterrand that, in fact, he had been entrusted with the task of executing him. This, according to Mitterrand, is what Pesquet said: "I've become more and more involved in the affair—the men in Algiers are holding me, and they also want to kill Mendès, Mollet, and Pflimlin. I don't want to be their accomplice. I'm risking my life to warn you—don't go and denounce me and hand me over to the police." Mitterrand concluded he had made a mistake in placing too much trust in a man who did not deserve it, in having taken pity on a former colleague in distress, and in agreeing to go along with the bit of playacting he was proposing in order to save him. The former Garde des Sceaux insisted he had acted in complete good faith.

Yet his thesis did not answer all the questions. Why had he proved so trusting of someone so obviously odd? Why, on the other hand, had he said nothing of it to his closest friends (Georges Dayan, above all)? Why had he not warned either the police or the legal authorities, an action that should have been the first reflex of a former Garde des Sceaux and minister of the interior? François Mitterrand was not exactly lacking in experience and ought to have learned to mistrust plots—and to have enough friends in the upper echelons of the civil service to know whom he could trust. In short, even Mitterrand's friends had to admit he did not have much evidence to demonstrate his good faith. "Looked at from a distance, that stag at bay left a rather disagreeable impression," noted François Mauriac, who was nevertheless soon to defend him.

The press, of course, changed sides. The Socialist Claude Fuzier wrote in *Le Populaire*: "Suppose Pesquet is lying—what does that make him? Suppose he is telling the truth—then M. Mitterrand does not come out of it very well, but M. Pesquet will not be given a certificate of virtue simply because he had lent himself to this comedy." In other words, the organ of the SFIO accepted as an admissible hypothesis that Mitterrand was a man of no great worth.

In the corridors of *France Observateur*, the journalists were organizing a curious test: chairs were arranged up to the height of the Observatoire railings and everyone attempted to jump or step over the obstacle in order to demonstrate it was possible to surmount the hurdle as the senator had done. The entire editorial staff, of course, roared with laughter, and concluded there was every reason to doubt it. Such was the climate at the time. Radio and television (which were controlled by the government) and the right-wing press were even less sympathetic.

An isolated François Mitterrand bitterly defended himself. He wanted to protect his honor. On October 30 he wrote in *L'Express*: "Yes, I have been taken in by them. They have been waiting for me for five years; for five years I have been moving among traps and pitfalls. And on Thursday night, October 15, I fell into their ambush. I have never stopped turning over the matter in my mind and my heart is still oppressed by it. . . . Because a man came to me, confided his hesitation in shooting, asked me to help him save himself, five years of prudence, analysis, and patience suddenly collapsed and I find myself faced with solitude and the anguish of questions asked." His distress sounded genuine.

The hunted man was at least to find illustrious defenders, beginning with François Mauriac, who wrote in his *L'Express* column:

Mitterrand has paid dearly for being less strong than his enemies themselves believed him to be. And I am grateful for his weakness. It shows he belongs to a different species than those who have tripped him up and who, no doubt, guessed his secret weak spot. . . . Mitterrand was capable of trusting a depraved man who claimed to be unburdening his heart to him. . . . He could have been a writer like myself, telling stories instead of living through them. He has chosen to live them. But the consequence of this choice is a hardening of one's nature. He has hardened himself, I imagine, as much as would have been required at a time other than this. But today, it is the time of murderers.[12]

In the next issue of the same weekly, Pierre Mendès France threw his authority and prestige onto the scales, telling how a man, entrusted with the task of murdering Mendès France, had once warned him of it under the seal of secrecy:

I admire the assurance of those who declare, judge, and condemn with such severity, and who explain what they would have done in his place. Perhaps they would be less sure of themselves if, like him, like me, they had received over the years horrible letters of threat and blackmail; if their wives, their children had also been harassed; if they had had crude abuse shouted at them in the streets, through the cowardly medium of an anonymous telephone message, or in the columns of a newspaper specializing in defamation; if they had felt the fury and hatred of men hiding in the shadows, who promised them day after day the fate of a Jaurès or a Jean Zay, if not that of Salengro. Let those who are so certain of themselves reflect for a moment and examine their consciences: perhaps they will then view the statements and insinuations that have circulated recently with less credulity and less self-satisfaction.

This was clearly and well said. Although, during the affair of the leaks, Pierre Mendès France had shocked and hurt François Mitterrand with his hesitations (even his suspicions), this time he did not stint with his support or qualify his commitment. It is true, though (and this is a law of the political world), that opposition, especially when at the bottom of the curve, brings together men who become separated when in power because they are in fact rivals.

After the attacks of the press and his enemies, another danger threatened the senator from the Nièvre. The prime minister, Michel Debré, summoned the procurator of the Republic and, on October 27, the courts demanded the lifting of parliamentary immunity from François Mitterrand, who was charged with contempt of court for having "concealed valuable evidence that was in his possession." Clearly the Gaullist government intended exploiting to the full the opposition politician's silences and omissions concerning his relations with Robert Pesquet. But for anyone who knew François Mitterrand's psychology, this was a crude maneuver: in trying to plunge Mitterrand's head in the water, Michel Debré instead provided the man he was trying to drown with the raft that was to save him.

Until then Mitterrand, surrounded by sneers and opprobrium, had not known whom to blame for his plight, if not himself. Robert Pesquet? What interest would there be in exchanging words with a man whom he should never have agreed to see in the first place?

The press? It was impossible to stop people from laughing without making oneself an even greater object of ridicule. But a prime minister who dared claim he was bringing you through the courts, who had once come in person to beg your indulgence and insist upon his good faith in your office of Garde des Sceaux in the Place Vendôme—that was too much, that was unforgivable.

For that same Michel Debré had himself been in the position of a defendant in January 1957. It was claimed he had been one of the men behind the bazooka attack directed against General Salan, the commander in chief of Algeria, which had cost the life of one of his officers, Major Rodier. Two thugs, Kovacs and Castille (of the same type as Robert Pesquet), had tried to implicate Senator Michel Debré, a Gaullist and virulent opponent, and a young unknown deputy named Valéry Giscard d'Estaing. And what had François Mitterrand done when the judges had advised him to request the lifting of parliamentary immunity from Michel Debré? He had summoned his opponent to the Place Vendôme and asked him to explain his actions, and, having listened to him, he decided not to implement the judges' request.

Pierre Nicolaÿ, then head of François Mitterrand's office, recounts: "Michel Debré was a friend; it had taken me a week to get through to him and persuade him to come and explain his position to the minister. When he came, he lost his temper. Yet our intentions toward him could not have been better. We acted entirely correctly with him. . . . His thanks was to bar my career throughout the Fifth Republic. . . ."

Nearly three years after this serious incident, François Mitterrand had reasons for thinking he was not being paid back in kind, a realization that gave a new edge to his indignation. And wasn't an opponent in his own class the best of therapies?

On November 18, when the rapporteur, an independent republican named Delalande, formally accepted the lifting of parliamentary immunity while stressing that "the senate's decision did not in itself in any way stain the honor of François Mitterrand," Mitterrand himself rushed to the rostrum and delivered a passionate plea that was a list of charges against the government as well as a defense of his own cause. Indeed, he delivered two fierce blows to his accusers. First, he revealed that, on the afternoon of October 22 (the same day Pesquet issued his denunciation in the press),

Maurice Bourgès-Maunoury, a former prime minister who was not among Mitterrand's personal friends, told the head of National Security that he, too, had been threatened in exactly the same way a month before and had immediately informed his minister. Mitterrand added: "From October 22 to November 3—that is, for twelve whole days—the government kept silent, thus preventing the law, the police, and myself, as well as public opinion and yourselves, from contradicting the main charge directed against me—namely, that I was the instigator of a fake assassination attempt." And the senator from the Nièvre pointed out, suddenly triumphant: "Bourgès was subjected to the same scenario, the same technique, the same agent provocateur, who, as you have admitted, was none other than Pesquet."

Second, since attack is the best means of defense, François Mitterrand set about recounting in detail, in the midst of an astonished silence, the bazooka affair. He described a politician in a highly uncomfortable position who acknowledged "the existence, in the file, of incriminating evidence and disturbing confessions." On the rostrum, Mitterrand described the scene in the Place Vendôme, revealed the man who had stood opposite him and been subjected to those accusations:

He would explain everything later, he said. He only needed a little time. But he would not have enough time, if, setting the legal machinery in motion, I threw certain names on the tender mercies of public opinion without further examination, . . . if I requested the lifting of parliamentary immunity. Yesterday's opponent did not hesistate to demand the guarantees of the law— and he obtained them. What could be more natural? The man who nervously paced up and down the room did not hesitate to request the protection of the government when he felt his rights were in danger—and the government protected him. . . . That man is the prime minister, Michel Debré. [Then followed various disturbances on the benches.] Ladies and gentlemen, there are certain things one has no right to do: to play, or allow others to play, with the honor of a political adversary and try to disqualify the opposition by abusively tarring it with criminal deeds.

François Mitterrand had scored a point—a very big one. The astonished senators, now unsure of what to do, decided it was a matter of urgency to postpone their decision and send the file before the ad hoc commission. Gaullist Jean-Louis Vigier, who had not spared François Mitterrand at the time of the leaks affair, made honorable amends. "Do you accept the measures that have been taken against him?" he asked the parliamentarians. "An attempt has been made to disturb his balance, and I would like to be sure it has not succeeded."

Yet those feelings were short-lived. Questioned at the end of a cabinet meeting, the head of government muttered a laconic: "M. Mitterrand has lied yet again." In the atmosphere of the time—when Gaullism and its leaders were in triumph—that was enough. The senators recovered. The battle was not yet over; they had nearly been taken in by eloquence. Now they saw nothing but the opponent: on November 25, by a large majority (175 votes to 12 abstentions, 77 senators not taking part in the vote), the lifting of François Mitterrand's parliamentary immunity was passed. Although the Communist group, a few Socialists like Gaston Deferre and Emile Aubert, and a few individuals like Edgar Faure, Pierre Marcilhacy, and Edgar Pisani supported him, the whole Right—from Jean Lecanuet to the Gaullists—and most of the SFIO senators voted against him.

Thus, on December 8, the Observatoire affair ended with the indictment of François Mitterrand. It ended because, paradoxically, the legal process was not carried any further—as if the government, satisfied it had shaken an opponent, was trying to avoid controversy and the embarrassment of a trial. When, during the presidential campaign, the Gaullists wanted to exploit the Observatoire affair to embarrass the candidate Mitterrand, the general refused: "We must not attack the honor of a man who might one day be president of the Republic," he replied, according to Léon Noël.

In fact, the target had already been reached. From then on, a shadow of doubt hovered (and still hovers) over the opposition leader.[13] Of course, nobody really believes any more that François Mitterrand was the instigator of the mock assassination attempt. But many people still wonder what his precise role was in that shady affair. He probably believed a plot was being devised against

him. A month before the Observatoire affair, his friend Bernard
Finifter had gone to Jean Verdier, director of National Security,
asking for a bulletproof vest, without saying for whom it was intended. And the previous summer Mitterrand had said: "I have to
sleep in a different place every night because de Gaulle wants to
kill me."[14] No doubt, too (and this is the opinion of many of his
friends), he wanted to turn to his advantage and to the detriment
of the government a threat in which he really believed. By getting
caught in too fine a net, he was to pay dearly for trying to be too
clever. Even today some of his followers admit they do not really
understand what happened. They even admit that the more their
leader tried to explain it to them, the more confused the affair
seemed.

In any case, it left deep marks on Mitterrand himself and had a
decisive effect on his political development. Those close to him at
the time noted two very different attitudes in him. After Pesquet's
revelations, he was dejected, distressed, almost prostrate. Several
people saw him with tears in his eyes. Some were even afraid he
might make some desperate gesture. And then Michel Debré arrived. François Mitterrand immediately bounced back.

From then on, he was able to steel his will and recover a role
and his authority. He was to rebuild his career, stone by stone,
against the Gaullist enemy. "Against the supposedly impenetrable
obstacle, there now came on the scene amour propre, that terrible
desire to be oneself, to prove to oneself before proving to others
that everything is always possible providing one is determined
enough."[15] The essence of Mitterrand is there.

From then on, he was no longer the same. He vowed an inveterate
hatred for the Gaullists and for those who supported the regime.
Hatred of the bourgeois reappears in his writings like a refrain:
"At Jarnac, at Nevers, in my Paris street, in my stalag alleyway, I
had already met them. In a way, I was one of them; because we
had the same background, because we spoke the same words in
the same way, because we had received the rudiments of the same
culture, because we wore the same clothes, they treated me as an
accomplice or a partner—until the day I realized we had nothing
to say to one another, the day I could bear to hear them no longer."[16]
And again: "For ten years (ten years too many) I was close to that

milieu of the *Tout-Paris*, which endlessly repeats the same things in the same tone of voice without ever growing tired of them, convinced it exercises a government over morals, whereas it no longer even inspires fashion. I was attracted, yes, by what now exacerbates me: the cocktail of little drugs a society administers to itself year in and year out—a society that believes it is quelling pressures when it has only needs!'"[17]

"The Observatoire was a social break for him—he isolated himself, then reconstructed a character for himself," notes André Rousselet. Georges Beauchamp relates: "Danielle was wonderful for him. She kept telling him: 'You've nothing in common with those people [the bourgeois].' "[18]

Mitterrand also knew whom he could depend on. His friends were still there. He realized that when, a week after the lifting of his parliamentary immunity, Georges Dayan and André Rousselet took him off to the Hôtel Moderne, then a favorite haunt of the Left, where they had gathered together some fifty followers. François Mitterrand arrived, very pale, very tense, in an atmosphere no less so. Then he started to talk. Those who were there listened to a flow of words all about dignity, injustice, and honor. He talked on and on, and, miraculously, like a lark intoxicated with its own song, he relaxed, recovered his color. The atmosphere subtly changed and became warmer. When he finished talking, his friends surrounded him, applauding. Not everything was lost: his friends were there.

Communist friends from the Resistance then began to drop in on him in his office. He made this admission to Robert Paumier: "Our sin would be to allow de Gaulle to give himself a successor." Yet he was still a long way from being able to stop the general. But he knew more than ever who his enemy was, and from that moment, rediscovered his destiny.

ABSOLUTE EVIL

After the Observatoire affair, François Mitterrand, not down, but seriously wounded, meditated on his life. It is easy to imagine him, walking alone through the misty forests of the Morvan, pondering his grievances against a regime born in equivocation, on the edge of legality; against the general, who was taking all power for himself without protest from the people; and against Michel Debré, who had had the temerity to try to teach him a lesson, and who assumed the airs of a statesman. Above all, Mitterrand cursed an evil destiny that had cut his career short—a malevolent fate that had brought him so many trials.

Fortunately, he still had the instinct that drove him to fight and to say no: no to conservatism, but also to the reforms of the Fifth Republic; no to the bourgeoisie, to its men, its works, and its pomps. The man from the Nièvre was becoming the "Mr. Nyet" of the Fifth Republic. For him, it was not enough to oppose. He did much more: he rejected in advance, fought systematically, opposed on principle. The Republic of General de Gaulle was evil incarnate to Mitterrand, so he became the St. George of good, pursuing it relentlessly.

Later he declared: "As the leader of the RPF, General de Gaulle behaved toward the Fourth Republic in an extremely demagogic way, blinded as he was by the ambition to recover a power he had imprudently abandoned. He was indeed a master in the art of unconditional opposition."[19] But did it occur to Mitterrand that this definition might quite easily be applied to himself?

In fact, although the year 1960 saw him astonishingly silent (L'Année politique does not mention his name once; he needed a little more time before resuming the attack), from 1961 on he was to launch a series of unremitting verbal attacks on the regime. In his eyes, there was nothing good to be said about it.

In an article in L'Express of July 1961, which cannot be read today without a smile, he writes: "Personally, I believe aspirations to the presidential regime correspond in France to an admission of failure. The presidential regime tends to personal power." And on July 17, 1962, he declared to the senate: "Well, yes, this regime which, it is said, has no name—which, it is wrongly claimed, is situated between the presidential and parliamentary regimes—has never borne anything but one name at any time, and that is dictatorship." And on July 5, 1961, he told the senate: "A regime, M. le premier ministre, that prefers popular ovations to votes of confidence in the parliament—a regime that takes account of the threat of crowds more than of the violated law—is not a Republic."

When, in August 1962, after the assassination attempt at Petit-Clamart that nearly cost General and Mme de Gaulle their lives, the president announced his intention to propose by referendum the election of the head of state by direct universal suffrage, the future Socialist leader responded indignantly. Again in *L'Express*, under the headline "Custard Tart," he wrote: "This reform is not aimed at endowing France with stable institutions. It tends to perpetuate the present adventure. . . . The time will come when one will be able to discuss the comparative merits of parliamentary democracy and presidential democracy. Then we shall compare the list of advantages against the list of disadvantages presented by this custard tart the presidential regime has become."

The method used (the referendum) did not meet with Mitterrand's approval either. "One is already astonished at the ingenuity of certain law professors," he wrote sarcastically, "who see being hatched by the grace of a fake referendum and a glaring omission in article eighty-nine the presidential regime of their dreams." This was a double no, to both form and substance.

The French did not share his opinion, ratifying the project by 62.5 percent of the votes cast.

The electors of the Nièvre did not hold his hostility to the referendum against him this time and, a month later on November 18, elected him once more to the Palais-Bourbon. In the midst of the Gaullist landslide (the UNR won 31.9 percent of the votes and 233 deputies), the pure, uncompromising opponent regained his seat and a platform better suited to the polemical ferocity of his talent.

Any subject was grist for his mill: de Gaulle's *force de frappe* (France's independent nuclear deterrent) in particular and defense policy in general, foreign policy, African policy, social policy, the new municipal electoral law, and so on.

On the *force de frappe*, he declared in the National Assembly on January 24, 1963: "On the basis of an independent, national atomic force, which is no more inside Europe than it is inside the Atlantic Alliance, there is no possible constructive solution . . . among our partners of the European Six. Are you so sure our national atomic force will not, in the years (if not in the months) to come, give rise to serious difficulties? For example, what will you do

if one of the Six demands, as would be quite normal to an ally possessing this force, to share its secrets, or even to use its atomic
weapons? . . ."

On foreign policy, he jibbed at "the irritation and neglect it shows
with regard to the United Nations," and, on several occasions,
attacked the Franco-German treaty that had been signed by Chancellor Adenauer and General de Gaulle. In January 1963, he declared: "You believe reconciliation between the French and German
peoples is good and necessary in itself. But there is nothing to stop
you from asking whether it was urgent to stress at this point the
particular understanding between the two states. There is no reason
why you cannot question the timeliness of this Franco-German
agreement."[20]

On African policy, he declared on June 10, 1964: "An attempt
is being made to replace the community with agreements of cooperation, but . . . the policy of aid to the developing countries,
the policy of leadership in the Third World, is merely the result of
an incredible series of failures in every area of foreign policy." In
1966, he wrote in *Combat républicain*: "The underlying content
of Gaullist foreign policy is essentially negative. . . ." Or again,
addressing Georges Pompidou, he said: "Your policy is a sort of
Poujadism magnified to the dimensions of the universe."

Mitterrand found no good whatsoever in the government's internal policy—it was all to be scrapped. Did the government want,
as in July 1963 (after a series of spectacular strikes in the Paris
transport system), to draw up legislation affecting strikes—that is,
to establish a compulsory five-day warning? Yet, in 1947, François
Mitterrand, who had warmly approved of various governments'
firmness on such occasions, now denounced "the enterprise that is
first of all an attack on individual rights that have been recognized
since the advent of democracy . . . and is now an attack on the
collective rights of trade unionism and the right to strike." "From
an excessive power to constitutional failures, from arbitrary acts
to denials of justice," Mitterrand wrote, "you are trying to give
absolute power the sanction of the law."

On the legal system, the establishment of special courts to deal
with matters affecting state security aroused his anger: "To my
mind," he said, "they contradict the very principles of the republican state."

The educational system, Mitterrand declared, benefited only "the privileged classes, those of the lower- and upper-middle class—in fact, those determined to enter and win the educational rat race."

On the public service, he condemned the widening of the regional prefects' powers (during the first stage of the Fifth Republic, he even refused to go to the prefecture of the Nièvre to avoid greeting a representative of that accursed regime, which he regarded as being "the grip of the central power and administration on local liberties"). This was a familiar target.

Economic policy inspired Mitterrand even less. He blamed it, of course, and pleaded for a "use of democratic planning, better-balanced regional plans"; he attacked "the hesitations of industrial decentralization"; and he demanded "the municipalization of building land." But he always posed the most clearly economic questions in institutional terms. For there he was more at ease—there he could criticize better.

Mitterrand stuffed his interventions with references to the coup d'état of December 2 (1852) and endlessly exploited the comparison between the Gaullist regime and Napoleon III's despotism (the comparison being, of course, not with the great Napoleon).

When, on March 20, 1964, the government set about altering the municipal electoral law (for towns of over thirty thousand inhabitants), introducing the majority principle of blocked lists, François Mitterrand almost became the champion of a form of proportional representation he had once so forcefully attacked. This was so much so that Marius Durbet, the conservative mayor of Nevers, feeling there were limits to one's patience, interrupted the speaker to remind him of a few personal memories: "You say that proportional representation had many virtues. Of course, it is equitable. But I have lived with you as a municipal councillor. Must I remind you that because of that system, none of my original budgets, supplementary budgets, or administrative accounts were passed by the opposition majority, of which you were part and which did everything to prevent me from running my city?"

Interrupted in this way, Mitterrand did not lower his guard; on the contrary, he redoubled his aggressiveness: "This electoral bill," he declared, "is in direct line with the arbitrary texts that were recently imposed on municipal housing, in direct line with the abuses revealed by the composition of the communes and regional structures, and in direct line with the Napoleonic power accorded the prefects, whom you expect to carry out your instructions wherever possible before the first ballot. . . . What this bill does is add one more tool to the panoply of personal power." And he concluded: "Long ago, Gaullism was a mystique; rather late in the day, you have made it a policy; now you are making it a form of cooking."

In the atmosphere of the time, anyone who threw such banderillas with such zeal was obviously exposing himself to the Gaullists' ire. Whenever François Mitterrand spoke in the National Assembly, the Gaullists unleashed their anger on him, reminding him of "the *francisque* and the Observatoire." On May 21, 1964, for example, two Gaullists, Gabriel Kaspéreit, deputy for Paris (ninth arrondissement), and his colleague Pierre Bas (pronounced Basse—fourth arrondissement), outdid themselves, provoking a serious incident. While François Mitterrand was vilifying the minister of the interior, Pierre Bas shouted out: "M. Frey did not jump over the Observatoire railings!" Tempers rose and Mitterrand hit the bull's eye with his reply: "M. Bas and I have known each other for a long time, ever since the time when, as minister of France overseas, I had to reprimand him."

There was a storm in the assembly. At the end of the debate, Pierre Bas, a former civil servant in the Ministry of France Overseas, asked to speak, defying François Mitterrand to explain when, where, how, and why he had committed an administrative offense and what punishment he had received. The accuser was extremely vague in his replies. But he proposed forming a jury of honor. Unfortunately, agreement could not even be reached on the procedure to be followed.

The next day, Pierre Bas, whose anger had not diminished, met François Mitterrand in the library of the National Assembly. He threw himself at the deputy for the Nièvre and struck him—without even resorting to the customary challenge.

Thus occurred another scandal in the Palais-Bourbon, echoes of which reached the press. It was an episode that was soon forgotten, except by the deputy for Paris, who still claims it as his first act of resistance against socialism, and for the deputy for the Nièvre, who saw it as further proof of the masked violence of that "dictatorship in kid gloves."

François Mitterrand's pugnacity tended to overheat; gradually it made him the most feared opposition speaker—even if his opponents pretended not to fear him. Questioned about him one day, Prime Minister Georges Pompidou remarked, exasperated: "Everything he says has no bearing on anything. Mitterrand is the very image of what France no longer wants to see again—in short, he is nothing but a ghost."[21]

When one goes into opposition, it soon becomes convenient (after the initial period of frustration—the loss of power, prestige, and conveniences, the humiliation of defeat) to represent a counterpower, a new form of influence. One feels less powerful, of course, but in an infinitely more comfortable situation. Removed from the daily worries of government, the complexity of decision making, the weighing of contradictory arguments, and the thanklessness of administration, two attitudes are possible: either one is convinced of one's uselessness and adopts a serene resignation, or one continues to say no and ends up considering oneself some kind of Joan of Arc, a savior of France. François Mitterrand "owed his personal and political salvation to the insolence of his rejection."[22]

Always saying no places one on the side of the just since one rejects any compromise, since one substitutes the desirable for the possible and the ideal for the real, since one can dream, in the name of morality and justice for the weak and oppressed, of all the utopias the man running things has no time to think about. In opposition François Mitterrand, the moralizing Catholic, could indulge in his favorite activity: the lyricist with his love of words could allow himself to be carried away by his inspiration, the literary man could coin phrases, the politician could theorize at leisure.

As if to create a character for himself and justify himself, the deputy for the Nièvre took up his pen. In publishing *Le Coup d'état permanent* in 1964, he confirmed his position as one of the foremost and most determined adversaries of the regime. The book is a well-written pamphlet. It is a pamphlet because it seeks to be neither just nor lucid, but to wound, to avenge (in particular, against Michel Debré). It also aims to remind the world that its writer has talent and is available for any struggle against Gaullism.

In these pages, everyone and everything "gets it": Gaullism, of course, but also the institutions, the notables, the bourgeois, who have certainly become his enemies:

> I call the Gaullist regime a dictatorship because, when all is said and done, that is what it is like; because it is moving ineluctably toward a continuous strengthening of state power; and because it no longer depends on him [de Gaulle] to change direction. I am quite willing to concede that this dictatorship was established despite de Gaulle. I am quite willing to call this dictator by a pleasanter name: *podestà*. A king without a crown seems to me even more to be feared.

But it is perhaps on the subject of the Constitutional Council that François Mitterrand allowed himself to become most polemical: "The Supreme Court of the Musée Grévin [the famous Paris waxworks museum], the pitiful hat of a pitiful democracy, is defended by no one. Set up to force the legislator to respect the limitations placed upon his sphere of activity . . . it never had any other purpose than to serve as de Gaulle's errand boy whenever the general thought fit to use it for that purpose."

And, to reinforce his thesis, he quotes a sentence written by Senator Marcilhacy in *Le Figaro* of February 22, 1960: "It seems to me that its [the Constitutional Council's] role is to force the law to serve the state."[23]

Mitterrand concludes this very well-written polemic:

> The power of a single man, even if consecrated for a time by general consent, is an insult to the people, to the citizens. . . . The abuse lies not in the use it makes of its power, but in the very nature of that power. . . . There can be nothing but an unconditional opposition when it is a question of substituting one system of government for another. To make this or that minor change to absolute power, to adapt it, to correct it, is already to come to terms with it. It is to act out the part of His Majesty's opposition, which participates in the regime and supports it just as much as does the majority.

François Mitterrand's readers were warned. If one day he returned to power, it would be to destroy those institutions and construct a new regime. At least, that is what he said.

THE FIRST CANDIDACY

No one would have envied the situation of the senator for the Nièvre in the years immediately following the Observatoire affair. Of course, he had kept a handful of faithful friends and his local support. But as for the rest, the UDSR was in ruins, his personal reputation badly damaged, and his future prospects bleak. Gaullism, his absolute enemy, was still in triumph. And the non-Communist opposition did not regard him kindly.

His efforts to join the various groups that had emerged in that opposition (such as the UFD), which he had patiently begun as soon as the general had returned to power, were suddenly impeded. The parties being formed in this political area preferred him outside. Charles Hernu, a new friend and former deputy of the Front républicain who had been swept aside by the landslide of 1958, an organizer of the very Mendésist Club of Jacobins, put out feelers on Mitterrand's behalf asking leaders of the new PSU,[24] which had brought together various politicians of the "small Left" (Gilles Martinet, Jean Poperen, Edouard Depreux, Pierre Bérégovoy, Pierre Mendès France, Michel Rocard), what kind of reception François Mitterrand would get if he asked to join. The answer was hardly encouraging. It was, in fact, a resounding no: not a single one of them said yes. The Autonomous Socialist Party did not want François Mitterrand's support, the most vehement opponent being Alain Savary.

How, then, could he exist politically? How could he make his weight felt? How could he emerge from isolation? With all the patience and obstinacy of a mountaineer, François Mitterrand began one of those climbs about which only he had the secret. Assisted by Charles Hernu, who made the introductions, he went from club to club, association to association; whatever bore, proudly or timorously, the colors of the non-Communist Left, but lay outside the traditional machines (SFIO and Radical party), was a fair target.

Fortunately, the times were auspicious. The year 1958 saw the smashing of many traditional party machines. In Paris (but also in the provinces), there had sprung up dozens of circles and clubs attended by senior civil servants, trade unionists, university teachers, and young employers who could not feel at home in any of the political parties, who regarded the ideologies and structures of the parties as archaic, who were still mistrustful of the Gaullists (the end of the Algerian War increased the numbers of these), and who were agitating together to revive the Center and Left.

All these groups took up a great deal of François Mitterrand's time. Like a ferret, he went out every weekend, scouring the country for audiences outside the main political institutions. Always enterprising, he founded, together with a number of independent-minded men close to radicalism and socialism, the Ligue pour le combat républicain. His new colleagues included the journalist Joseph Barsalou, editorial writer on the powerful *Dépêche du Midi*, the faithful Louis Mermaz, and Ludovic Tron, a Left-inclined *inspecteur des finances* who was not without money of his own. In May 1963, the Ligue linked up with Charles Hernu's Club of Jacobins. Thus was born a new association, the Centre d'action institutionelle (CAI), which set out "to make the democratic ideal triumph in France" (it was a vague program, as one can see).[25]

As if by chance, François Mitterrand became its first president. The executive committee of the association comprised Charles Hernu, Georges Beauchamp, Louis Mermaz, and René William Thorp, chairman of the French Bar Council. The landscape was hardly changing: the same men came together and carried on as usual. It was a question of getting known and holding the stage: on September 15, 1963, at Saint-Honoré-les-Bains in François Mitterrand's constituency, this little group organized a "luncheon of a thousand," to which eight hundred local politicians were invited. The idea was to revive the great ancient tradition of republican banquets. Charles Hernu remembers the aims of the meeting: to confederate the democratic socialist Left, for, he explains, "only a body containing the men of the old parties and clubs would be capable of getting the Left out of the rut into which it had slid since 1958."

One aim can hide another: the other, longer-term grand design was obviously to put up a single candidate for the presidential election. François Mitterrand sensed the importance of this constitutional innovation, which he had opposed. The next such election would be in 1965; it was urgent to rally the flock. He declared: "Why not come together as soon as possible? Tomorrow, nothing will be like yesterday if we make up our minds."

From then on, the president of the CAI could legitimately declare he was no longer either alone or outside the mainstream. Indeed, he was very free in saying so and in repeating it, his speeches invariably beginning with some such words as "My friends and I think," "My friends and I consider," and so on. Having felt abandoned and even rejected for so long, how pleasant it must have been to speak in the plural—at least for a time. When François Mitterrand later took control of the Socialist party—and even more when he was in the Elysée—he graduated to use of the sovereign *I*, which he was to employ (indeed, almost abuse) very freely.

Of course, the group was careful at the "luncheon of a thousand" (which was in fact eight hundred) not to mention a candidacy for the future presidential election. Yet François Mitterrand certainly had his own ideas on the matter:

> From 1962—that is, since the time it had been decided the election of the president of the Republic would take place by universal suffrage—I knew I would be a candidate. When? How? I could not predict it—I was alone. I had neither support nor party, nor Church, nor counter-Church, nor newspaper, nor current of opinion. I had no money, and I could expect none of the traditional, if discreet, sources of distribution that are all too well known. . . . These were all reasons not to be a candidate. But there were just as many reasons why I should be.[26]

This fierce opponent of electing the president of the Republic by direct universal suffrage was thus working out his strategy solely in terms of his candidacy in such an election. With his usual obstinacy, his rare ability to conceive subtle, complex, secret plans, Mitterrand knuckled down to the task early in 1963.

This is understandable: having decided that evil lay in Gaullism, it was easy to find good in the non-Communist Left. For a man imbued with Christian nostalgia and feeling, what could be more natural than to want to be a good shepherd? But Mitterrand was still not accepted in the community of the Left.

Although it was relatively easy for him to impose his authority among the *"clubistes"*—those somewhat muddleheaded amateurs neither obsessed with hierarchy nor concerned about who to put up as candidate—his official entry into the non-Communist Left would be more difficult. There the party machines put in the way of newcomers their two principal forces: inertia and "jobs for the boys." There he was expected to provide accounts of his good intentions and to justify past actions. These posts were jealously competed for.

Fortunately, in those early 1960s, the situation was no longer sewn up. The SFIO was in a pitiful state (in the legislative elections of 1962, it had just achieved its worst result—11 percent—in over half a century); its titular leader, Guy Mollet, had been since the Algerian War the most disputed man of the Left. The Radicals had barely managed to survive the war. Careerists were looking toward Gaullism.

Since not every way was closed off in the non-Communist Left, François Mitterrand set about using his usual tactic of infiltrating from the edges. At this time indeed, Georges Brutelle, assistant general secretary of the SFIO, was making a number of attempts to revive his party. He organized conferences and seminars, in which there recurred the obsessional question: how is the Left to be revived? "Guy Mollet had given me the green light," he explained, "but on one condition: I was not to invite people who might offend him." He therefore refrained from inviting François Mitterrand. But once again, Mitterrand sent one of his friends as a scout. In the PSU it had been Charles Hernu; this time it was Beauchamp, one of his most faithful friends, who suggested inviting the former minister. "I thought about it," Georges Brutelle recounts, "but was afraid of what Guy Mollet's reaction would be. . . . Then I made up my mind. At the beginning, Mitterrand was very discreet, but very assiduous—he was always there."

François Mitterrand had to be content with the short periods of time allotted to him to make speeches. He was not a fashionable figure but a newcomer who had to prove himself. Patient and imperturbable, he acquiesced. And since he was a much better speaker than many of the others, he often won support. No matter that he was criticized for the length of his speeches—in a few minutes everything could be said, above all, his loyalty to the socialist Left.

Before his audiences, which included (on a personal basis) members of the SFIO, Radical party, PSU, UDSR, clubs, and trade unions (particularly the teachers' and young farmers' unions), he tirelessly repeated: "I say at once to our organized socialist friends: there is no divergence between us. . . . When it is a question of choosing one's friends, one's enemies, one's struggle, the future one imagines for one's country, I genuinely believe the socialist choice is the only response to the Gaullist experience. This is my position of principle, and I do not feel I have to take examinations every six months in this area."

That was clear enough. The man who, as a child, sang "I am a Christian, that is my glory" now sang out with the same fervor "I am a socialist, that is my vocation." But if he sang loudly, it was because such a long apprenticeship was being imposed upon him. Many saw him arrive with a smile playing around the corners of his mouth. He felt people's reticence toward him, knew their mistrust. As a neophyte of socialism, he still had to prove himself.

And he did—in the end, prejudice was overcome. With each day grew the numbers of those who were willing to admit that so resolute an opponent, so fierce an adversary of Gaullism—a member of the Rassemblement démocratique in the assembly presided over by Maurice Faure, a former minister of the Front républicain who remained faithful to Guy Mollet to the end—was, if not a brother or relation, at least a fit ally, especially since, sustained by the faith of recent converts, he was now advancing by leaps and bounds. On December 10, 1963, Mitterrand wrote in *Le Courrier de la Nièvre*: "My attitude toward the Communist party is simple: anything that helps in the struggle against and victory over a regime tending to the dictatorship of a single man and the establishment of a single party[27] is good. Four or five million electors—who belong to the people, who are workers—vote Communist. To neglect their help and votes would be either culpable or, quite simply, stupid."

Thus François Mitterrand had quite overtly contravened the great taboo of the non-Communist Left, which, at this time, regularly rejected any electoral alliance with the Communist party. In other words, he was beginning to turn the SFIO to the Left.

Unfortunately, he was not alone in eyeing the presidential election. While he was undergoing this hasty preparation for his entry into socialism from the outside, with the idea of catching up with (and even going beyond) all those laying claim to the candidacy on the basis of seniority, other (indeed more senior) men were on their way.

On December 18, 1963, Gaston Deferre, mayor of Marseille and Guy Mollet's eternal rival inside the SFIO, declared his intention of being a candidate. He had been encouraged by small associated groups, especially in the Club Jean-Moulin and by the brilliant journalists on L'Express. These last had, so to speak, a left-wing sensibility, but had realized before the others that the presidential election would now be the determining event of French political life. These modernists had even carried out a public opinion poll to define the type of head of state the French would like to see succeed General de Gaulle. Thus they had learned that the French wanted, above all, stability, security of employment, and a political relaxation; that they accepted without any special enthusiasm the institutions of the Fifth Republic (contrary to a large section of the political class, which hated them); and that they wanted a president who was closer and more human—less heroic, in fact. L'Express published these results, which caused quite a stir. All that remained was to find the candidate who measured up to these requirements.

In order to win 50 percent of the vote, this ideal individual would have to obtain the votes not only of the entire Left (Communists included) but also of the Center. The program was vast, and riddled with contradictions. There could be no question of negotiating with the Communist party, but it was also impossible to ignore its electors. It was necessary to interest the MRP (or what remained of it) while remaining firmly on the Left. What was needed, then, was a new man, a modern socialist—one who was open, a man of dialogue, not too fixed in his views. One name emerged, that of Gaston Deferre, whose image at the time was more or less the exact opposite of what it has become today. For a time he was to bear the weight of the aspirations of all those young men on the Left and Center-Left who wanted their country to move with the times.

François Mitterrand had no choice. Since he wanted to be of the Left and was anxious to participate in this modernist current, he had to applaud it—which he did without wasting a day. In *Le Monde*, he wrote: "We asked for a captain to lead the French team that is to fight personal power. I approve Gaston Deferre's decision, I tell him there will be many of us ready to lend him a hand. I believe M. Deferre's candidacy is good for the opposition."

Good for the opposition? Perhaps, but not for him. He had just been overtaken. All that was left for him to do was to turn himself into a faithful member of the team—until something better turned up.

Mitterrand took part in the meetings of Horizon 80, the association supporting the candidacy of the Marseille mayor, but did not show great zeal: "He arrived very late at the meetings," says Claude Estier (which surprised no one). He also took part in a few public meetings, in which he did not emerge as a very enthusiastic advocate of the operation. All the same, Olivier Chevrillon, current president/managing director of *Point* and then a great supporter of the Marseille mayor (even placing the Council of State at his disposal to organize his campaign), today attests to François Mitterrand's "perfectly correct behavior."

Sometimes Mitterrand even admitted his reservations. Thus, on June 7, 1964, before the Convention des institutions républicaines (at a time when Gaston Deferre's candidacy was at its zenith), he declared: "Deferre exists; he is a socialist. He is the elected representative of his own party and he is a candidate. Our duty is to find out how we can help him. It is without the slightest hesitation—*though I have many criticisms to make of him* [my italics]—that I feel it necessary to support Deferre."

Did he hope to see other possible partners of the Marseille mayor torpedo Deferre's attempt (thereby opening up the way)? It is quite likely. Gaston Deferre's candidacy came up against too many habits, upset too many party machines, aroused too many old hostilities. And in any case, the mayor of Marseille was not a model of political skill. It was not just to defeat General de Gaulle that he threw himself into the race; he also wanted—and said so, and his supporters repeated it—to change the rules of the political game.

His aim was the birth of "a grand federation that would bring together the whole of the non-Communist Left and Christian democrats"—again, a vast program, which immediately revived the rather dusty quarrel between the clericals and anticlericals.

From the outset, Gaston Deferre had against him his old enemy Guy Mollet—"my best electoral agent," General de Gaulle quipped. The leaders of the MRP, driven in this direction by their membership, collaborated—but reluctantly. They wanted to change but not renounce their beliefs. The process was going round in circles. The unions, interested in the beginning, began to worry about the candidacy's partisan character. How was the insoluble problem of the Communists to be resolved? The equation was always the same: one wanted the Communist party electors, but had to pretend to ignore its leaders. Gaston Deferre's anti-communism was so overt and overwhelming that he did not dream for a moment of negotiating with them. Indeed, during the municipal elections of 1965 in Marseille, he had to fight on a double front: against the Gaullists on his right and the Communists on his left. He won, ruthlessly ridding himself of the few local Socialists who had made a pact with the Communist party.[28] And, at the beginning of 1965, he firmly committed himself to ignoring the party, if not its electors: "If I am nominated on February 3 by the extraordinary national congress of the Socialist party, I shall not open up talks with the Communist party (PC). I shall not negotiate with it. I shall not accept a common program."

On June 18, 1965 (a doubly happy anniversary for the Gaullists), Gaston Deferre's attempt collapsed: the marriage did not take place between the Socialists and centrists, and the grand federation was torpedoed. The Communist party was delighted; the party machinery now breathed more freely. For François Mitterrand, the way was open. He had proved himself, more or less, to be a man of the Left; he had been loyal. Now he could put his plans into operation.

But how? Through his friends, as always. They began to spread the rumor of his candidacy, all—Charles Hernu, Claude Estier, Roland Dumas, Georges Dayan—playing their parts. One took charge of the centrists, another of the Socialists, still another of the Communists. The division of labor was carried out in terms of affinities and connections. On the Socialist side, it was Charles Hernu who acted as chief scout. He confided the proposed candidacy to Georges Brutelle, who did not prove to be hostile. A dinner with François Mitterrand in a Latin Quarter restaurant was arranged between the two men. Brutelle promised to discuss it with Guy Mollet, whose grip on the SFIO had been strengthened by Deferre's failure. And, before going off on holiday to Hossegor, Mitterrand met the Socialist leader to get him used to the idea.

At Hossegor, where he was kind enough to give an interview to several journalists, François Mitterrand refrained from telling them of his plans. He knew that Maurice Faure, president of the Radical party, was about to throw his hat into the ring and that Guy Mollet would also view this candidacy kindly since he was determined to avoid another SFIO candidacy and a new Deferre affair at all costs. At the Communist party, Waldeck Rochet ("the only Eurocommunist there has ever been in the Communist party"), who wanted to give his party a French touch, did not wish to present a candidate; he favored a candidacy of the Union of the Left. The barrister Antoine Borker, himself a member of the Communist party, personal friend of Charles Hernu, and a participant in meetings organized by the bar chairman René William Thorp,[29] informed François Mitterrand's friends of this. Borker was sure the Central Committee of the Communist party would support a Mitterrand candidacy on condition that a meeting take place; the Communist party wanted to emerge from its ghetto and open up a dialogue with the non-Communist Left.

The deputy for the Nièvre guessed the time was ripe. He weighed the situation, pondering his chances. He was well aware that to take off he would definitely need the votes of Communist electors. But he did not want a formal meeting: opinion was not ready for it, and all the groups on the democratic Left strictly ruled out such a possibility. The chairman of the General Council for the Nièvre (which Mitterrand had become that year) certainly wanted to take into account the feelings and views of the Communist party in his campaign, but not to argue with the party over ideology or program.

Before announcing his candidacy, Mitterrand still had to be sure that Maurice Faure was not going to do the same, that Gaston Deferre would not make a comeback, that Pierre Mendès France would publicly declare his support, that Guy Mollet would say yes, and that the Communist party would not say no (that is, would come round to supporting him in the end). Such a series of obstacles would have discouraged many a man, but not François Mitterrand. Such obstacles have always strengthened his resolution.

An unquestionable man of the Left, the barrister Pierre Stibbe certainly was not kindly disposed toward Mitterrand, writing in *Le Monde* that, in confronting General de Gaulle, the Left should be represented by "some morally irreproachable person." In the political class, everyone realized at once this was a slur on Mitterrand, who was being rejected in advance.

Knowing the psychology of the future president, it is not difficult to imagine what happened next. Cut to the quick and feeling attacked, François Mitterrand put on his armor. His decision was made: he would be a candidate. As he later admitted, "Pierre Stibbe's article accounted for 30 percent of my decision to go ahead. I could accept anything except a moral challenge. That article would have removed my final hesitations if I had had any. It was repeated here and there that I was 'vulnerable.' Since my honor and will were not at the disposal of anyone, I continued to forge ahead."[30]

Mitterrand still had to win over others and pick up speed. The PSU, the small, left-wing socialist party, proposed the candidacy of Daniel Mayer, irreproachably left-wing and a man of unquestioned honor, if lacking in obvious charisma. And why not Mendès? The small, modernist Left would have been delighted to propose its hero, who at least benefited from untarnished prestige and well-tried authority. Yet Mendès France could not make up his mind. Always happy to be asked, P.M.F. has always felt some melancholy pleasure in saying no (though some see this as a touch of masochism, his friends prefer to see it as an edifying example of all too rare integrity). A determined opponent of the president of the Republic's primacy and of his election by direct universal suffrage, the former prime minister did not want to be compromised by getting involved in a mechanism he had always opposed. And, of course, it must be said (and even emphasized) that no one was very optimistic about the outcome of the fight. "Mendès France," Gilles Martinet explains, "had still not recovered from the 80 percent of yes votes in the 1958 constitutional referendum. He thought that against de Gaulle, a candidate of the Left would not get more than 20 percent of the votes—perhaps 25 percent, if one could count on a full Communist turnout. And for him, 25 percent was failure. He could not envisage it."

When François Mitterrand announced his candidacy, the first opinion polls gave him 11 percent, rising to 16 percent, of the vote. Jean-Jacques Servan-Schreiber, inspired as usual, was to write on October 25 that François Mitterrand, "proposed by decrepit and hostile party machines," could expect no more than 20 or 25 percent—the weakest total, he went on, the Left ("Communists included") had ever had "since the Second Empire."

In other words, no one was promising the deputy for the Nièvre a crown of roses. But no one realized, or wanted to acknowledge, that 25 percent—20 percent even—was for him an enticing prospect, a certificate of rehabilitation. And if he ever went beyond this quarter of the vote, even by 1 percent, he would at once become a man of considerable importance in that Left, sunk as it was in the slough of despond.

So on September 8, 1965, François Mitterrand set out on his journey, without confusing speed with haste, but without wasting time. He began by telephoning Gaston Deferre—a way of paying his respects—to ask for his support. The mayor of Marseille, forced to send the elevator back and in fact quite pleased to forbid an SFIO rival to play the card that had eluded him, gave his support, in principle, on one condition: there would be no negotiations with the Communist party. That same day, at his home in the rue Guynemer, Mitterrand received a visit from Mendès, who encouraged him in private, but preferred to wait for the general to declare his intentions before applauding in public. At nine o'clock, Mitterrand was with Daniel Mayer to ask him: "What will you do if I am a candidate?" Mayer replied that he was ready to step down. But he, too, had been given discreet, private encouragement from Mendès, which Mitterrand did not care for at all. That same evening, though, there was good news: returning home at eleven o'clock to join his henchmen (Dayan, Hernu, Dumas, Beauchamp, Estier, and Legatte), Mitterrand learned that the Communist party preferred him to Daniel Mayer. There was light on the horizon.

The next morning at half past nine he dashed over to see Maurice

Faure, telling him, among others, of the Communist support. The deputy for the Lot, gravely concerned, warned Mitterrand "against the risk of being accused of reviving the Popular Front." But before flying off to Greece, Faure gave him formal assurance that he would not stand against him if the SFIO supported him.

All that remained was to convince Guy Mollet, who received him in his office (or rather, his citadel) in the Cité Malesherbes dominated by portraits of his mother and Léon Blum. Mitterrand decided not to pull his punches: "I've already obtained Waldeck Rochet's agreement," he announced proudly. Guy Mollet, who did not want to hear anything about a Socialist candidacy—especially not that of his old enemy, Daniel Mayer[31]—was ready to give his consent, but only on one condition[32]: that François Mitterrand swear on his honor that he had had nothing to reproach himself with in the Observatoire affair. The promise was made and sworn on the spot.

"Say I'm a candidate, then," Mitterrand said.

"When will you declare your candidacy?" Mollet asked.

"In two hours."

"You certainly don't waste time. Think about it a little longer," the Socialist leader advised, somewhat nonplussed.

The text of the declaration of candidacy had already been written. François Mitterrand communicated it by telephone to the Agence France-Presse: "For me, the main task is to oppose arbitrary, personal power, narrow nationalism, and social conservatism, with a scrupulous respect for law and liberty. We must be determined to grasp all the opportunities offered by Europe and the dynamism of ordered expansion through implementing a democratic plan."

Once again, François Mitterrand had given fate a push—alone. Just as he had taken it upon himself to go and meet General de Gaulle at Algiers, so he made himself into the candidate of the Left.

The circumstances were favorable to the audacious. There was no other obvious candidate. Among the official leaders of the Left, each was concerned above all with preventing one of his rivals from emerging. François Mitterrand, on the other hand, represented very little more than himself. "It was the mediocrity of the Left leadership that allowed Mitterrand to become a candidate," Ernest Cazelles remarks.

All that remained was to gain the definitive support of the Communist party—that is, to obtain its support, without having to beg for it. It was important, therefore, to avoid any symbolic meeting that might offend both the electors and the leaders of the non-Communist Left. The Communist party held a meeting of its Central Committee to decide its attitude. François Mitterrand immediately fled to Brussels, on no particular business, and got Roland Dumas to take a letter to Waldeck Rochet. The next day, the general secretary of the Communist party declared in his report: "We Communists have always been for the Union of the Left." One more hurdle had been cleared: François Mitterrand was now enthroned. There was no precedent for this. The decision had not been made without stormy arguments within the Communist party, which was concerned above all with emerging from its solitude. "Mitterrand has the great merit of removing the obstacle of anti-communism," Jacques Duclos was to remark.

Did this mean that the Left, for once officially brought together (if not united), was singing in unison? Of course not: in the SFIO, there was endless grumbling; in the executive committee, which had to ratify the decision to support Mitterrand, there was certainly no unanimity; Guy Mollet was forced to confirm his support, but with altogether less enthusiasm. In an interview to *Paris-Presse* some days later, he explained, rather oddly: "We shall not drop Mitterrand now that we have decided to support him. But what is true is that I would have preferred the candidacy of M. Pinay, for he would have obtained the most votes in the family of the liberal democrats."

The mystique of the Union of the Left had certainly not yet taken hold in the Cité Malesherbes.

And what of the Radical party? "Several weeks after the Socialists and Communists, the Radical party rallied round. It did so in its own inimitable manner, at the same time inviting people to vote for Jean Lecanuet," Mitterrand recounts in *Ma part de vérité*.

And the PSU? No sooner had François Mitterrand made public his seven options—among which one might note his intention of doing away with the regime of personal power and the "ineffective, ruinous, and dangerous"[33] nuclear strike force, as well as his wish to reserve public funds for the state educational system—than his good comrade Edouard Depreux, national secretary of the PSU, wrote in *Tribune socialiste*: "Feeble and skillful (or if you prefer, feebly skillful), his seven options reveal a banality and poverty of thought. The result of so mediocre an operation is easy to predict: 5–6½ million votes out of 22–24 million voters; it is toward such a defeat that we are moving." One could hardly have been less enthusiastic and inspiring.

Indeed, the PSU almost outdid itself with its lack of enthusiasm. The organization's general secretary, Marc Heurgon, declared before his friends: "The Right is not presenting Pesquet, so why should we present Mitterrand?" Nevertheless, the party called on its members to vote in his favor, but on the one astonishing condition that they not take part in the campaign. This idea of supporting without participating (passed by 300 votes out of 544—67 having voted against, including Pierre Bérégovoy and Jean Poperen, who would have preferred a proper commitment) came from a young unknown member named Georges Servet. Those in the know are aware that hiding behind this pseudonym was a senior civil servant named Michel Rocard. "That marked the beginning of his rise in the party," Gilles Martinet observes.

The "left-wing intelligentsia" was no more enthusiastic. On October 4, two of its most celebrated editorialists tried to revive the idea of a Mendès France candidacy. In *Le Monde*, Professor Maurice Duverger wrote: "We must choose a candidate whose personality inspires confidence."

In *France Observateur*, Georges Daniel asked: "Why not try now to achieve the unity of the opposition? Why not P.M.F.? All those who have seen him agree in thinking he is ready to assume such a responsibility."

Jean-Paul Sartre gave Mitterrand no warmer a welcome. In the November issue of his review *Les Temps modernes*, he wrote: "To vote for Mitterrand is not to vote for him, but against personal power and against the rightward rush of the Socialists. Many people will vote for Mitterrand without illusions and without enthusiasm."

There was certainly no outbreak of joy at François Mitterrand's candidacy. Among the gloomy faces, André Ribaud seemed almost enthusiastic when he described the candidate in his famous column in *Le Canard enchaîné* as:

He was a man between two heights and two ages, with a pleasant face that brought a twinkle to the ladies' eyes. His ambition was such as to employ all sorts of talents to arrive at the highest fortune; he was rich in gifts, fertile in opinions, resources, and devices. He had a plentiful wit, but one so guarded and sometimes so labyrinthine that he would lose his way in his detours and be entrapped in rough country, dotted with the forests of outlandish intrigues, from which he emerged only with difficulty, although he had a cool head and was very capable of taking upon himself the cares of the state.

Others lent support. Gérard Jaquet declared in *Le Populaire*: "François Mitterrand has consistently and vigorously fought against the general's policy of personal power. He is unquestionably a man of the Left."

Finally, on October 28, with six weeks to go before the election, Pierre Mendès France gave Mitterrand his unreserved support in *France Observateur*: "Mitterrand is the best candidate to bring together all the democratic and socialist votes. I do not see how one could hesitate any longer. . . . I vote for him, and I would ask all those who trust me to vote for him, too."

All in all, the most positive support still came from the Communists, who, having decided once and for all to support François Mitterrand, did not go back on it and were careful not to display their doubts in public.

Mitterrand did not seem overconcerned when such support often took the form of a hangman's noose, holding him up while strangling him at the same time. He turned poverty into wealth. He had realized that the logic of the presidential candidacy was the primacy of a man, not of a party machine.

Thus it was all the better he had no party. Parties encumbered his rivals, and in any case, he had friends and also the former prisoners. They would take the place of a party machine. For no one from either the Socialist or Radical parties rushed in to help him organize his campaign. He had to rely on the old veterans, who were always the same: André Rousselet, Georges Dayan, Georges Beauchamp, Claude Estier, Louis Mermaz, Roland Dumas, Marie-Thérèse Eyquem, his brother Robert—and the former prisoners of war. Louis Deteix says: "I went to see him and left with a roll of posters, which I stuck up myself in the region of Clermont-Ferrand." Mitterrand himself explained: "The former prisoners were my first departmental delegates for my campaign. At night I slept in the homes of those men, most of whom I hadn't seen since the war."

And although he had no party, he was soon to turn the fact to his advantage. On October 9, before his friends of the Convention des institutions républicaines, he averred: "I shall not be a robot. I am a man of neither a party nor a coalition of parties. I am a man of a fight."

He was already looking further ahead. While the party apparatchiks were still thinking in terms of opposing Gaullist power, Mitterrand was broadening the campaign's scope: "The Left could not be absent," he declared in the Nièvre. "We are at the bottom of the mountain; we shall have to climb much further. Many things will have to change before the Left revives. I am seeing to it."

And as if to inaugurate a word that was soon to become the fetishistic leitmotiv of his vocabulary, he was carrying out the first "synthesis" in his overall program—a synthesis that still looked more like skillful patchwork. To concoct his program, the deputy for the Nièvre borrowed bits from everybody: from the Communists, a few nationalizations, the rejection of the Europe of trusts and cartels, and the determination to fight against the two military blocs' logic of confrontation; from the SFIO, the indignant condemnation of the regime's economic and social policies, and the ardent defense of Europe and the Atlantic Alliance; from the Radical party, the defense of basic individual liberties (he promised the revocation of the constitution's article sixteen—an article, in his eyes, validating dictatorship—and of article eleven on the referendum. "If I am elected," he promised, "it will not be I who initiates policy, but the National Assembly!" He also said: "We must eliminate the privilege of the president of the Republic, who believes, according to a famous tag, that the whole state resides in him and that the will of the whole people is enclosed in his."); from Pierre Mendès France, a few serious, austere arguments: lastly, from Gaston Deferre, two or three examples of unbearable situations and the nationalization of the business banks.[34]

Yet Mitterrand's most personal contribution concerned women. This seemed very bold at the time. Indeed, the candidate officially opted in favor of contraception and women's sexual freedom. This extremely bold statement originated, according to the writer Gabriel Matzneff, in a lunch in the rue Guynemer. On that day, the feminist novelist Benoîte Groult apparently "sold" the idea to the candidate, guaranteeing him a substantial female vote. "Do you really think so?" the prudish but freethinking Catholic asked in some doubt. Groult was able to convince him, and he kept the idea (later being glad he had).

The platform raised nobody's enthusiasm, but satisfied everyone, including an increasing proportion of the French electorate. As the campaign progressed, François Mitterrand attracted larger and more enthusiastic crowds to his meetings. The campaign culminated in Toulouse, where between the two rounds thirty-five thousand supporters gave him a standing ovation. Carried away by this fervor, he addressed his audience not with his usual solemn *"Françaises et français"* but with *"Citoyennes et citoyens"*—"citizens." The people of the Left existed—he had just encountered them.

It was a decisive moment, according to all those there at the time. That evening, the main opposition candidate was transformed into the leader of the Left. Even his wife—and this was by no means the least important event—found in it an invitation to commitment. "Danielle has had a revelation," Georges Beauchamp noted. "Before, she was hostile to politics; now she feels she must commit herself to the cause."

The leader of the Left did not, of course, have a very assured doctrine. Thus, between the two rounds of the election he was to plead on television for both the freedom of the commercial enterprise and a rebirth of the state's role, which was to "decide" (in particular, where investment was concerned).

What was the Left for Mitterrand?

On May 22, he expressed himself on television (where he was not at ease and where everything was done to prevent him from being so): "The Left is whatever fights for individual liberties, for justice, for social equality. . . . It is those who fought in 1848, for ten-year-old children not working more than twelve hours a day . . . ; in 1936, for the struggle for holidays with pay and the forty-hour week; in 1965, for a stricter definition of an incomes policy, economic expansion, and a determined defense of peace. . . . Our aim is the well-being, the happiness of men and women."

At Lyon, he exclaimed, waxing more and more eloquent as he went on: "The Left is French generosity. It is associated with the misery of the people, but also with its hopes. The Left means love between peoples, love between men." As can be seen, it had a great deal more to do with good, Christian, humanist feelings than with Marxism.

Nevertheless, feeling the popular current bearing him up, the candidate grew more lyrical each day and, in a sense, was not misguided in doing so. Indeed, the result exceeded everyone's hopes (including his own). At the first round, he obtained 32 percent of the votes cast, thus giving quite a jolt to General de Gaulle; at the second, he did even better, obtaining 45 percent of the votes (among which he accepted, without the slightest complaint, without for a moment rejecting them, without the Left taking it into its head to shout "Fascism will not pass," the votes of the extreme right-wing candidate, whose campaign manager was Jean-Marie Le Pen).

"I don't intend to spend my time analyzing the votes" was Mitterrand's comment after the fact. Jean Lecanuet's centrists also voted for him in large numbers.

Complaining, sighing, putting on a good face, everyone had to agree that the election had been a personal success for François Mitterrand. True to himself and ignoring the usual politenesses, the loser refused to congratulate the winner, General de Gaulle.

On December 19, 1965, the candidate of the Left became its natural leader. Of course, the Left was still divided and a long way off from any prospects of governing, but it had managed to get the sick man out of the bedroom in which he had been confined for years and persuade him to begin his convalescence.

At a private party organized at the home of Georges Bérard-Quelin, a newspaper tycoon, François Mitterrand exclaimed: "At the present time, there is a regime that is dying, a Left that is being born, and a Republic that will revive. The battle begins again this morning."

François Mitterrand was determined to give the quite new title "leader of the Left" a new content. Those who, in the party machines, were under the illusion that, after the presidential election, things would carry on as before (and who even wanted them to) were sadly mistaken. They were not yet at the end of their troubles. Jean Daniel noted at the time that throughout the campaign, François Mitterrand had violated the machines of the left-wing parties—"a salutary violation" he wrote. In fact, the violation had only just begun.

THE COUNTERPRESIDENT

On December 5, 1965, François Mitterrand became an authenticated man of the Left—thanks to the eleven million votes given him by electors who would now carry much more weight than the few hundred delegates at the party congresses of the non-Communist Left.

François Mitterrand was discovering (and, whether liking it or not, all the Left was discovering with him) that a presidential election did not simply make the victor a president: the challenger would become the leader of the opposition. In 1965, no thinker or strategist of the Left had yet taken that fact into account. Most people had imagined that when the result was declared—and no one doubted the victory would go to General de Gaulle—François Mitterrand would sink back into the ranks, enjoying no more than general esteem. Like a good republican, having carried out his duty he would become once more one leader among others (but not the first), taking into account his own limited following and the fact that the intellectuals were not rallying to him. After meeting Mitterrand in November 1966, Jean Daniel wrote in *Le Nouvel Observateur*: "Not only does this man give the impression he does not believe in anything—when facing him, one even feels guilty at believing anything. . . . Almost despite himself, he insinuates that nothing is pure, that everything is sordid, that no illusion is permitted, so that in the end one is supposed to conclude that after all, all in all in this shabby world, Guy Mollet was not as bad as people said." In short, they had expected Cincinnatus and found Caesar. (They should have been on their guard: Mitterrand already had the Roman's profile.)

Although François Mitterrand accepted the results gracefully, he wanted more. The election had whetted his appetite. He was now enjoying (for the first time in his life) the intoxicating delights of popularity. His more than honorable performance gave him a quite new authority, and since he was not a man to doubt himself, he was easily persuaded it was he who would revive the Left. No—it could only revive with him.

There was no question now as during his lengthy novitiate (1959–65, six long years) of forming pacts, moving around discreetly, wheedling, pleasing, cajoling—in other words, of taming. On December 5, he was like a person who had won the lottery. Before, he had pleaded—now he exerted his authority. Where he had been patient, he now stormed. Where he had made suggestions, he now gave orders. If anyone disagreed with him, he immediately threatened to withdraw from the fight. He wanted to be the sole leader of the entire opposition.

Mitterrand had few troops of his own and no deputies; his weapons were eloquence, celebrity, recourse to public opinion against the party machines, infiltration of those machines when possible. In short, the manner was very like cunning.

Since the failure of Gaston Deferre and his grand federation, the Left had been looking, in innumerable meetings and conferences, for a formula of unity that would not simply be uniformity, but would above all allow each of its party machines to survive, each of its leaders to preserve his title.

On the initiative of Mitterrand's Convention des institutions républicaines, a meeting was held on July 13, 1965 (that is, before the presidential election), bringing together the SFIO, Radical party, UDSR, and clubs. The best known contributors were Guy Mollet, Gérard Jacquet, Radicals Jacques Maroselli and Robert Fabre, and, of course, Charles Hernu, Georges Beauchamp, and Louis Mermaz. At this meeting the principle of a federation was decided on and Georges Brutelle, deputy general secretary of the SFIO and a great advocate of the renewal of the Left, was given the task of drawing up a charter, which would be presented on September 7.

On September 9, François Mitterrand declared himself a candidate for the presidency of the Republic. As a result, when the Federation of the Democratic and Socialist Left (FGDS), which brought together the SFIO, Radical party, and Convention des institutions républicaines (that is, the Mitterrand club), saw the light of day, it had no choice: its first president (the presidency, it had been decided, would rotate every six months, thus giving everyone a chance) could be none other than François Mitterrand.

Mitterrand made a first tentative appearance in an interview in *L'Express*: "I have no intention of breaking up the parties. I believe in the dynamism of my candidacy. I shall throw all my weight behind an electoral campaign of a quite new style and quite new kind for the legislative elections of 1967."

Those who could read between the lines already realized this rotating presidency was not intended to rotate for long, and that if Mitterrand did not become president of the Republic, he would at least be president of the FGDS—if not for life, at least until 1967.

Things were easier after the December poll. The deputy for the Nièvre had one priority: to get his Radical and Socialist partners to accept that his Convention was now the third partner in the coalition, that it deserved equal status and treatment. To achieve his ends, he used just one method: bluff. "It was really quite simple," a leading member of the current Socialist party remembers. "Everyone who came to his meetings—and everybody came—was asked if he would be so kind as to give his name and address; these were then added up as if they represented members." One day an exasperated Ernest Cazelles spread the rumor that the Convention was handing out membership cards free to swell its numbers.

François Mitterrand was furious: "I demand an investigation," he declared, knowing perfectly well as a good strategist that attack is the best form of defense. The others calmed him down. Once again, they had no choice: when he declared that since December, the number of new convention members had been outstripping those of the other parties (the FGDS had no individual membership), the leaders of the SFIO and Radical party were not convinced. They found it difficult to believe that this sudden influx of members was putting such an unaccustomed burden on the postal services. But the man who had managed to get 45 percent of the nation's votes was not to be contradicted.

Since the method had worked so well, Mitterrand used it again. He took it upon himself to put Guy Mollet—Guy Mollet, general secretary of the SFIO, former prime minister, and (until then) the most powerful if not most popular man of the Left—in his place. According to Mitterrand, Mollet had wanted to minimize the influence of the convention. As motive for his anger, François Mitterrand took out of his pocket a circular addressed by the SFIO leader to his departmental heads urging them to limit the convention's influence by creating so-called Clubs Jean Jaurès, which were supposed to counterbalance the convention's clubs. "My friends and I will leave the Federation," François Mitterrand threatened, "if we are not given our rightful place."

Guy Mollet had no intention of pursuing the controversy in public. The legislative elections were to take place the following year; it was hardly the moment to put a brake on the new movement's dynamism or break with the principal motivating force behind it.

By imposing his demands and exerting pressure, François Mitterrand got his way. In mid-March 1966, a few days before the Convention's congress at Lyon, he called on Guy Mollet, telling him he wanted to bring about a fusion of the Federation parties. He added that this fusion would need at its head a strong power endowed with authority, especially where choosing an electoral candidate was concerned, and that what he intended to propose was nothing less than the formation of an FGDS countergovernment modeled on the British Labour party shadow cabinet. This three-point program took Guy Mollet's breath away: the SFIO leader begged him not to rush things, to think about it further. "I have thought about it," François Mitterrand retorted, very counterpresidential, and then decided to make public what he had just whispered in private.

Three days later at Lyon, the president of the FGDS declared that he was in favor of a fusion of the Federation's three component parts, meanwhile telling his partners: "In a real federation, one ought to have at its head a strong central power, possessing ultimate authority over matters of common interest. . . . A true federation is the least we can demand if our agreement is to remain." In other words, François Mitterrand was refusing to accept a figurehead presidency. Once again he was threatening his partners with a break: it was take it or leave it.

The demands that followed Mitterrand's firing of his first shot were not inconsiderable:

- A single candidate to represent the Federation in each constituency, outgoing deputies being automatically adopted if they so wished (this went a long way toward calming the anxieties of the Socialist and Radical deputies).
- A single parliamentary group in the National Assembly after the elections of March 1967. (At the time, Socialists and Radicals formed two different groups, while the Convention des institutions républicaines had only one deputy: the deputy for the Nièvre.)
- Lastly, the formation of a "countergovernment" made up of members of the three groups, each matching a particular ministry.

The idea was met with a chorus of indignant objections by the entire Left. The Communist party was furious since it was not associated with the affair; above all, it feared being excluded once again from a Left that had only just been reunited. The Socialists protested angrily. Along with Guy Mollet, they felt that although the idea was not bad, it was dangerous to distribute portfolios since those who held them would immediately become targets for the government. And the Radicals preferred, they explained gravely, the term *"équipe de contestation"* (debate team) to that of countergovernment.

François Mitterrand, however, was not concerned with these semantic quarrels. He was determined to pursue the path he had laid down. On April 29, after innumerable meetings, the executive committee of the Federation finally gave in and entrusted "President" Mitterrand with the task of forming the first "countergovernment of the Fifth Republic."

Just in case certain individuals were still under any illusion, François Mitterrand's first comment was unequivocal: "I shall assume the task of appointing this team myself." Although a determined opponent of General de Gaulle's personal power and the Fifth Republic's institutions, which gave too many prerogatives to its leader, François Mitterrand instinctively reacted quite differently when it came to himself. Since he was the symbol, he must be the leader—in which case he had nothing against plenary powers. Applying this same logic, he declared (more sincerely than ironically) after he had entered the Elysée: "The institutions? With anybody else, they are dangerous. They were dangerous before me, they will become so after me."

Meanwhile the "counterpresident" formed his team. Guy Mollet was given defense; Radical René Billières, education and culture; Gaston Deferre, social affairs; Robert Fabre, environment; Pierre Mauroy, youth. "Ah! Guy Mollet and I had to go to the rue Guynemer three times to persuade him to take Mauroy. He didn't want him," Ernest Cazelles remembers. Marie-Thérèse Eyquem (a member of the Convention) was given women's affairs—an idea that had not yet occurred to those responsible for the country's government. Charles Hernu was the general secretary of this countergovernment.

Since the government of the Right met every Wednesday at the Elysée, the government of the Left assembled every Thursday—and, like the Right, published its communiqués and offered its comments to the press.

There was much amusement at the expense of these gentlemen, playing at being ministers, and at François Mitterrand, acting out the role of head of state. People might smile, but it made no difference. They soon got used to the idea of listening to the opinions of the "counterpresident," who was even beginning to look the part. If the general gave a press conference, then, the following week, François Mitterrand gave his, and it was well attended.

"It was quite simple," Pierre Mauroy remembers with a smile. "From the moment François Mitterrand became president of the FGDS and the countergovernment, not a single communiqué could be issued from the SFIO: nobody would have been interested."

The same phenomenon took place in the National Assembly. In each great debate, François Mitterrand took upon himself the role of principal opposition speaker. At the height of the famous Ben Barka affair (the kidnapping of the Moroccan opposition leader in Paris), Mitterrand was the government's accepted opponent. On television and radio, he became one of the most frequently invited opposition spokesmen (though he complained, not without reason, of being ill-treated by the state-run French Office of Television

Broadcasting). Gradually he learned to use the word *socialism* quite naturally. Since it was difficult for him to appear the innovator, he declared one day in all seriousness to Guy Mollet, with whom he had gone to London: "There is no age for becoming a socialist: look at Jaurès and Blum." The general secretary of the SFIO was not very convinced. For him, one was born a socialist—one did not become one (Mollet was always to doubt the socialist sincerity of the new converts of the Federation, and especially of its leading member).[35]

Whatever reservations there may have been, François Mitterrand imposed his authority and behaved like a charismatic leader. This was true enough in the everyday life of the Federation; it was even more noticeable when it came to defining broad strategy outlines, especially the crucial ones concerning the Federation's relations with the Communist party.

"From now on, the privileged ally of the FGDS is the Communist party," Mitterrand declared in June 1966. Gaston Deferre, who was still dreaming of an alliance with the centrists, berated the president of the Federation: he did not care for the fait accompli technique. The radicals jibbed. At a meeting of the FGDS, François Mitterrand, while protesting that they should not reject any progressive Republicans, made it quite clear to the mayor of Marseille that he had no intention of telephoning him for permission whenever he wanted to open his mouth. And he threatened (once more): "I came here with the intention of refusing to allow my mandate to be renewed. If you renew my mandate, it will be on the basis of what I have said today." It was renewed—up until the legislative elections. They had no choice—they never had any choice.

Since the presidential election, the deputy for the Nièvre had been almost obsessed by the birth of a popular current, which now needed cultivation and development. He took particular pride at having "lifted the Communist party out of the ghetto." Feeling stronger within the non-Communist Left, he even agreed (as the Communist party had tirelessly urged) to plan a solemn meeting of the two factions of the Left, an unprecedented event under the Fifth Republic.

The meeting took place in December 1966. François Mitterrand led the Federation delegation; Waldeck Rochet, the Communist party delegation. There was no question of a common program, despite the express wishes of the Communist party. All that emerged from the meeting was a statement drawn up by the two parties, of which Jacques Fauvet was to write in *Le Monde* on December 23, 1966: "It is something of a report, something of a catalog, and something of a semicontract." Above all, it was a preelectoral agreement with a promise of automatic withdrawal in the second round in favor of the best-placed candidate of the Left.

But although he gave "priority" to the alliance with the Communist party, François Mitterrand did not forget the others: ideally, he would also have liked to reach agreement with Jean Lecanuet's Centre démocrate, not to mention the PSU and Pierre Mendès France.

The trouble with the Federation was that it had an electoral future only with Waldeck Rochet's votes and a future in government only with Lecanuet's. That is why, up until the elections, although he was negotiating with Waldeck Rochet, François Mitterrand did not miss an opportunity to praise the republican virtues of Jean Lecanuet, who had come out against personal power by running against General de Gaulle. Scarcely had he launched this compliment to his right than he caught himself and, turning to his left, declared: "For me, nothing is more important than the Union of the Left, which obviously includes the Communist party." Then he added, for the ears of the centrists: "Priority does not mean exclusivity." Mitterrand was walking a tightrope. His progress led Raymond Barillon to write in *Le Monde*: "Not having the power to impose his views or settle disputes, he constantly has to protect himself on his right and on his left, to balance, to calibrate, to alter his aim as soon as he has fired."

There was some success, however: after a great deal of hesitation, the PSU finally signed an agreement with the FGDS.

The FGDS presented or supported 430 candidates. It had 91 former deputies. It got elected 116 of its candidates, including 17 members of the Convention (among them Georges Dayan at Nîmes, André Rousselet at Toulouse, Claude Estier, Louis Mermaz, and Georges Fillioud). In several cases (a rare event and certainly proof of goodwill) the Communists even withdrew in favor of Convention members who had come behind their candidate in the first round but were better placed to win in the second. "They were not so generous with the Socialists," Ernest Cazelles remembers. The Communist party had not forgotten that thanks to François Mitterrand, it had broken out of its isolation.

The majority remained a majority by one seat. It could console itself with the thought that the opposition was divided: although the centrists belonged to it in principle, they would never have anything to do with the Communist party.

François Mitterrand had not exactly triumphed, but he had done extremely well.[36] He was certainly not modest about his achievement, for in April 1967 he declared, without the trace of a smile, that he was "ready for power" and able to lay down a program.

Georges Pompidou, the by now experienced prime minister, irritated by an arrogance he regarded as quite unjustified, snapped at him in the National Assembly: "For whom are you speaking with so much assurance? . . . You are at the head of a group of 121 deputies; the so-called United Left has about 200 deputies; the majority, some 240. Are you, then, trying to make us believe that you have won, like those rugby supporters who, on the night of their club's defeat, explain that they might have won, that the ground was not good, that the referee did not see everything? . . . You have won, have you? In fact, you have lost . . . for the third consecutive time. . . . That will allow your young supporters to gain experience, M. Mitterrand, and M. Mermaz to become more gracious."

THE TRAPDOOR OF MAY 1968: THE LAST DUEL WITH MENDÈS

At the beginning of 1968, the president of the FGDS could well be optimistic. In three years, he had assumed the role (which he had carefully written himself) of challenger to the general. Time was on his side; the resident of the Elysée was beginning to look his age and seemed less at ease in the economic field (where France's battles now lay) than in the stormy tumults of history.

More out of lassitude than anything else, de Gaulle put Georges Pompidou back at the Matignon; with his slender majority in the National Assembly, the general was beginning to look like an athlete who had given up competing. A young minister who had recently been turned out of the government, Valéry Giscard d'Estaing, was huffing impatiently, beginning to assemble his own supporters, and coming out with cutting remarks about "the solitary exercise of power."

In the cantonal elections of October 1967, 49.8 percent of eligible votes (that is, a clear majority of the votes cast) were for left-wing candidates. The Left was in the middle of a big reconstruction plan. The idea was still the same: to rebuild a great non-Communist party. The clubs argued, the party members were growing impatient, the readership were in conclave. Members of the SFIO, Radical party, and Convention now seemed ready for that further step François Mitterrand had been asking for since 1965. The horizon was brightening.

On the matter of the alliance with the Communists, things were not too bad either. In February 1968, the Federation of the Left and the Communist party signed a common platform. The word *common* concealed very little agreement and a great deal of divergence on Europe, the Atlantic Alliance, the extent of nationalization, and the Middle East. No matter: for the first time, something was emerging beyond purely electoral agreements that looked like the sketch of a plan for government. François Mitterrand, with four years ahead of him before the next presidential election, knew he had plenty of time to bring the Communist party gradually to a more realistic position, providing he too made the few symbolic steps that would be necessary when the time came. The strategy was clear and the time scale propitious. For the president of the FGDS, things were slowly going in the right direction.

Curiously enough, Georges Pompidou, who then appeared to be an immovable prime minister (he had been at the Matignon for six years) also seemed quite pleased with himself. To a meeting of the Gaullist party, the Union of Democrats for the Fifth Republic at Ajaccio in March, he more or less declared that the future looked good. It is true that at the château, as the Elysée was known, no clouds could be seen. On January 1, while presenting his good wishes to the French nation, the general had given every reason for hope:

What will 1968 turn out to be like? The future does not belong to men, and I am not predicting it. Nevertheless, when one considers the way things look, it is with real confidence that I look to the future of our country over the next twelve months. . . . It is difficult to see how we could be paralyzed by crises like those we have suffered so much from in the past. On the contrary, as the desire for renewal continues and its promoters (especially the young) do their work, there is every reason to hope that our Republic will find ever more active and wider help. In any case, in the midst of so many countries shaken by so many crises, ours will continue to set an example of efficiency in the conduct of its affairs.

Some time later Pierre Vianson-Ponté, a great specialist in France's political climate, wrote an article for his newspaper, *Le Monde,* that was to go down in history: "France is bored," he observed. . . . "Our public life today is characterized by boredom. . . ." And he concluded: "Excitement and imagination are as necessary as well-being and expansion." In the higher reaches of the political and social world, these remarks found a ready echo. People nodded over dinner tables before drinking large glasses of champagne and turning out the lights. Yes, prosperity was getting boring, well-being was palling, peace monotonous. Nevertheless, the storm was brewing, though neither on the Right nor on the Left, neither in the government nor in the opposition, did anyone hear the rumble of distant thunder.

With the coming of spring and rising of the sap, certain curious news items did reach their ears, however. Students in the lycées and universities were getting restless and smashing odd bits of equipment. At Nanterre, small Maoist groups were laying down the law and jeering at the young Communist deputy Pierre Juquin, an intellectual (and graduate of the prestigious Ecole Normale Supérieure) trying very hard to look fashionable. The Communist party was not at all pleased at these demonstrations by young bourgeois attacking it from the left. Others were quite delighted: anything to embarrass the Communist party. No one paid any attention to what was happening in Germany or in the American universities—they were all too bored.

Suddenly the earth moved and everything collapsed. It was May 1968. One by one the universities in Paris and in the provinces went on strike. The weather was magnificent, it was warm, *"la contestation"* (confrontation) appeared—soon the word was on everyone's lips. The walls of the Latin Quarter and Paris campuses were covered with graffiti: the old intellectual and moral order was being derided. The bourgeois university was being rejected. The students announced they would no longer be the agents of capitalist exploitation (they started a fire at the Bourse, that temple of capitalism). The consumer society (another term soon to be on everyone's lips) was rejected. Students demanded an end to hire/purchase practices, the daily grind, fidelity, obedience, male chauvinism, the conveyor belt, work, respect for the bureaucrats. Instead everyone was urged to enjoy. It was written on the walls: the young students whose hair was getting longer and ties were disappearing dreamed of self-management, love, solidarity, creativity, idleness, lack of respect, and fraternity.

The old order imposed its nuclear power stations, nuclear strike force, and Concorde. May 1968 advocated a pastoral, ecological economy. Cars were symbolically burned. Fathers would delve and mothers spin; everyone would go off and make pottery in the Larzac and drink goat's milk. Everyone would make love (one couldn't fall in love with a growth rate). The real life would begin.

The government was disconcerted. First it decided to open the Sorbonne, then to close it, depending on its mood. Then it gave up making decisions, because no one obeyed them. At first the general spoke of "childishness." Alain Peyrefitte, minister of education, denounced the activities of "irresponsible groupuscules."

The Left was no more receptive. It wanted at all costs to pour the youthful events into the old, rather rusty molds: May 1968 heralded the eternal return of June 1936, of the Popular Front. It was "May 1958 turned inside out," as Georges Séguy declared.

And what of François Mitterrand? From the early days of May, he had at least realized something had been happening since April. On May 8 he declared in the National Assembly: "Although youth is not aways right, the society that mocks it, misunderstands it, and strikes it is always wrong." But he had certainly not grasped the events' scope. The first two weeks of the month saw him concerned, above all, with Guy Mollet, drawing up the statutes of the new parties rather than dissecting the cultural groups of confrontation.

On May 13, after the first serious incidents, a large demonstration composed of students and members of the Left set out for Denfert-

Rochereau via the Latin Quarter. As the demonstrators marched, they shouted, "Dix ans, ça suffit!" ("Ten years are enough!") for the ears of General de Gaulle. François Mitterrand demanded the freeing of the jailed students, an amnesty for those found guilty, and discussions about the university's future.

But it was another May 13 that was still of passionate concern to him: that of 1958. In the Salle Pleyel, he gave a lecture whose theme had been decided on long ago: "May 13, Ten Years After." Still, he did refer to present events: "This afternoon, you have witnessed a reflex of the country's good health. The Left must learn to be less a sort of museum for great memories and more a place in which youth can feel at home."

On May 14, the students erected barricades and defied the police. France was astonished. François Mitterrand addressed Georges Pompidou: "It is time, it is high time, the government got out!" Then he launched the traditional slogan against repression. He criticized Christian Fouchet, minister of the interior, for the way the police gave chase to the students and arrested them, even on private premises: "There are many ministers of the interior ["of which I was one," he clearly implied] who do not confuse order and brutality, citizens' security and provocation." Pierre Mendès France, though approached by Michel Rocard to become the spokesman of the angry students, preferred to say nothing. But François Mitterrand provoked Georges Pompidou to a verbal duel. The students could not have cared less, making it quite clear they were absolutely indifferent to the political debate.

When the strike of wage earners was triggered, or when it was taken over by the General Confederation of Labor (the Communist trade union organization), showing the leftists where the true revolutionary force was situated, politicians of all persuasions clearly saw there was something artificial in the conjunction of two movements so alien to one another, but did not know what words to use or tone to adopt. Their world of black cars and Republican palaces, their office meetings and committees, their negotiations around platforms, plans and reports—all this suddenly seemed ridiculous. To the protagonists of May, the politicians belonged to another planet. A symbolic fact often noted was that neither the students nor the workers were ever for a moment tempted to march to the Palais-Bourbon.

On the other hand, politicians were not exactly conspicuous at the barricades—François Mitterrand no more than anyone else. "Can you see him, going off and being addressed as *tu* and heckled by bearded students?" one of his friends asked. Yet he lived on the edge of the same Latin Quarter, within earshot of the demonstrators. A few months later he was to say to Pierre Bénichou, a journalist on *Le Nouvel Observateur*, how happy he had been that his two sons had taken part in the May movement—that he would have been very disappointed had they shown a lack of interest in it. But each age has its own pleasures, and François Mitterrand was playing with the grown-ups. He had no intention of appearing to take over the student movement, preferring instead to embody the political alternative, for it now seemed that office might be within reach. Events were rushing ahead, disorder was spreading, and the government was losing its grip.

On May 24, before General de Gaulle's unfortunate intervention offering the rioters, who couldn't have cared less, a referendum on participation, Mitterrand declared: "The government no longer has reality, authority, or credibility. The prime minister must set an example: he must resign. Then the new process will be set in motion, at the end of which a full response will be given. . . . The general must accept that it's all over."

As he had long ago read in the Bible, François Mitterrand believed judgment day had come. After the general's speech, he published a statement, as did most political leaders: "The general imposes a plebiscite at a time when workers, peasants, students, and teachers are seeking dialogue." He declared once again that the Federation of the Left would reject the referendum. Pierre Mendès France echoed him: "A plebiscite is not a matter for discussion, but for struggle." Waldeck Rochet, general secretary of the Communist party, commented in turn: "The Gaullist regime has had its day: it must go."

In other words, France's politicians were still playing the old political game: the president made a speech and the opposition leaders took up their positions. Neither side was really aware that the ground was being pulled out from under them, that their declarations had no impact whatsoever.

Observers who, out of sheer habit, continued to analyze the floods of declarations and takings of stands, thought they could detect, among other things, a new Mendès-Mitterrand alliance, so close did their points of view and approaches seem. But instead, May 1968 saw the last single-combat duel between the two men.

Pierre Mendès France, who since 1958 had endlessly predicted that this regime born of riot would perish by riot, believed the events were giving him striking confirmation. The regime was paying for its original sin. For the first time since 1955, when his government had been overthrown, he believed his hour had come. Gilles Martinet supports this view. Indeed, from May 21 onward, a Pierre Mendès France support association had been set up. It brought together a large number of well-known university teachers, including Jacques Monod and Laurent Schwartz. Groups of student rebels even went to visit the sage of the rue du Conseiller-Collignon, for whom they showed particular consideration: for them, he was quite different from those "political zombies" whom they castigated so readily.

Although he was president of the FGDS and a tireless worker in the cause of Left unity, François Mitterrand had no right to such homage (even if Daniel Cohn-Bendit felt "he might always be useful").

On May 23, the two leaders of the non-Communist Left met in the rue Guynemer to review the country's situation. Each was on his guard; both soon realized that once again they were not on the same wavelength. The deputy for the Nièvre knew perfectly well that the political leaders were alien to the student explosion. Pierre Mendès France, who had become deputy for Grenoble, stressed the responsibilities of the opposition, especially in the event of a collapse of the government's authority.

On that same evening, there were new incidents in the boulevard Saint-Michel. It was always the same ritual: cars were burned and barricades erected. "We should go over," said Charles Hernu, a friend of both men, who was there at the time. François Mitterrand pondered. P.M.F. advised against going. Relieved, the president of the Federation agreed.

But the next day, Mitterrand learned that the seemingly cautious Pierre Mendès France, accompanied by Marie-Claire de Fleurieu and the lawyer Georges Kiejman, had gone off to the rue Soufflot, into the midst of the disturbances, and talked with the students. He concluded that P.M.F. had not wanted to go to the Latin Quarter in his company, that he had tried to play his own game. The former prime minister denied this, of course, denied he had intended going all along, but François Mitterrand did not believe him, and immediately set about planning a riposte.

On May 24, the day of the general's broadcast, a huge student demonstration was planned around the Bastille: France was paralyzed by strikes and the crisis was almost reaching its climax. When, during a meeting of the executive committee of the FGDS, the president of the Radical party, René Billières, suggested that "under the circumstances, the Federation ought to approach Mendès, who has the ear of the students." François Mitterrand, stung to the quick, snapped: "If you want to replace me, you should say so frankly." Guy Mollet tended to agree with Billières and, though he had often been opposed to Mendès, he was close to believing that, under the circumstances, Mendès represented the Left's best chance.

François Mitterrand was downcast; even more, he was deeply hurt. For three years he had plowed the political field for the FGDS, pushing the plow, spurring on those oxen he felt (with some justification) would not have budged an inch without him. He had obtained results that were regarded as more than creditable. Then, at the first opportunity, Pierre Mendès France suddenly appeared as the supreme savior. Although he had been elected at Grenoble in 1967, it was thanks to the support of the FGDS—yet, he had done nothing for the Federation of the Left in three years. And François Mitterrand's partners in the Federation, still fascinated by the myth of the former prime minister, seemed quite ready to drop him without batting an eyelid. It was too unjust.

Fortunately for Mitterrand, the Communist party would have nothing to do with what might look, near or far, like a left-wing de Gaulle, a providential savior. And the Communists were worried because the Mendès France support committees, which advocated his return to power, were spreading. In Le Monde, Alfred Fabre-Luce praised Pierre Mendès France's "stature and international authority," concluding: "In 1958, our politicians went to Colombey to seek out a hermit. I propose an open-air conspiracy to seek out in the National Assembly another solitary man. . . . P.M.F. to the

Elysée!" And Pierre Abelin, deputy-mayor of Châtellerault, also launched an appeal to Mendès.

That men identified with the Center (like Pierre Abelin) or the Right (like Alfred Fabre-Luce) should offer their support to the deputy for Grenoble was enough to arouse the suspicions of the Communist party. Such suspicions deepened when, on May 27, seventy thousand students brandishing red and black flags gathered in the Charléty stadium shouting out their hostility toward the parties and trade unions, castigating Gaullism, but also yelling "Séguy resign!" (Séguy was general secretary of the communist-led CGT.) They spared only one well-known politician, the only one indeed to back by his presence those sacrilegious slogans: Pierre Mendès France.

At the same time, the Communist party was beginning to wonder whether François Mitterrand was not himself part of the Mendès plot (they should have known him better). But he was about to make his move.

On May 28, Mitterrand summoned the press to the Hôtel Intercontinental. Under the blinding lights and clicks of the cameras he declared:

> There is no longer a state, and what has taken its place does not even possess the appearances of power. What I propose to de Gaulle and to the French nation is a plebiscite. If he does not get its approval, he must go. . . . What allows me to consider such a departure is that, after all, General de Gaulle might understand where his duties lie. We must forestall that power vacuum by setting up a provisional government of administration composed of ten men selected without regard to outdated notions of balance and excluding no one on principle. To form such a government I would consider first Pierre Mendès France. And, for the presidency of the Republic, universal suffrage will decide. But I am already telling you I am a candidate.

This was certainly giving destiny a push. Like de Gaulle ten years earlier, François Mitterrand was setting in motion the process that might lead him to power. He had also taken P.M.F. unawares, not having warned him of what he was going to say; the former prime minister learned the news on the radio and felt outmaneuvered.

Although François Mitterrand had paid him the honor of proposing him for the Matignon on a provisional basis, he was keeping the essential role—the Elysée—for himself.

In the FGDS, reactions were good. Everyone felt that the formula was viable and that a plausible way out was being presented to the nation. François Mitterrand was warmly congratulated by Guy Mollet, Pierre Mauroy, Louis Mermaz, and Gaston Deferre. They had not seen that the president of the FGDS had shocked people. His tone had been that of a schemer. On television, he looked like an apprentice dictator; he frightened people. When Pierre Mauroy got home, he had the unpleasant surprise of being greeted by his wife in these terms: "What have you just done? Are you crazy?"

Pierre Mendès France, who had not yet appreciated this gap, still grumbled (but, after all, he had always made it clear that electing the president of the Republic by universal suffrage was not to his taste). However, he could hardly allow himself to refuse this division of tasks—especially since Eugène Descamps, leader of the Confederation français démocratique de travaille (CFDT), the union organization most sympathetic to the aspirations of May, had declared: "Mendès is quite capable of assuming, together with the parties of the Left, responsibility for the government." Even Jean Lecanuet himself applauded: "If P.M.F. can guarantee the safeguard of our liberties, if he carries out a European and social policy, we shall not haggle over the men he chooses to work with." A consensus was emerging. And Jean Daniel wrote in *Le Nouvel Observateur*: "He is of an impressive calm and determination. . . . History is at last giving him the role that is his, one that can only be first." Mendès was acclaimed everywhere (or almost)—but for a temporary job.

Everyone agreed that there should be a government of the Left emerging out of May, but with whom? The Communists wanted to be represented, and they went to see François Mitterrand in the rue Guynemer to tell him so.

"How many Communist ministers will there be?" Waldeck Rochet asked.

"At least one," François Mitterrand replied.

"That isn't a lot," Waldeck Rochet observed.

"Public opinion must get used to seeing you back in government."

"The more Communist ministers there are, the sooner people will get used to it," François Bulloux, the deputy for Marseille, retorted with a smile.[37]

Could the May rebels have a share of power? Pierre Mendès France wanted them to, and told Mitterrand so when he met him at Georges Dayan's home in the rue de Rivoli. Mitterrand replied: "You realize this will mean a break with the Communist party."[38]

"We cannot cut ourselves off from those who represent youth," Mendès retorted.

"Then appeal to men who are entirely above reproach, like Professors Kastler and Monod,"[39] Mitterrand said.

Several such cuts and thrusts followed. The two men finally reached agreement, but it was already too late. Events, which were developing at a rapid pace, left them behind. After his brief flight to Baden-Baden in Germany, the general returned home, determined to run things with a firm hand. He had had doubts, and had taken a break. He came back and spoke on the radio, castigating "yesterday's politicians" who wanted his job, giving up the idea of the referendum, keeping Georges Pompidou at the Matignon, and announcing the dissolution of the National Assembly, to be followed by fresh elections.

His moment of weakness had served him well. His mysterious absence had taken people by surprise and created suspense; his return made the whole thing look like a trick. The majority, a number of whose members had hesitated and even succumbed,[40] recovered its nerve. Very soon there was euphoria. At the procession on May 30 along the Champs-Elysées, the Gaullists shouted: "De Gaulle is not alone" and "Mitterrand, you won't be president."

A furious president of the FGDS commented on the general's broadcast thus: "The voice you have just heard is the voice of 18 Brumaire, it is the voice of December 2, it is the voice of May 13, it is the voice that is inaugurating an insolent, minority government against the people, it is the voice of dictatorship. The people will silence that voice."

From then on the Gaullists, who had been so afraid and sometimes proven so craven, once again made him their scapegoat. They even charged the FGDS president with going outside the law when he submitted his candidacy for the presidency of the Republic. But François Mitterrand had merely exploited the theme of the power vacuum and made clear what his own position would be in the event of de Gaulle's resignation (which the general himself had envisaged). It was not, therefore, illegal to replace him by election.

On the other hand, Mitterrand was paradoxical, imprudent, and even something of a poor loser when he spoke of "dictatorship" at a time when the head of state was asking for the matter to be settled by universal suffrage. And it certainly was settled—in a most unequivocal way (and not in the direction hoped for by the Left).

The electors, at first somewhat well-intentioned toward the students, soon became exasperated by the endless street theater and especially by the strikes. In the countryside and suburbs, people could not understand why young people from good families would want to burn cars and, in the municipal housing estates, people did not like the sight of privileged youngsters castigating the consumer society. It was time for common sense to prevail. A lesson was about to be given to those believed, rightly or wrongly, to be close to the rioters and strikers, beginning with François Mitterrand, who already wanted to replace *"le grand Charles"*—again (for a time at least) the paragon of virtue.

The Left suffered a catastrophic defeat at the legislative elections. The FGDS had had 118 deputies; it was left with 57. The Communist party had only 33 deputies left of its former 73. François Mitterrand himself only just scraped through at the second round, and all his friends in the Convention were defeated without exception. Within the FGDS there was only one tenable, logical conclusion: the personal candidacy of François Mitterrand spelled disaster.

Trouble deepened. In August, Soviet tanks invaded Czechoslovakia; the Prague spring was over. The majority was quick to exploit the event: any alliance with the Communist party, it was said, would bring the Red Army closer to the gates of Paris; those who advocated such an alliance were either accomplices or irresponsible. People were sometimes convinced of this.

Once again, François Mitterrand experienced one of those dizzy falls a strange destiny has reserved for him, one that made his detractors say he was "a born loser," had "the evil eye," would "never succeed," and would "never get to the Elysée." Fêted in

1967, Mitterrand had become in 1968 the object of widespread resentment.

As he walked home, he had plenty of time to measure his stock by the looks people gave him. "I'm the most hated man in France," he confided to Michèle Cotard. But he added at once: "But this allows me to hope that one day I shall be the best-loved man." François Mitterrand never gave up.

THE DESCENT INTO HELL—NEAR EPINAY

An eternal Sisyphus, who saw as in a nightmare the rock rolled back to crush him whenever he neared the summit, François Mitterrand had to begin all over again in the early summer of 1968.

Those who in May had been pleased to count themselves among his friends turned away from him by July. In the National Assembly, those left-wing deputies who had escaped the great electoral wash exuded ill-temper and rancor. Their success, they made quite clear, was due solely to their own merits—the Mitterrand label had been a heavy burden to bear. Those who had been defeated charged Mitterrand with being solely responsible for their misfortune. As proof, they cited the fact that those closest to him, the members of the Convention, had all been defeated—and some, including the faithful Roland Dumas at Brive, in the first round. François Mitterrand, who, in adversity, is seldom a good loser, denounced the political and psychological trick that had been played on him: "It's a holdup thought out, planned, and carried out by specialists!"[41] But that never consoled the deputy who had lost his seat.

Public opinion was no kinder. The man whom the French in 1965 had regarded as "brave," "eloquent," "talented," above all, "interesting," now emerged from the opinion polls as "ambitious," "arrogant," "a demagogue," and "the wrong man for the times." And these descriptions were never to leave him. The man who had once been celebrated for his charm now inspired fear: he was criticized for his overly liberal use of sarcasm; for his disturbingly sidelong, shifty looks; for his excessive ruthlessness. And was he really always as respectful of the law as he tried to make out? people wondered. After the May episode, even if the charge was not well founded, it was felt one could no longer trust him. And on television, a great many men of talent, celebrity, or respectability stressed all his unfortunate defects.

Times were hard for everyone. General de Gaulle did not really succeed in winning back the hearts of the French people: what they had voted for was perhaps not so much the man of June 18 as a return to law and order—and the reopening of the gas stations. And what of the Gaullists? He guessed they were busily engaged in their own affairs, already looking to Georges Pompidou and dividing up the inheritance. So the general thought (to be reassured or to challenge fate?) of organizing another referendum, as if no sooner had he been reelected than he wanted to put his title in jeopardy once again.

On the Left, things were no better. Guy Mollet, racked with pain, sick, gloomy, disillusioned, shut himself up more and more in his smoke-filled office, as if to protect himself from the prevailing winds, to chew over the cud of bitterness. His party, which he loved so much, was in a sorry state; Pierre Mauroy had eluded his grasp and was looking greedily in the direction of François Mitterrand. Finally, Prague had revived all his fury against and mistrust of the Communists. Of course, the French Communist party had disapproved of the intervention of the Warsaw Pact troops, but only to qualify its criticisms and shamefully accept the normalization that followed.

After the torments of May, Guy Mollet wondered who could unify a Left split between rebellious students and social democrats, modernist technocrats and revolutionaries, pro-bourgeois workers and proworker intellectuals. He thought more and more of retiring from political life and said so. He even summoned his presumptive heirs, Pierre Mauroy and Claude Fuzier, telling them what he was feeling. And he gave them their parts.

Mollet felt all members of the Convention should really belong to the Socialist party (the radicals had already let it be known they would not join), but that François Mitterrand should not be its first leader. A party man was needed. Mollet hesitated between Mauroy and Fuzier, in the end choosing Mauroy. The man from Lille would have the first place; the Parisian, the second. From then on, it was up to them. So that he wouldn't leave in an atmosphere of failure, Mollet was very anxious for the launching of the revived party to be his last public legacy.

Throughout several meetings in October, the SFIO and the Convention tried to draw up the doctrinal bases of the new party. François Mitterrand felt the wind was against him: no one dared bring up the question of the leadership in his presence. He knew why, and in the end he snapped: "In the new party, of which I shall be a member, I shall not be a candidate for any post."[42] At the congress of the Convention des institutions républicaines that took place at Levallois-Perret on October 5 and 6, François Mitterrand unburdened his fury before his friends: "I find it difficult to accept being criticized for not doing what nobody wanted me to do—that is, for bringing more unity to the Federation. Do you imagine that, taking the Left as it was, it was possible, just like that, with a flick of the wrist, to convince it of the need for unity— a Left that has been shut up behind its barriers, its vocabulary, its rehashed hatreds through half a century of socialism applied at the wrong time and in the wrong way?"

Socialism? Yes, after the trials of May, which went some way toward renewing politicians' imaginative powers and reawakening intellectuals' theoretical fertility, the president of the FGDS thought the moment had come to present his vision of things. He then laid out a few broad outlines: "I believe in the socialization of the principal means of investment, production, and exchange. . . . I believe in the usefulness of an important public sector able to take the reins of the economy as a whole."

Taking their line from him, his friends in the Convention drew up a brave declaration of principle (which, after a few years in power, they would no doubt have emended somewhat):

Because they are serious democrats, Socialists feel real democracy cannot exist in a capitalist society. In this sense, the Socialist party is a revolutionary party. The aim of socialism is the common good, not private profit. The gradual socialization of the means of investment, production, and exchange is its indispensable basis. Indeed, economic democracy is the distinctive characteristic of socialism. . . . The Socialist party proposes to replace gradually capitalistic ownership with social ownership, which may take on many different forms and which the workers must be trained to administer. . . . Socialist transformation cannot be the natural product and sum of reforms correcting the effects of capitalism. Its purpose is not to improve a system, but to replace it with another.

This conception of French-style socialism was not particularly original, but it showed that the members of the Convention, a disparate group of individuals who had come from the fringes of Marxism or from a Center-Left that had grown progressively more pink, was not deaf to the cause of May. Their condemnation of profit (which they were to rehabilitate in 1982, under the reign of necessity) sounded like an echo of the angry students' slogan, "One does not dream about a growth rate."

On the Right as on the Left, it was a race to see who understood best (retrospectively) the aspirations of the young people of 1968. Jacques Chaban-Delmas proposed his "new society" and Valéry Giscard d'Estaing his "gentle growth." (In a fashionable conference organized at UNESCO in 1972, Giscard did not hesitate to declare: "I am an objector to growth.")

Mitterrand was not far behind. Many people date his official conversion to socialism from this time. *Conversion* is certainly the right word. When he explains this event at length in his best book, *Ma part de vérité*, he does so in religious terms. The former pupil of the Angoulême priests gives this definition of the Left:

> Personally, I would say it is justice. I was not born on the Left—still less a socialist, as people know very well. . . . I shall merely make my case worse when I confess that I later showed no precocity. I could have become a socialist under the shock of ideas and facts, at the university, for example, or during the war—but no. Efficient grace took a long time to reach me. I had to be content with whatever grace did come, and I received a share of it, like everybody else. . . . I obeyed, I suppose, a natural inclination, which was both firm and fragile. . . . No, I did not meet the God of socialism on the way. I was not awoken at night by that unknown visitor. I did not fall to my knees and weep for joy. I did not go into one of its churches. . . . Socialism has no God, but it has at its disposal several revealed truths, and in each chapel, there are priests who watch over them, decide disputes, and punish offenders, catechumens among catechu-

mens filling the narthex. I read the sacred books and heard the preachers: faithful to their religion, they taught the power of facts. . . . Alas, socialism produces more theologians than servants. . . .

One could hardly adhere to socialism in a more religious spirit. A little later Mitterrand told Jean-Marie Borzeix that he had understood injustice upon reading the Sermon on the Mount. Indeed, François Mitterrand's development is shared by a number of Catholics, disillusioned with Christian democracy and propelled to the Left by the Algerian War, who discovered something like spiritual exaltation in the May students' protests against the materialism of the consumer society. Even the Catholic hierarchy subscribed to this, with greater or lesser enthusiasm, and the newspapers wrote that the Church was "moving to the Left." The Sunday after Ascension in the year of grace 1968, Msgr. Marty, archbishop of Paris, declared from the pulpit in Notre-Dame: "We challenge a society that ignores men's profoundest aspirations. God is not a conservative. God is for justice." The bishop of Bordeaux Msgr. Maziers, addressing an audience of workers shortly afterwards, gave his own definition of the class struggle, calling it a "fraternal, collective struggle" workers had "been forced to wage for so long in order to take part in a more human way in the life of the world." Breton priests announced to their astonished flock that "there are only historical misunderstandings between socialism and Christianity."

In fact, in the 1960s, a section of the clergy (especially the younger priests and chaplains to the Catholic action movements) no longer concealed its socialist commitment. Although most still distrusted Marxism, some felt they had discovered in self-management (a 1968 concept particularly cherished by the CFDT, the main non-Communist trade union organization) a solution to the world's problems that was both socialist and Christian. The de-Christianization of the working class haunted them with remorse, and the development of their thinking was not to be without political consequences: although in 1974, 77 percent of practicing Catholics voted in the second round for Valéry Giscard d'Estaing, three years later, in the municipal elections of 1977, the transfer to the Left

of over two million Christians largely explains the triumph of the
Socialists.

François Mitterrand did not follow the same path as most Catholics. For years, he had been separated from them. And thinking
of the youth he had been in 1936, he was to admit: "Since the
Church, whose precepts I had continued to observe, was not in the
camp of suffering and hope, one had to join that camp, I told
myself, without her. And so I left my father's path, only to find it
again all the more surely."[43] This last sentence almost says it all.
Mitterrand has the same scruples as many priests or lay Catholics,
has the same feelings of remorse, and has been under the same
influences. On top of all this—and this is no small matter—only a
single way was open to Mitterrand's ambition: that of the Left. As
a result, the Church and her stray sheep, having parted on the
Right, were to find themselves in neighboring provinces after May
1968.

Guy Mollet, a dyed-in-the-wool atheist, never believed in the
sincerity of this conversion: "Mitterrand did not become a socialist," he said. "He learned to talk like one—a different matter!"[44]

The president of the FGDS might recite his new creed every day,
but the SFIO family still regarded him, in that summer of 1968,
as a plague bearer—one who, moreover, was contagious and should
therefore be dropped as soon as possible. In the Federation's executive committee, Arthur Notebart (a deputy for the Nord), Max
Lejeune (a deputy for the Somme), and Charles Loo (a deputy for
Marseille) raised the hue and cry. Some even went so far as to ask
(very discreetly) Gaston Deferre to exclude Mitterrand from the
FGDS group in the National Assembly. Guy Mollet opposed this
and, presaging the storm, gave his absolution to the neophyte. On
November 5 on Europe 1, he declared that the poor showing of
the Left in the legislative elections could not be blamed on François
Mitterrand. But it was too late. The deputy for the Nièvre, deeply
angered, cut short these maneuvers and submaneuvers and announced, before its leading members, that he was resigning from
the FGDS.

"I am not giving up the fight," he went on. "The Federation
must now go forward and transform itself." Did he believe they
would now rush in and try to keep him? In any case, after this

adieu (which was really a good-bye), no one moved. Only Pierre Mauroy and Robert Fabre came to shake his hand. It was hard—very hard.

But although he had abdicated, the proud leader of the FGDS was not giving up. As in the past, whenever he had to resign himself to take a few steps back, it was in order to move forward later with increased determination. As Claude Estier remarks, "he felt he had been subjected to such injustice that he decided not to depend in the future on ungrateful party machines and leaders who might let him down. His decision to lead a great party of his own stemmed from that experience."

Incredibly, three years later François Mitterrand achieved his aim. On June 21, 1971, a month after his triumph at Epinay, he explained to *L'Express*:

By inclination, perhaps, I am a solitary man. In the UDSR and in the Convention, I worked through small groups of individuals, not through a mass party. Gradually I have discovered what, for me, is now the truth. Socialism represents the only response to the world's problems today. Of course, for many, socialism is not yet a very clear idea. Nevertheless, everyone realizes it is a choice leading to the end of the present system in which money is king, in which ownership of the means of production determines political power, and in which everyone is mere appearance. Socialism means the people together taking hold of their own destiny. And it means learning to shoulder responsibilities. It is in itself revolutionary, for it is a break with the established economic and social order. But there is not the least chance of success without the formation of a great party. Having realized that, I drew the obvious conclusion. I was finished with small groups.

Finished with small groups? It would prove easier said than done, taking him over three years. Yet once again, Mitterrand demonstrated his talent for remedying the most unfavorable situation and turning it to his advantage.

Early in 1969, the political class as a whole mobilized for the referendum campaign demanded by General de Gaulle, with two reforms on the agenda: the replacement of the senate by a chamber bringing together representatives of all the economic, trade union, and social forces of the nation (the wish to establish "participation" had thus been translated into a structure that appeared to some as a resurgence of corporatism), and the establishment of regional reform. The general had warned the nation it would be all or nothing. If the referendum were rejected, he would leave immediately.

The Left, the centrists, and Valéry Giscard d'Estaing campaigned against it. François Mitterrand did, too, of course. But his "friends" in the SFIO, fearing the effects of his unpopularity, deliberately kept him out of the television campaign. Putting on a brave face, he waged a very active campaign of his own against what he called the "plebiscite."[45]

The general was beaten. On April 27, 53.1 percent of the votes cast were against the referendum. That evening, Charles de Gaulle let it be known he was leaving the Elysée and retiring definitively to Colombey-les-Deux-Eglises. Disproving all François Mitterrand's prognoses, the general took his leave, like a perfect democrat. The deputy for the Nièvre had lost an adversary whose very size had given him the illusion of comparable greatness.

A new presidential race began. Georges Pompidou, a tough opponent, was already on the starting line. Mitterrand reflected. He began by saying he was a "candidate with nothing." But the faithful Louis Mermaz and enterprising Roland Dumas were already, as it happened, busily collecting the signatures of local representatives necessary to any presidential candidacy.

François Mitterrand was not a man to wallow in illusions: the year 1969 looked much less favorable than 1965. It was impossible in the climate of the time to present Socialists and Radicals with a fait accompli. The Communists regarded him with more suspicion than before: he was at the bottom of the heap and they were not going to put themselves out to save him. Jacques Duclos even said rather cruelly: "Mitterrand represents no organization. He is moved only by ambition and sees the Left as a Spanish inn."[46] In fact, Mitterrand still suspected the Socialist leaders of sending discreet emissaries to Waldeck Rochet and his assistant (a certain Georges Marchais) to bar his candidacy.

The Left was so disorientated and in such poor shape that Guy

Mollet referred to the possible candidacy of a highly regarded scientist, Jean Rostand. In fact, Mollet would not have looked askance at the victory of Alain Poher, president of the senate, whose chances opposite Georges Pompidou were not to be dismissed. However, a candidate had declared himself from within the SFIO, Gaston Deferre, who, in a spirit of revenge, had decided to try his luck this time, still without making any compromise with the Communist party.

The Union of the Left was on fire. The PSU presented a brilliant, talkative young candidate who wanted to reconcile leftism and reformism. In May 1968, this individual had scared P.M.F. by proposing, in response to the rebels' aspirations, the establishment of district revolutionary committees in each town. This honorable tax inspector of Huguenot background was to campaign on a motorbike. His name was Michel Rocard.

This time, the Communist party decided to compete under its own colors. There had, through Claude Fuzier, been a few contacts with the Socialists, but since May (and, above all, since Prague) there had been a decided cooling on both sides. He therefore made it quite clear to Guy Mollet that Communist votes would never go to Gaston Deferre. Oddly enough, since apparently everyone was trying to respond to the aspirations of youth, the Communist party launched into the battle a mustachioed veteran, a former pastry cook with a strong, rolling Pyrenean accent, who, with his jovial smile, would have looked like everyone's ideal grandfather if his anything but kindly eyes had not sent a shiver down the backs of even the least impressionable.

In order to get to the starting line, Gaston Deferre had to force the hand of his comrades somewhat. Guy Mollet had first thought of Christian Pineau, and Alain Savary was also ready to throw himself into battle. But on May 4, at the congress at Alfortville, the mayor of Marseille came out on top. *Le Monde* noted it had come about "thanks to an utterly manipulated congress, in which the mandates were distributed arbitrarily; use had even been made of the mandates of absent federations."

Claude Estier was to comment: "Gaston Deferre had been nominated; it requires a great deal of imagination to declare that he has been appointed by the new Socialist party."[47] Whom could

Gaston Deferre call on to help him and form a presidential ticket in the American style? Pierre Mendès France himself. Throughout the campaign, the duo were to indulge in a strange, lugubrious television number, playing the roles of interviewer and interviewee. "For three weeks on end, one would see alternating or cohabiting on the television screen for the few minutes granted the Deferre-Mendès tandum two candidates looking very sorry for themselves, as if they had just left the funeral for socialism—even when they were accompanied by the excellent Roger Priouret, who was certainly one of the best French journalists around, but not one whose tone is most likely to bring joy to the hearts of the French people," wrote Jean Lacouture, who nevertheless was very favorably disposed toward Mendès France.

To mitigate his gloom somewhat, François Mitterrand could at least tell himself that he remained the only symbol of the Union of the Left and that no one had taken that title from him. He was to console himself soon enough when, on June 1, 1969, the score for the Left fell. *Fell* is the appropriate word, for Gaston Deferre (in supreme humiliation) scarcely received more than 5 percent of the vote. He was just (only just) reimbursed for the cost of his posters, pamphlets, and circulars. Pierre Mendès France, who in 1965 had feared he would only get 25 percent of the vote, had to share this meager patrimony with his friend Gaston.

Jacques Duclos, who had pulled off a very fine, almost light-hearted campaign (after him, the Communists forgot the recipe), obtained 22.51 percent of the vote. For the Socialists, it was a cataclysm. This, of course, would serve François Mitterrand's purposes. What was needed, in a word, was the Union of the Left.

While his comrades bandaged their wounds, Mitterrand began one of those tours of France that had become familiar to him. Preaching the union and renewal of the Socialist party, he had some great successes. At Chambéry, before an audience of two thousand, he declared: "If divisions were removed at the top [of the SFIO], an enormous popular current would see the light of day." A few days later, invited by the RTL, he went on: "Without a great democratic and socialist party, the Left is disorientated and unbalanced." Everywhere he repeated the same thing: "the non-Communist Left lacks a catalyst."

There was a difficulty, however—and a not inconsiderable one. The spot was already taken. In July 1969,[48] the SFIO met in conference with the hope of effecting a face-lift (it had been decided, all the same, to call the party from then on the Socialist party) and chose as its first secretary (the title, too, was new) Alain Savary. Guy Mollet, who was stepping down, had managed to impose his will for the last time by barring the way to Pierre Mauroy, to whom he had once promised his succession. But Mauroy had committed the cardinal sin of displaying too early a tendency to independence and an ill-concealed liking for François Mitterrand.

The new leaders exercised their new power by scuttling the FGDS group in the assembly, which now became the Socialist group. Of course, François Mitterrand was cordially invited to join—as an ordinary deputy. But either Mitterrand's taste for the heights or his wounded pride persuaded him otherwise. Rather than remain anonymous, he preferred to sit from that point on among the handful of nonparty deputies.

It was too much. His efforts to unite the ununitable had failed. And he was no more successful in trying to influence the Socialists from a small independent group devoted to him personally. Since power on the Left passed through the leadership of the Socialist party, he would do everything possible to get the job.

Every two years, in that particular political family, there took place what Mitterrand called the "great Easter"—a congress in which (in theory, at least) the leader democratically submitted himself for reelection. How could he transform the theory into practice and thereby remove the outgoing leader? It was obviously a long shot for someone who had never belonged to the party and whose very adhesion to socialism was so recent it might seem more than a little suspect in the eyes of old party veterans.

In fact, circumstances were rather favorable for anyone capable of deciphering men's passions. The holder of the coveted post, Alain Savary, a very honorable man, exerted little influence over his membership. He had embarked on a halfhearted ideological debate with the Communists, out of which could emerge neither dynamism nor enthusiasm.

And in any case, questions of personality weighed far more heavily in this ancient machine with its accumulation of failures, compromises, and divisions. Where failures were concerned, Gaston Deferre certainly took some beatings. The mayor of Marseille attributed the extent of his failure to the old Molletist machine and was ready to do anything to "de-Molletize" the Socialist party; he had had enough of being relegated for twenty-five years to the minority of the party. Pierre Mauroy, bitter at being deprived of the post of first secretary at the last minute, was ready for revenge. The CERES of Jean-Pierre Chevènement, Didier Motchane, and Georges Sarre—young wolves with already-sharp fangs whom Guy Mollet had taken on, encouraged, and flattered—had soon become convinced that Mollet himself and his acolytes were the main obstacles to any real development in the party. It was these three men who launched the first assault. In 1970, Didier Motchane gave the signal when he blamed the "nonentities"—"those generals, who always lie and are always beaten, occupying the Cité Malesherbes"—for all the party's misfortunes. Not given to subtleties, he castigated "that astonishing gang of gentlemen-bourgeois and proletarian bourgeois." After this first salvo fired by one of his confederates, Jean-Pierre Chevènement launched in. He declared: "The Socialist party has become an obstacle to the Socialist party." Such a statement had to be punished, and a furious Alain Savary suspended him for six months.

François Mitterrand was not slow to realize how he could exploit this odd situation. He did his sums and concluded that Mauroy, Deferre, and those they carried with them formed a very sizable minority with the Socialist party. The CERES represented 7 or 8 percent of the vote at a party congress; if the members of the convention were added, a majority could be built up—providing it kept together and realized it could only achieve anything if it did so. "It was a terrific bluff. Mitterrand got Savary to believe his friends numbered over fifteen thousand, when actually there were only three thousand of them," recounts Jean Poperen, who did not at the time belong to the Mitterrand clan. Everything was now ready to put the Mollet-Savary axis into the minority.

However, there were a number of things still left to be done. To begin with, if Pierre Mauroy was to bring all his votes with him, he had to be the sole boss of the Nord federation. This required the agreement of Augustin Laurent, the Socialist patriarch of Lille.

But the gods were with Mauroy: at the municipal elections of March 1971, Augustin Laurent handed over to him the keys of the great city's town hall—and therefore of the Socialist federation.

It was also necessary that former enemies, the extreme left of the Communist party, the CERES, and the right wing of the Socialist party (Mauroy and Deferre) should agree to combine their votes. This was not so simple: it was an uneasy marriage. The CERES dreamed of a revolution engineered with the Communist party. At Lille and Marseille, on the other hand, the alliance with the centrists was the rule. Indeed, Alain Savary had charged Gaston Deferre and Pierre Mauroy with associating with reactionaries in the elections of March 1971. The insolent young men in the CERES went further. For them, the mayor of Marseille represented the diabolical temptation of the "third force," an object of permanent exorcism.

But it is well known that in politics (in François Mitterrand's, especially) ideology is fine providing it does not impede the march to power. Jean-Piere Chevènement, Gaston Deferre, and Pierre Mauroy, all of whom were dying to get onto the platform, were forced to outdo one another in the political game. Meanwhile, Pierre Joxe and Claude Estier went on talking to Alain Savary and Guy Mollet, hinting, without promising too much, that their boss was supportive.

François Mitterrand was prudent enough not to be too much in evidence. In this affair, he used the spider's strategy, silently spinning his web with the help of his friends and waiting for the flies to get caught in his toils. His childhood in the Charente had taught him that flies were not caught with vinegar.

It would take too long to narrate in detail all the comings and goings between the "conspirators" during the spring of 1971. They met secretly, in twos, threes, and tens, in constantly varying formations, until, little by little and with great stealth, they finally all met together. Since they could not unite on policies, they had to unite on (or rather, against) personalities: Guy Mollet and Alain Savary.

At these meetings, François Mitterrand (in a way no one else can match when he takes the trouble) used all his charm, coaxing those there, mocking those who were not, dangling a radiant future before the ambitious, discussing doctrine with those whose tastes lay in that direction. For when it came to manipulating men (he had known the recipe since the Resistance), he was inimitable. "Imagine, he even took us off to a cabaret," recounts a still-wondering Paul Mauroy.

The predictable result (except to Alain Savary and his friends, who never imagined the CERES would make such an about-face) occurred at the Epinay congress: the coalition of "conspirators" had become a majority. The suspicious Guy Mollet and innocent Alain Savary had been magnificently outmaneuvered. Mollet tried to reassure himself, repeating: "With his face, Mitterrand won't last two years."

On June 16, François Mitterrand became first secretary of the new Socialist party. He did not even have a membership card. Two months later, when interviewed by Marcelle Padovani for *Le Nouvel Observateur*, he said: "The Epinay congress proceeded with the implacable logic of life against whatever threatens or destroys it. It proceeded outside the control of the leadership and specialists. It expressed the wishes of the grass roots. If you compared it with an abstract painting, I would readily admit . . . the Epinay congress was not lacking in a certain aesthetic rigor."

He certainly had a way of putting things. Mauroy and Deferre, Chevènement and Estier, Mollet and Savary must have rubbed their eyes when they read these words. At the Epinay congress, neither Mollet nor Savary smiled. They were witnessing a great spectacle: radiant, talented, charming as he could be when he had won, François Mitterrand indulged in a great lyrical outpouring on the platform. From that point on, he would lay down the law of the socialism he embodied. And what a law it was: "Anyone who does not accept the break with the established order and capitalist society cannot be a member of the Socialist party," he declared. "Revolution is break. Our base is class confrontation. The real enemy is the monopoly of money—the money that corrupts, buys, crushes. The king money that ruins and corrupts even men's consciences."

The delegates gave him a standing ovation. They did not know or did not notice that this condemnation of money had once been propounded, almost word for word, by an old man to whom they were not particularly well disposed: Pétain. No matter—the festival reached its climax and the new party boss, who had just preached revolution, class confrontation, and a break with the established order, went on: "We must reconquer the ground lost to the Communists." This was logical enough, but he at once added, more surprisingly: "We must reconquer the liberals, and those of no party." He then raised his fist and sang the "Internationale"—for the first time in his life.

It had been a good day's work.

FRANÇOIS MITTERRAND AND HIS FRIENDS

Those who wish to understand François Mitterrand cannot ignore the character and style of his relationships with friends. He is (and has always been) the core of a circle that exists only for and because of him. Actually, there are several circles, each alien to the other, of whose subtle interrelationships he is a sensitive but tyrannical master.

A few dozen men and women may, without exaggeration, claim to have his confidence. The less shrewd or subtle dare to imagine they have it all, when in fact, each possesses only a part of it.

Only one man, Georges Dayan, enjoyed the unique privilege of knowing he was the friend of all the François Mitterrands. The rest are allowed to know only one of the innumerable facets of his personality—and woe to anyone who ventures beyond the permitted bounds. "One may know things or secrets about him, but only on the express condition that one doesn't let him see one knows them," says one of his closest friends.

Any attempt to push open one of François Mitterrand's doors without being invited is to risk having it banged in one's face. Not many have taken that risk. The president has always made certain to calibrate what he reveals of himself to others: a fraction of his past, memories, tastes, interests, hopes, and even loves.

On the other hand, those who are closest to him among the young socialists who entered the Party under his reign (and often because of him) affect an astonishing indifference to his past, almost a refusal to know what he was like before. For them, François Mitterrand is the father, the prophet of a French-style, just, and moral socialism.

Those who know where he came from (for lack of knowing where he is going) marvel at his pliability, and are quite prepared for any number of sudden transformations they dare not even imagine. They feel anything is possible with him. And, of course, from their first meetings, all had guessed (or now convince themselves they had guessed) that their "friend" had a destiny.

"He's a very special kind of person. I had an intuition of his future the first time I met him," attorney Jacques Ribs confesses. Dozens of people speak of him in the same vein. Many, having soon become convinced he would go far, did not hesitate to hitch themselves to his star—some out of ambition, most by a tacit acceptance of his superiority.

"I have organized the whole of my life in relation to him," declares Georges Beauchamp without hesitation, though he was given (or claimed as reward, after 1981) only a modest seat on the Conseil économique et social and that celebrated Légion d'honneur (which has been the right of all those whom chance or choice have placed on the Socialist president's road). "But my real reward," he goes on, "is that we call each other *tu*." People on the Left or the Right might well retort: "And a lot of good it's done you!" But, in the clan, no one would dare laugh at such words. Using *tu* is the supreme decoration, the grand cross of the order of Mitterrandism.

Instinctively, his friends became his liege men. "I think I chose him because he is naturally the sovereign," admits André Rousselet, who has become president of the Havas agency under Mitterrand's reign. And he continues: "After 1981? Nothing has changed between us. He has always been the president."

No one in Mitterrand's entourage has ever questioned his primacy; no one has ever thought of setting himself up as a rival or competitor. Serving the man, if not always his ideas, is the rule of the game. Deep down one may not entirely accept his choices, one may frown disapprovingly or be secretly exasperated, but he is never to be blamed.

Few of those around him ever dare to argue with him, still less actually to oppose him. For François Mitterrand immediately turns every disagreement into a personal quarrel. The questioner or the skeptic soon finds himself vilified as an ungrateful deserter. If Mitterrand feels suspected or judged, he immediately freezes and deploys his defenses: the look in his eyes hardens; the pouting mouth, with its "superior" air, becomes a cruel jaw revealing the sharp teeth; the color drains from his face; he exudes bitterness; affection evaporates; and the curtain falls. As with electricity in a storm, communication is suddenly cut, to be reestablished a few minutes later, or during some subsequent visit, or never at all. "He places people in the position of being terrorized at the very idea of displeasing him," remarked someone long acquainted with this feudal setup.

Not everyone, however, is treated in the same way. Indeed, from some he tolerates—even almost expects—intellectual independence (providing it is not disturbing in a lasting way). Over the years he has put up with the outbursts of a Pierre Joxe, whose intelligence he respects and whose fidelity he is certain of (the two indispensable prior conditions). In the case of Chevènement, who played no small part in Mitterrand's takeover of the Socialist party in 1971 and took a decisive role at the Metz conference in 1979 by removing Michel Rocard from the presidential candidacy, Mitterrand accepts his independence while prudently limiting it, dropping him for a time, but never forgetting to take him back when it pleases him. From the moment Gaston Deferre gave up any attempt to be top dog, Mitterrand put up with outbursts, indiscretions, and excessive language he would have tolerated in no one else. Downplaying his moralistic inclinations, Mitterrand did not even take offense at the repeated shortcomings for which the municipal administration of Marseille was noted. In the case of Laurent Fabius, who dazzled him with his neo-Giscardian vigor, Mitterrand pretended to ignore the almost cavalier way in which the young minister addressed him as "President" at cabinet meetings. With so much admiration in the tone of voice, Mitterrand could forgive him a great deal; it did not prevent Fabius from being made prime minister.

But in most cases, the slightest shortcoming receives an icy response. Friendship with François Mitterrand involves an extreme code of behavior to which everybody must submit. One must know how to judge the mood of the moment, calibrate the degree of welcome possible in any one day, understand when to keep quiet, speak, or disappear. "One must be able to sense whether or not one is on the same wavelength," notes a close colleague, well used

to this curious liturgy of friendship. "François Mitterrand represents the triumph of the unstated or the merely hinted at. When
things are going well, one has a vague, almost physical sense that
things *are* going well. And when things are going badly, one feels
so embarrassed one wants to run away."

Although he tends to mock or despise others' protocol, François
Mitterrand is very good at imposing his own in a ritual that is more
patriarchal than monarchic. At Latché, his refuge in the Landes,
guests are assigned their places at the table and roles in the conversation upon arrival. Being allowed to stroke the donkeys or take
the ritual walk through the forest with the dogs will, for them, be
the supreme reward. Strolling through the forest, the master of the
house—always decked out in a way some might find picturesque,
others incongruous, the most cherished accessory being the beret,
which, despite its highly national character, is not the most status-
lending item of masculine attire—sometimes unburdens himself
and even goes so far as to listen to others. More often, however, he
indulges in a monologue for miles on end on the subject of the
seasons, the clouds, or the quality of the light.

Many close friends who have gone down from Paris with the
hope of passing on some urgent message or long-cherished idea
have had, if the atmosphere was not right, to pack their bags and
return to the capital, mission unaccomplished.

The harem is also subject to sudden thunderbolts: out of the
blue, the grand vizier falls for some new favorite. In the twinkling
of an eye, old friends are banished and made to bide their time.
Such favorites have included Jacques Attali, Jack Lang, Régis Debray, and Jean-Edern Hallier. To win over François Mitterrand, it
is better to be a rising star than someone who has reached the
zenith. He cares neither for the unknown nor for those who have
arrived. Being celebrated at least once in the pages of *Le Nouvel
Observateur*, *Le Monde*, or, more recently, *Libération* is the best
passport to one of these sudden friendships. One must write well,
perhaps sing, or even have a talent as a theatrical director. Arriving
from some Latin American country (or, failing that, from some
Mediterranean land) with one's works under one's arm is also a
good introduction. Some connection, however distant, with the late
Salvador Allende, Fidel Castro, or Papandreou has been known to

open the doors of the Elysée and even those of Mitterrand's private home in the rue de Bièvre—or at least put one in line for the Légion d'honneur (which, since 1981, has been compulsively and liberally dished out as if it were some national candy).

But, in order to find a lasting place in the monarch's affections and network of his friendships, it is not enough to shine. The most useful quality is the ability to show devotion and admiration—the latter especially, perhaps. In this regard Jacques Attali, with his look of a devoted young owl, has done as well as anyone. First he managed to pass himself off as a latter-day Pico della Mirandola, writing a few abstruse and controversial books, then serving as an economics tutor; since his entry into the Elysée as the president's alter ego, able to present the best possible picture each day, Attali has become transformed. Indeed, he has become indispensable: a daily confidant, companion on the president's walks round the gardens, source of new ideas (some good, some less so), he must always be there, ready to inscribe in history the president's slightest deed. He builds up his exclusive, jealous happiness—a bit more than yesterday, but less than tomorrow—in familiar contemplation of the master. Knowing the president is there in the office next door, that he will soon appear, call him, smile at him, consult him, tell him some news, or try out some idea on him—this is what constitutes Attali's happiness. To the envious exasperated by his influence, the head of state replies that Attali is the most intelligent of all, that he "already belongs to the year 2010." And some, not lacking in common sense, smile to themselves: "The year 2010? We have to get there first."

And what of Jack Lang? François Mitterrand, who in many ways has kept his provincial outlook, immediately decided this university teacher turned man of the theater personified true Parisian chic. All witnesses confirm this: the shy, introverted native of Jarnac seems to have been completely taken in by this man of youthful looks, carefully tousled hair, and clothes of a yachtsman on the waterfront, so good at conveying his overflowing enthusiasm for cultural matters in an endless stream of left-wing jargon. How, too, could Mitterrand resist a spontaneity that made Lang fling his arms around people (preferably the rich and famous) as if they were old pals? André Malraux used to take General de Gaulle off to museums before the morning bell sounded. Jack Lang, on the other hand, has no rival in getting the Socialist president to turn up, at the right time, at "in" (even "underground") spots, where he can breathe the spirit of the time, and at places where he ought to be seen. Perhaps it was this taste for the limelight that made Mitterrand declare, the day after May 10: "The French have crossed the frontier separating night from daylight."

And Régis Debray? This intellectual of such a bourgeois background and so romantic an appearance, who was so clever with words and yet always childish in his judgments ("Cuba, island of liberty!" was his first motto), played, for the first secretary of the Socialist party, the role of Christopher Columbus, discovering America—Latin America—for him. In the eyes of the ordinary party member, this intellectual freedom fighter, friend of Che Guevara, and one-time inmate of a Bolivian jail, embodied the struggle against American imperialism.

Jean-Edern Hallier merely passed through the Mitterrand court. One day, in a generous mood, the first secretary of the Socialist party, not yet in a position to hand out the Légion d'honneur, declared this disillusioned angel to be "the best writer of his generation." This compliment, which would have earned Mitterrand the eternal devotion of any ordinary man or even a Norman writer, aroused in this crazy Celt the passion of a praying mantis. And, once crowned, François Mitterrand was very nearly torn to pieces by the suicidal talent of a writer who had dazzled him so much but was now for him a poor specimen of the species.

These courtiers must not just learn to endure the king's whims. When one loves, one does not count the cost. For over thirty years, all of François Mitterrand's friends have learned this—sometimes at their expense. This man, so impatient to beat down the wall of money, does not concern himself with vulgar necessities. He never has any cash on him, in large or small denominations.

Jacques Bloch-Morhange, not one of his close associates, provides valuable testimony:

> We were going down his staircase—he lived on the second floor—when his wife, opening the apartment door, made a sign to him that there was something urgent she wanted to tell him.

He climbed back up a floor, listened to her, fumbled in his pockets, failed to find what he was looking for, and returned to the first floor in order to ask me if I could lend him a hundred francs because his wife needed it to buy the food for lunch and, as it happened, he had absolutely no money on him that morning. Of course, I lent it to him. To my knowledge he still owes me it. Too late now![49]

This habit has never stopped Mitterrand from generously inviting many of his familiars to restaurants. But they must understand they will have to foot the bill. "Pay it and we'll settle up later," the master invariably says, before disappearing. Usually, that is the end of it. One lady, the object of his tender attentions, joked affectionately: "He cost me a lot of money because he was always without ten francs for coffee or twenty francs for a taxi."

Yet François Mitterrand is not insensitive to the misfortunes of his own people. Although he does not care for weddings or christenings, he is tireless when it comes to visiting friends in hospital (Jean Chevrier, owner of the Hôtel du Vieux-Morvan at Château-Chinon, where the deputy for the Nièvre formerly had his winter and summer quarters, was visited regularly once a week by the head of state when he was in hospital during the spring of 1984).

Nor does he miss a funeral. Like all great Christian romantics, he is familiar with death. His predecessor, Valéry Giscard d'Estaing, did not wish to accept that history is tragic; François Mitterrand knows it is (some even maintain he hopes it is).

He is never more sure of himself, more master of his feelings, than under the most trying circumstances: he was profoundly moved by the murder of French soldiers in Beirut and the assassination in the rue des Rosiers. At such times he is at his best. Never more than under such tragic circumstances does he have the knack of finding the right words, the right facial expression, the right gestures. On such days, many French people of all parties feel he possesses greatness.

"And for his friends' widows, he is incomparable," one of his closest colleagues confided in admiration.

This monarchical temperament, this organization of friendship always intended to give him the first role, stems no doubt as much from his organizing ability as from his affections. Even if he cultivates friendships that bring him nothing, over the years Mitterrand has been able to form a phalanx of faithful followers consisting of the most devoted members of his entourage, on whom he has been able to depend absolutely in conquering the UDSR, setting up his clubs, launching his assaults on the Socialist party, and, eventually, taking over the Republic itself. Surrounded today by a plethora of zealous underlings, hundreds of Socialist deputies, and thousands of Socialist party members, his convictions remain intact: "With sixty well-placed friends, you can hold a country, you can hold France," he once imprudently confided.

Perhaps the president remembered the imaginary dialogue between Lenin and Trotsky in Curzio Malaparte's *The Technique of the Coup d'Etat*, in which Lenin maintains that if one is to conquer power, one must be based in the masses, while Trotsky declares that, on the contrary, one only has to have a few men placed at strategic points to get the same results. According to these arguments, the head of state would seem more of a Trotskyite than a Leninist.

In any case, his sixty-odd friends, some famous, some not, are of every kind. What is there in common between a Jean Védrine and the Marquis de Saint-Périer, Mitterrand's golf partner under the Fourth Republic who drove him to the fairway in his Rolls-Royce? What kinship can be detected in the freemasonry of Mitterrandism between those of the Charente and those of the Nièvre, those of the Resistance and those of the bar, those of the opposition and those in power?

All have at least one point in common: not one is a worker. Is this not, paradoxical though it may seem, proof that François Mitterrand really is a socialist?

THE FOREIGN PRINCE

It needed an individual as complex, diverse, and even baffling as François Mitterrand to give a soul to that creaking machine that was the Socialist party in the early 1970s. Arriving at the headquarters in the Cité Malesherbes, a former private house, an old, badly proportioned building bequeathed by the SFIO, the new first secretary discovered a strange patchwork, a bizarre conglomerate consisting of old, sentimental SFIO notables fond of their food and wine; young, half-repenting Leftists, who, after wandering from one small political group to another, had found in the mass party some memory of May 1968's crazy fraternity; severe economists who commented learnedly on the growth rate without imagining for a moment that it might collapse; engineers stifling in their laboratories for whom socialism represented the Western frontier; *grands bourgeois* (often from the Protestant or Jewish upper reaches of society), from whom a little financial aid could be asked at election times (in exchange for which they could shake the plumber's hand with a sense of uniting in a common cause); careerists; a handful of adventurers; Christians with a social conscience ready to sacrifice their political virginity for the salvation of the world; a few progressive-minded employers ready to embrace the prospect of self-management (preferably in their competitors' enterprises); and, above all, teachers—primary school teachers, lycée teachers, university lecturers and professors—whole trainloads of teachers of every type and category.

The task of seducing them, bringing them together, and motivating them required means François Mitterrand was not entirely devoid of. First, he had a gift for words. The first secretary had just reread certain good authors: Proudhon, Marx, Jaurès, Hegel, and Blum. Armed with these ingredients and a few pinches of Christianity, he was ready to invent a socialism of his own, as others had invented the nouvelle cuisine. In language very reminiscent of 1848, in which there was much talk of man's dignity, of love of liberty-equality-fraternity, he spoke a written language and hinted at a rosy future in which "man will dominate the machine," in which the poor will be rich and the evil rich punished, in which money ("king money") will be dethroned.

Mitterrand had a particular gift for the broad vision. When he pursued an argument, he could pad it with historical references, suddenly moving his audience by introducing some childhood memory or impressing them by slipping in a quotation from Renan, Michelet, or Lamartine. And, to make them laugh, he would take a swipe at the Right. (In some congresses, the mere name of Lecanuet, delivered with a hardly perceptible snigger, was enough to trigger off giggles in the hall.) On his lips, the word *gauche* (left) took on an almost magical power. All in all, even if his speeches had not yet reached their ultimate perfection, this music was harmonious enough to seduce the ears of such diverse people.

At first, many party members and leading personalities called him (among themselves) "the foreign prince," and some even "the accursed prince." But gradually he imposed his authority. "Jean, étonne-moi!" ("Jean, surprise me!") Diaghilev had demanded of Cocteau. Mitterrand, too, could surprise. He was not like any other boss. "Guy Mollet's working hours were sacrosanct," Pierre Mauroy recounts. "We knew he was there in the building from morning till night. We expected to be summoned into his office and to take the brunt of his abuse. François Mitterrand, on the other hand, only spent one or two hours a day in the building—and it was never at the same time. He would arrive, unexpected, ask one of us to walk through the capital with him, then we all had dinner together. We spent some magical moments with him."

He certainly surprised, this prince who arrived at the Cité Malesherbes always driven by young ladies who were constantly changing (at the time, the Socialist party could not afford to give its leader a chauffeur and he himself could hardly drive). Gradually party members began to learn Mitterrand's curious eccentricities. Although he never wore a watch or carried money, he constantly dragged around, in an inside coat pocket, an odd bundle of folded, rumpled papers, which were almost stuck together and which he carefully transferred from one coat to another when he changed. It was just possible to make out a crumpled postcard; old, yellowed newspaper clippings; a dry flower; and, on bits of paper, in scribbling whose mysteries he alone could decipher, innumerable telephone numbers and some precious quotation. In a restaurant, before going to the table, he would extract from this bric-a-brac a tiny card, scarcely larger than a postage stamp, on which he noted the names of those he had invited and the places he had assigned them around the table. At meetings of the executive committee or secretariat (which he sometimes deserted to make a private telephone call)—and supposedly sometimes even at cabinet meetings— he occasionally removed this "little pile of secrets" from his pocket, and, under the intrigued gaze of his neighbors, spent a few happy moments with that piece of his private life.

In a few months the new first secretary was to shed his old dress habits and adopt quite new ones. To adapt to his flock, this man who had known nothing but dark suits, white shirts, and black ties—the dress of any possible minister under the Fourth Republic—now adopted lighter colors, turtleneck sweaters, corduroy trousers—clothing more associated with the teaching profession. But, above all, he achieved his own synthesis of Blum and Jaurès, borrowing the broad-rimmed hat of the former and loose scarf of the latter. Later, when he was better integrated into the Socialist International, he sometimes wore the sailor's cap, after the fashion of Helmut Schmidt. The habit may not make the monk, but it at least makes the convert.

Mitterrand also tried his hand at the rites and practices of the popular festival. He was not entirely at home here, however, which sometimes caused some curious scenes. Thus, during the summer of 1972, to celebrate his twenty-five years as a parliamentarian, he organized a great fête at Château-Chinon. The whole party was there—all his faithful followers, all his friends. His good, delighted townspeople watched such celebrities as Dalida and Roger Hanin, Mikis Theodorakis, and Paul Guimard pass by. An unknown man arrived in a Rolls: only those in the know knew this was the Marquis de Saint-Périer. People pointed out the novelist Edmonde Charles-Roux, who had made a few purchases on the way at Vézelay (including a boa in orange wool, which she promised to offer as a model to her friend Yves Saint-Laurent).[50]

François Mitterrand, who felt at home on his own territory and among his friends, wrote: "Men who claim to be in politics without remaining in permanent contact with simple people are merely ignorant technocrats. I learn much more by spending an hour in a fairground than by pouring over thick files."

Was this an expression of unconscious snobbery? Not at all. The first secretary simply wanted to emulate Jean Jaurès, who had related the following incident: "This afternoon, instead of going to work in the chamber library, I went to see an old cobbler in Auteuil, who doesn't know who I am but wants to convert me to socialism. Would you believe it? I get a lot out of what he tells me as he pulls on his awl. Thanks to that good man, I realized there is a lot wrong with the trade unions."

The contact with "simple people," as François Mitterrand calls them, does not exclude a certain distance adopted toward members of the party. The man from Jarnac realized that in order to ensure his peace of mind, he would have to rule the Socialist party as a sovereign—and that he could do so.

To begin with, he had the necessary prestige and uniqueness. When Mitterrand speaks, there is silence; everyone soon learns to keep quiet and drink in his words as an elixir of truth. If some chatterbox breaks the rules, a dark, imperious gaze is turned upon him, causing him to wish the earth would swallow him up. Each week in the party weekly, *L'Unité*, Mitterrand's bucolically political (and very often moralizing) page (which might be better termed his private journal entry) almost takes on the authority of a pontifical bull. In the party branches, it is awaited, dissected, commented upon. Often people wish it were less anecdotal, but they are proud of it, too: it is certainly a change from the customary wooden language of the parties.

To reign, or perhaps simply to surprise, Mitterrand divides. This complex man seems to protect himself by confusing things. On a single subject, he hands out the same task to several investigators, who discover (often quite by chance) that there are others in competition with them. This leads to deep jealousies, great disappointments, and nagging anxieties. If only, to get some post of responsibility, it was enough to work hard. But the latest comer may suddenly interest the prince and carry off the title, and "in the twinkling of an eye a destiny is made that completely disrupts another," confided one who has benefited and then suffered in this way. Thus the novelist and historian Max Gallo owed his post as government spokesman to a particularly good performance on the television books program *"Apostrophes."* The three or four claimants who had been slaving away for months displaying their merits had no alternative but to go into collective mourning. Thus at the Grenoble congress Mitterrand offered Pierre Bérégovoy a job at party headquarters after meeting him in the bathroom. To animate a party like the Socialists, one must know how to impress people, one must have a sense of "theater." But above all, one must have the skills of a juggler, and in this François Mitterrand has no equal.

For a man who claims to be hopeless at figures and mathematics, he deserves the Field Medal (the Nobel Prize for mathematicians) for his algebra-like achievements in politics. He has an equation permanently to solve: knowing his own tendency within the Socialist party is represented symbolically by the letter A, that of Pierre Mauroy by the letter B, that of Michel Rocard by the letter C, and that of Jean-Pierre Chevènement by the letter E (tendency D, representing the influence of women in the Socialist party, soon sank without trace), his whole problem, given the primacy of parameter A, is to express his personal power in an equation. From congress to congress, the forces have shifted. Thus at Pau in 1975, the equation was: $A + B - E =$ my personal power (the Rocardians were not yet organized). At Nantes in 1977, it was the same. But at Metz in 1979, everything changed, the equation becoming: $A + E - B - C =$ me.

In other words, whereas at Metz, Mauroy and Rocard formed an alliance and challenged his authority, François Mitterrand soon managed to bring under his wing the CERES, that turbulent left wing that had helped him so much to seize power at Epinay and that, since 1973 (the ingratitude of kings), he had thrown into the minority, the Socialists' purgatory.

To buttress his personal authority Mitterrand has always had recourse to the same methods—first, a permanent mistrust nothing can disarm. "I remember the unease that reigned at certain meetings of the executive committee when the first secretary tore to pieces, like a tiger with its teeth in its prey, André Boulloche, Alain Savary, Claude Fuzier, and other poor devils, who, unhappily for them, had taken it into their heads to oppose him."[51] And then Mitterrand threatened to resign. When the CERES, Pierre Joxe, and Claude Estier wanted to distance the Socialist party from the Common Market, François Mitterrand wrote to Pierre Mauroy, telling him he was prepared to return to Colombey-Latché if people were no longer willing to follow him. The results? The recalcitrants, with ropes round their necks, voted unanimously against their ideas. He resigned again—or rather, threatened to but everyone dissuaded him—when certain party organizations needed a lot of coaxing to support the nomination of those *petits bourgeois*, the left-wing radicals. The first secretary would not tolerate his allies being treated that way. So he placed his friends as sentinels to keep an eye on all the strategic points—an old habit.

Georges Dayan became his spokesman in the executive committee: in Mitterrand's absence, he could express his views for him. Georges Beauchamp was his special representative on the party's finance committee. Guy Penne was always sent off to settle conflicts. Charles Hernu was given the job of testing the climate (and sometimes even of playing the role of a kamikaze to test the party's resistance on subjects that might evolve). Mitterrand had even worked out a method for this: when the subject was too delicate for the first secretary to be involved personally, Charles Hernu published an article on the matter in *Le Monde*; the reactions were then noted, and the first secretary had only to work out a synthesis of cleverly prepared positions.

When Mitterrand's authority over the party grew stronger, he almost made his hegemony official. Side by side with the regular governing body of the Socialist party (eleven national secretaries and eight delegates), he appointed special representatives answerable only to him and, following a favorite technique, made their tasks deliberately duplicate those of other members. This was an excellent way of oiling the cogs. Soon political decisions were being made in informal conclaves meeting at his home in the rue de Bièvre. Gradually the first secretary became the "party regent."[52] These methods inevitably created a stormy situation within the party, resulting in a strange relationship of fear and dependence between the party and the master. The number of courtiers increased and the court grew larger. François Mitterrand himself was not at all averse to this. "This changing, dynamic party, traversed by various currents, has a strong hold on my affections just as it is, even when it irritates me—even because it irritates me," its first secretary wrote.[53] It may have irritated him, but it also tired him. And if François Mitterrand imposed his authority on this disparate assemblage it was partly because he worked hard on it and could claim personal success for results that got better each year (80,000 members in 1971; 100,000 in 1973; 150,000 in 1975).

Each year he undertook a tour of France (he is without peer where detailed knowledge of the country is concerned, leading the life of a mere commercial traveler, going to the most out-of-the-way spots to sell that perishable commodity, socialism). His colleagues and underlings admired the vitality of this then fifty-six-year-old man who was willing to travel in uncomfortable night trains in order to find himself, in the early hours of the morning, pale, without even having had time to shave, in front of a meager gathering of party members hungry for hope. Jokers have even remarked that if Joseph Mitterrand, his father, had taken as much pains to sell his vinegar, it would now be the national drink.

Twice, however, François Mitterrand hinted that he was growing tired of this kind of life. In May 1972 he wrote:

Each week I go out to the provinces, where I visit Socialist federations and hold public meetings. On Saturday or Sunday I go back to the Nièvre, where I chair the sessions of the General Council at least six times a year. In Paris, Wednesdays and Thursdays are taken up with meetings of the national secretariat and executive committee of the party. On top of that, I have few evenings that are not taken up with working parties or branch meetings. I am not complaining, but when one has to add to this timetable a parliamentary debate, the writing of an article, the planning of a book, the preparation of a broadcast, I do sometimes—yes, I must admit—feel tired.[54]

And again in May 1973 he wrote: "I find it hard to overcome my tiredness at the end of the week. The trouble is I find it difficult to break the rhythm I have imposed upon myself. I find rest such an effort that I often give up trying."[55]

What is it that drives him this way? "After a quarter of a century of parliamentary life, my life's ambition is not to go to the Elysée," he wrote in *La Rose au poing* the same year (1973), just after signing the Common Program with the Communists. This is hard to swallow, for less than a year later, there he was opposite Valéry Giscard d'Estaing—a determined candidate who only narrowly missed being elected. Yet many of those close to him have been tempted to believe him when he declares: "If I had a patent of nobility, I would take the one I derive from my Socialist comrades. If I am to leave a trace in history, it is not the worst furrow." Of course, after the Epinay congress, some Socialists felt an instinctive distrust for this much too clever leader, but as they observed the devoted way he worked for the party, they came to believe there was more sincerity than calculation in what he did.

Throughout those years, François Mitterrand played the role of first secretary so well that he became the very embodiment of the job in the eyes of the party membership. He acquired his legitimacy by remaining the most determined opponent first of Georges Pompidou, then of Valéry Giscard d'Estaing, never having a good word to say for either. He consolidated his position in his negotiations with the Communist party, which were virtually trials of strength. Finally, he crowned it with his party's almost constant electoral progress. So he soon won the hearts of the party membership. Everything and anything was expected of him; people would do anything for him.

Yet he sometimes sorely tried his comrades. At the end of 1971, he suddenly disappeared without leaving a trace. Where was he? What was he doing? Who was he with? Nobody in the party knew. For several days, the Cité Malesherbes had lost its captain. Some feared he had been kidnapped. No one guessed that, in fact, he was in India—in Calcutta, to be precise.

He had been invited there by two members of the community of the Frères du Monde, Françoise and Léo Jallais, to see for himself what real misery was like. He had accepted—out of a desire to understand, and perhaps out of Christian scruples. There was also another possible reason: in the Bangladesh crisis, André Malraux was on the side of the Bengali freedom fighters, and was thus overtaking François Mitterrand on his Left. In this trip, too, Mitterrand was not without courage. He slept on a straw mattress on the ground in a Bengali camp—incognito, of course.

But the conflict became acute. The Pakistani air force bombed Indian airports and Indira Gandhi proclaimed a state of emergency, closing the airports. The first secretary was trapped. He had to seek help, make contacts (and thus abandon his anonymity). Mitterrand learned that a French journalist was staying at the Ritz Intercontinental Hotel in Calcutta, and he called on him. Jean-Claude Guillebaud, then special correspondent for the *Sud-Ouest*, saw the deputy for the Nièvre arrive in jeans and a bush hat. They had lunch together. Guillebaud was with a Frenchwoman, the companion of a Bengali poet, who was acting as an interpreter—a young sari-clad woman from a wealthy family in Lyon. She turned to François Mitterrand and asked: "Are you a journalist, too?"

No, Mitterrand replied, but he needed journalists—a journalist, at least, to tell everyone back home where he was and what he was doing. The Agence France-Presse was notified. The editorial offices were astonished and moved. The first secretary wrote to Pierre Mauroy, the party's number two person, a letter that was to be read out to the rather astonished comrades of the executive committee: "I needed to renew contact with true misery outside the padded walls of European politics. The reason for the discretion I am requesting of the party lies in my wish to avoid any artificial fuss or publicity."

Where publicity was concerned, he had no chance whatsoever. On his return, he was forced to organize a press conference, in which he admitted: "I found myself as disoriented [at Calcutta] as Fabrice del Dongo at Waterloo." And, perhaps to avoid the artificial, upon his return he began preparing the Socialist program, convinced more than ever that the castes (which, translated, meant the French bourgeoisie) had to be put out of harm's way.

The first secretary, who had just run off on a private escapade, was definitely in the thick of things. An imposing list of tasks faced his party: restoring its financial health; proving it could respond to any government initiative; scoring points at elections; winning over the working class; rebalancing the Left to the detriment of the Communist party; preparing for negotiations with the Communists (and, with this in view, working out its own theory of socialism).

Scarcely had he arrived at the Cité Malesherbes than he entrusted Pierre Joxe (one of his long-standing Marxist friends) and the young Jean-Pierre Chevènement (who dreamed of a break with capitalism and a marriage with the Communists) with the task of setting out the somewhat confused and often contradictory convictions of French socialism.

For several months, two hundred experts slaved away, providing note after note, preparatory document after preparatory document. "What a lot of gibberish!" the style-conscious prose writer and lover of the classics sighed more than once as he made his acquaintance for the first time with this new jargon with its mixture

of Marxism, economism, sociology, extravagant rhetoric, and pe-
dantry.

The leaders of the CERES, it is true, delighted in their task.
Where neologisms were concerned, they were unbeatable. One day
Didier Motchane, a somber theoretician whose enthusiasm knew
no bounds and sometimes led him to the most outrageous conclusions, was interrupted by an exasperated first secretary: "Motchane, who do you think you are—Lenin? And what if I were
Lenin?" The onlookers watched in astonishment, embarrassed smiles
playing around their lips. "We nudged one another under the table," delightedly recounts one of those who attended the meeting.

Whether Leninists or not, the Socialists brought forth a program,
which left any form of social democracy a hundred leagues behind.
The fundamental official aim of "Changer la vie," as it was called,
was workers' control in the enterprise—self-management (a word
that was to disappear completely after the victory of the Left). It
was decided to nationalize credit, those enterprises whose main
customers were the government, and all those enjoying a monopoly.
The Molletists surreptitiously introduced, to the great satisfaction
of the CERES, a clause that was to inspire the use of a great deal
of ink: "At the request of the workers concerned" in any enterprise,
the nationalization of that enterprise would be considered. In the
majority, this blunder (which had surprised François Mitterrand
himself) was soon exploited and raised the specter of wholesale
nationalization. May 1968 was not far behind.

In foreign policy, Atlanticists and neutralists, Europeans and
anti-Europeans, advocates and opponents of the nuclear deterrent
confronted one another inside the Socialist party. The Chevènement
project was attacked by Arthur Notebart, a deputy for the Nord,
as a "diarrhea of anti-Americanism." André Chandernagor, deputy
for the Greuze, added: "It may well be brilliant, but it must also
be comprehensible."[56] When points of view are so contradictory,
François Mitterrand, hesitant in such matters by nature, invariably
chooses a middle road. Thus, on the subject of the nuclear strike
force, which was later to become a component part of the Socialist
doctrine but was then still widely challenged, Mitterrand made this
Solomon's judgment: "The only logical policy would be neutrality,
but it is inconceivable."

A great deal of discussion took place in all the party branches and federations, and innumerable amendments were produced. Some concerned serious matters (abortion or the death penalty); others belonged instead to the symbolism of the Left (the abolition of television advertising, which was seen as an abominable illustration of the consumer society to be gotten rid of as soon as possible, and of the first class in the Paris métro).

In economic matters, an ingenious aim was laid down: "The search for a model of growth that excludes profit and is exclusively devoted to men's happiness" (a prospect that seems amusing after several years of Socialist zigzagging in power).

It was this text that was the basis of the bitter negotiation and bargaining with the Communist party and from which the Common Program of the Left emerged. Its propositions were so contradictory and outrageous that they led the majority to believe it gave them a weapon that would stop the Left in its tracks. However, the opposite happened. Attracted by the sound and fury of the great ideological debate taking place within the Socialist party, people flocked to join the party. The Left became fashionable once more; it was not until 1981 that the movement shifted the other way.

But since there were nevertheless critics and since refutations were being planned, François Mitterrand took up his pen to explain his position, reject the accusations, become the natural leader of the entire united Left—and finally, to enter the temple of socialist thinkers. Thus he drew up a sort of record of his thoughts and feelings of 1972–73.

La Rose au poing[57] is almost entirely devoted to the number one enemy: capitalism. It was necessary to plan for the advent of economic democracy, the starting point of which remained, he wrote in the style of Maurice Thorez, "the collective appropriation of the major means of production, investment, and exchange." There was in France, he assured his readers, a class dictatorship—a dictatorship of the privileged—which was no less real than the Soviet *nomenklatura*, even if, he admitted (having to at least appear objective), "its manners are more refined." In August 1972, he explained his ideas to Roger Priouret[58] in these terms:

> I have become convinced that the economic structure of capitalism is a dictatorship and that for me, it represents a danger to that love of liberty lying deep within me. My reflex has not

been an ideological one, but first one of sensibility, then of politics. . . . From my upbringing I acquired the susceptibility of a
petit bourgeois who does not like people walking over him, who
belonged to a very liberal, proud family living on the edge of the
bourgeoisie. . . . It was this sensibility inherited from my youth
that convinced me that the real bottleneck was the economy.

Everything always went back to Jarnac.

As the years passed (up till 1981), his analysis remained the
same. Thus, in *Le Monde* in 1976 he wrote: "Socialists believe that
the capitalist system is the root of all evil; that the supreme law of
profit has as a natural consequence the elimination of individual
or collective aspiration to such values as beauty; that the ruling
class persists in diminishing imagination, diversity, knowledge, and,
still more, the demand for responsibility, that cutting edge of a
civilized society."

Where institutions are concerned, the constitution must be reformed, he continues in *La Rose au poing* (this had been his obsession since *Le Coup d'état permanent*). The mandate of the head
of state must be reduced to five years and the referendum must
not be used as a plebiscite. Article sixteen ("the dictatorship article") must be revoked; the prime minister must be given back
the full autonomy given him by an article twenty that was never
applied and never respected; and, lastly, the Constitutional Council
must be replaced by a Supreme Court. He concludes: "The time
is past when one could get oneself elected on the Left in order to
govern on the Right. . . ."

To Jean-François Revel, who questioned him with a touch of
anxiety, François Mitterrand replied in *L'Express*: "The mutation
we are proposing must culminate in the abolition of capitalism. . . . There can be no coexistence between socialism and private
monopolies. . . . We believe in self-management socialism. I have
had drawn up, chapter by chapter, the number of new civil servants
that the application of the Common Program would involve: it is
not as high as you think. The Common Program is less statist than
M. Giscard d'Estaing's pseudoliberalism." "What would happen
if, in a nonprofitable enterprise, the workers had a vote and decided
it should nevertheless continue?" Jean-François Revel asked. Fran-

çois Mitterrand replied: "No. The state would settle the matter within the framework of the national plan."

In 1965, the left-wing candidate declared he was favorable to free enterprise—providing the state decided its investment programs. Yet in 1973, he favored self-management—on condition that the state, not the workers, made the decisions. Is there not a contradiction here? "No, it's dialectical," replies his entourage, who since 1971 have become used to the way Mitterrand's mind works.

This perhaps touches on the most mysterious characteristic of his strange personality: no sooner has he formulated a thesis than he maintains, in his own manner, its antithesis. "He is like yin and yang, but both at once," notes a half-amused, half-admiring hierarch of the Socialist high society. "As soon as François Mitterrand has made a decision, he at once begins to vaunt the advantages of the choice he did not make," one of his ministers adds.

Is this Machiavellianism? It is by no means certain. Although Mitterrand's nature complements his self-interest, he always reacts in such a way that the choice of alternative remains his alone (which is probably confirmed by events). This shocks those who do not know him well and has contributed a great deal to his image as a cunning politician, ever ready to change his mind or reverse a decision. But this is the way he is: whatever he says always corresponds to some part of himself. Michel Jobert, who for two years has closely observed this shifting, multifaceted man who is never entirely the same nor entirely different, notes in rather poetic terms: "Mitterrand is like water, which one moment is there, trembling on the soft leaves of an aromatic plant, and, the next, is no longer there, having turned into evening mist, morning fog, or, thirsty insect, which either drinks it then or stores it away for the arid days of summer. . . . Mitterrand is H_2O, sometimes mist, sometimes rain, or snow: he flows and, if he is stopped by some obstacle, he tries to get round it. . . . He is an ongoing force, but one whose outlines are difficult to discern."

Through ambiguity, hard work, distance, oratorical skills, a monarchical tone, a touch of cruelty, an art for setting off one tendency against another, François Mitterrand has become sole captain of the Socialist ship—a ship that was, until quite recently, moving forward. Where in 1968 the FGDS obtained only 16.5 percent of the vote, in the legislative elections of 1973 its candidates collected 20.8 percent (left-wing Radicals included). The Communist party was still ahead, with 21.4 percent of the vote. But the rebalancing of the Left had begun. Of the eighty-eight Socialist deputies, forty had not sat in the previous assembly. So Pierre Mauroy, Jean-Pierre Chevènement, Alain Savary, Pierre Joxe, and Jean Poperen arrived at the Palais-Bourbon for the first time. And with them returned the defeated candidates of 1968: Louis Mermaz, Georges Fillioud, and so on.

But three years later, at the cantonal elections of 1976, the Socialist party could claim to be the first party in France, with 26.5 percent of the vote. This time the Communist party, despite having (with 22.8 percent) increased its proportion of the vote, was overtaken. The rebalancing of the Left was achieved.

At the municipal elections of 1977, it was a landslide. The Left—Communist, Socialists, and Radicals combined—reached the (unprecedented under the Fifth Republic) figure of 54 percent of the vote and took 155 of the 221 communes of over thirty thousand inhabitants. The Socialist party captured forty-one of the big cities from the majority; the Communist party, twenty-two.

Finally, at the legislative elections of 1978, the gradual progress was confirmed since the non-Communist Left got 25 percent of the vote and, for the first time at this type of election, outstripped the Communist party, which was stuck at 20.6 percent. Meanwhile, the Union of the Left broke up and the Communist party, charged as being responsible, was internally divided. The Socialist party, despite its progress, did not reach the heights (30 percent) that had been promised by several public opinion polls. What political commentators call the "polling-booth effect"—that is, the sudden, last-minute reflex of fear felt by the elector at the prospect of a change in the majority—had a lowering effect. All the same, the graph of votes cast continued to rise.

This electoral progress, of course, had its setbacks. Two events apart from the breakup of the Union of the Left hampered François Mitterrand's long march: his defeat at the presidential elections of 1974, and the emergence of a rival within the Socialist party, Michel Rocard.

In 1974, François Mitterrand once again narrowly missed becoming president. On April 4, President Pompidou died quite suddenly. Without bothering much about a decent waiting period, the political class unexpectedly threw itself into a presidential election.

This time, the Left turned unanimously to the first secretary of the Socialist party. Everyone swore (Communists included) to bring their colors to the camp of justice. How could Mitterrand resist the affectionate pressure of so many friends and comrades? How could he not try his luck when such a united and growing mass was behind him? How could he dare disappoint such hopes? An extraordinary congress of the Socialist party met hastily at the Palais de la Mutualité and begged François Mitterrand, with 3,748 votes out of 3,748 (an odd, almost totalitarian vote), to be a candidate.

Le Nouvel Observateur asked bravely: "Who can beat Mitterrand?" The question was all the more judicious in that Claude Perdriel, owner of the weekly, had promised to devote himself heart and soul to the cause of the Socialist candidate for the duration of his campaign.

François Mitterrand felt drawn to the heights, so he set up his offices in the Montparnasse headquarters. In those futuristic premises, he was enthusiastically joined by his personal friends: André Rousselet, Louis Mermaz, François de Grossouvre, Joseph Francheschi, Charles Hernu, Claude Estier, Jacques Attali, and Christian Goux (a distinguished economist whom Mitterrand called "one of the truest interpreters of Marx").[59]

François Mitterrand led a campaign that was as active as it was short. Very soon his main adversary became Valéry Giscard d'Estaing. Georges Pompidou's minister of finance prevailed over the Gaullist Jacques Chaban-Delmas. The growing crisis (450,000 out of work, 11.5 percent inflation) formed the main theme of the debate, even if no one really showed any appreciation of its scope. The Socialist leader explained that liberalism and capitalism were entirely responsible. Giscard d'Estaing retorted that the program of the Left would make the present crisis much worse.

Modernism prevailed over socialism. François Mitterrand was beaten by a hair (getting only 49.3 percent of the vote)—it was becoming a habit. This time, the Communist party was left far behind. It had played the game with irreproachable discretion, providing votes and making itself almost invisible.

But destiny was certainly ruthless. The first secretary of the
Socialist party was fifty-eight. For the first time, he publicly showed
his disillusion and fatigue. To his friends, who had gathered in the
Montparnasse offices the day after the defeat, he confided: "I felt
myself ready to govern France. I think I would have made a good
president. Do not despair, the Left will soon win. It will not be I,
though, who will lead it to power, but you. Meanwhile, the struggle
goes on." "We were all heavyhearted," Georges Beauchamp remembers. "Most of us were holding back our tears." To Jean Daniel,
who called on him a few days later, the defeated candidate confided:
"I shall never be in a better position again. I was ready for government. I had the physical capacity required—it may now dimin-
ish. It would have given me great pleasure to be president of the
Republic. But it isn't of fundamental importance to me."[60]

There was a slight consolation; the day after the defeat, François
Mitterrand had never, according to the opinion polls, been so high
in public esteem: as good Gauls, the French always prefer the man
who comes second. His party benefited from this. During the summer of 1974, membership of the Socialist party grew hundreds at
a time. The federation secretaries were overwhelmed, assailed by
neophytes anxious to work for the party—so much so that they
were even tempted to turn people away. The failure of May was
perceived in the camp of the defeated as a moral revenge. They
knew, they believed, they were convinced that next time power
would be theirs.

For the time being, however, François Mitterrand had to confront
another worry. As if 1974 had not been bad enough, the Socialist
congress on October 12 and 13 announced that Michel Rocard was
joining the Socialist party.

At first glance, however, the news did not seem at all bad. Everyone (or nearly everyone)—beginning with Pierre Mauroy, who was
largely responsible—was delighted that such a man would be joining the party. The CERES itself was happy to welcome a comrade
who was so fervent an advocate of self-management. The arrivals of
such well-known individuals as Jacques Delors, Edmond Maire, Edgar Pisani, or Hubert Dubedout (the mayor of Grenoble) made a
great deal less stir, but were just as agreeable. This new blood would
revitalize the socialist family, now on the way to reunification.

For his part, François Mitterrand was not at all averse to welcoming men who, formerly, had humiliated him by barring his entry to the PSU and had not refrained from criticizing his activities under the Fourth Republic. During the summer, however, Jean Poperen, also a former member of the PSU, warned the first secretary: "I know Rocard and his friends. You are letting a virus into the Socialist party."[61] But Poperen was teased for his anti-Rocardian obsession, which had led him to call the young technocrat (who had opposed the Union of the Left) "Rocard d'Estaing." And nobody listened to him—except a few men like Pierre Joxe and Claude Estier, who also expressed their reservations. They feared Rocard's arrival would complicate relations with the Communist party and the CGT, relations that had improved since the signing of the Common Program.

The first secretary did not listen to them, however. He was convinced that Rocard would not carry much weight opposite himself in the party's leading circles. He was delighted Edmond Maire was introducing a tone that was not exactly common in the Socialist party—that of the working class. Lastly, the mayor of Grenoble, who had turned his city into a field of social experiment, symbolized for many a generation of competent, dynamic men of the Left. All in all, François Mitterrand concluded that this party congress had done a good job.

At first this impression seemed to be confirmed. Up until the legislative elections of 1978, everything went well. The press turned Michel Rocard into a fashionable figure. At the Pau congress in January 1975, his speech was well received. Thanks to him, it was said, the Socialist party at last had a serious economist in its leadership. Soon he was being presented as François Mitterrand's favorite son; there were even comments about the new grip former members of the PSU were getting on the Socialist party. Many people (such as Georges Séguy) were worried about Michel Rocard's overly favorable reaction to the Sudreau report on enterprises, which he called a "hymn to the glory of the capitalist enterprise." But the reservations of the Communists hardly disturbed Mitterrand; these were attributed to the rancor aroused in their ranks by the attitude of Michel Rocard, the man of Charléty, in 1968. And it was thought they would get over it.

Good relations between François Mitterrand and Michel Rocard seemed to have been reestablished. When *L'Expansion* organized a forum to enlighten the employers as to the Socialists' intentions, the two men were even seen together declaring in chorus that the market was still the best system for regulating the economy, and that the number of nationalizations would not go beyond that proposed in the Common Program.

But in July at the Nantes congress, Michel Rocard distanced himself. He seemed to want to reassure the management and middle management in the enterprises, who tended to support the Center, if not the Right. And, in doing so, he worried the Mitterrandist majority, which he was already irritating by his modernist intellectual manners. To many, the one-time revolutionary of 1968 seemed to be turning into a reformist, which was sacrilege. And he didn't stop there: in September, in a debate on Europe 1 with Jean-Pierre Fourcade, he chose to speak more as an administrator than a politician—even more sacrilege. The Communists began to grumble that they had been right all along and berated quite mercilessly a man who "wanted to run the French economy in the Swedish or German style."

At this point the Socialist leaders drew up his balance sheet. Here was a man who antagonized the Communists, but who, on the other hand, had the ear of the "class enemies," the economic circles he reassured. Here was a man who was in fashion, whose style pleased, whose audience was growing both outside and inside the party exactly at the moment François Mitterrand's star was beginning to wane. As time went on, Rocard's more or less permanent battles with the Communists raised doubts as to the advisability of the Union of the Left's strategy; the breakup of that union merely added to the sense of disillusion. François Mitterrand was aware more than anyone of this shift in opinion. Indeed, he had had doubts about the union for a long time. In September 1975, in one of those seminars so beloved of political scientists (this one taking place at Gouvieux, in the Oise) he declared: "The succession is not open." To make quite certain the signal would be received, he had confided to Gilles Martinet, a friend of Rocard's: "The party is not for the taking. It is already taken."

This, however, did not prevent a war of succession. It began in March 1978 on the evening of the second round of the legislative elections, elections that the Left nearly won, but eventually lost. That evening the whole of France witnessed the first thrust.

On French television Michel Rocard (who had just been elected deputy for Yvelines), his hand on his heart, his eyes half cast down, launched into a great act of critical introspection that seemed quite spontaneous. In fact, he had prepared a text, heavily amended, which he had before him. This text explained that the strategy adopted by the Left was probably not the best. In living rooms all across the country, this man who beat his breast so honestly and "talked straight" seemed appealing enough. All the criticism was heaped on the other Socialist leaders, who usually appeared on the platforms and did not have the courage, it was thought, to come and stand with their opponents in front of the cameras on the night of a defeat.

Over the next few days, things did not improve. Whereas Michel Rocard was praised in most quarters, François Mitterrand, who embodied the Union of the Left, was regarded as responsible for the electoral defeat and was criticized on every side. The left-wing writer Pierre Bourgeade wrote: "He should retire. . . . He would then combine skill with greatness" (thus repeating—like a boomerang?—François Mitterrand's words to General de Gaulle in 1968). In *Le Quotidien de Paris*, the left-wing (and sometimes extreme left-wing) Gaullist Maurice Clavel openly urged Mitterrand to retire. In *Paris-Match*, Jean-Edern Hallier coldly ordered: "François Mitterrand, retire!"

A bitter deputy for the Nièvre (whose feelings are perfectly understandable) wrote in his journal: "I now expect from Archimides' principle a sum of doubts, insolence, and insults exactly equal to the sum of praise, support, and oaths of fidelity that moved me in the opposite direction."

However, he was not a man to be beaten so easily. He sprang back: "Do not believe that the ambition to be president of the Republic at all costs is the motivating force behind my activity. . . . But, after all, the normal end of term in 1981 is not far off." A few days later on March 30 he declared: "In 1981, the Communists will have their own candidate. For us, there are three possibilities: myself, Pierre Mauroy, and Michel Rocard." He seemed quite untroubled.

Meanwhile, his friends, thinking it might prove useful, got a

motion adopted unanimously at the first meeting of the Socialist
group in the assembly declaring its "affectionate loyalty" to its
leader.

Socialist hearts were filled with affection for him, but they were
also realistic: public opinion polls showed Michel Rocard was gaining in popularity. When invited to comment on them, Rocard explained to the press club of Europe 1 that the French probably
appreciated a certain "political style" and were moving away from
a certain "political archaism." François Mitterrand did not care
for this at all, soon realizing it was he who was being called "archaic."

From then on, the competition was wide open. Many thought
they already knew who would win. On September 23, *Le Monde*
carried the headline: "Rocard wants to run for the Elysée in 1981."
Le Nouvel Observateur was ready to close the Mitterrand chapter:
"Attachment to a man must not compromise the necessary debate."
As he toured the country, Raymond Barre thought he could announce: "Like Faust, Mitterrand signed a pact; he must now pay
for it."

Inside the party itself, the first secretary's halo was dimming.
The man who had once been called "the Prince" with defiance,
but above all with respect, was now referred to in the branches as
"Tonton" ("Uncle"). It was certainly more affectionate, but the
French always show affection for losers. Pierre Mauroy made it
clear that "for 1981, the most qualified candidate is still François
Mitterrand"; that "still," however, did not please the ears of the
first secretary.

Meanwhile, Michel Rocard was everywhere: on television, on the
radio, in all the newspapers. He was the darling of all the media.
Le Nouvel Observateur interviewed him and, by way of introduction, Jean Daniel wrote: "Pierre Mauroy might have the party one
day, but not the country. Michel Rocard might have the country
one day, but not the party." He had already stopped talking about
François Mitterrand.

Was it time to make preparations for his retirement? To visitors,
the first secretary talked about death, said how tempted he was to
turn to writing as a career, hinted that life in the country had its
charms.

Were these feints or ruses? The Metz congress was not far off. And François Mitterrand was determined to hold onto power. At the moment when the defeat of the Left had struck him, he had been given an opponent like a gift from heaven. For he always bounced back to win *against* someone. And there a man stood, blocking his way, in his own party. Mitterrand would simply rally his forces against him and find in that struggle a new dynamism.

To begin with, as usual, he sent his friends to carry out the initial skirmishes. On June 21, 1978, Edith Cresson, Louis Mermaz, Charles Hernu, Lionel Jospin, Jean Poperen, and a few others made public what they called a "contribution of the thirty," intended for use at the forthcoming congress, in which they referred to the important role they had played in creating the Socialist party, reaffirmed their support for the Union of the Left, and stigmatized "any attempt at a supposedly technological and modernist solution that might place our party in mortal danger." Rocard was tied to the pillory.

Pierre Mauroy, who had not been told of the operation, felt excluded. He then learned that without telling him, Mermaz had been in talks with members of his own federation of the Nord with an eye on the forthcoming congress, and that he had also made overtures in the direction of the CERES. The mayor of Lille exploded angrily, threatening: "If Mitterrand signs an agreement with the CERES at Metz, then I shall join Rocard." Mistrust was everywhere.

But François Mitterrand did not stop there. He entrusted Paul Quilès, a somewhat cold, methodical graduate of the Ecole Polytechnique, to work on the federations for the forthcoming congress. And to assist him, he appointed Jean Auroux, Henri Emmanuelli, and Christian Nucci. Furthermore, every Thursday, a working party met in the rue de Bièvre: there, around the faithful Georges Dayan, were Pierre Bérégovoy, Jacques Attali, Pierre Joxe, Laurent Fabius, and Paul Quilès. These men were unknown (or at least very little known) to most French people, but they became famous when François Mitterrand later repaid their loyalty in 1981—or 1984.

They soon spread the rumor throughout the party that "the Rocard candidacy was wanted by the Elysée to divide the Socialist party, that it provided Giscard with an opponent he would have no difficulty beating." It seemed leading Socialists were lining up to strike the deputy for the Yvelines. On November 23, Gaston Deferre, president of the group in the National Assembly, declared on the radio: "Rocard's speech is like that of a tax inspector talking about balancing the budget. If that is what you want politicians to do, then Messrs. Barre and Giscard d'Estaing are already waiting. These policies are strangely reminiscent of those of Pierre Laval." A pained Rocard denounced this political calumny.

François Mitterrand felt things were going his way once more. He attacked—and liked it. He commented ironically on those who, "as others cultivate cannabis, cultivate moods—those gentle, yet deleterious drugs." He set out, once again, on his tour of France, courting the old guard of the old SFIO: Notebart, Ernest Cazelles, Jacques Piette, and Claude Fuzier. He forged new locks and reinforced his camp.

As a result, on December 20, 1978, Mauroy and Rocard signed a common "contribution." It bore four hundred signatures, including those of Jean-Pierre Cot (whom Mitterrand had, on his arrival in the Socialist party, taken under his wing) and Françoise Gaspard, the young mayor of Dreux. François Mitterrand did not take at all kindly to this. He began by delivering his usual angry threat: "If I don't win at the Metz congress, I shall resign." At this point, Rocard committed a blunder that made passions even keener. During a television broadcast, he declared: "If we win in April [at the congress], Pierre Mauroy will become first secretary" (the implication being that he himself would be a candidate for the presidency). From the next day forward, the knives were out. The Mitterrandists had no trouble denouncing the operation carried out against their leader. And, since things were going so well for them, they were not content to stop there: they called Michel Rocard a traitor. The Rocardians, on the other hand, responded by calling François Mitterrand an elderly monarch, a symbol of impotence and economic incompetence.

Their offensive changed the arithmetic in the Socialist party: Jean-Pierre Chevènement had to become an indispensable ally of François Mitterrand if the leader was to win at Metz. The deputy for Belfort did not take long to be persuaded: for him, the Rocard-Mauroy alliance corresponded to a right-wing offensive sustained by the analysis that "capitalism is merely undergoing a crisis of adaptation that in no way brings its existence into question."[62] It was clear that CERES was joining the Mitterrand camp out of doctrinal purity. "In the French Left, probably no one has done more than I to fight social democracy," pleaded Michel Rocard on French television. This seemed extremely odd since everyone regarded him as a Social Democrat, but it was all part of his charm.

On both sides, friends were solicited. Although the contribution launched by Michel Rocard and Pierre Mauroy was signed by four hundred leading figures (including thirty-nine deputies and ten senators), the appeal of the first secretary's supporters collected five hundred signatures (including thirty-nine deputies and thirteen senators), while that of CERES included six deputies, three senators, and thirty-six members of the executive committee.

On January 19 at Arras, a skillful François Mitterrand declared: "I would give up being a candidate in the presidential elections if that would save the unity of the party." Michel Rocard's televised response, on February 10, 1979, was innocent enough: "If François Mitterrand is a candidate in the presidential elections, I shall not be." And, to get back in favor with his Marxist-inclined comrades, he went on: "I am not at all antistate. . . ." His advisers were tearing their hair.

The Metz congress was poisoned with hatred. For the first time, François Mitterrand was booed on arrival. The confrontation between him and Michel Rocard took the scholastic form of a debate on the two cultures coexisting within French socialism—a debate that would cause quite a few smiles today. On the one hand, there was the Jacobin centralizing tradition and, on the other, a desire for decentralization and self-management. "Everything depends in the first instance on the transformation of the economic system, which posits in clear terms the problem of property," said the first secretary. Michel Rocard, in contrast, claimed that one had to take account of the laws of the market. François Mitterrand's friends retorted that Rocard "overestimated economic constraints." No one was under any illusion that this was simply a battle of ideas: it was a duel to the death between two men who wanted the same job.

The final thrust was delivered by the first secretary's young squire, Laurent Fabius. With his pile of degrees, he was well qualified to settle the matter: "Between the plan and the market, there is us: socialism." It was certainly a vague formula, but it meant something very precise. Rocard was a beaten man. As he listened, François Mitterrand seemed to be swallowing some particularly delicious sweet.

The die was cast: the first secretary had won his congress. Thanks to the CERES, which joined the majority, Pierre Mauroy (who had preached so ardently for a synthesis, wanting to reconcile the irreconcilable) and Michel Rocard went into the minority.

Shortly afterward, though it is difficult to establish any causal link between the two events, the Socialist party lost its title as the largest party in France in the European elections. With 23.53 percent of the vote, it was overtaken by the Gaullist UDF, which obtained 27.6 percent.

After the summer interlude, the battle began again, for what had been at stake—the presidential candidacy—was still at stake, and the time of reckoning was approaching. François Mitterrand began to have doubts: his stock was falling. On September 30, he said: "Only when the insults directed against me cease will I wonder whether I can still serve. As long as they continue, I believe that the time for my retirement has not yet come." On another occasion on television, he declared: "I disturb a lot of people—the establishment, with all the means at its disposal; a large part of the press; Georges Marchais; many newspapers claiming allegiance to the Left; even the United States or Moscow—but I like that. I am convinced I am propounding the right policies."

Yet the opinion polls still seemed to favor his opponent: according to them, Michel Rocard was the best candidate for the presidency of the Republic. François Mitterrand attempted a counterattack by declaring to six thousand members at a meeting at the Porte de Pantin: "Do you think it is public opinion polls that decide policy in the Socialist party? Comrades who enjoy popularity must be respected. But Socialists must not allow the decisions they make to be dictated from outside." His friends echoed him. "The Socialist party will not allow itself to be influenced by the opinion polls," stormed Paul Quilès. Louis Mermaz confirmed that opinion polls were "the biggest swindle ever encountered in the history of the Fifth Republic"—and so on. Yet, whatever they did, whatever they said, those terrible polls were believed in by many people—so much so that a number of leading Mitterrandists began to change sides and join the deputy for the Yvelines.

In September 1980, the first secretary's friends urged him to put himself more unequivocally in the running. "You don't have the right not to be a candidate, if only for the future of the party." But, undaunted, he replied: "Before the right time is not the right time."

On October 19, Michel Rocard, tense as ever, announced his candidacy from his town hall at Conflans-Sainte-Honorine. "He's misfired," the press commented, for once reserved. Nevertheless, the Mitterrandists were not at all pleased. On October 23, an act of sacrilege took place. Rocard held a meeting at Epinay, where branch members cried: "Rocard, president!" It was as if Calvin were preaching in St. Peter's.

François Mitterrand kept silent, but this was too much. Claude Estier, who knows him well, now says: "I am sure the way Michel Rocard announced his candidacy made François Mitterrand present himself." It was always the same reflex: whenever an enemy or rival came forward, François Mitterrand sprang back.

On October 26, at Marseilles, he said: "If the membership asks me to do so, I shall be a candidate." His camp (that is, his friends, who controlled a majority of the federations), along with large numbers of members, were not slow in asking him to do so. Michel Rocard, as he had promised, stepped down—he had no choice. And the man who had been so decried, so rejected by the opinion polls and the French voters, was to enter the Elysée. He had benefited from the circumstances and from his opponent's weakness. Well advised by his aides, he was able to turn his handicaps into advantages: his age and his past made him seem to be a man of experience; his authoritarianism was presented as a sign of character; his mysterious ambiguity became serenity. He even filed down his teeth to reassure people.

On May 10, 1981, François Mitterrand was elected president of the Republic. He ought to have thanked Michel Rocard—but this, of course, was the last idea that would have entered his head. Ingratitude is an attribute of princes—even foreign princes.

THE ALLIANCE WITH THE DEVIL

In the sunniest days of the Union of the Left, François Mitterrand's
friends declared: "No one could be more anti-Communist than he.
His feelings haven't changed." Yet he had wanted the union with
the Communist party and had put it into practice, helping the
Communist party emerge from its ghetto and inviting four of its
representatives to join his cabinet.

Since the early 1960s, Mitterrand had realized that to knock the
man of June 18 off his pedestal he would have to bring together,
without being overly fastidious, all opponents of Gaullism. The
electoral law, the majority ballot—for which he had struggled so
hard under the Fourth Republic—emphasized bipolarization, making a union with the Communist party almost inevitable.

Since the only justification for this marriage was the conquest
of power, the satisfaction of his own purposes, François Mitterrand's attitude could be regarded as indicating extraordinary cynicism, even as a mortal sin. But, at the same time, his efforts to
reduce the Communist party's influence—always his intention—
certainly deserve a plenary indulgence.

François Mitterrand is both the man through whom the Communists returned to power for three years and the man who helped
impose upon them the cruelest decline in their history.[63] Anyone
attempting to analyze his character cannot find a better illustration
of his duality.

At first, opportunity made the thief. In 1965, the Communist
party was trying to change both its image and its strategy. The
long reign of Maurice Thorez had just come to an end: the immovable Son of the People had died the previous year. The process
of de-Stalinization had begun; the Party wanted to return to parliamentary politics in the full sense. It now knew the Fifth Republic
was there to stay and isolated opposition would be ineffective. What
it sought was a kind of certificate of republican honor, which it
believed an alliance with the Socialist party would effect. The Communist leaders could hardly see any risks in the operation. Their
Party was strong, firmly rooted, highly structured, while that of
the Socialists was bloodless: in such a partnership, the Communists
would set the tone without difficulty.

François Mitterrand, on the other hand, realized from the outset that a union with the Communists might weaken the Communist party machine and strengthen the Socialist tendency. It was an audacious bet. Very few people at the time, on the Left or on the Right, would have bet on its success. Many even regarded the deputy for the Nièvre as reckless, imprudent, and overconfident. But he stuck to his opinions. In June 1972, after signing the Common Program of the Left, he confided to his friend Patrice Pelat: "One day, the French will thank me for ridding them of the Communist party."

He kept to his course and subsequent events seem to have proved him right: at the dawn of the Fifth Republic, the Communists were still winning 20–22 percent of the vote, while the SFIO had slumped to 11 percent; by 1984, the power ratio within the Left had been exactly reversed. Indeed, from his own point of view, François Mitterrand may have succeeded in his aim too well: the Communist party has fallen back so much that the Left itself has become a minority.

From the outset, it is true, the Communist party leadership made a serious mistake: by not presenting a candidate in the first round of the 1965 presidential election, it made the Socialist party the natural beneficiary of unity. Since the union took the form of François Mitterrand's single candidacy, the Communist party allowed its votes to go to its Socialist partner. This led its electors into bad habits. In 1974, the same mechanism brought the same results. Symbolically, the Communist party had admitted that in the Union of the Left, it was the junior partner—the tender, rather than the locomotive.

It was an infernal trap. The day after the presidential election of 1974, Georges Marchais, the Communist party general secretary, declared: "In 1981, we shall have our own candidate." But it was too late. They should have realized that the first time round.

The Communists' second error was signing the Common Program. After 1965, Waldeck Rochet never gave up trying to persuade the Socialists to draw up a proper contract for government. François Mitterrand, whose eye was fixed on the horizon of the Elysée, had warned his new comrades at the Epinay congress: "There will be no electoral alliance if there is no electoral program. There will

be no common majority if there is no majority contract. There
will be no government of the Left if there is no contract of government." All these "ifs" seem to imply that he did not agree. The
first secretary's ingenuity consisted of dragging his feet and letting
his future partners believe he was not keen. As the weeks went by,
he tested the water's temperature like a swimmer afraid to plunge
into the cold. He would dip in a toe, quickly retreat, making a face,
and then finally, pretending to summon up his courage, slowly
come back, each time keeping his foot in the water a little longer.
This curious ritual delighted his Communist partners, convincing
them they would end up drowning their Socialist allies.

In the end, the Common Program was joyfully adopted: the
Socialists had given in on a few additional nationalizations and a
range of social benefits, and the Communists were willing, on the
subject of the alternative ballot, to leave the last word to the electors.
But the precise content did not really enthuse either party. Jean
Poperen, who was both an important actor and a shrewd observer,
noted at once: "The virtue of the Common Program is not so much
its technical content as its political significance."[64] The important
fact was that this text gave the Communist party a certificate of
citizenship and the Socialist party a certificate of membership in
the Left.

As for the rest, it was an unconsummated marriage—feeling did
not enter into it, and each was thinking of the dowry brought by
the other. Scarcely two days after the signing, François Mitterrand
declared cynically at Vienna, before the suspicious jury of the Socialist International: "Our fundamental aim is to build a great
Socialist party on the ground occupied by the Communist party,
in order to prove that out of five million Communist electors, three
million are quite capable of voting Socialist." The union was more
like a combat, a competition.

At the same time (but this was to be known only three years
later), Georges Marchais, the new general secretary of the Communist party, presenting a secret report to the Central Committee,
warned his comrades: "On fundamental matters, the ideology of
the Socialist party remains absolutely reformist. . . . The permanent
features of the Socialist party are, apart from its apparent or real
desire to promote social and democratic reforms, the fear that the

working class and the masses will begin to move; hesitation at waging the class struggle in the face of big capital; the tendency to compromise with capital and to collaborate with class enemies. These features have not disappeared since the Epinay congress."[65] When a marriage takes place with such feelings on both sides and there are witnesses to prove it, it would have little difficulty being annulled even in the court of Rome.

Begun in such a spirit, the union could not but be quarrelsome and fragile. Yet for two years, from 1972 to 1974, the Communist party seemed to play the game. The legislative elections of 1973 appeared to give them encouragement: although the Socialist party made progress, the Communists revived. The wave of May 1968 had left it no more than twenty-three deputies; the ballot of 1973 brought it forty more.

In 1974, the death of Georges Pompidou took everyone by surprise. Georges Marchais still felt too new in his post, too much of a beginner, to risk competing himself. So François Mitterrand was the new candidate and the Communist party a good partner. Things were going very well. Between the two rounds, the general secretary of the Communist party summoned Claude Estier (who had always had good relations with the Communists), and told him: "We don't want to embarrass François Mitterrand—we'll be fairly discreet where ministerial posts are concerned." And when the Soviet ambassador, Chervonenko, called on Valéry Giscard d'Estaing to inform him that Moscow's preference went to him, the Communist party, genuinely hurt, was furious.

But the very day after this near victory, it was clear who had benefited on the Left: six legislative by-elections were organized in the autumn. Five times out of six, the Socialist party came first in a dazzling move ahead—by 10 to 15 percent. And in the sixth constituency (in the Dordogne), the only one in which the Communists came out on top in the poll, its candidate, Yves Perron, was beaten in the second round because a large number of Socialist votes had not been transferred to him. This was definitely a sore point.

There could no longer be any doubt: the union profited whomever embodied the Left. The political bureau did its accounts: since the Socialist candidates were definitely advancing to the detriment of the Communist party, the union ceased to represent salvation and was now viewed as a hell. From that day on, it was condemned. The Union of the Left ceased to exist by late 1974.

As always (but enough attention is never paid to them) the party leaders set the tone. In November Roland Leroy explained at Limoges: "In the name of a supposed rebalancing of the Left, there is an attitude aimed at weakening the position of the Communist party and that is thus in line with the plans of big capital." A few weeks later, Georges Marchais was thundering at Vitry-sur-Seine, "We cannot be reduced to a supporting role," while Pierre Juquin, zealous as ever, announced "a certain convergence between the plans of the bourgeoisie and the aims of the Socialist party."

On November 8 François Mitterrand declared: "You have no reason to entertain doubts about yourselves—the Socialist party needs no crutches. The quality of the union derives from a quiet, conciliatory strength with regard to the Communist party." In other words, from that point on the Socialist leader was acting without paying too much attention to the Communist leadership, but without forgetting to address the Communist electors.

Nevertheless, the gunfire from the Communist party continued throughout 1975. The cantonal elections of 1976 confirmed their plight: the Socialist party came out on top, while the Communists failed to make progress. And whereas the Communist electors observed exemplary discipline, Socialist electors were mysteriously absent from the polling booths as soon as they were required to vote for a Communist candidate.

If the break was not yet openly acknowledged, it was because the municipal elections of 1977 were approaching and because the electoral system drove both parties to the union. The Communist party suddenly adopted a more gentle tone. The Socialist party, relieved, accepted more discipline, imposing single lists on its more recalcitrant deputies. As a result of this remission, the Communists took twenty-two towns of over thirty thousand inhabitants. This was always worth having, especially from a financial point of view. Jean-Pierre Chevènement's CERES similarly presented them with Reims and Saint-Etienne.

But the remission was not to last. Scarcely had the new mayors settled into their town halls than the polemics resumed. The Socialists were accused of every sin in the book, of betraying the Common Program and of moving to the Right. *L'Humanité*, the Communist daily newspaper, published, at a highly opportune moment (the day before a television debate between François Mitterrand and Raymond Barre), a detailed account of the Common Program's costs (and the sums involved were indeed astronomical). With such ammunition, Raymond Barre, like a cat toying with a mouse, had little difficulty beating his opponent. Mitterrand, mortified at looking like a student failed by a smooth-talking teacher, was to entertain a long-lasting animosity toward his ruthless examiner. Then as if by chance, at Châtelleraud on July 3 during a cantonal by-election, Edith Cresson lost because a large number of Communist votes failed to be transferred at the second round. The local federation had done its duty.

Throughout the summer, the polemics continued. The Communist party demanded an updating of the Common Program's economic side. Instead of making the program more moderate because of the economic crisis, the Party wanted to extend it in an almost provocative way, demanding wholesale nationalizations and social benefits as if the country were entering a period of astronomic growth. François Mitterrand did his best to negotiate with the Communist leadership, giving a little here while trying to resist there, enduring a few sleepless nights. But whatever he said or did, the Communist party would not budge. The break had finally come. And it occurred in a live television interview on the eight o'clock news.

Although the Left might well have been the favorite before the legislative elections of 1978, the Socialist party might well see the opinion polls giving it splendid scores (up to 30 percent of the vote), the Communist party, with its usual zeal, set about spoiling everything. This chronic discord placed in the electors' minds a seed of skepticism that was just enough to rob the Left of victory. As a result, against all expectations, the outgoing majority retained control of the National Assembly.

These results gave pleasure to at least two: Valéry Giscard d'Estaing, who concluded that he could not be beaten in 1981; and the Communist party, which concluded that François Mitterrand could not win the presidential election.

For three years, the disunion of the Left was celebrated each week by some new vitriolic attack. Lionel Jospin concluded: "The Communist party wants to prevent the advent of a government of the Left in France." It could not have been any better put.

If the Communists thought that this would lead François Mitterrand to give up, they misjudged him. After the defeat of 1978, he was still declaring: "I have no judgment to pass on Georges Marchais. He has been the expression of the collective will of the Communist party leadership and perhaps of the strategy of international communism. I believe it is the French people who will have the last word. It will not be possible for the Communist party to carry out an operation that, after destroying the chances of the Left in 1978, will end up by destroying itself." In other words, he was saying, "I am carrying on."

In 1981, the Communist party campaign was particularly malevolent with regard to François Mitterrand. Georges Marchais even went so far as to say Mitterrand was even more to the Right than Valéry Giscard d'Estaing. On March 5, Charles Fiterman (who, three months later, was to be a minister) declared before the secretaries of the party federations: "Mitterrand is not offering new policies—his positions converge with the politics of the Right." But, as everyone knows, it was the Socialist candidate who won, while the general secretary of the Communist party obtained only a humiliating 15.3 percent of the vote. He was fourth; Mitterrand first. It was a day of mourning in the Place du Colonel Fabien (the famous Communist party headquarters, built by the celebrated architect Oscar Niemeyer).

After the legislative elections, the Communist party had to drain the cup to the dregs. Since the party was no longer in control of events, it pretended, if not to organize them, at least to keep an eye on them. Thus, four Communist ministers were to do their duty for three years. The Communist electorate had proved to be too much in favor of unity for the leadership to resist the tide. After going through the motions of a negotiation, the political bureau allowed the comedy of participation to go forward.

The early days were sweet indeed. The Socialists opened the floodgates, loading the good ship France with costly gifts. The country went into debt, devalued the franc, unbalanced the budgets, distributed the fruits of a nonexistent growth, led the people to believe they could work less and live better in the midst of an international slump. In short, they implemented everything Georges Marchais had demanded with his "updated" Common Program.

This bad vaudeville act was suddenly interrupted by the "pause"— that is, the period of "Socialist rigor." The Communist party was worried; it protested, but kept quiet. "We want to remain in the government," its spokesmen repeated on every possible occasion— at least up until the end of the legislature (and why not) of the president's seven-year term. In fact, they stayed until the municipal and European elections. The Communist party hoped to benefit at least from its participation in the government by preserving its municipal bastions and demonstrating that it was beginning its recovery; Communist leaders were convinced 15 percent of the vote was an absolutely rock-bottom figure that did not correspond to the party's real audience.

The truth was much more cruel: the Communist party lost the municipalities won in 1977. The discovery of fraud and various irregularities forced it to abandon ten more. Its image seemed very tarnished indeed. In the European elections, with 11 percent of the vote, it had sunk to its 1928 percentage.

The union had served it ill, disunion had further weakened it, the polemical war with the Socialists had diminished it still further, and participation in the government had devalued it. The party now had no alternative but to retreat to its crumbling citadel— with the hope of regaining strength in opposition.

If only the alliance with the Socialist party and experience had changed it. Of course, it no longer used the same language. As François Mitterrand himself remarked,[66] the times had gone when Maurice Thorez could coldly write: "That sinister Blum, that cunning politician, that disgusting Tartuffe, that hypocrite so hideous he nauseates those who have to get near him despite their repulsion, that political scum with his repugnant reptile's contortions and hisses, that jackal Blum, that scoundrel, that supplier of the prisons, that stool pigeon Blum." Beside such a torrent of insults, Georges Marchais seemed urbanity itself.

And it was very far from the time when Communist Youth placarded the walls of Paris (after the Liberation) with posters that

read: "France is only our country—the USSR is our fatherland."
Communist leaders no longer referred, like Etienne Fajon, to the
"unconditional solidarity with the USSR," and no longer wrote,
like André Wurmser (in 1957): "Every man has two nations: his
own and the Soviet Union."[67]

So the language had changed. What about the substance? The
Communist party had changed too since it now accepted (on the
whole, if not in detail) the institutions of the Fifth Republic, the
Common Market (in principle, if not in form), the nuclear strike
force (provided it was not too powerful), parliamentary democracy,
and even the renunciation of the myth of the proletariat's dictatorship. But who believed, on all these points, in its absolute sincerity? And who believed it was entirely independent of Moscow?
François Mitterrand, "ally" that he was at the time, wrote in 1978:
"The decisions made in Paris by the leadership of the French Communist party usually correspond to the requirements of a world
strategy originating in Moscow." On the Euro-missile affair, on
Afghanistan, on Poland—indeed, on hundreds of occasions—the
Communist party had adopted positions highly agreeable to the
Kremlin bosses. Finally, who would believe the Party had really
changed its nature? "Democratic centralism" continued to reign.
The general secretary and his clan always set the pace.

In short, if François Mitterrand, aided by circumstances and the
Communists themselves, had managed to reduce (for the moment)
their influence, he has not succeeded in changing the nature of this
Leninist party (nor has he ever claimed he could).

On the other hand, he himself had to hand over a few reluctant
presents as dowry. Without the Communist party, the Socialists
would not have adopted so radical a program, would have shown
less enthusiasm for nationalization, would not have felt forced to
indulge perpetually in double-talk (sometimes liberal, more often
collectivist; sometimes favoring self-management, more often
statist; sometimes displaying sympathy for the Third World, more
often for the Atlantic Alliance; sometimes vindictive, sometimes
realistic).

Above all, the Communist ministers, during their three years in
power, installed men here and there who, though certainly competent from their point of view, were in key positions to observe

the workings of government. Furthermore, they put in place (especially in the nationalized industries) mechanisms that gave their Party (and especially the Communist CGT) money and power.[68]

It was, therefore, a high price to pay. But in exchange, François Mitterrand was given the present of his dreams: the Elysée.

7

POWER

LOST ILLUSIONS

WHEN HE ASSUMED POWER, FRANÇOIS MITTERRAND DREAMED
—convinced by his own language, enthused by his own mythology,
and contaminated by twenty-three years of opposition—that he
would remake France in his own image. It was to be an ideal France,
radiating his social generosity and redistributive philosophy. Under
his vigilant guidance, the state would have the efficiency and greatness of the scales of justice. "I am the only one who is able to
overcome unemployment," he had repeated endlessly throughout
his presidential campaign.

For three months, the polemics on employment between Mitterrand and his opponent, Valéry Giscard d'Estaing, were very like
the impossible dialogue between a prophet and an accountant.

Faced with such an example, he was certain, the country would
appeal to him to establish a just balance. He would be de Gaulle's
counterpart, his symmetrical opposite. He would be a just, social-
minded de Gaulle—that is, a left-wing de Gaulle. It would be he
who would put this regime, built upside down, back on its feet.
History would appreciate his achievement.

At first, President Mitterrand's installation in the Elysée benefited from a dazzling state of grace that went well beyond the frontiers of the people of the Left. In June 1981, 74 percent of France's citizens declared they were happy with his election. The French like novelty.

In bringing the Left to power, French society really wanted to postpone once more the purgatory of economic rigor. Valéry Giscard d'Estaing and his prime minister, Raymond Barre, had tried to convince them of the need for austerity and sacrifice. Far from agreeing with them, the French had preferred to crown the man who promised that with him, they would work less and live better.

Where the Right carried out a policy based on the social market economy (record unemployment benefits [90 percent of wages], a generous social security system, and stable purchasing power), the Left promised that it would pursue bolder, more protective policies. It would reform the country's economic structures without affecting the lot of the poor, the weak, or the wage earners.

And, in fact, in that France (then the fifth economic power in the world), Socialist generosity was soon to lavish its benefits. The recipes of the Popular Front of 1936 were immediately taken off the shelf, dusted, and put in place. The minimum wage was increased, together with pensions and other benefits of every kind. The working week was reduced (thirty-nine hours paid at forty). A fifth week's holiday with pay was given, and the retirement age was reduced for all (sixty instead of sixty-five). A great stimulus was given to ordinary people's consumption habits, which, it was believed, would unfailingly increase the growth rate. "I spend, therefore I am" might have been the government's motto. Nicole Questiaux, minister of state concerned with "national solidarity," repeated several times in the media: "I am not the accounts minister"—an understatement if there ever was one.

A start was made on the long list of promised reforms. The cure-all of nationalization inaugurated what Pierre Mauroy called the "bedrock of change." Everywhere the state became the natural repository of the general interest and of individual happiness.

And what of the prime minister, Pierre Mauroy? He was the reverse of some Marxist ayatollah. This warmhearted man had believed, from his childhood in the tough, hardworking Nord, that socialism went hand in hand with personal happiness and love of one's neighbor. "Son, raise your cap when a worker walks by," his schoolteacher father had told him. When he passed his *baccalauréat*, his father allowed him, as a reward, to join the Socialist youth organization. Affable, generous, voluble, idealistic, Pierre Mauroy fully embodied the first phase of the seven-year term.

In his speeches, he mingled history and politics, producing a rosy picture of France that seemed to have come straight out of Zola's novels. This tall, strongly built man with fine hands (like those of a bishop, made to distribute largesse and to bless) had a certain notion of France: as a people of ordinary folk, poor but hardworking and honest, threatened by a few "big guys" who had to be brought down.[1]

During the first year of his seven, François Mitterrand was enthroned on a cloud. "We were intoxicated," he was later to acknowledge (a royal plural suggesting that the error was a general one). On the international stage, French diplomacy reflected the presidential optimism. It was a time when the head of state became the bard of a worldwide new deal to rally the North and South to the idea of a concerted worldwide economic revival, which he hoped would precipitate the economic revival everyone throughout the world was yearning for.

At first, then, there was a combination of a political analysis (the need to satisfy the traditional left-wing electorate), an overly optimistic view of the international situation, an idealized vision of France's economic and industrial reality, an underestimation of existing constraints, and a belief in the correctness of the Keynesian policy of sustaining demand (on which the theory and practice of the more modern Left had been based in France since 1945—Mitterrand's pope, Pierre Mendès France, included).

Empowered with this logic, François Mitterrand did not restrain his enthusiasm before the monument to the Revolution in Mexico City. On October 21, 1981, he exalted the idea of a reform of the world economic order through the transformation of the relations between the rich North and poor South. He launched his famous "greetings to the humiliated, to the sequestered, to the brutalized priests, to the landless poor," then went on, with a marked lack of humility, to declare: "Our ideas are contagious—they will travel round the world."

But what is left of those promises of spring 1982? Technically, nothing—or very little. The economy consists of nothing but figures (and it was not long before these were all bad). Deficits mounted: national indebtedness climbed to dizzy new heights. For the French, the situation had turned sour. Like a hydra-headed monster, unemployment was trying to crush the Left. Pierre Mauroy fought valiantly to keep unemployment, as he put it, "at the crest of two million." The figure was soon exceeded; lines lengthened at the employment offices.

A prisoner of the superstitions of the Left, François Mitterrand very soon became a prisoner of the crisis. Up till the summer of 1982, none of the new princes seemed to have any doubt as to the road to be followed. None, that is, except Pierre Mauroy—who, as early as the spring of 1982, having been alerted by his experts, was with heavy heart considering taking the ailing economy in hand—and Jacques Delors, minister of finance, who, convinced of the urgent need for a "pause," wanted to publish the catastrophic financial figures for April and May 1982 but was dissuaded from doing so by those around the president who, he was told, was not to be "irritated" or "distracted" from the huge task awaiting him at Versailles.

For the summit of the seven great industrial countries was being held that year in the royal city. For François Mitterrand, it would be the last attempt to save his initial program. It became—such is the irony of fate—the very symbol of both his illusions and the distrust on the public's part.

This was because the "president's Promethean ambition" soon led him astray. The trilogy—the Versailles summit (June 7), the press conference (June 9), and the devaluation of the franc (June 13)—begun in pomp and splendor, ended in confusion and contradiction. The summit had failed (each leader maintaining his own position); the overly euphoric press conference aroused hopes the devaluation cruelly dashed only four days later. For the French people, the president's language and prestige had been devalued along with the franc.

Of course, for each stage in this triptych, François Mitterrand had his explanations: if Versailles had failed, it was because France had faced up to American pressure (in fact, a few courteous words from Ronald Reagan's advisers had naïvely been welcomed as agreement to the French propositions for reforming the international monetary system); if there had been disparity (to say the least) between the press conference of June 9 and the government's austerity plan of June 13, it was because people had not paid sufficient attention to the long preliminary declaration that had nevertheless stated the urgent need for drastic measures. Mitterrand had used an analogy with mountain climbing to explain that after a flat stretch, there would now be a mountainous stretch—but no one could ever have imagined this analogy meant a wage and price freeze and a sudden increase in taxes for both private individuals and enterprises.

The prime minister, Pierre Mauroy, had not reached the end of his troubles. He very soon realized the situation was even worse than the French leader suspected. Wisely, he concluded, his heart growing heavier with each passing day, that the austerity adopted would not be at all enough. Other steps, other constraints, other sacrifices would unfortunately be necessary. He was convinced of this while at the same time deploring it.

François Mitterrand would hear nothing of it. He refused to accept that his experts' calculations had been so inaccurate, taking as a personal affront the prospect of having to carry out an austerity program such as the one that had been envisaged by Raymond Barre—indeed, the very program he had once so sneered at. Thus the head of government adopted a policy of increased austerity the head of state would not accept, resulting in a cacophony of different voices emerging from the government.

François Mitterrand, like a caged lion, tried to break out from behind the humiliating bars of austerity. Finding himself unable to do so, he settled into it unwillingly, denying there had been any change. He invented a formula that was to mark an epoch, referring to the "parenthesis of rigor"—an optimistic way of reducing major trials that would, of course, be lasting as certain unfortunate, but ephemeral events.

Curiously enough, Pierre Mauroy, who was more aware of the constraints, also used ambiguous language. On television he denied having a new austerity plan already prepared, declaring ingenuously: "All the economic lights are green." This led the opposition to retort that Pierre Mauroy was color-blind.

In private, the prime minister complained bitterly about those he had nicknamed the "evening visitors," those familiars of François Mitterrand—Minister of Social Affairs Pierre Bérégovoy, industrialist Jean Riboud, and Minister of Industry Laurent Fabius—who played the role of tempters, appearing when the offices were shut. They defended a thesis that sounded extremely attractive to left-wing ears: "Austerity is not compulsory; in order to fight unemployment, we must temporarily abandon the European monetary system and get growth moving again."

The approach of the municipal elections (March 1983) led the head of state to give in to his natural inclination: temporization. More than ever, it was critical to wait—which he did, forcing his colleagues to do so, too.

But the French were not taken in. They felt the effects of austerity, they worried about rumors that things were going to get worse, and they were frightened at hearing the government make statements not in accord with its actions. As a result, they supported the opposition in the opinion polls. On the whole, they gave the benefit of the doubt to the leaders of the Social-Democratic Left (Jacques Delors, minister of finance, and Michel Rocard, minister of the plan). In contrast, they were very harsh indeed toward the president and his prime minister, each of whom in private blamed the other for the low ratings. To his close friends, François Mitterrand confided: "Pierre Mauroy's credit has been undermined and I have suffered as a result."

In fact, it was the whole Left that had suffered in the municipal elections—it lost control of thirty large towns and cities. The opposition was victorious, but not triumphantly so. After the first round, it hoped to be able to win about fifty towns. But, in the second round, the working-class vote managed to save several old bastions of the Left. In Marseille, the second city in France, Mayor Gaston Deferre, the minister of the interior (who had run the city for thirty years), had arranged an apportioning of the electorate so judicious that, although he won fewer votes than his opponent, he managed to keep more seats and get himself reelected.

The situation could not have been worse: the results were bad enough for the government's standing to deteriorate still further, yet not catastrophic enough to force it to adopt drastic measures.

A crazy week followed, during which François Mitterrand oscillated like a pendulum between two directions: either he should
increase austerity, according to the dictates of international competition (in which case the minister of finance, Jacques Delors, who
had propounded this thesis, ought logically to go to the Matignon);
or he should choose the road of isolated national growth, with
France closing her frontiers and leaving the European monetary
system (in which case Pierre Bérégovoy, advocate of this option,
or even Louis Mermaz, president of the National Assembly, ought
to become prime minister). One thing was clear to all: Pierre Mauroy would have to go.

For a week, before an astonished public, nothing happened and
rumor ran riot. At lunchtime one heard that Pierre Bérégovoy's
chances were increasing, while, by dinner, Jacques Delors was the
favorite. The president took advice and reflected. He was, it was
said, determined to hesitate. At one point, Jacques Delors almost
got the job. Punctilious and clumsy, though, he spoiled his own
chances by demanding guarantees from the president (to be made
minister of finance and prime minister, as Raymond Barre had
been before him). This was a big mistake: François Mitterrand was
not a man to allow his hands to be tied. The ultimate surprise was
that in the end, austerity was increased, a new devaluation was put
into effect (the third since 1981), and Pierre Mauroy succeeded
himself.

STUPOR ON THE LEFT

There then began a period of transition that was to last for a year.
In left-wing terminology, certain words and phrases such as *socialism*, *break with capitalism*, and *pediment of change* disappeared. A new term—*modernity*—appeared on the scene, discreetly
at first, then with increasing insistence. The young Laurent Fabius,
the head of state's ambitious favorite, spoke of little else. The
president, who had just come back from the United States, told
how astonished he had been on his visit to Silicon Valley.

While the president was converted to modernism (which for the
traditional Left is a new idea), the French people grumbled more
and more. The opinion polls showed that never had a president

been so unpopular (though, of course, taxes and unemployment never having been so high no doubt explained this).

Against this background of unpopularity caused by the economic failure of the Left was to be grafted a specifically political problem (see chapter 2): the great quarrel concerning the religious schools. In its program, the Left had proposed integrating the private schools into the public sector in the name of the sacrosanct principle of "a unified secular public service." As soon as it ventured to apply its ideas, it was met by opposition of quite unexpected virulence. Each week tens of thousands (soon to be followed by hundreds of thousands) of parents demonstrated their absolute rejection of the policy. They wanted to be allowed to send their children to the school of their choice.

Confronted by the extent of the protest, François Mitterrand, who had at first encouraged the minister of education Alain Savary, in the end dropped him and retreated. The minister learned of this about-face on television, like everybody else. A man of honor, he resigned immediately. Pierre Mauroy, anxious about his left-wing image, well aware that his government was coming to an end, seized the opportunity and resigned in turn. A page had been turned.

Pierre Mauroy was succeeded by Laurent Fabius, then thirty-seven. In order to represent modernization and bring words and acts into greater harmony, the president chose the man who was the youngest, the most brilliant (Fabius was a graduate of the Ecole Normale Supérieure, the seedbed of French academic excellence, and the Ecole Nationale d'Administration, France's foremost business school), the most patrician (his father is a celebrated antiques dealer, his mother an excellent horsewoman, and his wife an heiress of a fortune in her own right), the closest to him personally (he had worked for Mitterrand for ten years), and above all, the most ambiguous (when Fabius was in opposition, and in the early days of the government, he gave the impression he belonged to the more extreme majority tendency in the party; as soon as his responsibilities—or ambition—increased, he became the spokesman of the more moderate clan). At the Hôtel Matignon, Fabius deliberately proved more concerned with good administration than with socialism. Indeed, he was quick to go on television and explain that without modernization, productivity, work, effort, competition, a balanced budget (in 1981 he had been the most spendthrift minister of the budget), and rigor—yes, rigor—there was no salvation. The Communists took to their heels, attacking the government for its "many convergences with the Right."

The president himself did not lag behind. François I gave way to François II. The first strove to leave his mark on history; the second governed with a view to ending his term in the best possible light. He radically changed direction. He had adulated the state; now he decreed that its grip had to be loosened. He had increased taxation; now he declared that its burden was too heavy. Enterprises had been subject to a mass of controls; now they had to be given back their freedom. The ranks of the civil service had been swollen; now sackings were the order of the day. Change had been the key word; now there was still change, but in the opposite direction.

"I could have been Lenin," the president once confided to a few visitors in the Elysée. In the autumn of 1981, he had even threatened his opponents with a radicalization of his policies. More prudently, preferring to listen to what the opinion polls and ballot boxes were telling him, he moderated them instead.

Paradoxically, François Mitterrand's Socialist regime converted the French to the liberal religion, the doctrine of free enterprise: a diminished state, less taxation, fewer laws. Socialism in power had given birth to a new individualism. It was a curious transformation.

The president was not credited either with these changes or with their virtues. For the French, François Mitterrand was the man who had tried in vain to oppose the changes that had had to be made to a policy he had begun.

But he was really the man of illusions. For it had been an illusion to promise to overcome unemployment and the economic crisis without the power or knowledge to do so. Soon, in all official speeches, the battle against inflation replaced the battle for employment.

Up until the legislative elections of March 1986, the Left tried hard—with François Mitterrand at its head, for he had become the advocate of the outgoing majority (now reduced to the Socialists alone since the Communists' departure)—to carry off an extraordinary act of political sleight of hand. Indeed, it focused all its efforts and arguments around a single obsessive theme: the victory over rising prices. It even presented itself as the champion in Europe of the struggle against inflation (and blatantly manipulated figures to boot). It boasted it had succeeded where the Right had failed, refraining from mentioning that it had itself failed in an area where it had promised success. But the memory of the French electorate was not that short—as it showed by electing a right-wing majority.

The Socialist party racked up an honorable score (32 percent of the vote). Nevertheless, the Left had been soundly beaten. Of course, the institutions of the Fifth Republic had, for the first time in its history, elected a complete legislature (five years). But despite the changes in the electoral law, the Left had nevertheless lost the legislative elections—just as it had lost in turn the cantonal elections (1982), municipal elections (1983), European elections (1984), and, finally, regional and legislative elections (1986).

For his part, François Mitterrand remained in place as the constitution dictated. But he had to preside over a right-wing Council of Ministers after appointing its leader, Jacques Chirac, as head of government. He could not prevent the new prime minister from implementing policies that were exactly the reverse of those he had advocated in 1981.

The president had lost the election, but he had not been knocked out.

THE POISONED KISS

If there is one area in which François Mitterrand has shown clear-sightedness and perseverance since 1965 (the year he first ran for president), it is in his relations with the Communist party.

From the earliest days of the Fifth Republic, he had realized that without the Communists, he would have no majority—and therefore never get to the Elysée. To those who criticized him for selling his soul to the devil to get power, he retorted: "You will see that the Union of the Left will benefit the Socialists and harm the Communists."

At the time this was an idea verging on heresy: the Communist party was then a powerful machine, with several hundred thousand members, controlling the key unions and innumerable other associations. It then had the support of 22 percent of the French electorate.

Next to this powerful battleship, the Socialist party looked like a delicate corvette: it had scarcely 15 percent of the electors; its prestige had been in tatters since the Algerian War; and it was in desperate financial straits. So, for the Socialist party, the Union of the Left looked to most people like a *liaison dangereuse*.

François Mitterrand gambled that he could anticipate events. He sensed that under firm guidance (his own), the Socialist party could become the front-runner. This is precisely what happened. The only unexpected (but considerable) flaw in this audacious maneuver was that the operation succeeded so well, the Communist party was weakened far beyond what was expected, and, despite a spectacular recovery, the Socialist party did not make up in influence what the Communist party had lost. As a result, what was a gain for the Socialists became a loss for the majority. With 32 percent of the votes cast in March 1986, the Socialist party today is the largest party in France. But taken as a whole, the Left reached a ceiling of only 45 percent of the vote. Paradoxically, the triumph of the Socialist party has brought the defeat of the Left: the trap into which François Mitterrand led the Communist party has now caught its author. The situation has all the ingredients of an ancient tragedy.

There can be no doubt that the Communist leaders reacted fairly quickly (and have, in fact, since 1974) to limit the damage threatening them. During the 1981 presidential campaign, they did everything possible to impede François Mitterrand's impetus and destroy his reputation on the Left. Charles Fiterman (later to become the most senior of the Communist ministers in the government) declared that the Socialist candidate was as harmful and dangerous to the workers as Giscard or Chirac. Georges Marchais, the Communist candidate for the presidency, laid into the "Gang of Three" (Giscard, Chirac, and Mitterrand) with equal vigor. But these exhortations had no effect. The people of the Left so clearly chose the Socialist champion in the first round that the Communist party had no choice: in the second, they instructed their supporters (amounting to 16 percent of the total vote) to vote for François Mitterrand. After all, how could they give their followers glimpses of a bright future yet dare to deprive them of the only remaining left-wing candidate—especially when he had twice, in the same circumstances (in 1965 and 1974), been the candidate of the Left as a whole?

For the Communist party, the worst was yet to come. The bosses in the Place du Colonel Fabien hoped their pitiful result would at least allow them to remain outside the government. They were able to believe this until after the legislative elections of June 1981, for the Socialists had obtained a majority of seats in the National Assembly alone. To the Communists' great delight, they realized that François Mitterrand could govern without them.

At the time, many leading Socialists (including Lionel Jospin) felt that the ministerial participation of the Communists was not obligatory, while the opposition shuddered with horror at the idea that the Soviets could infiltrate the workings of the state.

This did not take into account François Mitterrand's obstinacy. His personal history, he explained, "had since 1965 been identified with the Union of the Left." He had a moral debt to the Communist electors. He wanted to keep his word to them, however difficult his relations might be with the Communists at the top. So he decided, despite the preferences or warnings of many of his friends, to give a few symbolic portfolios to the Communists. In the end he gave them four: transport, health, occupational training, and the civil service.

The conservative press immediately shrieked with horror. True, the representatives of the Communist party were only to run one ministry out of ten; true, they were deprived of the key portfolios (no accident). Nevertheless, for the first time since 1947, Communist leaders sat in the Council of Ministers. And in France, the railways were under the authority of the minister of transport, while the civil service gave access to the entire public sector. The Communist CGT was actually given new advantages, enabling it to consolidate its organization inside French railways and to plant its members in key civil service posts. As for the Ministry of Health, its plans for reform raised such an outcry on the part of the medical profession that, a few months later, the job had to be given to somebody else.

For a year—the time of harmony between the Socialists and

Communists—the risk of the Communist party infiltrating the state apparatus gave nightmares to some sectors of the population, including trade unionists, the well-off, and the liberal intelligentsia. It was even said that Mitterrand's fate would be the same as that of Kerensky.[2] Looking back, such fears appear to be fantasies. In practice, the influence of the Communist ministers on the making of government policy proved very slight. Contrary to fears, especially current in Washington, Socialist France, far from becoming a shaky ally within the Atlantic Alliance, displayed far more determination and loyalty than it had under earlier presidents. Similarly, whenever a choice presented itself inside the European community between the spirit of solidarity and the temptation to retreat out of national interest, Paris always acted honorably. In a way, the very presence of Communist ministers in the government forced François Mitterrand and Pierre Mauroy's cabinet to behave in such a way as to give no grounds for suspicion.

As soon as economic realities imposed their law on the left-wing government—as soon as it had to move from social distribution to administrative austerity—relations deteriorated. Soon *L'Humanité*, the Communist daily newspaper, adopted a very oppositional tone. The CGT showed its displeasure and even threatened the government with national strikes (though it lacked the means of organizing them). Through leaks it was learned that Communist party representatives were expressing increasing opposition to the new policies in the Council of Ministers. Irritated but not surprised, François Mitterrand then admitted at a spring 1984 press conference that a "clean sweep would be necessary." This, of course, did not make relations with the Communists any better. In various by-elections, the Communist party, far from gaining from its participation in the government, continued to shed supporters.

Indeed, the disillusion of the Communist electors was clearly perceptible: a detailed analysis of the ballot revealed that many of them had abstained, while in some cases, they had even gone so far as to make a protest vote for the extreme Right. Everything was ripe for a break: on the international scene, the presence of the Communists in the government irritated Soviet leaders, while in France itself the Communist party continued on its inexorable decline whether in government or in opposition. Between 1981 and 1986, the Communist party was to drop from having 16 percent of the vote to having under 10.

That the Communist party had remained a sort of foreign body inside the government became obvious when it left in July 1984. Seldom had a political decision of such importance been received with so little interest—the reason being that it had been expected for so long. Even those who in 1981 had been up in arms at the danger when the Communists entered the government saw them leave without even thinking of celebrating, so expected was the epilogue.

In all fairness, François Mitterrand should have been praised for contributing in this way to the decline of the Communist party. Unfortunately, justice is not the rule in politics, and now that the Communist party was no longer an object of fear, the Right did not regard François Mitterrand as a savior. On the contrary, its theoreticians explained that the Communist party had not been killed off by the president of the Republic, but had strangled itself: its leaders were tired; the Soviet model was no longer an inspiration; its remedies for the crisis were not taken seriously by anybody; even its organization, which remained the most authoritarian party machine in France, discouraged young people from joining. Still, it had to be admitted, the president of the Republic deserved some praise at least for effecting this longer-term development. On the other hand, it brought no short-term electoral solution. If the Left were to succeed in reconquering parliamentary power, the Socialist party would have to start expanding again, this time to the detriment of the Center, not the Communist party, which was a risky business altogether. This would be so unless François Mitterrand himself, as a new candidate and newly elected president, could create such dynamism that the party managed to achieve a majority on its own.

CONTINUITY

French foreign policy is based on a few simple ideas: national independence, balance between the military blocs of the world, the construction of Europe, the right of peoples to self-determination, the development of poor countries . . . In it can be seen both the traces of a furrow dug by the thousand-year-old destiny of the oldest nation in Europe and the special mark left on a nation by its leaders. From the first day, I encountered on this terrain the support of the overwhelming majority of French people.

In these words François Mitterrand began his *Reflections on French Foreign Policy*, a long book published just a few weeks before the legislative elections of March 1986.

The publication date was carefully calculated to coincide with a contest that the president of the Republic knew only too well could not be favorable to him. It was a skillful maneuver and indeed one that had been anticipated the previous summer when a widely discussed article by Roland Dumas, foreign minister and a close friend of the head of state, propounded much the same theme. Under the all-embracing title "Consensus," Dumas set out to demonstrate in the columns of *Le Monde* that whoever emerged victorious in the elections, there could be no question of the French altering such a popular, effective, and incontrovertible foreign policy. The word *continuity* was not mentioned, but the concept imbued the whole article. Roland Dumas' skill lay in presenting agreement on foreign policy as a rallying on the part of the French people to François Mitterrand's theses, whereas, in fact, it would have been truer to say that François Mitterrand had rallied to the classic doctrine of the Fifth Republic.

To tell the truth, in 1981, the new president's choices in this field had come as something of a surprise, both in France and abroad. Those possessed of a good memory would certainly have been astonished by the policies advocated by the victor of May 10. After all, he had poured enough scorn on his predecessors in the area of international relations, which, as the time for presidential elections approached, increasingly became his own chosen field. He had wholeheartedly opposed General de Gaulle's policy of nuclear independence; he had solemnly blamed him for leaving NATO; over and over again he had declared his disagreement with Gaullist policy on the Middle East. He had regarded Georges Pompidou as a halfhearted European. He had harassed Pompidou and Valéry

Giscard d'Estaing in turn on what he regarded as their overly close relations with Leonid Brezhnev. He had condemned French military intervention in Africa—particularly in Chad and Mauritania. He had made arms sales the very symbol of political cynicism and shortsighted *realpolitik*. For over twenty years he had consistently refused to vote for the military budget. He had regularly poured scorn on the Foreign Affairs budget; each year, in the National Assembly, he had reserved his greatest oratorical skills to indict whoever happened to be the unfortunate holder of the Foreign Affairs portfolio.

Under Giscard d'Estaing, the worse the opinion polls became, the greater Mitterrand's fury and the more wounding his sarcasm. Even initiatives on European matters found no grace in his eyes. The creation of European councils to bring together heads of state, the election of the European parliament by direct universal suffrage, and the establishment of the European monetary system did not come about on their own, but Mitterrand never accorded the French president any credit for them.

On his accession to power, one might well have expected a complete change of course.

Abroad, especially across the Atlantic, the worst was expected. There was nothing reassuring about the triumph of this left-wing government, elected on an ultra-interventionist platform, with nationalistic overtones. The participation of four Communist ministers in the government (for the first time since 1947, that is to say, since the outbreak of the Cold War) was regarded with suspicion. How could one trust an ally that allowed declared adversaries to sit at the very heart of state power?

In Brussels, at the seat of the European Economic Community, it was feared that a few independent measures would be taken. Had not the government of Pierre Mauroy decided to abandon the European monetary system? Would nationalization be compatible for very long with the free-enterprise logic of the Common Market? And was not one of the Socialists' aims the distinctly odd idea of limiting external trade to 20 percent of the gross internal product? Was not France about to succumb once more to the old demons of Colbertism and archaism?

None of the anticipated changes came about. In the end, François

Mitterrand's foreign policy was to be marked much more by continuity than by bold change. His principal mark, for he did leave a mark, was to dress up very old ideas in new clothes. Though he never admitted it, he simply stepped into his predecessors' shoes.

Yes, there were some changes, but they were ones of style, not substance. The advent of a Socialist president, itself, could not but be a fact of major importance. The event left its mark on the world—though largely by statements of moral intent and symbolic gestures. No sooner was he elected president than François Mitterrand, visiting the famous aeronautics exhibition at Le Bourget, took a bold initiative. He demanded that the French military aircraft presented to him be disarmed to demonstrate his notions of peace and his distaste for the export of French military equipment. The climate seemed to be changing. On a visit to Mexico, the president delivered a homily celebrating the virtues of the poor made hungry by the great capitalist powers. His words had quite an effect in the two Americas—especially when it was learned that France was proposing to deliver military equipment to Sandinista Nicaragua, and that the dazzling Jack Lang, his minister of culture, went off to Cuba to pay homage. Once there, Lang declared, without a trace of hesitation, that "Cuba is a courageous country that has every right to choose freely its own political regime." The statement caused a scandal and was (wrongly) assumed to have had the backing of the Elysée.

Another significant gesture was the much trumpeted visit to Israel, including a speech to the Knesset. It was the first time in many years that a French head of state had made an official visit to Tel Aviv and Jerusalem. He arrived as a friend and was received as an ally. Although François Mitterrand claimed to support the rights of the Palestinian people, his mere presence in Israel, let alone his warmth on the occasion, were felt in the Arab capitals to mark a change of direction.

There followed a whole series of exercises in political gymnastics intended to ingratiate France with the Third World that looked very like an attempt to expiate the sin of colonialism: Algerian gas benefited from highly favorable terms (highly unfavorable to the French taxpayers). Foreign Minister Claude Cheysson was tireless in visits and speeches intended to demonstrate French affection— though little of practical use followed those visits.

Lastly, defense of human rights took its place in the new French diplomacy: the head of state gallantly raised the problem of Sakharov under the gilded ceilings of the Kremlin—to the great consternation of Soviet officials.

During the first years of Socialist power, it seemed that a new tone had come in with the new personnel. A combination of amateurism and moralism seemed to have transformed the prevailing atmosphere. And yet, as time passed, French people began to see the germ of tradition beneath the chaff of words. To Washington's great relief—and to his own, perhaps, as well—the Socialist president turned out to be the most dependable of European allies.

During François Mitterrand's seven-year term, the great strategic question in the West was the development of Pershing II and cruise missiles, in response to Soviet SS 20s. The European leader who proved to be Washington's most consistent supporter was unquestionably President Mitterrand. In his famous speech to the Bundestag, he came out unhesitatingly in favor of Washington's position. Quite obviously, the presence of Communist ministers in his government, far from tying his hands, tended rather to drive him to demonstrate where his true friends were to be found.

During the earliest years of his term, Mitterrand even declared that he would not go to Moscow, and that he would receive no visits from his Soviet counterparts until the rights of the Polish and Afghan peoples were respected. The expulsion of fifty Soviet "diplomats" from Paris was also intended to illustrate this hard line. Whether socialist or not, France remained well and truly within the Atlantic Alliance.

And he proved himself a European. From the outset of his seven-year term, the economic policy of growth through consumption raised the question of whether the franc should leave the European monetary system. For several years "Europeans"—and others not so "European"—constantly argued about the advisability of such a step. After endless ambivalence, François Mitterrand decided in favor of the "European" solution. He displayed the same outlook when the question of Spain and Portugal's entry into the community arose, or when it became urgent to find solutions to the budgetary deadlock in Brussels. Socialist France remained to the end Europe's good pupil.

In Chad and Lebanon, François Mitterrand followed in his pre-

decessors' footsteps. He had condemned interventions into the
affairs of Colonel Qaddafi, yet, when his turn came, he, too,
intervened. He had warned against sending French forces to Lebanon, yet he sent them and then deplored the deaths, receiving
news of them with a suitably tragic countenance. Under him, France
remained the protector of the countries of black Africa; and, under
him, France was anxious to protect its influence in the Middle East.
Under François Mitterrand, Franco-African summits went on much
as before (except that they cost more). France remained France.
So, when called upon to continue as before, Mitterrand's diplomacy
was ever ready. But when it tried to innovate, the results were less
happy: France wanted to relaunch the century-old debate on North-
South relations and the aid given by the rich countries to the poor
ones—to no avail. The one great idea of the regime was to reestablish an international monetary system by preparing a new
Bretton Woods Conference—it still has not taken place. François
Mitterrand favors a reexamination of the prospects for a combined European defense (although he opposed the European
Defense Community under the Fourth Republic). Nothing has
yet come of it.

He can claim credit, however, for one success: the development
of the Eureka Project, of a technological Europe that, after its
first hesitant steps, is now making progress. On the other hand,
although he opposed President Reagan's Strategic Defense Initiative, he has been unable to discourage his European partners
from taking part in it. Even his wife, Danielle Mitterrand, herself
an ambitious advocate of human rights at the beginning of
the reign, seems to have lost some of her enthusiasm as the years
pass.

To be fair, one has to admit that the Socialist president has been
lacking in neither style nor a certain panache. He has irritated his
counterparts in both the White House and the Kremlin. Certainly,
he has never been underestimated. But in matters of substance he
has fallen short of his ambitions. He wanted the voice of France
to be heard in a new way. This never came to pass. For example,
after France's initial chilly relations with the Soviet Union, nobody
knows precisely why, but relations have suddenly become warmer.
(In the meantime, the fate of the Afghans and Poles has not im-

proved.) For most French people the main thing seems to be that French foreign policy continues, despite the electoral ups and downs. The esteem with which François Mitterrand is regarded by certain right-wingers is surely tempered by the fact that he has not carried out a truly socialist foreign policy.

EPILOGUE

IN 1981, WHEN THE VICTORS WERE BEING ASKED WHAT French-style socialism was, they replied proudly in one voice: "It's the alliance of socialism and time."

Their right-wing predecessors had held the reins for twenty-three years. Now that the Socialists had won, thanks to the institutions established by General de Gaulle, they in turn were to benefit from the same favors of destiny. To be fair, they did not count on being in power for twenty-three years, but fourteen years (two seven-year terms) seemed reasonable enough. Led by a president to whom they accorded all the stature of a statesman, armed with their program, proud of the correctness of their theses, they displayed all the naive self-assurance of the newly rich—plus a good conscience, their distinctive mark.

Unhappily for them, though, the state of grace was soon exhausted; by-elections, local elections, and general elections soon dissipated their illusions. Legislative socialism was not made to last, governmental socialism would be beaten, popular socialism was in mourning, and ideological socialism was in full retreat.

There was only one escapee from this sinking ship: presidential socialism, in the person of the indomitable François Mitterrand.

Faithful to himself and his own course, the head of state, so recently a conqueror, promptly fell back into the abysses of unpopularity. Never had a president in office known such disfavor. But unlike his predecessors, no sooner had he touched rock bottom than he was already plotting revenge.

March 1986 sounded the knell for the Left—and the beginning of a resurrection for François Mitterrand. Paradoxically, it took a return of the Right to power for the man in the Elysée to regain popularity for a second time, to arouse almost a new wave of fervor. Once again, ambiguity suited him wonderfully. Had he not been the inspiration and best interpreter of the policies carried out for the past five years—the very same policies that had just been rejected? Had he not proudly claimed their paternity during the campaign? And had he not held a meeting to galvanize the Socialist troops—he, a president of the Republic in office, forgetting his duty to remain above the battle, descending from the Elysian heights to plunge furiously into the mêlée of the legislative elections as if he were just an ordinary Socialist party first secretary?

As the leader of the losing side, François Mitterrand ought logically to have suffered the same fate as his party. Some members of the opposition had even prophesied during the campaign that a defeat of the Left at the legislative elections would drive an exasperated crowd to the Elysée demanding his resignation. A few days before the ballot, some of those close to him spread the rumor that he would resign in any case, of his own free will, if his friends were defeated. When the day of the ballot came, however, there was no question of this. Having been elected for seven years, François Mitterrand was quite determined that his rights would be scrupulously respected. He had, it is true, taken part in the campaign; he had accepted his share of the responsibility. But constitutionally his mandate was not in question.

Rebels as they are in ordinary life, the French are great legitimists in important matters. And these were important matters. So they considered François Mitterrand quite right to remain in office, providing he loyally abided by the rules of the game.

The French had clearly voted for the Right. In the new majority, Jacques Chirac's "Gaullist" RPR won more votes and seats than the other groups. Under the circumstances, the president of the

Republic prudently (or realistically) felt he had no choice. He had toyed with the notion that if the Right failed to win a decisive victory, he would turn to his old Gaullist accomplice, Jacques Chaban-Delmas, Georges Pompidou's former prime minister, but even more important, Mitterrand's friend for thirty years and colleague in the Mendès France government. Similarly, if the UDF, the Center-Right grouping that had formed an electoral alliance with the RPR, had won roughly as many seats as the RPR, he might have been able to call on Valéry Giscard d'Estaing. (In either case, he would have been given an affirmative reply.)

But François Mitterrand's great manipulative skills have always been in knowing how to turn bad into good. This time, the promptness with which he summoned Jacques Chirac to form a government (scarcely twelve hours after the final result) was regarded by the French as proof of fair play. The president was respecting the institutions. Better still, the man who had spent so many years fighting General de Gaulle's constitution was becoming its guardian, the man through whom the tables of the law would be applied. He demonstrated their viability, however complicated things looked. A left-wing president of the Republic with a right-wing National Assembly (and therefore government)—such a thing had not been seen for twenty-three years. The Gaullists had always warned against such a prospect. The most Mitterrandist Socialists were those who expected the worst possible mess to emerge from such a situation, while Raymond Barre sounded the death toll of the Fifth Republic and foresaw a return to the bog of Fourth Republic–type parliamentarianism.

Yet nothing of the sort happened. People very soon realized that the president presided, the government governed, the majority obeyed, and the opposition opposed—in short, that the constitution was being applied. It may not have been a traditional application that prevailed, but it was certainly a more literal one. According to article twenty, the head of government (the prime minister) directed governmental policy. For the first time in twenty-three years, power had crossed the Seine, leaving the Elysée for the Matignon.

So was "cohabitation" working? Scarcely had François Mitterrand installed Jacques Chirac than, in a message to the parliament (communicated in advance to the prime minister), he wrote out the rules for parliament with all the scrupulousness of a lawyer. He called on all of France to testify to his goodwill, but he also laid down the limits beyond which he would not allow the prime minister to go (for example, in effecting certain denationalizations, or what in legal terms would challenge certain social acquisitions).

Everything was clear. Even under Jacques Chirac, the old Mitterrand style of mingled complexity and ambiguity continued. Let us consider complexity first. In foreign policy, which throughout the Fifth Republic had been the domain of the president, power sharing was required for the first time. The head of state would, of course, continue to occupy the first place: he would symbolize France, represent the nation on great occasions, and even be able to influence policy. In practice, every week Mitterrand receives the foreign minister and defense minister, and every two weeks, the minister of cooperation, all of whom keep him informed on what they are doing and respect his predilections.

But Jacques Chirac plays a role in this—and a greater one than any of his predecessors. He accompanies François Mitterrand to the European summits and those of the great industrialized countries. The ambassadors appointed by the Elysée must now meet with Chirac's approval. If one of them does not (as, for example, in the case of Eric Rouleau, former *Le Monde* journalist, great friend of the left-wing Arab leaders, and faithful friend of François Mitterrand, who appointed him to Tunis), he must hand in the keys to his embassy. All in all, however, the broad lines of foreign policy are not a matter for disagreement, and each difficult decision reveals a certain schizophrenia.

The celebrated refusal to allow American bombers to fly over French territory on their raid on Tripoli was the result of a consultation between the head of state and the prime minister. Although agreement was reached, it was not without serious arguments. On other important matters—President Reagan's Strategic Defense Initiative, for example—Mitterrand's hostility is completely out of tune with Jacques Chirac's moderate sympathy. In fact, the Elysée preaches the "no, but" (no in principle, but French enterprises have a right to take part), whereas the Matignon prefers the "yes, but" approach (yes in principle, but respect the independence of France and her specific interests).

Until March 16, 1986, foreign policy was solely the head of state's affair. This power is now divided; it is not the only one. There is another area of codecision: the appointment of senior civil servants. Constitutionally, it is a matter for the Council of Ministers, with the agreement of the head of state. In practice, Jacques Chirac has the right to propose; François Mitterrand, to veto.

Usually the president accedes to Chirac's requests, providing the forms are respected and the pace does not seem too rushed. The Elysée wishes to be kept informed in advance of the Matignon's intentions, otherwise the president refuses if necessary to allow a particular appointment to be placed on the agenda of the weekly cabinet meetings. He has been known to do this for several weeks in succession, as, for example, over a new presidential appointment to the Crédit Agricole (a state-run investment bank for the farming industry). He also insists that senior civil servants or heads of public enterprises who have been removed from their jobs by the new government be duly compensated; further, he insists that these compensations be specified in advance. On this matter the executive definitely has two heads. Which of the two gives in more often? François Mitterrand, if he allows Jacques Chirac to appoint his own men to the more important jobs (though the president wages a rearguard action, doggedly defending his own men). As a result, much time is wasted and a great deal of haggling goes on in each ministry, echoes of which reach the outside world.

Ambiguity comes into its own every Wednesday after the meeting of the Council of Ministers. On that day, two spokesmen officiate in turn, implicitly in confrontation. First Alain Jupé, budget minister and government spokesman, expatiates on the excellence of the decisions made that morning. Then Mme Gendraux Massaloux, spokesman for the Elysée, points out the dangers involved in implementing such policies. An odd kind of stereo echoes in the ears of public opinion and sows discord in editorial offices. Is the president of the Republic as much of an arbiter as he claims? Indeed he is: Mitterrand exploits any opportunity to heap scorn on the government and therefore, by implication, on its head. Seldom does a speech, an inauguration, or a visit to the provinces end without some mocking formula emerging on the failures and inadequacies of the Right—and on the virtues and ambitions of the Left.

To the French, who seem so pleased with this cohabitation (their unconscious ideal having always been that the Right and Left should work together), Minister of Justice Albin Chalandon was not wrong in declaring that the prime minister had the advantage of governing between the cross fire of two oppositions: one in the parliament, the other in the Elysée. For the time being, this strange situation benefits the president (but for how long?).

The Socialists appreciate Mitterrand's warnings, still regarding him as their effective leader and the embodiment of their hopes. The right-wing electors are grateful to him for calling on Jacques Chirac and for avoiding a constitutional crisis. Partly out of cowardice, partly out of prudence, the French seem quite happy with this perverse situation.

Cohabitation will last for another year at most, since the next presidential elections will theoretically take place in the spring of 1988. But who can be certain how long the experiment will last? A crisis is always possible. It could come from François Mitterrand or from Jacques Chirac. But the prime minister is master neither of the timetable nor the terrain. If he resigned, nothing would stop the head of state from calling on someone else to run the government (thought it would have little chance of success, it is true). And if Chirac left the Hôtel Matignon for the second time (the first having been in August 1976 under Valéry Giscard d'Estaing's presidency), his image would be tarnished, his legitimacy split asunder, and his abilities as a possible unifier seriously undermined.

The choice remains with François Mitterrand. He can allow the experiment to continue to the end of his normal term, counting on the fact that economic difficulties, continuing unemployment, the discontents of various sectors, and the short time remaining at the government's disposal for carrying out its policies will erode the regime's capital of goodwill before the decisive vote.

He could also alter the timetable by resigning. Many of his friends, to whom he confides nothing (one of them complained bitterly, "I don't even know if he confides in himself, or whether his left hand knows what his right hand is doing"), support this hypothesis. Most of them earnestly want him to run again. Despite the plethora of candidates from the point of view of the Socialists, he is still the best. So they hope he will alter the timetable. Although a crisis might make François Mitterrand run again, the possibility of elections at the end of the presidential term does not in any way imply that he will do so. And, in any case, people are whispering in his ranks that by 1988 François Mitterrand will be seventy-two—quite old to begin a new seven-year term.

Everything depends on Mitterrand's decisions and preferences. Either he is thinking, above all, of the image he will leave in history, in which case it seems certain that he will prefer to end his term in office on a wave of regained popularity (he would then be the first Socialist to have entered the Elysée by universal suffrage, and, having made a success of government changes, inaugurated cohabitation, and consolidated the Fifth Republic, would have almost equaled, in his own mind, General de Gaulle himself—the model, the reference, the rival, the commander); or he will prefer politics to history, revenge to legend, in which case he will run again, set out for battle once more, and lead his troops back into power. But that would imply that he still believed in socialism—precisely at a time when his followers are desperately looking for new ideas.

Clearly this consummate politician is determined to hesitate.

NOTES

CHAPTER 1

1. Interview in the magazine *Lire*, July 1978.

2. Students or ex-students of the Ecole Normale Supérieure, one of a number of *"grandes écoles"* in which France trains its intellectual elite. Entry is by open competition; the successful pursue their studies at the University of Paris while enjoying the additional privileges of board and special tuition [translator's note].

3. An electoral alliance formed by the Radical, Socialist, and Communist parties that was to form the Popular Front government (1936–38) under the Socialist leader Léon Blum [trans.].

4. The seat of the Chambre des Deputés, the lower house of the French parliament [trans.].

5. The Panthéon, the building devoted to the nation's heroes, though secularized under the Revolution has always kept its original status as a church and is still surmounted by a cross.

6. The civil administrator of a *département* appointed by the central government [trans.].

7. Coincidence: Mme Jeannine Alexandre Debray, mother of Régis Debray, adviser at the Elysée, published in late 1981 a biography of Victor Schoelcher.

8. The church of Sermages in the Nièvre.

9. Jacques Chardonne, *Le Bonheur de Barbezieux* (Paris: Stock).

10. Interview with François Mitterrand, *L'Expansion*, August 1972.

11. François Mitterrand, *La Paille et le grain* (Paris: Flammarion).

12. Every summer, François Mitterrand goes to meditate in that tiny church. He is thinking, it seems, of choosing the adjoining graveyard as his last resting place. A photograph of it now stands on the mantelpiece of the president's office in the Elysée.

13. Recounting his first escape at the ambassadors' lecture in May 1947, François Mitterrand said: "As I walked, one memory obsessed me: that of the dishes that used to be served at home during family festivities two or three times a year. I remembered in particular a duck with orange and for five days I walked thinking of that duck with orange."

14. Mitterrand, *La Paille et le grain*.

15. François Mitterrand, *Ma part de vérité* (Paris: Fayard).

16. When he fell, all dressed up, into the Dronne at the age of seventy-five (a small bridge having collapsed), he yelled out quite imperturbably, calmly observing the bank, to his terrified tenant farmer: "Go on, then, pick up my hat before it blows away!"

17. Mitterrand, *Ma part de vérité*.

18. Ibid.

19. The Socialist (now Communist) party newspaper, founded by Jean Jaurès [trans.].

20. Interview with François Mitterrand, *L'Expansion*, August 1972.

21. Claude Manceron, *Cent mille voix par jour pour François Mitterrand*.

22. With all due respect, this promotion seems somewhat improbable, since Angoulême was not the last stepping-stone to the Gare d'Austerlitz in the hierarchy of the Paris-Orléans Company.
    In the columns of *Who's Who*, before his first candidacy for the

presidential election, François Mitterrand, who at the time wanted to embody the Union of the Left, wrote somewhat overmodestly under the heading of father's profession, "railway worker." After consultation with his brothers, he changed this in later editions to "employee of the Paris-Orléans Railway Company," then to "industrialist."

23. And he sold his property at Touvent, to the despair of his grandchildren. Today, still profoundly affected by the event ("it was my first mourning," he has admitted), the president of the Republic always urges his friends never to sell a family house. And each summer he goes back to Touvent to try to persuade the present owner to sell him part of his land.

24. Interview in *L'Expansion*, 1972.

25. Interview in *Le Quotidien de Paris*, August 1981.

26. However, he presented himself as an Indépendant (conservative) at the Jarnac municipal elections and failed to get elected. Not everyone was suited to universal suffrage.

27. In 1934, in *Service public*, de La Rocque outlined his program as follows: it consists of strengthening the executive, extending the powers of the president of the Republic and limiting those of the parliament, reconciling capital and labor, regulating the right to strike—measures in favor of workers and the family. In 1958, Joseph Mitterrand might well have been a Gaullist.

28. This was a right-wing, nationalist, largely anti-Semitic movement led by Charles Maurras. It gained widespread support, particularly among intellectuals, through the newspaper of the same name up to 1940, when it supported the Vichy regime of Marshal Pétain [trans.].

29. Interview in *Le Quotidien de Paris*, August 1981.

30. Interview in *L'Expansion*, August 1972.

31. Mitterrand, *Ma part de vérité*.

32. Interview in *L'Expansion*, August 1972.

33. One of François Mitterrand's schoolfellows, now president of the L'Oréal company.

34. He is a great lover of hunting, an aristocratic sport that clashes with his older brother's profession of socialism.

35. Interview in *Le Quotidien de Paris*, August 1981. Boulanger, a former general in the French army, led a movement in the late 1880s for "strong government." In 1889 he was implicated in an attempted coup d'état and fled the country [trans.].

36. François Mitterrand, *L'Abeille et l'architecte* (Paris: Flammarion).

37. Mitterrand, *La Paille et le grain*.

CHAPTER 2

1. A banal translation of her French title, "ministre de la condition féminine" [trans.]!

2. Bérégovoy, in Socialist party jargon.

3. During his first presidential campaign in 1965, François Mitterrand had almost caused a scandal by coming out in favor of contraception.

4. Jean Guitton, *Une Mère en sa vallée* (Paris: Fayard).

5. These are questionable arguments: a public inquiry carried out by *La Croix* in December 1980 revealed, on the contrary, that private education was definitely open to all. According to these statistics, pupils' parents had the following professions (by percent): farmers (8), workers (16.6), junior office workers (10.5), middle management (21.4), employers (only 16.85), and members of the liberal professions (only 12.5).

6. In François Mitterrand, *Ici et maintenant* (*Here and Now*, a title with religious associations) (Paris: Fayard).

7. Later, as minister, François Mitterrand always put a car at the canon's disposal when his old friend was staying in the capital.

8. François Mitterrand, *La Paille et le grain*.

9. The Collège Saint-Paul took in several African pupils, whom the Mitterrand family invited to Jarnac for the shorter school holidays. Among them was Alphonse Boni, former president of the Ivory Coast at Abidjan, who became a member of François Mitterrand's office when Mitterrand was made minister for France overseas.

10. Mitterrand, *L'Abeille et l'architecte*.

11. Mitterrand, *La Paille et le grain*.

12. A former pupil, who for a long time sat next to him in class, Guy Dupuis (later Brother Guy), related the story in *Paris-Match*.

13. Mitterrand, *L'Abeille et l'architecte*.

14. Mitterrand, *La Paille et le grain*.

15. Ladies, acting *in loco parentis*, with whom boarders were allowed to spend their Sundays during term [trans.].

CHAPTER 3

1. On an official visit to Savoie in September 1984, the president, who had just appointed to the Matignon the almost advanced liberal Laurent Fabius, declared: "Socialist I was, Socialist I remain. That is, I intend to lead society in that direction."

2. Nobody had so far noticed it.

3. Father of Pierre Guillaumat, ex-president of the company Elf-Aquitaine, accused by the Socialists in the famous affair of the "sniffer" planes.

4. Father of Pierre Marcilhacy, who was to be appointed to the Constitutional Council in 1983.

5. President Mitterrand never wears a watch.

6. "Bloc-notes," *L'Express*, 1959.

7. A religious congregation particularly devoted to the figure of Our Lady.

8. As is shown by the room he was to occupy for years at the Hôtel du Vieux-Morvan: a mean, formica-topped table, a bed covered with crimson-colored velvet, a small sink, and no bathroom.

9. Jacques and Bernard Marot, Jean Ferréol de Ferry, Jean Roy, Henri Thieullent, Louis Gabriel Clayeux, François Dalle, and André Bettencourt (who arrived at "104" just as François Mitterrand was doing his military service).

10. An obvious reference to the papal prohibition of Action française.

11. The Croix-de-Feu movement, led by Colonel de La Rocque, who, as we have seen, had already attracted François Mitterrand's father, was dissolved on June 18, 1936. Its power and discipline had made it one

of the groups most feared by the left-wing parties. Originally it recruited solely from among those who had been decorated with the croix de guerre (hence its name) during the 1914–18 war, but it later expanded, setting up parallel youth organizations, particularly the Sons of Croix-de-Feu and the National Volunteers. By early 1935, it had over 260,000 members in a state of permanent mobilization, able to respond immediately to any uprising led by the Communist (or any other left-wing) party. During the Popular Front period, each demonstration by supporters of Colonel de La Rocque was countered with big public meetings organized by the Communists and Socialists.

12. In his book *Les Non-conformistes des années trente*, Jean-Louis Loubet del Bayle declares that in the years 1937–38, François Mitterrand was an active propagandist on the monthly *Combat*, for which many right-wing intellectuals wrote (including Thierry Maulnier, Drieu La Rochelle, Robert Brasillach, and Claude Roy, Mitterrand's friend from Angoulême).

13. This small organization, which was actually called the Secret Committee for Revolutionary Action, practiced secrecy and cultivated mystery. It criticized Maurras for not daring to step outside legality in order to defeat the parliamentary Republic. In answer to the street demonstrations and factory occupations carried out by the members of the Communist party, it advocated recourse to violent action. It castigated the Popular Front and big business alike. It had a few arms caches, especially in the Paris sewers, and its networks were responsible for several assassination attempts. War was to divide the Cagoule. Most of its members were active collaborators; others fought in the Resistance or on the side of the Free French.

14. Former French consul at São Paulo, elected in 1984 on the Le Pen list for the European elections.

15. Méténier was thus described by Philippe Bourdrel in his book *La Cagoule* (Paris: Albin Michel).

16. Ibid.

17. Ibid.

18. Ibid.

19. Jeantet was to be one of his proposers for the *francisque*.

20. Herbert Lottman, *Pétain* (Paris: Seuil).

21. Mitterrand, *Ma part de vérité.*

22. Europe 1, August 1984.

23. Mitterrand, *Ma part de vérité.*

24. Action française's small "private army" [trans.].

25. Maurras, too, was very anti-German.

26. In the review *Montalembert.*

27. After Henri de Montherlant's suicide, François Mitterrand confided to the writer Gabriel Matzneff: "Drieu La Rochelle and Montherlant, the masters of my youth, are dead."

28. In an interview with Roget Priouret in 1972, François Mitterrand declared: "I am an antimilitarist. I refused to do my military training."

29. In the review *Montalembert.*
    His close friends remember a match with Félix Gaillard one Sunday at the house of Marcel Bleustein-Blanchet (Robert Badinter's father-in-law) during the Fourth Republic, when Mitterrand almost gave himself a heart attack trying to beat a better player.

30. She carefully preserved them, wrapped in her daughter's baby clothes.

31. His mother's death had such an effect on him at the time that he asked one of his friends: "Is it silly to love one's mother?" Later, over the dinner table, he would suddenly ask the lady next to him: "Did you love your mother?"

CHAPTER 4

1. Two French generals who were ardent advocates of French Algeria, the doctrine that Algeria should remain part of France (a view shared by the entire French population of Algeria and most of the French nation). When it became clear that General de Gaulle did not share this view, instead favoring a policy of moving toward Algerian independence, Salan and Jouhaux led a revolt of the French army in Algeria against de Gaulle's authority—a revolt that soon turned into an attempted putsch [trans.].

2. However, their surprise was scarcely justified: during the 1974 presidential campaign, Valéry Giscard d'Estaing, when questioned on the

transfer to Douaumont of Philippe Pétain's remains, had replied in the negative; but the candidate of the Left, François Mitterrand, had promised after his election to organize a conference bringing together representatives of the parliament, government, and war veterans' associations for the purpose of "proposing solutions to this matter of contention." The Socialist hierarchs probably paid no attention to these words (which in any case suffered the usual fate of electoral promises: oblivion).

3. Mitterrand, *La Paille et le grain*.

4. It was he who introduced to the first secretary of the Socialist party a number of brilliant men on the Council of State, to which he had been appointed under the reign of the broad-minded Giscard d'Estaing. Jacques Attali and Laurent Fabius were among his protégés.

5. Referring to his captivity in 1947 at an ambassadors' lecture, he recounts: "Being unable to raise my right arm, since a shell splinter was lodged in my shoulder, I was transferred to a small factory where they made fruit juice. My job consisted of separating the rotten apples from the good ones." He still has a tiny piece of shrapnel in his right shoulder blade.

6. *Mitterrand La Paille et le grain*.

7. Curiously enough, he has said very little about this second attempt, accounts of which vary from one biography to another. Indeed, he has always remained very reticent about all three escapes, and has never tried to make political capital out of them. His brother-in-law, Roger Hanin, has always regretted this (if Michel Picar and Julie Montagard, the enthusiastic authors of a book devoted to Danielle Mitterrand, are to be believed).

8. The *hommes de confiance* were prisoners to whom the Germans left certain responsibilities in the everyday running of the camp.

9. In *Dossiers PG rapatriés*, a rare work (only three hundred copies were printed) edited by Jean Védrine, who brought together about one hundred accounts by former prisoners.

10. The Radical-Socialist party, one of the largest and most influential of the parties under the Third Republic, remained a potent force under the Fourth, and finally disappeared during the Fifth. Its name was misleading: it was in no sense a socialist party. Rather, it was

an anticlerical party of the Center, roughly equivalent to the British Liberal party of the time.

Up to the Fifth Republic, the French prime minister was referred to as "president of the council [of ministers]." However, I use the current term *prime minister* for convenience [trans.].

11. In Védrine, *Dossiers PG rapatriés.*

12. Supporters of General Giraud, a World War I hero, who escaped from German captivity in 1942. He promised Pétain not to join de Gaulle, but later escaped from France to head a contingent of French troops under the Allies' command. For a time he came to a working arrangement with de Gaulle, but this broke down in 1943 because of Giraud's ultraconservative views [trans.].

13. In Védrine, *Dossiers PG rapatriés.*

14. In Mitterrand, *Ma part de vérité.*

15. Charles Moulin, *François Mitterrand intime* (Paris: Albin Michel).

16. "And this," he was to say in his 1947 lecture, "was one of the things I learned during my captivity. I realized the extent to which the social classes, heredity, education, and upbringing produced quite different results—not according to the category of origin, but according to the personal reflex of the man himself. And one saw men whom one would never have suspected of possessing this dignity show more courage than those whom, in advance, one would have believed to be worthy men."

17. During his presidential visit to Israel, François Mitterrand invited the son of his dead comrade to accompany him.

18. Mitterrand, *La Paille et le grain.*

19. Ibid.

20. Ibid.

21. Moulin, *Mitterrand intime.*

22. According to the written testimony of Jean Védrine (who was nevertheless not a direct witness), approved by François Mitterrand in *Dossiers PG rapatriés.*

23. In *L'Homme libre,* September 6, 1944.

24. Quoted by Georgette Elgey, *Histoire de la IVe république* (Paris: Fayard), Vol. 1, *La République des illusions.*

25. As Georges Baud, another former prisoner, puts it.

26. Védrine, *Dossiers PG rapatriés*.

27. Ibid.

28. Later, as a young minister, he would present a reproduction of the Vézelay poster to all the foreign diplomats with whom he had dealings.

29. In *Paris-Match*, September 1944.

30. Emile Poulat, *Eglise contre bourgeoisie: Introduction au devenir du catholicisme actuel* (Paris: Casterman).

31. That is, all the political regimes since the Revolution of 1789.

32. December 1942.

33. A faithful follower of the marshal and a former prisoner. Pierre Limagne writes in his *Ephémérides des quatre années tragiques* (Paris: Bonne Presse), May 9, 1942: "Simon Arbellot, who has just been to Germany, not this time as a prisoner, but as an official journalist, gave a lecture to the recipients of the decoration and told them of his certainty of Hitler's victory."

34. In the review *Ecrits de Paris*, January 1966.

35. Védrine, *Dossiers PG rapatriés*.

36. In *Ecrits de Paris*.

37. He himself gave the names of Jeantet and Arbellot to Franz Olivier Giesbert, the author of one of his biographies, *François Mitterrand ou la tentation de l'histoire* (Paris: Seuil).

38. In exchange for which the Communist Pierre Bugeaud was willing, on his side, to tone down an enthusiastic article he had written to the glory of Stalin.

39. Head of the Army Resistance Organization, which was more Giraudist than Gaullist.

40. Jean-Marie Borziex, *Mitterrand lui-même* (Paris: Stock).

41. "I obtained this information from the Central Bureau for Information of Free France," Maurice Schuman now notes, "so I reported young Morland's courage on a broadcast from London. That is why when Georges Pompidou, during a debate in the National Assembly, brought

up the whole story of François Mitterrand and the *francisque*, I wrote to him to tell him that Mitterrand had been a great resister!' "

Max Fleury, head of a Gaullist network, remembers: "I was at the Salle Wagram, just behind him, when François Mitterrand attacked Laval. I remember applauding; his courage made a great impression on me."

42. Both still ignore the existence of a third movement, the CNPG, which was Communist.

43. It will be noted that in his book on the Army Resistance Organization, Colonel Dainville makes no mention of this flight.

44. Mitterrand, *La Paille et le grain*.

45. Awarded the Grand Cross of the Légion d'honneur in 1983.

46. Paul Paillole, head of counterespionage at Vichy, comments: "All the planes that brought resisters out were British. In London, we were dependent on the British. What I think the general meant to suggest was that Mitterrand did not belong to the Gaullist networks—that is, to the Central Bureau for Information of Free France."

47. Mitterrand, *Ma part de vérité*.

48. Commenting on this episode, the first secretary of the Socialist party even went so far as to declare before journalists: "De Gaulle wanted to kill me!' "

49. I have already indicated the links between him and the Mitterrand family.

50. Védrine, *Dossiers PG rapatriés*.

51. Philomène Mercier adds: "He came back to see us in 1952. He was then a minister. His wife stayed in the car. He said to us: 'One day, I will be prime minister' " [interview with the author].

52. Their partners called this movement the PINMIT, the abbreviation of Pinot-Mitterrand.

53. Henri Frenay, *La nuit finira: Mémoires de résistance, 1940–1945* (Paris: Laffont).

54. The Liberation of Paris took place on August 24, a week later.

55. Frenay, *La nuit finira*.

56. Mitterrand, *Ma part de vérité*.

57. A story that will certainly bring a smile to the lips of more than one visitor forced to wait for hours on end to see the first secretary of the Socialist party.

58. Charles de Gaulle, *War Memoirs*, vol. 3, *Salvation*: 1944–1946 translated by Richard Howard (New York: Simon and Schuster).

59. *Les Clartés du jour* (Paris: Plon).

60. Alain de Boissieu, *Pour combattre avec de Gaulle* (Paris: Plon).

61. *Tout commence à Alger, 1940–1944* (Paris: Stock).

62. The same church in which Marie-Louise Terrasse and François Mitterrand worshipped during their engagement.

63. *Les Miroirs parallèles* (Paris: Calmann-Lévy).

64. Ibid.

65. Ibid.

66. Michel Picar and Julie Montagard, *Danielle Mitterrand* (Paris: Ramsay).

67. Mitterrand, *Ici et maintenant*.

68. Hélène Vida, *Mes hommes politiques* (Paris: Belfond).

CHAPTER 5

1. Jean Daniel, *Le Nouvel Observateur*.

2. She was to leave him a collection of snuffboxes.

3. A well-known figure in French advertising, founder of Agence Publicis, the leading French advertising agency [trans.].

4. The certificate allowing someone to practice as a barrister. A law passed in April 1954 under the Laniel government was to allow holders of law degrees, acquired before 1941, to practice the profession without having passed this additional examination.

5. Picar and Montagard, *Danielle Mitterrand*.

6. He was one of the protectors of those who financed the Cagoule and gave important jobs in his firm to leading Cagoulards, including Corrèze, Harispe, and Eugène Deloncle's son.

7. Picar and Montagard, *Danielle Mitterrand.*

8. A first Constituent Assembly, elected on October 21, 1945, had drawn up a bill that, though supported by the Communists and Socialists, was rejected by 53 percent of the electors during the referendum of May 5, 1946.

9. The MRP was a postwar party of the Catholic Center, similar in outlook to the Christian Democratic parties in other countries [trans.].

10. The Section française de l'Internationale ouvrière was the old name of the Socialist party, prior to its reconstruction in 1969 [trans.].

11. In *Libres*, 1939.

12. As the body that distributed subsidies to politicians and parties favorable to the theses of the CNPF was then called.

13. Mitterrand, *Ma part de vérité*, dialogue with Alain Duhamel.

14. Since the legislative elections of 1986, the Right is no longer the opposition, but the majority [trans.].

15. Oddly enough, this document can no longer be found, since the *Barodet* of 1946, in which all the candidates' professions of faith are collected, has disappeared from the library of the National Assembly.

16. His list, known as the Union démocratique et de defense républicaine, benefited at the time from Radical but not Socialist support. It was nevertheless the time of the Republican Front and of the alliance with the Mendésist Radicals, Guy Mollet's SFIO, and Jacques Chaban-Delmas' Social Republicans.

17. Max Lejeune, who had preceded him a month before in this job, had this correction: "In fact, the Communists had gone on strike because I had handed back to the Ministry of Armed Forces the trucks requisitioned in 1945 for the repatriation of prisoners and which since then had been used almost exclusively by the Communists to take their supporters to public meetings."

18. *L'Expansion*, August 1972.

19. Ibid.

20. In 1953, when François Mitterrand was president of the UDSR, an association of UDSR journalists was founded whose purpose was not only to bring together sympathetic journalists, but also to attract

members of the press to that party. It should also be noted that it was a UDSR leader, Jean Marin, who was appointed by André Bettencourt in 1954 managing director of the Agence France-Presse. François Mitterrand was sufficiently interested in the Agence to have proposed a bill in 1949 concerning its statutes. As one of his former government colleagues comments: "Mitterrand was unrivaled in his relations with the press."

21. Eric Duhamel, *L'UDSR* (master's thesis, 1983).

22. Still a determined advocate of proportional representation.

23. A bill to return to balloting by arrondissement, which did not get any further, had led to hasty (and of course controversial) new constituency boundaries.

24. During his campaign in the legislative elections of 1956, he often attacked the Communists and their beliefs. André Rousselet remembers him saying: "Who is interested in Marxism nowadays, except a few old English ladies?"

25. Interview with Paul Guilbert of the *Quotidien de Paris* in 1977.

26. In *Paris-Match*.

27. Ibid.

28. Interview in *L'Expansion*, August 1972.

29. Interview with the author in 1984.

30. François Mitterrand had fits of dizziness and often fainted. Jean Dayan, Georges's brother, a physician by profession, then had to administer injections through his suit before he went on the platform at meetings.

31. Testimony of the Abbé Coudreau.

32. At the time, the RPF, which had done very well in the municipal elections, demanded (in vain) that the legislative elections be brought forward.

33. In other words, by de Gaulle when he was in power.

34. Indeed, the day before in his speech, François Mitterrand had declared: "A movement, however powerful it may be, that rests on the authority, intelligence, or prestige of a single man is already fragile. . . . The other day Dussort asked me the following question: 'Is

it true that you said at Dijon that we should be equally suspicious of a fascism from the East as of a fascism that seems to find its expression in one man [in other words, General de Gaulle]? Did you really say that?' To which I replied to him in private: 'It is not exactly what I said, but I will be careful not to deny it.' "

35. Duhamel, *L'UDSR*.

36. Testimony obtained by the author.

37. Compare with Duhamel's thesis in his *L'UDSR*.

38. According to René Puissesseau, *Le Monde*'s special correspondent.

39. On the eve of the previous elections, the Vatican newspaper had called on the faithful, in scarcely veiled terms, to vote for the Popular Republican movement.

40. Jacques Bloch-Morhange, *Le Grenouille et le scorpion* (Paris: France Empire, 1982).

41. A minister for the Associated States had just been created to administer Indochina, Morocco, and Tunisia, which were protectorates and therefore came under the Foreign Ministry. The Ministry of the Interior had full authority over the three departments of Algeria (including the Sahara), Réunion, Guiana, and the West Indies.

42. François Mitterrand, *Présence française et abandon* (Paris: Plon, 1957).

43. Ibid.

44. François Mitterrand, *Le Coup d'état permanent* (Paris: Plon, 1964).

45. René Pleven was prime minister from July 1950 to March 1951; Henri Queuille succeeded him until August 1951, at which time René Pleven returned to the Matignon.

46. François Mitterrand, *Aux frontières de l'union française* (Paris: Julliard, 1953).

47. Alain de Boissieu, *Servir de Gaulle* (Paris: Plon).

48. Testimony of Maurice Decisier, Jean-François Rives (then regional head in the South) and Henri Verdier (inspector of administrative affairs who was also kicked out).

49. Mitterrand, *Ma part de vérité*.

50. Mitterrand, *Présence française et abandon.*

51. Paul Henri Siriex, *Félix Houphouët-Boigny: L'Homme de la paix* (Paris: Seghers).

52. Elgey, *La République des illusions.*

53. Paul Henri Siriex gives another version. In his book (see above), written with the blessing of the Ivory Coast president, he notes: "In the conversation, the minister was neither threatening nor bullying, but neither was there any written agreement, duly checked and signed. This really was to fail to understand the way Houphouët's mind worked. No, really, it was inconceivable he would give in to any kind of blackmail or to increased pressure, any more than one can imagine the minister resorting to this, without contradicting the spirit that had inspired his approaches."

54. Coulibaly, Félix Tchicaya, Hamari Diou, Houphouët-Boigny, Gabriel Lisette, and Mamadou Konaté.

55. Mitterrand, *Présence française et abandon.*

56. Mitterrand, *Le Coup d'état permanent.*

57. Siriex, *Félix Houphouët-Boigny.*

58. And yet the young minister ought to have reassured those ultras. In the spring of 1951, he had expressed his approval in the National Assembly of the brutal manner in which the high commissioner, Pierre de Chevigné, had reestablished order in Madagascar after the violent riots of 1947. He declared that he had visited the local prisons where, he said, "the conditions of detention were very acceptable for a democratic country like ours."

59. Mitterrand, *Ma part de vérité.*

60. During the debate concerning Pierre Mendès France's investiture. But since Mendès did not win a vote of confidence in the assembly, he did not become prime minister. The crisis was to last thirty-six days and end with the formation of the Laniel government.

61. Mitterrand, *Ma part de vérité.*

62. *L'Année politique,* 1954.

63. Bloch-Morhange, *La Grenouille et le scorpion.*

64. Jacques Julliard, *La IVe république* (Paris: Calman-Levy, 1968).

65. Through him, Jean Marin (UDSR) was made head of the AFP, while Jacques Marot, a journalist on the AFP and another friend from "104," was promoted.

66. Bloch-Morhange, *La Grenouille et le scorpion.*

67. An electoral alliance, the leaders of which were, with Pierre Mendès France, the Socialist Guy Mollet, the Gaullist Jacques Chaban-Delmas, and François Mitterrand.

68. Mollet declared in March 1956 in the National Assembly: "We shall maintain indissoluble links, but they will be freely negotiated and accepted." He was saying, in other words: "Lay down your weapons and you will then be able to choose freely the only solution offered you."

69. From October 30, 1954, to January 31, 1961, 222 political prisoners were executed for supporting the rebellion.

70. Jean Lacouture, *Pierre Mendès France* (Paris: Seuil, 1983).

71. *L'Année politique*, 1957.

72. At the time, she also went to see de Gaulle:
    "Why are they doing that?" she asked.
    "It brings immediate results," replied the general.
    "But it will turn against us in the end."
    "They aren't intelligent enough to realize."
    Germaine Tillion begged the general to do something, make some gesture, issue a statement.
    He replied, "Whatever I say, it will be misunderstood by somebody."
    In 1957, in *Jeune Afrique*, she commented: "He was not then a man who thought of returning to power."

73. Julliard, *La IVe république.*

74. He no longer belonged to the new government formed by the Radical Maurice Bourgès-Maunoury.

75. *L'Année politique*, 1961.

76. Paul Guilbert, interview in *Le Quotidien de Paris.*

77. Debate in the senate, July 5, 1961.

78. Jean-Noël de Lipkowski remembers a lunch at his mother's in the boulevard Saint-Germain (she was herself a deputy). The guests included François Mitterrand, Roland Dumas, Georges Dayan, and Patrice Pelat. As he entered the elegant apartment, the deputy for the Nièvre (who did not exactly live in a working-class suburb) exclaimed, half in jest: "Ah, les beaux quartiers!"

79. Lacouture, *Pierre Mendès France.*

80. And yet, in his letter of resignation, he wrote to Guy Mollet: "It was absolutely necessary to provoke certain acts that might serve as testimony of rebirth, trust, and hope, without which our eviction from Algeria will take place sooner or later. We have a right to prevent that eviction."

81. Guilbert, interview in *Le Quotidien de Paris.*

82. As the saying goes: "Algiers is terrible, you go in on the Left and leave on the Right."

83. For the Socialists, any expeditionary corps, whether to Suez (or, more recently, Chad and Lebanon), has a right to the title of "peace force," providing it is sent by a left-wing government. Similarly it was not desirable to speak of the Algerian "War"; officially, this was "pacification." War became war once again, and the forces of peace were suddenly turned into troops in the service of imperialism, as soon as the Right returned to power.

84. Interview with Franz Olivier Giesbert.

85. Interview with the author.

86. Author's interview with Jean-Noël de Lipkowski.

CHAPTER 6

1. Mitterrand, *La Paille et le grain.*

2. An illustration of that decidedly crazy month was the attitude of the general secretary of the SFIO, described by Serge and Merry Bromberger in their book *Les 13 complots du 13 mai* (Paris: Fayard):

   During those twenty-one days of crisis, Guy Mollet was the most French of all the French. He held every possible opinion at once, followed every course of action at once. He had secret contacts with the general's office after May 13 and understood the position of the French in Algeria; while preaching firmness against the rebel generals, he was negotiating with de Gaulle's collaborators and at the same time organizing a republican defense with other parts of the Left. He maneuvered to open the way to the general while encouraging Pflimlin to stay put. He shared all the feelings that divided the nation. The supreme honor of his life was to be received at Colombey.

3. Julliard, *La IVᵉ république.*

4. Mitterrand, *Ma part de vérité.*

5. Ibid.

6. Interview with Franz Olivier Giesbert.

7. Mitterrand, *Ma part de vérité.*

8. Interview, *Le Point,* 1973.

9. Moulin, *Mitterrand intime.*

10. Mitterrand, *Ma part de vérité.*

11. Among the more perplexed were Henri Frenay, who lived in the same building as François Mitterrand. On the very night of the affair, Mitterrand gave him a quite obviously different version. A close friend of the couple and godfather to Gilbert Mitterrand, Henri Frenay then decided to break with the man who had been his friend.

12. Even when he wanted to be friendly, François Mauriac never managed to be entirely indulgent. The following week, taking up Mitterrand's defense once again in reply to Robert Lazurick (who had written in *L'Aurore*: "In the eyes of his political friends, the author of such retractions will remain definitively disqualified"), the Catholic novelist added *in fine* on the former minister: "I never took him for a saint."

13. A man like Pierre Viansson-Ponté, then political editor of *Le Monde,* who regarded himself as a "political sympathizer," felt he had been duped: on the evening of the pseudoassassination, Mitterrand, with his hand on his heart, had told him no more than half the truth.

14. Testimony of Jean-Jacques Servan-Schreiber.

15. Mitterrand, *Ma part de vérité.*

16. Ibid.

17. Mitterrand, *L'Abeille et l'architecte.*

18. Mme Mitterrand went to see Pierre Lazareff, at whose home the couple had often spent weekends during the Fourth Republic, to criticize him vehemently for the uncomplimentary headlines in *France-Soir* and to inform him that their friendship was at an end.

19. Mitterrand, *Ma part de vérité.*

20. In February 1958, the same François Mitterrand confided to Jean-Noël de Lipkowski: "Franco-German reconciliation is very important—European unity must be based on the Paris-Bonn axis."

21. Georges Suffert, *De Defferre à Mitterrand* (Paris: Seuil).

22. Borzeix, *Mitterrand lui-même.*

23. It will be remembered in the footnotes of history that, while president of the Republic, François Mitterrand appointed Pierre Marcilhacy as one of the nine sages of the Constitutional Council—and that Marcilhacy did not refuse the appointment.

24. Born in 1960 out of the fusion of Gilles Martinet's UGS and the Parti socialiste autonome, created the year before by such dissidents of the SFIO as Edouard Depreux.

25. The CAI was soon to be linked with various clubs (the Jean-Moulin, the Tocqueville Circle of Lyon, and so on). This movement was to culminate in the birth of the Convention des institutions républicaines, which, in fact, was to be the party of François Mitterrand's friends.

26. Mitterrand, *Ma part de vérité.*

27. Contrary to what a vain people might believe, the single-party system referred to here was not that of the Communist regimes, but that dreamed of by General de Gaulle.

28. Later, it is true, Gaston Deferre shared a list with the Communist party. Within the Socialist party, evil tongues murmured that his third marriage, to Edmonde Charles-Roux, played no small part in his political development. As we know, the novelist was a firm believer in the idea of an alliance with the Communist party. She often signed appeals launched by the party, honored its receptions by her presence,

marched, arm in arm, with Henri Krasucki—while wearing Chanel suits.

29. So-called legal conferences, rather like opponents to Gaullism in the early 1960s.

30. Mitterrand, *Ma part de vérité*.

31. Having nevertheless deprived Daniel Mayer, after the Liberation, of the job of general secretary of the party, Guy Mollet never forgave him. That is how politicians are.

32. Testimony of Ernest Cazelles.

33. François Mitterrand, even though he later became a supporter of the nuclear strike force, never voted in favor of a military budget in twenty-three years.

34. In 1963, the mayor of Marseilles promoted a bill to do just this.

35. Quoted by Philippe Alexandre in *Le Roman de la gauche* (Paris: Plon).

36. At the first round, on March 5, 1967, the Left (Communist party, FGDS, and PSU) obtained 43.51 percent of the vote.

37. Claude Estier, *Journal d'un fédéré* (Paris: Fayard, 1970).

38. The version of this meeting given by Jean Lacouture, which is therefore that of P.M.F. himself, is much cruder than Claude Estier's: "Mitterrand, visibly exasperated, did not spare him: 'The Communists don't want you as prime minister. But they'll agree to your being given a portfolio, perhaps that of education. . . .' When Mendès retorted that the new forces—the unions, students, and peasants—must be represented in the government, François Mitterrand interjected, on the subject of the students: 'Do you want me to give a job to Geismar? The whole thing would collapse.' [In fact, P.M.F. was thinking of the eminent scientist Jacques Monod for education.]"

39. Estier, *Journal d'un fédéré*.

40. François Mitterrand says he has kept in a safe dozens of letters from Gaullists offering him their services.

41. *L'Année politique*, 1968.

42. Where persecution was concerned, the Gaullists did not lag behind. They removed him from the seat he had occupied in the Strasbourg

Assembly under the previous legislature. He then retorted: "The UNR honors me once again by attacking me, which I accept with a little disdain and contempt."

43. Mitterrand, *Ma part de vérité.*

44. Alexandre, *Le Roman de la gauche.*

45. He said no for five reasons: 1) he wanted to protest against the president's assumption of powers that the constitution did not give him; 2) in his eyes, the referendum was illegal and anticonstitutional; 3) regionalization without decentralization, he said, was a trap; 4) the division into twenty-one regions was, he believed, dangerous for the unity of the nation; 5) finally, one could not give one answer to two different questions.

46. *L'Année politique,* 1969.

47. Estier, *Journal d'un fédéré.*

48. François Mitterrand refused to take part in that congress, to which he had nevertheless been invited, because he was not its organizer.

49. Bloch-Morhange, *La Grenouille et le scorpion.*

50. Recounted by Carmen Tessier in "Les potins de la commère," *France-Soir.*

51. André Salomon, *Parti socialiste: La mise à nu* (Paris: Robert Laffont, 1980).

52. Ibid.

53. Mitterrand, *L'Abeille et l'architecte.*

54. Mitterrand, *La Paille et le grain.*

55. Ibid.

56. Albert du Roy and Robert Schneider, *Le Roman de la rose* (Paris: Seuil, 1982).

57. Published by Flammarion in 1973.

58. In an interview in *L'Expansion,* August 1972.

59. On this subject, he wrote in *L'Abeille et l'architecte:*

Intellectuals (and especially economic theorists) who feel solidarity with that historical struggle have a decisive role to play. They are needed to help break up the established ideological bloc, to take apart the various parts of the state machine, and, on the basis of their thought, open the way to socialism. . . . As Marx did a hundred years ago, it is thus desirable to take up and deepen the critique of the present political economy, of the class in power—to have the many theoretical works on the economy and society develop and provide the tools for a critique of a declining order.

60. Quoted by Giesbert in *François Mitterrand ou la tentation de l'histoire*.

61. Quoted in du Roy and Schneider, *Le Roman de la rose*.

62. *Le Monde*, January 4, 1979.

63. The Communist leaders, retreating into a backward-looking view of French society, confined within their ideology, unhealthily attached to the USSR, compromised by the failure of the Soviet model, by the Poujadist campaigns, and by a string of betrayals not so much shocking as all too visible, were also largely responsible for it—especially, as we shall see, since they made one tactical error after another.

64. Alexandre, *Le Roman de la gauche*.

65. Quoted by Etienne Fajon in *L'Union et le combat*.

66. Mitterrand, *La Paille et le grain*.

67. Quoted by Elgey in *La République des illusions*.

68. Compare with the book by Denis Jeambar, *Le Parti communiste dans la maison* (Paris: Calmann-Lévy).

CHAPTER 7

1. Thus in the plan he put before the Socialist congress at Bourg-en-Bresse in the autumn of 1983, he dreamed of breaking up the press empires so as to leave only small, courageous newspapers (preferably those promoting the right policies) that would all be assisted by the socialist state.

2. A famous Russian social democrat, who, after sharing power with the Bolsheviks, was brutally removed by them.

INDEX

Abbas, Ferhat, 177
Abelin, Pierre, 276, 277
Action française, 15, 33, 46, 48, 96
Affair of the leaks, 178–83
Africa, 146, 153–69, 196–98, 238, 353, 356
Ahmed, Hocin Ait, 203
Albrecht, Bertie, 115
Algeria, 58–59, 119, 177, 244, 285
  de Gaulle and, 185, 211–17
  Pflimlin and, 211–14
  revolt by Algerians, 185–206, 210
  revolt by French troops, 206, 210–17
Alibert, Raphaël, 48, 79
Alleg, Henri, 194–95
Allende, Salvador, 298
Alliance Democratique, 121
Arbellot, Simon, 84, 85
Aron, Raymond, 195

Attali, Jacques, 298, 299, 317, 323
Aubert, Emile, 233
Aumeron, General, 190
Auriol, Vincent, 129, 131, 134, 135, 139–40, 174
Auroux, Jean, 323
Avinin, Antoine, 98–99, 143

Baecque, François de, 205
Baker, Josephine, 97
Barangé law, 149
Bardo treaty, 169, 187
Barel, Virgile, 129–30
Barillon, Raymond, 268
Baron, Albert, 72
Barrachin, Edmond, 123, 132
Barre, Raymond, 322, 324, 333, 339, 342, 344, 361
Barrès, Maurice, 16
Barsalou, Joseph, 244
Bas, Pierre, 240
Batten, Van, 84, 87

Bauchard, Philippe, 117
Baud, Georges, 77–78, 84, 87
Baudrillart, Msgr., 71
Baumel, Jacques, 90, 142, 143, 149
Beauchamp, Georges, 135–36, 146, 163, 165, 167–68, 174, 218, 220, 235, 296, 308, 318
  FM's candidacy and, 244, 246, 253, 257, 259, 262
Bechard, Paul, 166
Ben Barka affair, 266
Ben Bella, Ahmed, 200, 203
Benet, Jacques, 43, 44, 55, 74, 79, 88, 90, 91, 97, 101
Bénichou, Pierre, 274
Bénouville, Pierre de, 29, 47, 90
Berard-Quelin, Georges, 260
Bérégovoy, Pierre, 22, 23, 59, 243, 256, 306, 323, 343, 344
Berthouin, Fernand, 210
Bertin, Jean, 104–105
Bettencourt, André, 79, 88, 92, 177
Biaggi, Jean-Baptiste, 46, 51
Bidault, Georges, 141, 146, 171, 181, 210
Biget, Maître, 70, 72–73
Billières, René, 210, 266, 276
Bleustein-Blanchet, Marcel, 120
Bloch, Pierre, 96
Bloch-Morhange, Jacques, 152, 172–73, 300–301
Blum, Léon, 2, 50, 125, 135, 137, 139–40, 305, 335
Boissieu, Alain de, 107–108, 158
Bonnefous, Edouard, 147, 151, 218
Bonnet, Christian, 218
Bonte, Floribond, 129
Borel, Suzy, 79
Borgeaud, Henri, 191

Boris, Georges, 176
Borker, Antoine, 251
Borzeix, Jean-Marie, 285
Bouchaud, Canon, 28
Boudiaf, Mohamed, 203
Boulloche, André, 307
Bourdan, Pierre, 143
Bourdet, Claude, 90
Bourgeade, Pierre, 321
Bourgès-Maunoury, Maurice, 118, 192, 193, 200, 204, 232
Bourgignon, Fred, 15
Bourguiba, Habib, 203
Boutemy, Emile, 123–24
Bouvyer, Jean-Marie, 46–47
Brainville, Yves, 72
Bréaud, Jean, 76
Brezhnev, Leonid, 353
Brusset, Max, 121, 124
Brutelle, Georges, 246, 251, 262
Bugeaud, Pierre, 101, 104
Bulloux, François, 279

Cagoule, 46–48, 79
CAI (Centre d'action institutionelle), 244–45
Caillau, Michel (Michel Charrette, Michel Chambre), 91–96, 98
Camaret, Michel de, 47
Capitalism, 313–15, 319, 324–25
Capitant, René, 142–46
Carrel, Dr. Alexis, 83
Carreyrou, Gérard, 117
Castelnau, General de, 14
Castro, Fidel, 298
Catholicism, 83, 167
  FM and, 6–9, 15–16, 26–27, 123, 124
  Gouze family and, 112–16
  issues important to, 80
  prosecution of priests and, 166–68

Catholicism (*cont.*)
    secular education and,
    14–15, 23–27
  swing to the Left, 82, 141,
    285–86, 303
Catroux, General, 201
Cazelles, Ernest, 254, 263, 266,
    268, 324
CERES (Centre d'études et de
    recherches socialistes)
    (Center of Socialist Study
    and Research), 292–94,
    307, 312, 318, 323, 325,
    326, 332
CFDT (Confédération française
    démocratique de travaille)
    (French Confederation of
    Democracy and Labor),
    278, 285
CG(N)PF (Confédération générale
    nationale du patronat de
    France) (General National
    Confederation of French
    Employers), 48
CGT (Confédération générale du
    travail) (General
    Confederation of Labor),
    225, 273, 277, 337, 350
Chaban-Delmas, Jacques, 101,
    152, 172, 178, 182, 193,
    198, 200, 210, 284, 317,
    361
Chalandon, Albin, 364
Chalvron, Bernard de, 79
Chandernagor, André, 312
Charente region, 6–17 *passim*
Charpy, Pierre, 180
Château, François, 72
Chevalier, Jacques, 178, 186, 190
Chevalier, Pierre, 143, 157
Chevènement, Jean-Pierre, 25,
    297, 332
    reorganization of the Left and,
    292–94, 307, 311, 312,
    316, 324

Chevrier, Jean, 301
Chevrillon, Olivier, 249
Cheysson, Claude, 354
Chigot, Pierre, 84, 85, 87–88
Chirac, Jacques, 347, 348,
    360–64
Chiron, Pierre, 29, 30, 44
Claudius-Petit, Eugène, 80, 90,
    135, 136, 142, 143, 147,
    161, 191, 194, 218
    UDSR and, 135, 136, 142, 143,
    147, 152–53
Clavel, Maurice, 321
Clayeux, Louis Gabriel, 54
Clemenceau, Michel, 125
Clément, Léonce, 115
Clostermann, Pierre, 143
CNR (National Council of the
    Resistance), 90, 91, 99
Cohn-Bendit, Daniel, 275
Cold War, 144, 353
Collège d'Angoulême, 38–45, 165
Collège Saint-Paul, 25–35
    class system at, 27–28
    discipline at, 28
    FM at, 29–35
    politics at, 33–34
    strictness of, 28–29
Committees of Public Safety, 211,
    213, 215
Common Market, 307, 353
Common Program of the Left,
    309, 313, 319, 320,
    329–30, 333, 335
Communism, 2–3, 37, 48, 100,
    114, 127, 141–42, 192,
    195, 208
    affair of the leaks and, 178–83
    Africa and, 153, 159–64, 167
    anti-, 119–34, 144, 159–64,
    250, 328–37
    Czechoslovakia and, 280, 282,
    289
    decline of, 329–36, 347–51
    FGDS and, 265, 267–71

FM and, 34, 98–99, 133, 219,
222–23
  alliance between, 328–37
  candidacy of, 97, 247–58,
  288–95
  negotiations between,
  313–20
  as president, 334–37,
  347–51, 353, 355
  reorganization of Socialism
  and, 309–20
  Observatoire affair and,
  225–26, 233
  POWs, 98–99, 103–105
  student uprising and, 271–81
  USSR and, 336
"*Contestation la,*" 271–81
Convention des institutions
  républicaines, 249, 258,
  262–65, 270, 287
  socialism and, 281–84
Cornuau, Jean, 103–106
Cornut-Gentille, Bernard, 157,
  158
Cot, Jean-Pierre, 324
Cotard, Michèle, 281
Coty, René, 134, 179, 182
  Algerian crisis and, 193–218
  passim
Coudreau, Canon, 26
Coursol, Pierre, 78, 84, 147
Cremieux, Francis, 131
Cresson, Edith, 323, 333
Croix-de-Feu, 44–45
Cuba, 354

Dahuron, Abel, 227
Daladier, Edouard, 121, 122
Dalle, François, 16, 43, 44, 51,
  53, 56, 88
Dalida, 305
Danger, Robert, 126
Daniel, Georges, 256
Daniel, Jean, 184, 185, 261, 278,
  318, 322

Dayan, Georges, 56, 60–61, 130,
  148, 199, 204, 218, 220,
  228, 235, 250, 253, 257,
  268
  reorganization of the Left and,
  295, 308, 323
Dayan, Irène, 220
Debray, Régis, 298, 300
Debré, Michel, 143, 152, 172,
  182, 197, 211, 236, 241
  Observatoire affair and, 209,
  230–34
Dechartre, Philippe, 69, 85, 89,
  90, 91, 98, 99, 101
Deferre, Gaston, 154, 193, 200,
  219, 221–22, 233, 258,
  266, 267, 278, 286, 297,
  324
  candidacy of, 248–53, 262,
  343
  failure of the Left and, 289–94
de Gaulle, Charles, 2, 15, 45, 59,
  76, 175, 185, 186, 250,
  269, 270–71, 365
  Africa and, 153–55
  Algeria and, 185, 211–17
  FM and, 352
    break between, 102,
    106–108, 145
    election of 1965, 260
    hatred of, 222, 234–43
    as POW, 71–72, 86
    rise to power of, 205–19
    as wartime envoy, 89–99
  POWs and, 65, 90–94,
  104–108
  resignation of, 287–88
  Resistance and, 89–99, 102
  RPF and, 143–45
  student uprisings and, 273–80,
  282
de Gaulle, Geneviève, 137
de La Rocque, Rambaud, 15,
  45–46, 121
Delbecque, Léon, 210

Deleplace, General, 92
Delom-Sorbé, Maurice, 142
Deloncle, Eugène, 47, 48
Delors, Jacques, 318, 341,
    343–44
Delouvrier, Paul, 71
Democratic Parti socialiste
    démocratique, 121
Depreux, Edouard, 186–87, 223,
    226, 243, 256
Descamps, Eugène, 278
Desgraupes, Pierre, 62, 218
Deteix, Louis, 146–47, 148, 258
Dides, Jean, 179, 181
Dillard, Father, 67
Doriot, Jacques, 51
Dreyfus, Alfred, 11
Droit, Michel, 107
Dronne, Raymond, 86
Dubedout, Hubert, 318
Duchet, Roger, 125
Duclos, Jacques, 129, 179, 255,
    288, 290
Dumas, Roland, 168, 191–92,
    199, 218, 219, 220, 227,
    250, 253, 255, 257, 281,
    288, 352
Dupuis, Marc, 130
Durbet, Marius, 239
Duveau, Roger, 205, 215–16
Duverger, Maurice, 202, 256

Elgey, Georgette, 133
Emmanuelli, Henri, 323
England, 30
Estier, Claude, 183, 184, 204,
    250, 253, 257, 268, 287,
    331
    reorganization of the Left and,
    289, 293, 294, 307, 317,
    319, 327
Ethiopia, 50
Europe, 351–57

European Defense Community,
    151–52, 172, 356
Eyquem, Marie-Thérèse, 257, 266

Fabius, Laurent, 297, 323,
    325–26, 343, 344, 345
Fabre, Robert, 262, 266, 287
Fabre-Luce, Alfred, 276, 277
Fajon, Etienne, 336
Fascism, 44–54, 214
Faure, Edgar, 118, 132, 150,
    169, 172, 176, 219, 222,
    233
    affair of the leaks and,
    178–82
Faure, Maurice, 210, 247, 251,
    253–54
Faure, Paul, 121
Fauvet, Jacques, 182, 268
FGDS (Federation of the
    Democratic and Socialist
    Left), 209, 262–70, 291
    Communists and, 265, 267–70
    election results, 268–69, 280
    FM's resignation from, 286–87
    origin of, 262–65
    shadow cabinet of, 266
    student uprising and, 274–80
    aftermath of, 286–87
    three-point program of,
    264–65
Fifth Republic, 207–337
Fillioud, Georges, 268, 316
Finifter, Bernard, 67, 89, 110,
    234
Fiterman, Charles, 334, 348
Flandrin, Pierre-Etienne, 56, 121
Fleurieu, Marie-Claire de, 184,
    275
FLN (National Liberation Front),
    189, 192, 201, 202, 203
Florin, Abbé, 65, 72
Forcinal, Albert, 135
Forestier, Gilbert, 65

Fouchet, Christian, 178, 179, 273
Fouques Duparc, Henri, 190
Fourcade, Jean-Pierre, 320
Fourth Republic, 117–206
France, Anatole, 46
France: Revue de l'état nouveau, 48, 79, 82–83
Francheschi, Joseph, 317
Francisque, 83–87
Franco, Francisco, 47, 50
Frédéric-Dupont, Edouard, 167, 175
Free France, 89–100 *passim*
Frenay, Henri, 93, 99–108 *passim*, 115, 137, 142, 174
Fuzier, Claude, 228, 282, 289, 307, 324

Gagnaire, Etienne, 78, 101
Gaillard, Félix, 64, 118, 204, 210
Gaillard, Robert, 72
Gallo, Max, 306
Gandhi, Indira, 310
Ganeval, General, 205
Gaullists, 222, 270, 282, 326
  FM and, 144–46, 164, 240–50
  Observatoire affair and, 230–35
  resurgence of, 359–65
  UDSR and, 143–46
  see also de Gaulle, Charles
Gazier, Albert, 212
Gide, André, 52, 76
Giroud, Françoise, 120, 174, 176–77, 180, 183, 184
Giraud, General, 90–91, 95, 96, 97
Giscard d'Estaing, Valéry, 1, 18, 24, 218, 231, 301, 310, 314, 348, 352–53, 361, 364
  as candidate, 269, 284, 285, 288, 309, 317, 323, 324, 331–39
Gouin, Félix, 101
Goux, Christian, 317
Gouze, Danielle, 110–16
Gouze, Madeleine (Christine Gouze-Renal), 110–12
Gouze, Roger, 112–16
GPRA (Gouverment provisoire de la republique algérienne) (Provisional Government of the Algerian Republic), 197
Grossouvre, François de, 317
Groult, Benoîte, 259
Groussard, Colonel, 48
Guénault, Marcel, 87
Guérin, Henri, 77, 84
Guillaumat, General, 38
Guillebaud, Jean-Claude, 310
Guimard, Paul, 305
Guitton, Jean, 26, 39

Hadj, Messali, 189
Haedrich, Marcel, 78–79, 134, 138, 140
Hallier, Jean-Edern, 298, 300, 321
Hamon, Léo, 142, 152
Hanin, Roger, 305
Haour, Abbé, 40
Hernu, Charles, 243–44, 250–51, 253, 262, 266, 275
  reorganization of the Left and, 308, 317, 323
Herriot, Edouard, 121, 122
Heurgon, Marc, 256
Hitler, Adolf, 46, 49, 53
Houphouët-Boigny, Félix, 146, 154, 161–65

If, Simone, 22
Indochina, 149, 170, 172–73,
    175, 181, 189
Israel, 354

Jallais, Françoise and Léo, 310
Jaquet, Gérard, 257, 262
Jardel, Jean, 84
Jarnac, 6–17 *passim*, 74–76, 112
Jaurès, Jean, 2, 49, 305
Jeantet, Gabriel, 48–49, 79–80,
    84, 85
Jews, 60, 67, 76, 80, 83, 115,
    303
Jeze, Professor, 50
Jobert, Michel, 315
Jobit, Msgr., 31, 42, 50
Join-Lambert, Pierre, 77, 84
Joinot des Yvelines, prefect, 38
Jospin, Lionel, 59, 323, 334, 349
Jouhaux, Edmond, 59
Joxe, Pierre, 58–59, 297
    reorganization of the Left and,
        293, 307, 311, 316, 319,
        323
Julliard, Jacques, 175, 189–90,
    194
Jupé, Alain, 363
Juquin, Pierre, 271, 332

Kaspéreit, Gabriel, 240
Khider, Mohamed, 203
Kiejman, Georges, 275
Koenig, General, 178, 179
Kosciusko-Morizet, Jacques, 172,
    204, 205, 224
Kriegel-Valrimond, Maurice, 131

Labrusse, Roger, 180–81
La Chenelière, Major de, 97
Lacheraf, Mostafa, 203
Lacombe, Henri, 39
Lacoste, Robert, 172, 192, 193,
    201, 203, 204, 211

Lacouture, Jean, 175, 178, 186,
    217, 290
Landry, Colette Mitterrand, 47,
    56
Landry, Pierre, 75
Lanet, Joseph, 147, 148, 149
Lang, Jack, 4, 298, 299–300,
    354
Langeais, Catherine, *see* Terrasse,
    Marie-Louise
Laniel, Joseph, 169–73, 181–82,
    201
La Rose au poing (Mitterrand),
    313–14
Laurent, Augustin, 292–93
Laurent, Jacques, 48
Lavagne, André, 84
Laval, Pierre, 48, 77, 84, 85, 87,
    324
Lazareff, Pierre, 120
Lecanuet, Jean, 233, 255, 268,
    278, 303
Leccia, Bastien, 148
Le Coup d'état permanent
    (Mitterrand), 241–42, 314
Left, 113–14, 168, 178, 183–85,
    200, 270
    Christian swing to, 82, 141,
        285–86, 303
    election losses of, 343, 347,
        348, 359
    FGDS, *see* FGDS
    FM being driven, 182–83, 191,
        234–35
    FM's ascendancy to leadership
        of, 209, 215, 243–69,
        282–95
    FM's childhood and, 14–15, 34
    Gouze family and, 113–16
    new organizations within,
        243–45
    non-Communist, 243–51, 290
    questions that divided the, 2
    student uprising and, 271–81

aftermath of, 282–95
UFD and, 223
see also Communism; Socialism
Legatte, Paul, 175–76, 183, 253
Legendre, Jean, 181
Lejeune, Max, 193, 286
Lenin, V. I., 302, 312
Le Pen, Jean-Marie, 227, 260
Leroy, Roland, 332
Levaï, Ivan, 117
L'Hoiry, Dr., 29
Liberation, 99–108
Lipkowski, Jean-Noël de, 29,
    168–69, 199, 212
Loo, Charles, 286
Lop, Ferdinand, 51
Lorrain, Jules "Papa Jules,"
    7–17, 57
Lorrain, Ninie, 7, 8, 17–18
Lorrain, Robert, 11–12, 39
Lustiger, Msgr., 24

Magne, André, 77, 87, 88
Maire, Edmond, 318, 319
Mairey, Jean, 180
Malraux, André, 310
Marchais, Georges, 288, 326,
    329–35, 348
Marcilhacy, Maurice, 38
Marcilhacy, Pierre, 15, 233, 242
Marie, André, 129, 131
Maroselli, Jacques, 262
Marot, Jacques, 44–45, 54
Martinet, Gilles, 223, 226, 243,
    252, 256, 275, 320
Marty, Msgr., 285
Massaloux, Gendraux, 363
Massignon, Louis, 194
Masson, André, 87, 89, 100
Massu, General, 211
Matzneff, Gabriel, 259
Mauduit, Antoine, 78–79
Mauduit, Henri de, 158–59

Mauriac, François, 11, 38, 39, 54,
    76, 183, 223, 228, 229
Mauroy, Pierre, 58, 59, 266, 278,
    282, 287, 304, 307, 316,
    318
  failure of the Left and, 291–94
  as FM's rival, 321–26
  as prime minister, 339–45,
    350, 353
Maurras, 46
Mayer, Daniel, 129, 223, 226,
    253, 254
Mayer, René, 149, 151, 171, 189
Maziers, Msgr., 285
Mendès, Lily, 184
Mendès France, Pierre (P.M.F.),
    118, 134, 152, 174–85,
    219, 243, 268, 290, 340
  Algeria and, 186, 188, 189,
    191, 193, 217–18
  described, 174–75
  FM's candidacy and, 251–58
  Laniel and, 170–73
  Mollet and, 198–202
  Observatoire affair and,
    226–30
  student uprising and, 273–81,
    289
  UDF and, 223
Ménétrel, Bernard, 49, 85
Mercier, Louis and Philomène,
    97–98
Mermaz, Louis, 59, 218, 220,
    244, 257, 262, 268, 269,
    278, 344
  reorganization of the Left and,
    288, 316, 317, 323, 326
Méténier, François, 47–48, 79
Middle East, 352–56
Mitterrand, Colette, 47, 56
Mitterrand, Danielle Gouze,
    110–16, 120, 157, 235,
    259, 356
Mitterrand, François

Mitterrand, François (*cont.*)
  affair of the leaks and, 178–83
  Africa and, 146, 153–69,
    196–98, 238, 353,
    356
  Algeria and, *see* Algeria
  ambition, 134–41, 155, 224,
    236, 309, 321
  on the *Anschluss*, 53–54
  assassination attempt on,
    224–35
  Atalli and, 299
  Bas affair and, 240
  on bourgeoisie, 81, 234–35,
    242
  broadcasting strike, 129–31
  on capitalism, 313–15, 319,
    324–25
  on Catholicism, 26–27,
    114–15, 167–68, 286
  on chance, 20
  childhood of, 5–21
  Communism and, *see*
    Communism, FM and
  contradictions of, 22–27,
    36–37, 53–54, 102, 168,
    171–73, 312, 315
  as counterpresident, 261–69
  Dayan and, 60–61, 295
  Debray and, 300
  de Gaulle and, *see* de Gaulle,
    Charles, FM and
  described, 32–33, 38, 111,
    118–20, 155, 208–209,
    234–43, 257, 295–327
    "algebra" of, 306–307
    anti-Communism, 119–34,
      159–64, 328–37
    charity, 41
    charm, 293–94
    during childhood, 19–21
    clothing, 40, 134–35, 305
    contemporary leaders,
      174–75
    England, 30
  high society, 119–20
  as a "juggler," 306
  as leader of the opposition,
    261–69
  as "*le beau François,*" 127
  "little pile of secrets," 304
  lost election of 1968, 280–87
  manner of, 28, 30, 31, 174
  mistrust and suspicion,
    118–20, 150, 168,
    178–83, 252, 281–82,
    309–10
  music, 54
  oratory, 31–32, 231–32,
    235, 241, 246, 303–304,
    306
  personal authority, 307–308,
    315
  as POW, 72–73
  punctuality, 158, 176–77,
    249
  religion, 23, 26–27, 29, 31,
    34–35, 42–43, 80, 82,
    284–86
  in the Resistance, 88–89
  at school, 29–35, 41–57
  self-, 33, 34, 117, 234–35,
    287
  serenity, 117–18, 224
  sports, 30–31, 54
  tiredness, 309, 318
  tragedy and, 301
  "tu" and, 296
  writing, 41
  economics and, 50, 124–25,
    176, 313–15, 319–20,
    341–47, 350
  electoral system reform,
    132–33
  fascism and, 44–54
  on his father, 13
  FGDS and, *see* FGDS
  Fifth Republic and, 207–209
  as the "foreign prince,"
    302–27

francisque, 83–87
on freedom, 75
as Garde des Sceaux, 185, 186,
     192, 193, 200, 204, 219,
     228, 231
Gaullists and, 144–46, 164,
     240–50
Hallier and, 300
in India, 310–11
Lang and, 299–300
Laniel government and,
     169–73, 181–82
La Rose au poing, 313–14
as lawyer, 219
on literature, 20, 52
Ma part de vérité, 284–85
marriage of, 110–16
Mendès France and, 174–85,
     199, 251–58, 273–81
military and, 53, 56–57
MNPGD and, 98–108
on money and business, 16, 20,
     34, 81, 138–39, 287, 294,
     300–301, 303
as "Morland," 87, 90, 92–93,
     110, 115
as "Mr. Nyet," 236–43
  on African policy, 238
  on Constitutional Council,
     242
  on de Gaulle, 236, 242
  on economic policy, 239
  on educational system, 239
  on election reform, 237,
     239–40
  on *force de frappe*, 237–38
  on foreign policy, 238
  Le Coup d'état permanent,
     241–42
  on legal system, 238
  as opposition speaker, 241
  on public service, 239
  on strikes, 238
Observatoire affair and, 209,
     224–35, 254

on political parties, 81–82,
     257–58
on POWs, 66, 67–69, 82,
     101–108
as president, 327, 334–65
  change and, 346
  Chirac and, 360–64
  Communists and, 334–37,
     347–51
  early reforms, 339–41
  economic failures and,
     341–47, 350
  epilogue, 359–65
  expectations for, 4–5
  foreign policy, 351–57,
     362–63
  lost illusions, 338–44
  "modernity" and, 344,
     345–46
  secular education and,
     23–27, 345
  tombs visited by, 1–4
  unpopularity, 344–45
as presidential candidate,
     243–61, 316–27
presidential elections and, 237,
     245, 248, 261
*Reflections on French Foreign
     Policy*, 351–52
risk taking, 89
Rocard and, 297, 307, 316,
     318–27
royal kinship of, 11
as senator, 221, 223, 237
"simple people" and, 305
Socialism and, *see* Socialism
student uprising and, 271–80
  aftermath of, 280–87
supporters of, 89, 135–38,
     220, 226, 233, 235, 243,
     250–51, 257–58,
     295–302, 307–308, 323
"synthesis" of, 258
Terrasse and, *see* Terrasse,
     Marie-Louise

François Mitterrand (*cont.*)
  tours of France, 308–309, 324
  UDSR and, *see* UDSR
  ups and downs of career,
    208
  Vichy and, *see* Vichy
  women's rights and, 22–23,
    259, 307
  World War II and, *see* World
    War II
Mitterrand, Jacques, 17, 28, 40,
  96
Mitterrand, Joseph "Papa
  Joseph," 6, 8, 12–17, 76,
  309
Mitterrand, Pascal, 120
Mitterrand, Philippe, 17
Mitterrand, Robert, 14–18,
  29–30, 40, 71, 136, 257
Mitterrand, Yvonne, 6, 18–19, 57
MNPGD (Mouvement national des
  prisonniers de guerre et des
  déportés) (National
  Movement of Prisoners of
  War and Deportees), 91,
  98–108
Moch, Jules, 212
Mollet, Guy, 118, 170, 178, 205,
  228, 261, 272, 304
  Algeria and, 185, 186, 192,
    193, 212–14
  failure of the Left and, 282,
    286, 291–94
  FGDS and, 262–67, 276, 278
  FM's candidacy and, 246–55,
    288–89
  government of, 198–204
Monis, Ernest, 18
Monnet, Jean, 151
Monod, Jacques, 275, 279
Mons, Jean, 179, 180, 181
Monsour, Bernard, 72
Montagard, Julie, 110, 115
Montalembert, 18

Montalembert, 41, 44–45, 46, 53
Monteil, André, 151, 183
Montjoye, Jacques de, 78, 96
Montmaur, 78–79
Moreau, Paule, 148
Moreau, Robert, 100
Morocco, 169–71, 189, 203, 204,
  266
Motchane, Didier, 292, 312
Moulin, Charles, 98, 220
Moulin, Jean, 2–3, 90, 94
MRP (Mouvement républicain
  populaire) (Popular
  Republican Movement),
  121–23, 126, 129, 132,
  166–68, 248, 250
  UDSR and, 141–44, 146, 149,
    151
MTLD (Mouvement pour le
  triomphe des libertés
  démocratiques) (Movement
  for the Triumph of
  Democratic Liberties), 189
Munier, Jean, 89, 110
Muslims, 186–87, 191, 192, 203
Mussolini, Benito, 47–48, 50

National Catholic Federation,
  14–15
National Movement of Prisoners
  of War and Deportees, 98,
  101, 144–45, 147, 148
Neuwirth, Lucien, 225
Nicolaÿ, Pierre, 128, 136, 163,
  166, 179–80, 204, 231
Noël, Léon, 124, 219, 233
Notebart, Arthur, 286, 312, 324
Nucci, Christian, 323

Observatoire affair, 209, 224–35,
  254
"104," 38–45, 49, 52, 54, 74,
  79, 88

Ordioni, Pierre, 109–10
O'Reilly, Father, 41, 44, 46

Padovani, Marcelle, 294
Palewski, Gaston, 107–108
Panthéon, 1–4
Papandreou, Georges, 298
Parti de la réconciliation
    française, 121
Parti républicain de la liberté,
    123
Passy, Colonel, 97
Paternos, Father, 166–68
Paumier, Robert, 85, 98, 99, 235
Pelabon, André, 179
Pelat, Patrice, 62–63, 67, 69, 89,
    108, 110, 111, 329
Penne, Guy, 308
Perdriel, Claude, 317
Pernin, André, 100
Perrin, Joseph, 144–45, 147, 148
Perrinot, Abbé, 32, 143
Perron, Yves, 331
Pesquet, Robert, 226–34, 256
Pétain, Marshall Philippe, 45, 48,
    49, 59, 64, 79, 87, 141,
    294
  POWs and, 65, 70–72
  see also Vichy
Peyrefitte, Alain, 272
Pflimlin, Pierre, 204, 211–14,
    228
Picar, Michel, 110, 115
Pierron, Marcel, 70
Piette, Jacques, 324
Pilven, Pol, 79, 89, 92
Pinay, Antoine, 149, 171, 213
Pineau, Christian, 200, 289
Pinot, Maurice, 76–77, 84
  Resistance and, 87–98 *passim*
Pirou, Gaëtan, 39
Pisani, Edgar, 233, 318
Pius XI, Pope, 15
Platon, Admiral, 84, 85

Plazenet, Abbé, 40
Pleven, René, 95, 125, 174, 210,
    212, 218
  Africa and, 161–72 *passim*
  USDR and, 142–54 *passim*
Poher, Alain, 289
Polimann, Canon Angèle, 49
Pompidou, Georges, 24, 238, 241,
    269, 270, 273, 279, 282,
    288, 289, 310, 317, 331,
    352
Poperen, Jean, 59, 243, 256, 292,
    316, 319, 323, 330
Popular Front, 48, 62, 63, 113,
    254, 272, 339
Postel-Vinay, Anise, 137
Poulat, Emile, 82
Priouret, Roger, 290, 313
Prisoners of war, 60–74, 257–58
  anxiety of, 64
  blame for defeat, 63–64,
    70–71, 91
  camp spirit of, 64–65, 68
  de Gaulle and, 65, 90–91,
    93–94, 104–108
  escapes, 62, 67, 74–75
  FM on, 66, 67–69, 82
  organizations of, 64, 75–77,
    87–108, 144–45, 147
  politics, 69–72
  return of, 74–77
  university for, 72–73
  variety of, 66–67
  see also UDSR
Protestants, 7, 16, 303
Prouvost, Jean, 139
PSU (Parti socialiste unifié)
    (Unified Socialist Party),
    243, 246, 252, 255–56,
    268, 289, 319

Questiaux, Nicole, 339
Queuille, Henri, 124, 131,
    139–40, 174

Quilès, Paul, 59, 323, 326
Quilici, François, 190

Radical party, 139, 142, 145,
    146, 185, 210, 246, 251,
    255, 258, 282, 288, 307,
    316
  FGDS and, 262–67, 270
Ramadier, Paul, 126, 129,
    135–36, 174
Rastignac, Eugène de, 37
Raynal, Pierre, 147
RDA (African Democratic Rally),
    146, 154–68 *passim*, 183,
    196
Reagan, Ronald, 342, 356, 362
*Reflections on French Foreign
    Policy* (Mitterrand),
    351–52
Resistance, 81, 83, 87–99
  de Gaulle and, 89–99, 102
  FM and, 85, 87–99
  maquis, 78–79
  Vichy and, 78, 79, 87
Revel, Jean-François, 314–15
Revers, General, 88, 92
Rey-Herme, Father, 41, 43
Reynaud, Paul, 50, 125, 157
RGR (Rassemblement des gauches
    républicaines) (Assembly of
    the Republican Left),
    121–23, 142
Ribaud, André, 256–57
Riboud, Jean, 343
Ribs, Jacques, 296
Right, 3, 284
  FM and, 14–15, 70, 121–27
  prosecution of priests and,
    166–68
  resurgence of, 343, 347, 348,
    359–65
Rocard, Michel, 209, 243, 256,
    273, 289, 343

  as FM's rival, 297, 307, 316,
    318–27
Rocheboitaud, Jean, 29
Rochet, Waldeck, 97, 251, 254,
    255, 267–68, 274, 278,
    288, 329
Rops, Daniel, 39
Rosselli brothers, 46–47, 48
Rostand, Jean, 289
Roualle, Alain de, 123
Roudy, Yvette, 22
Rouleau, Eric, 362
Rousselet, André, 183, 205, 218,
    220, 235, 257, 268, 296,
    317
Roy, Jean, 54, 158
RPF (Rally of the French People),
    45, 125, 126, 130, 164,
    236
  USDR and, 143–45, 148
RPR (Rassemblement pour la
    république) (Assembly for
    the Republic), 360, 361
Rummelhardt, Father, 166–68
Russia, 336, 353, 355, 356

Saint-Périer, Marquis de, 302,
    305
Saint-Vincent-de-Paul
    Conference, 14, 41
Saivre, Roger de, 190
Sakharov, Andrei, 355
Salan, Raoul, 59, 213, 231
Salmon, Robert, 138
Santo, Emmanuele, 47
Sarrazin, Antoinette "Mamie," 7,
    19
Sarrazin, Pierre, 7, 17
Sarrazin, Yvonne "Lolotte," 7,
    19, 20
Sarre, Georges, 292
Sartre, Jean-Paul, 194, 256
Savary, Alain, 23, 24, 193, 200,

203, 204, 243, 307, 316, 345
failure of the Left and, 289–94
Schmidt, Helmut, 305
Schoelcher, Victor, 2, 3
Schoeller, Eugène, 120–21
Schuman, Maurice, 89, 126
Schuman, Robert, 129, 139, 151, 174
Schwartz, Laurent, 275
Schwing, Dr., 220
Secular education, 14–15, 23–27, 112–13, 149, 345
Séguy, Georges, 272, 277, 319
Sérigny, Alain de, 211
Servan-Schreiber, Jean-Jacques, 174, 176, 193, 224, 253
Servet, Georges, 256
SFIO (Section française de L'Internationale ouvrière) (French Section of the Worker's International) (Socialist party), 121–26, 129, 136, 186, 196, 223, 226, 228, 233, 246, 302–303, 324, 329
aftermath of student uprising and, 283, 286–91
FGDS and, 262–67, 270
FM's candidacy and, 248–58 *passim*
Mollet and, 198–204
UDSR and, 142–43
Siriex, Paul Henri, 161–62, 165
Social Catholicism, 11–12
Socialism, 2, 3, 113, 139–40, 143, 153
aftermath of student uprising and, 282–95
ascendancy of FM to leadership of, 207–209, 215, 243–69, 282–95, 302
compensation for maternity leave and, 22–23

electoral progress of, 315–18, 329–35
FM on, 36–37, 148, 247, 266–67, 282–87, 309
Mollet government and, 198–204
new convictions of, 311–13
presidency of FM and, 353–65
reorganization of, 288–95, 302–27
Rocard-FM conflict and, 297, 307, 316, 318–27
secular education and, 23–27
transformation of, 346
see also Left; SFIO
Soustelle, Jacques, 142, 143, 201, 211, 213
Spanish Civil War, 50
Stibbe, Pierre, 209, 252
Student uprising, 271–81
aftermath of, 282–95
Suez Canal, 200, 202–203

Taste, Henri de, 39
Ténard, Baron, 138
Terrasse, Marie-Louise (Catherine Langeais), 44, 47, 224
breakup of engagement, 75, 76, 108–10
courtship and engagement, 55–57, 61
FM as POW and, 62, 73–74
Thellier de Poncheville, Canon, 39
Theodorakis, Mikis, 305
Thévenin, Georges, 104, 105
Thieullent, Henri, 44, 50, 54
"Third force," 220–23
Third Republic, 45, 69
Third World, 238, 354, 355–56
Thorez, Maurice, 51, 128–29, 131, 160, 313, 328, 335
Thorp, René William, 244, 251
Tillion, Germaine, 137, 194
Touré, Sékou, 146

Trefusis, Violet, 119
Tron, Ludovic, 244
Trotsky, Leon, 302
Tunisia, 169–70, 187, 189, 203
Turpin, René, 180–81

UDF, 326, 361
UDSR (Union démocratique et
    socialiste de la Résistance)
    (Democratic and Socialist
    Union of the Resistance),
    80, 89, 119, 125, 126,
    131–32, 163, 168,
    171–72, 177, 183, 215,
    218, 220, 223, 243, 287
  Algeria and, 186, 191, 195–99,
    204
  appointment of FM to Ministry
    for War Veterans and,
    135–41
  competitors of, 141–49
  conquest of, 141–53, 302
  hopes for, 141
UFD (Union des forces
    démocratiques) (Union of
    the Forces of Democracy),
    223, 226, 243
Union démocratique et
    républicaine des
    indépendants, 125
Union of the Left, 251, 255, 269,
    289, 290, 316, 319–21,
    323, 329, 332, 347, 348,
    349
United States, 355, 356
UNR (Union pour la nouvelle
    république) (Union for the
    New Republic), 149, 237

Vadim, Roger, 220
Vatican, 137
Védrine, Jean, 26, 63, 64, 65, 78,
    84–85, 87, 88, 97, 101,
    136, 302
Vendroux, Jacques, 143
Vernay, Alain, 137
Verrier, Pierre, 86, 103, 104–105
Vianson-Ponté, Pierre, 271
Vichy, 48, 49, 59, 69–70,
    74–87, 115
  FM's work for, 75–78, 85–87
  francisque, 83–87
  Resistance and, 78, 79, 87
Vida, Hélène, 116
Vigier, Jean-Louis, 233

Warenghien de Flory, Bernard, 41
Whybot, Roger, 179
Williams, Philip, 121–22
Women deportees, 137
Women's rights, 22–23, 259, 266
World War II, 2, 53–54
  effects of, 59–60
  French defeat in, 63–64,
    70–71, 82
  Liberation, 99–108
  "Phony War," 57, 61
  prisoners of war, *see* Prisoners
    of war
  Resistance, *see* Resistance
  Vichy, *see* Vichy
Wurmser, André, 336

Zilbermann, 128
ZUT (Zigenheim Université
    temporaire), 72–73